Praise for the author

"Rebecca Solnit has the wide-foraging mind of a great essayist and the West-besotted soul of the recording secretary for your local historical society. . . . A San Franciscan, she's who Susan Sontag might have become if Sontag had never forsaken California for Manhattan. . . . Solnit's prose combines the imagery of a poet, the ideas of a theoretician, the rhythm of a thoroughbred, and the force of a Southern Pacific locomotive."
David Kipen, *San Francisco Chronicle*

"Solnit has emerged as one of our most gifted freelance intellectuals."
Philip Connors, *Newsday*

"Like a Mike Davis, Marshall Berman, or Simon Schama, Solnit is a cultural historian in the desert-mystic mode, trailing ideas like swarms of butterflies."
John Leonard, *Harper's Magazine*

"A guide of tremendous erudition and just as much common sense, capable of slipping almost imperceptibly from the personal mode to the analytical and back again without appearing self-indulgent." Andrew O'Hehir, *Salon*

"Passionate, potent, and to the point, Solnit's polemic embodies American political and social writing at its best." *Publishers Weekly*

"An extraordinary mind seizes hold of an unexpected topic and renders it with such confidence, subtlety, and grace that one finds it hard to remember what things looked like before the book appeared in the world."
Jim Lewis, *New York Times Book Review*

"An inspired observer and passionate historian, Solnit, whose *River of Shadows* (2003) won a National Book Critics Circle Award, is one of the most creative, penetrating, and eloquent cultural critics writing today."
Donna Seaman, *Booklist*

"Her gift for synthesis, her supple grasp of history, and her ability to shift smoothly from fact to metaphor without warning recalls another artful American writer: Henry Adams."
Mary Panzer, *Chicago Tribune*

STORMING THE GATES OF PARADISE

STORMING THE GATES OF PARADISE

LANDSCAPES FOR POLITICS

REBECCA SOLNIT

UNIVERSITY OF CALIFORNIA PRESS
BERKELEY   LOS ANGELES   LONDON

University of California Press, one of the most distinguished university
presses in the United States, enriches lives around the world by advancing
scholarship in the humanities, social sciences, and natural sciences. Its
activities are supported by the UC Press Foundation and by philanthropic
contributions from individuals and institutions. For more information,
visit www.ucpress.edu.

University of California Press
Berkeley and Los Angeles, California

University of California Press, Ltd.
London, England

Library of Congress Cataloging-in-Publication Data

Solnit, Rebecca.
    Storming the gates of paradise : landscapes for politics / Rebecca Solnit.
        p.   cm.
    Includes bibliographical references and index.
    ISBN: 978-0-520-25656-9 (pbk. : alk. paper)
    1. Political ecology—United States.   2. Human ecology—United
States.   3. Landscape assessment—United States.   4. United States—
Politics and government.   I. Title.

JA75.8.S65   2007
304.20973—dc22   2006035367

Manufactured in the United States of America

15   14   13   12   11   10   09   08
10   9   8   7   6   5   4   3   2   1

The publisher gratefully acknowledges the generous support of Peter Wiley and Valerie Barth as members of the Literati Circle of University of California Press.

Contents

Photographs

Introduction

Prisons and Paradises

I

It was a place that taught me to write. I had begun going to the huge antinuclear actions at the Nevada Test Site, sixty miles north of Las Vegas, in the late 1980s. The next few years of camping and committing civil disobedience by trespassing into this most bombed place on earth—the site of more than a thousand nuclear explosions that were only nominally tests—taught me other things as well.

Maybe the first was that the very term *place* is problematic, implying a discrete entity, something you could put a fence around. And they did: three strands of barbed wire surrounded this 1,375-square-mile high-security area—but it didn't keep in the radiation or keep out the politics. What we mean by *place* is a crossroads, a particular point of intersection of forces coming from many directions and distances. At the test site, some of the more obvious convergences or collisions involved the history of civil disobedience since Thoreau and the history of physics since it became useful for atomic bombs, along with the Euro-American attitudes toward the desert that made it possible to devastate it so wantonly, and the counter-history of the indigenous people of the region. During the decades of detonations, the radioactive fallout reached New England and beyond; protestors came from Japan and from Kazakhstan, as well as from New York and rural Utah. So much for fences.

The challenge of describing the austere sensuality of living outdoors in a harsh

1

and possibly radioactive desert under a spectacular sky, of doing so while contemplating the fate of the earth and playing tag with assorted armed authority figures, called forth a great collapse of category for me. I realized that in order to describe the rich tangle of experience there, I needed to describe, to analyze, to connect, to critique, and to report on both international politics and personal experience. That is, I needed to write as a memoirist or diarist, and as a journalist, and as a critic—and these three voices were one voice in everything except the conventions that sort our experience out and censor what doesn't belong. Thus it was that the distinct styles in which I had been writing melded. My 1994 book *Savage Dreams* (later reissued by the University of California Press) came out of this, but that was only the start.

Since then, I have been fascinated by trying to map the ways that we think and talk, the unsorted experience wherein one can start by complaining about politics and end by confessing about passions, the ease with which we can get to any point from any other point. Such conversation is sometimes described as being "all over the place," which is another way to say that it connects everything back up. The straight line of conventional narrative is too often an elevated freeway permitting no unplanned encounters or necessary detours. It is not how our thoughts travel, nor does it allow us to map the whole world rather than one streamlined trajectory across it. I wanted more, more scope, more nuance, more inclusion of the crucial details and associations that are conventionally excluded. The convergence of multiple kinds of stories shaped my writing in one way; this traveling by association shaped it in others. Early in my history of walking, I wrote that "if fields of expertise can be imagined as real fields, fenced off and carefully tilled, then the history of walking is a path that trespasses through dozens of fields." So are most unfenced lines of inquiry. I learned two kinds of trespassing at the test site, geographical and intellectual.

There I also learned that the sunset is no less beautiful when you are wearing handcuffs (or more so, as I discuss in "Justice by Moonlight"). That is to say, experience never gets sorted out, except by the mind that insists it must be, and the most truthful are the passionate impurists. One of the people I met at the test site was the landscape photographer Richard Misrach (whose pictures of clouds and skies are the nominal subject of "Excavating the Sky"). At the time, the early 1990s, he was making images that many people found deeply disturbing. I was told again and again that he was "glorifying violence" with his pictures of the rav-aged military landscapes of Nevada's endless expanse of military land. These crit-ics wanted the beautiful to be synonymous with the good, beauty never to be seductive unless that seduction was the path to virtue, evil to be easy to reject, and pictures about politics to be able to fit into the dry sensibility of photojournal-ism rather than the voluptuousness of large-format color photography. The envi-ronmental magazines mostly obeyed these mandates, as I have been complaining ever since: oil spills were always in small, ugly pictures; and the big color pictures of pristine nature excluded any sense of history, violence, or even, for the most part, decay. (Photographer Eliot Porter was at the root of much of this, as "Every Corner Is Alive: Eliot Porter as an Environmentalist and an Artist" elaborates, but it wasn't his fault; he was better than his followers.)

Richard's work challenged us to feel the conflicts of being fully present in a complicated world, and I was trying to do the same. We were not alone: perhaps that struggle to put the world back together was the major mandate of the late twentieth century. And we have, in many ways, by learning to think about the politics of food; by becoming more sophisticated about where the material objects and energy we use come from and go (thus the lingerie in "The Silence of the Lambswool Cardigans" and the nuclear waste and gold mines in the section "Trouble Below"); by learning to think about the world more in terms of systems than discrete objects; by pursuing ideas and histories across fields and genres; by remembering at last, those of us who are not indigenous, that all the terrain of the Americas has a human history as well. It was a long way back. I think of that fork in the road and the subsequent great divide as the Thoreau problem. It surfaces in considerations of his work again and again, and because Thoreau is so important to American thought (and to the writing in this book—he appears at least briefly in several of the essays), it seems worthwhile to revisit his seamlessness and the interpretive apartheid that divided up his territory.

Thoreau was emphatic about the huckleberries. In one of his two most famous pieces of writing, "Civil Disobedience," he concluded his account of his night in Concord's jail with these words: "I was put in jail as I was going to the shoe maker's to get a shoe which was mended. When I was let out the next morning, I proceeded to finish my errand, and having put on my mended shoe, joined a huck leberry party, who were impatient to put themselves under my conduct; and in half an hour,—for the horse was soon tackled,—was in the midst of a huckleberry field, on one of our highest hills, two miles off, and then the state was nowhere to be seen." He told the same story again in the other, *Walden*, this time saying that he "returned to the woods in season to get my dinner of huckleberries on Fair Haven Hill." That he told it twice tells us that he considered the conjunction of prisons and berry parties, of the landscape of incarceration and pastoral pleasure, significant. But why?

The famous night in jail took place about halfway through his stay in the cabin on Emerson's woodlot at Walden Pond. His two-year stint in the small cabin he built himself is often portrayed as a monastic retreat from the world of human affairs into the world of nature, though he went back to town to eat with and talk to friends and family and to pick up money doing odd jobs that didn't fit into *Walden*'s narrative. He went to jail both because the town jailer ran into him while he was getting his shoe mended and because he felt passionately enough about national affairs to refuse to pay his tax. To be in the woods was not to be out of society or politics.

Says the introduction to my paperback edition of *Walden* and "Civil Dis obedience": "As much as Thoreau wanted to disentangle himself from other peo ple's problems so he could get on with his own life, he sometimes found that the issue of black slavery spoiled his country walks. His social conscience impinged on his consciousness, even though he believed that his duty was not to eradicate social evils but to live his life independently." To believe this is to believe that the woods were far from Concord jail not merely by foot but by thought. To believe that conscience is an imposition upon consciousness is to regard engagement as a hijacker rather than a rudder, interference with one's true purpose rather than perhaps at least part of that purpose.

Thoreau did not believe so or wish that it were so—and he contradicted this isolationist statement explicitly in "Civil Disobedience," completed, unlike Walden, shortly after those years in the woods—but many who have charge of his reputation do. They permit no conversation, let alone any unity, between the rebel, the intransigent muse to Gandhi and Martin Luther King Jr., and that other Thoreau who wrote about autumnal tints, ice, light, color, grasses, woodchucks, and other natural phenomena in essays easily and often defanged and diced up into inspiring extracts. But for Thoreau, any subject was a good enough starting point to travel any distance, toward any destination. There were no huckleberries in his passionate defense of the violent abolitionist John Brown, but there were arguments about freedom in the essay on huckleberries written about the same time.

This compartmentalizing of Thoreau is a small portion of a larger partition in American thought, another fence built in the belief that places in the imagination can also be contained. Those who deny that nature and culture, landscape and politics, the city and the country are inextricably interfused have undermined that route for all of us, Thoreau's short, direct route so few have been able to find since. This makes politics dreary and landscape trivial, a vacation site; it banishes not merely certain thoughts—chief among them that much of what the environmental movement dubbed wilderness was or is indigenous homeland, a very social and political space indeed, then and now—but even the thought that Thoreau in jail must have contemplated the following day's huckleberry party, and that Thoreau among the huckleberries must have ruminated on his stay in jail. That alone is a major route to and fro, and perhaps the most important one. We are usually in several places at once, and the ways our conversations and thoughts meander is a guide to the connections between all things or any two things. People in cities eat the fruits of the country; people in the country watch the strange doings of city-dwelling politicians and celebrities on TV.

If "black slavery spoiled his country walks," you can imagine that it spoiled the slaves' country walks even more. Thus the unresisting walk to jail. "Eastward, I go only by force; but westward I go free," Thoreau wrote elsewhere, but the route to the free west (which, for slaves, was the free north of Canada) was not always direct. You head for the hills to enjoy the best of what the world is at this moment; you head for confrontation, for resistance, for picket lines to protect it, to free it, to make it better. Thus it is that the road to paradise often runs through prison; thus it is that Thoreau went to jail to enjoy a better country; and thus it is that one of his greatest students, Martin Luther King Jr., found himself in jail and eventually in the way of a bullet on what was called the long road to freedom, whose goal he spoke of as "the mountaintop." We were lucky at the Nevada Test Site in those days; the prison and the mountaintop were pretty much the same place.

Bertolt Brecht once wrote, "What kind of times are they, when / A talk about trees is almost a crime / Because it implies silence about so many horrors?" He wrote in an era when the trees seemed marginal to the realm of politics; in recent decades, everything from climate change to clear-cutting has made forests pivotal. To imagine the woods as an escape is to have already escaped awareness of the political factors weighing in on their fate and their importance. This is the most unfortunate way that schism has closed up. But it has also undone the false dichotomy between the city and the country: if the woods are being cut down to build houses, we can see the fate of the forest and its bodily remains in the new subdivision; we can protest it in the urban administrative headquarters or the overseas shareholders' meeting. Conventional environmental writing since Thoreau has often maintained a strict silence or an animosity toward the city, despite its importance as a lower-impact place for the majority to live, its intricate relations to the rural, and the direct routes between the two. Imagining the woods or any untrammeled landscape as an unsocial place, an outside, also depends on erasing the societies who dwelt and sometimes now dwell there, the original Americans. One more thing that can be said in favor of Thoreau is that he spent a lot of time imaginatively repopulating the woods around Concord with Indians and even prepared quantities of notes for a never-attempted history of Native America (and the third section of his *The Maine Woods* is mostly a portrait of the Native guide Joe Polis).

Not that those woods were unsocial even after their aboriginal population was driven out. "Visitors" is one of the chapters of *Walden*, and in this chapter (mentioned in "Jailbirds I Have Loved"), Thoreau describes meeting runaway slaves in the woods and guiding them farther on the road to freedom. Rather than ruining his country walks, some slaves joined him on them, or perhaps he joined them in the act of becoming free. Some of those he guided were on the Underground Railroad, in which his mother and sisters in Concord were deeply involved; and a few months after that famous night in jail, Thoreau hosted Concord's most important abolitionist group, the Concord Female Anti-Slavery Society, at a meeting in his Walden Pond hut. What kind of a forest was this, with slaves, rebels, and the ghosts of the original inhabitants all moving through the trees? He had gone to jail, of course, over his refusal to pay taxes because he considered both slavery and the war on Mexico immoral.

The American landscape in his time was crossed by many invisible lines: those that separated slave and free states; those that demarcated the rapidly shrinking Indian territory and the new reservations; those that laid out the new national borders drawn up at the conclusion of the war on Mexico, whereby the million square miles or so that had been Mexico's northern half became the U.S. Southwest. Even the name of the short-lived Free Soil Party of the 1840s implies that something as tangible as soil is embedded with something as immaterial as ideology. Though Thoreau remarked in his essay "Walking" that the principal surveyor of wild lands must be the Prince of Darkness, he himself was such a measurer of land. He knew that what exists as landscape for one kind of experience exists as real estate for another. Fair Haven Hill, up above the Sudbury River, may have been his favorite place of all, a promontory from whose rocky crest the view was considerable, but he surveyed a portion of it for Reuben Brown on October 20–22, 1851 (and did some surveying for his jailer, Sam Staples, on various occasions long after the famous night in jail).

You can see that two-mile journey from the jail to the berries another way. Thoreau began that essay/lecture on walking with, "I wish to speak a word in favor of nature, of absolute freedom and wildness." If he went to jail to demonstrate his commitment to the freedom of others, he went to the berries to exercise his own recovered freedom, the liberty to do whatever he wished—and the evidence in all his writing is that he very often wished to pick berries. There's a widespread belief, among both activists and those who cluck disapprovingly over insufficiently austere activists, that idealists should not enjoy any pleasure denied to others, that beauty, sensuality, delight all ought to be stalled behind some dam that only the imagined revolution will break. This schism creates, as the alternative to a life of selfless devotion, a life of flight from engagement, which seems to be one way those years at Walden are sometimes portrayed: escape. But change is not always by revolution; the deprived don't generally wish most that the rest of us would join them; and a passion for justice and pleasure in small things are not incompatible. It's possible to do both, to talk about trees and justice (and in our time, justice for trees); that's part of what the short jaunt from jail to hill says.

Perhaps prison is anything that severs and alienates; paradise is the reclaimed commons with the fences thrown down; and so any step toward connection and communion is a step toward paradise, including those that take the route through jail. In Thoreau's case, I think of the modern term *prefigurative politics*, which means that you can and perhaps ought to embody what you avow—that you cannot get to peace through strife, to justice by bullying; that you win a small victory by embodying freedom, justice, or joy, not just campaigning for them. In this sense, Thoreau was demonstrating on that one day in Concord in June of 1847 both what dedication to freedom was and what enjoyment of freedom might look like—free association, free roaming, the picking of the fruits of the earth for free, free choice of commitments—including those that lead to jail—and of pleasures. That is the direct route to paradise, the one road worth traveling.

III

Storming the Gates of Paradise gathers together nearly forty essays whose common ground is a concern with place, geography, land, environment, and an interest in reading them politically—and in understanding politics through place. Often the most and least tangible join forces: inchoate anxieties about the Other are manifest as an actual fence on the border; the cheap excuses of the war on terror turn into concrete repression on the streets of New York in "Jailbirds I Have Loved"; the Playboy Channel and nature calendars inform each other in "Tangled Banks and Clear-Cut Examples."

Places matter. Their rules, their scale, their design include or exclude civil society, pedestrianism, equality, diversity (economic and otherwise), understanding of where water comes from and garbage goes, consumption or conservation. They map our lives. Even the American Civil Liberties Union often overlooks that part of the First Amendment guaranteeing "the right of the people peaceably to assemble," since peaceable assembly has been not only assaulted in some places (New York City during the 2004 Republican National Convention, for example) but designed out of the landscape in others. Or has it? I have long believed that San Francisco's vibrant political culture comes in part from its very terrain: a pedestrian density, considerable street life, parks and plazas serving as focal points for public gatherings. Nonetheless, in the spring of 2006, Latinos turned what seemed to be the democracy-proof, automobile-dominated terrain of Los Angeles into the site of an exuberant, enormous gathering—perhaps a million or more—in defense of immigrant rights, making a city out of sprawl by acting as a functioning civil society within it (a core subject of "Nonconforming Uses: Teddy Cruz on Both Sides of the Border"). Which is only to say that the way we inhabit places also matters, and that comes from experience, imagination, belief, and desire as much as or more than from architecture and design. In other words, the mind and the terrain shape each other: every landscape is a landscape of desire to some degree, if not always for its inhabitants.

The fundamental desire could be described as the desire for paradise, or perhaps the demand for it—for the city on a hill; for a more perfect union; for getting to the mountaintop, in Martin Luther King Jr.'s sense as well as Thoreau's and Muir's; for the peaceable kingdom that devolves into the gated noncommunity but is also this country's rich history of utopian communities and social experiments. In this country, we immigrants have, since the seventeenth-century Puritans invaded the Northeast and the sixteenth-century conquistador Coronado clumped through the Southwest looking for Cíbola's Seven Cities of Gold, believed in paradise, sometimes as a birthright, sometimes as a goal, sometimes as something recently lost (for conservatives, that loss may be the patriarchal family that they imagine existed, like some primordial forest, uninterrupted from one coast to the other; for radicals, it's too often some simplified or entirely imagined version of society before technology or some other form of alienation intruded).

Paradises from the past are seldom useful as anything but rulers by which to measure the failures of the present, the failures that paradises of the future seek to fix—abolition, women's suffrage, labor rights, the civil rights struggle, the modern women's movement, environmentalism, and human rights movements, including those taking on the global economy. There's the paradise of the semi-fictitious pure place seen in nature photography and heard in environmental exhortations, the paradise of solidarity in political action, the paradise of memory and recognition transfigured. And then there are the ruins, the prisons, the radioactive lands, the endless battles between this country's myriad factions, each of whom is in one way or another storming the gates of paradise, trying to get inside their vision of a better world. The belief in an attainable paradise fuels the restless idealism that keeps this country agitated. This book tries to map a few of the infinite versions.

Neither definitions of paradise nor modes of attempted entry remain stable over time; this book may be in a roundabout way a chronicle of a rapidly evolving world. The earliest essay in the book, "The Garden of Merging Paths," was written as the World Wide Web was first becoming available to the most technologically advanced; by the time of an essay such as "Fragments of the Future: The FTAA in Miami," the Web had become a nearly ubiquitous and broadly accessible tool for organizing on behalf of global justice, for tracking issues, for finding alternative news. When the latter piece was published, in 2003, the World Trade Organization's future was still up in the air. As I write now, in late 2006, the organization seems largely defunct if not quite absolutely stone-cold dead, killed off by activists and by resistant nations in the global South, after the watershed moment when the WTO met in Seattle in November 1999.

These are the most concrete shifts. Rereading the essays that deal with representations of Native Americans, I can see that much has changed since I plunged into that arena in the early 1990s; rereading those that deal with U.S.-Mexico border politics and the demonization of immigrants, I can see that not enough has. Some of these pieces are more retrospective or concerned with phenomena—gardens, skies—that are more about the sea floor of culture than the shifting tides of politics; others deal with urgent issues—nuclear waste and other environmental disasters in the making—that remain unresolved. I changed, too: an earlier anthology of mine, *As Eve Said to the Serpent*, was subtitled *On Landscape, Gender, and Art;* in collecting these essays, I first measured the extent to which my writing had taken up urban life and contemporary politics, drawn in by the crises as well as the possibilities of both. One thing that decades of reading histories and occasionally participating in or witnessing the making of history has taught me is that the future is up for grabs. Nothing is certain except that we can, sometimes, with enough will and enough skill, shape it and steer it. Some of that skill comes from remembering the past and understanding the present, goals I have tried to serve here.

1

UNEVEN TERRAIN

The West

The Red Lands

〖2003〗

The West began at the pay phone at the gas station in Lee Vining, the little town next to Mono Lake on the east side of the Sierra Nevada, too remote for cell phones. I was standing around in the harsh golden light at seven thousand feet waiting to make a call when I realized that the man on the line was trying to patch up his marriage, and the task wasn't going to be quick or easy. "You just aren't going to let us get back together, are you?" he said in a tone at once supplicating and truculent. I thought that maybe she had her reasons and wondered how far away she was on the other end of the phone line.

At Lee Vining, named after a miner and Indian killer, the rain shadow begins: the Sierra, which are just a hair shorter than the Alps, scrape off the Pacific clouds and keep everything east of them arid. There are few real boundaries in nature, and this is one of the most astounding: from the west, you can hike up a green mountain slope and come to the divide, where you face the beginning of a thousand miles or more of desert, stand in patches of deep snow from the winter before, and look at a terrain where only a few inches of moisture a year arrive. In most of California, all water flows west to the Pacific, including that of the western slope of the Sierra; but on the Sierra's other side, it goes east, into salty bodies of water like Mono and Pyramid lakes, into sinks and subterranean spaces, into thin air. The Great Basin, so-called because its scanty water doesn't drain to any sea, is mostly a terrain of north-south-running ranges, sharp-edged raw geology, separated by flat expanses of sagebrush.

In the desert, plants grow farther apart to accommodate the huge root systems they need to collect enough water to live, and so do communities and ranches. Few but the desert's original inhabitants found it beautiful before cars. The extremes of heat and cold, the vast scale, and the scarcity of water must have been terrifying to those traversing it by beast or on foot. On a hot day, water is sucked straight out of your skin, and you can feel how fast dying of thirst could be; but this aridity is what makes the air so clear, what opens up those fifty-mile views. What feeds the soul starves the skin. Now, with air conditioning and interstates and the option of going several hundred miles a day with ease, desert austerity is a welcome respite from the overdeveloped world. The aridity and the altitude—the lowlands are mostly more than four thousand feet high—make the light strong, clear, and powerful; and the sky in these wide places seems to start at your ankles.

Because wild creatures too are spread far apart and often operate at night, because the colors and changes of the plant life can be subtle, it often seems as though the real drama is in the sky—not exactly life, but life-giving, the light and the rain. Summer thunderstorms in the arid lands are an operatic drama, particularly in New Mexico, where the plot normally unfolds pretty much the same way every day during the summer monsoon season: clear morning skies are gradually overtaken by cumulus clouds as scattered and innocuous as a flock of grazing sheep, until they gather and turn dark; then the afternoon storm breaks, with lightning, with thunder, with crashing rain that can turn a dusty road into a necklace of puddles reflecting the turbulent sky. New Mexico is besieged now by a horrendous multiyear drought, and, watching the clouds gather every afternoon as if for this dionysian release that never came, I felt for the first time something of that beseeching powerlessness of those who prayed to an angry, unpredictable God and felt how easy it would be to identify that God with the glorious, fickle, implacable desert sky.

Every summer I go to live in the sky, I drive into this vastness whose luminousness, whose emptiness, whose violence seem to give this country its identity, even though few of us live there. It's hard to convey the scale of the empty quarter. The Nevada Test Site, where the United States and the United Kingdom have detonated more than a thousand nuclear bombs over the past half century, is inside a virtually unpopulated airbase the size of Wales. Nevada is about the size of Germany and has a population of a million and a half, which wouldn't sound so stark if it weren't that more than a million of them live in Las Vegas and most of the rest in the Reno area, leaving the remainder of the state remarkably unpopulated. At one point, the state decided to capitalize on this and named Highway 50, which traverses the center of Nevada, "the loneliest highway in America."

From Mono Lake, I drove about forty miles on 120, crossing from California to Nevada at some point along the way; then a stretch along the Grand Army of the Republic Highway, Route 6, over to the small town of Basalt; and another hundred or so miles up to 50. At first, the country was high enough that it was green, beautiful, stark, and treeless. Then the altitude climbed a little into piñon pine and juniper country, before dropping down into the drabness of most of the Great Basin, the color of sagebrush and the dirt in between. A grove of trees is a sure sign of a ranch house and irrigation, though there are entire valleys—and a valley means a place five or ten miles wide and several times as long—in which no such ranch is to be seen. Highway 50 traverses a dozen of these valleys and passes; driven in a day, they pass like musical variations, with their subtle differences of color and form. One range looked like mountains, another more like cliffs, with tilted layers of strata clearly visible. One valley was full of dust devils, those knots of swirling wind that pick up debris and move it across the land, funnels that are the visible sign of the wind's entanglement in itself.

Most of California is west of the West: the vast arid expanses come to an end at the Sierra Nevada, the long wall of mountains on the state's eastern edge. West of the Sierra, a dramatic change in scale takes place, and the infolding, the lushness, the variety of the terrain seem to invite the social density and complexity of California, with its thirty-something million residents from all over the world. The two coasts often seem to me to be a pair of parentheses enclosing the inarticulate, unspoken, inchoate American outback, this part of the country colored red for Republican in the voting map for the last presidential election, when the coasts were Democratic blue.

The red lands are an outback, a steppe, a Siberia, far removed from the cosmopolitanism of the coasts. When I live out here, as I have for a week or so now and again over the past dozen years, it seems hard to believe in cities, let alone in nations, in anything but the sublimity of this emptiness. The Great Basin is wide open topographically but introspective in spirit, turned in on itself; and news from outside seems like mythology, rumor, entertainment, like anything but part of what goes on here, or doesn't, out here where the sparse population is interspersed with sites for rehearsing America's wars. A lot of people became preoccupied with Area 51, an off-limits part of the eastern periphery of the Nevada Test Site where aliens were supposed to have landed, or been captured, or had their flying saucers tested, and the logic behind the beliefs seemed to be equal parts creative interpretation of military secrecy and a sense that everything from outside was alien. But the absences resonate as much as the presences.

On another road trip a few years ago, we'd gotten on Interstate 50 farther west and driven through the part of the highway that is also the Bravo 17 Bombing Range, past the electronic warfare installations, past the fake town they practice bombing, to Dixie Valley, a ranching community whose population was forced out by sonic-boom testing in the 1980s. Fallon Naval Air Station—a naval base in this driest of the fifty states—was testing the military uses of sonic booms on livestock, school buses, and homes. Animals stampeded and aborted, windows shattered, people went off the roads, and the navy solved the problem by eliminating the population in this oasis where clear spring water breaks the surface of its own accord.

The few dozen houses had been burned to the ground, and tanks used for aerial target practice were scattered between them. As we looked at the ruins of one ranch house, an extraordinary sound erupted behind us. The best way I can describe it is as the equivalent of a chainsaw running up one's spine, a noise so powerful it seemed more physical than sound. I turned just in time to see a supersonic jet disappear again, after buzzing us from about two hundred feet. It came from nowhere and went back there almost immediately, as though it had ripped a hole in the sky. The wars fought in the Middle East have been fought here first, in strange ways that could make those wars more real but instead make them more removed.

Once, driving a back road in Nevada, I was stopped for half an hour by a road construction crew. The woman in the hard hat who'd flagged me down spoke wistfully of San Francisco when I told her where I was from. She'd visited once in high school and spoke as though the seven-hour drive was an impassable distance, and perhaps it was, for her. Her town was called Lovelock, and it had a few casinos but no movie theater or bookstore. When I think of how Americans could fail to measure the carnage caused by hundreds of bombs in one city by that of two hijacked airplane crashes in another, I think of her.

And I think of the wars fought for our cheap gasoline, the wars that make viable not just my summer jaunts but year-round homes sixty or seventy miles from the grocery store (to say nothing of military flights measured not in miles per gallon but gallons per mile). When the freeway clotted up with roadside businesses south of Salt Lake City, this seemed verified by an auto dealer with a flashing signboard: "Our Troops. God Bless Them." And maybe all the talk about freedom means freedom to drive around forever on cheap petroleum, out here in a terrain just a little less harsh than Afghanistan. Thomas Jefferson was afraid of the red lands, afraid that where the arable soil ended so would his arcadian yeoman ideal and Europeans would revert to nomadism. There's something roving and ferocious about the white West that suggests he's right; the United States is really more like the lands it's been bombing lately than like Europe.

Red for a kind of cowboy ethos that society is optional and every man should fend for himself. This vast space was where people stepped out of society when their domestic lives failed or the law was after them. The ethos, of course, ignores the huge federal subsidies that support cattle raising, logging, and mining, just as Republican tax cutters overlook the fact that the military they wish to expand consumes the lion's share of tax revenue. Western and action movies concoct endless situations in which belligerence is justified and admirable, in which a paranoiac autonomy is necessary; and the current president, like Ronald Reagan before him, portrays himself as a representative of these places and their cosmology, an act of self-invention as bold as that of any renamed outlaw. Reagan went from the Midwest to Hollywood; Bush is a product of East Coast privilege, even if he did go to flat, dry Midlands, Texas, to cultivate his insularity and a failed oil business.

Maybe the seductive whisper of these empty places says that you don't have to work things out, don't have to come home, don't have to be reasonable; you can always move on, start over, step outside the social. To think of a figure in this vast western space of the Great Basin is to see a solitary on an empty stage, and the space seems to be about the most literal definition of freedom: space in which nothing impedes will or act. The Bonneville Salt Flats—a dry lake bed in northern Utah—where some of the world's land speed records have been set, and Nevada's Black Rock Desert dry lake bed, where more speed records were set and the bacchanalian Burning Man festival takes place every September, seem to have realized this definition in the most obvious ways: speeding cars, naked, hallucinating, tattooed love freaks partying down. And, of course, the U.S. military training for foreign adventures. (In the first Gulf War, the commanders referred to the unconquered portions of Iraq as "Indian Territory.")

Easy though all this is to deplore on moral grounds, the place is seductive. There's a sense for me that all this is home, that every hour, every mile, is coming home, that this isolated condition of driving on an empty highway from one range to another is home, is some kind of true and essential condition of self, because I am myself an American, and something of a westerner. There's a bumper sticker that says, "I love my country but I fear my government," and, more than most nations, the United States has imagined itself as geography, as landscape and territory first, and this I too love.

A year ago, I was at a dinner in Amsterdam when the question came up of whether each of us loved his or her country. The German shuddered, the Dutch were equivocal, the Tory said he was "comfortable" with Britain, the expatriate American said no. And I said yes. Driving across the arid lands, the red lands, I wondered what it was I loved. The places, the sagebrush basins, the rivers digging themselves deep canyons through arid lands, the incomparable cloud formations of summer monsoons, the way the underside of clouds turns the same blue as the underside of a great blue heron's wings when the storm is about to break.

Beyond that, for anything you can say about the United States, you can also say the opposite: we're rootless except that we're also the Hopi, who haven't moved in several centuries; we're violent except that we're also the Franciscans nonviolently resisting nuclear weapons out here; we're consumers except that this West is studded with visionary environmentalists; and on and on. This country seems singularly dialectical, for its evils tend to generate their opposites. And the landscape of the West seems like the stage on which such dramas are played out, a space without boundaries, in which anything can be realized, a moral ground, out here where your shadow can stretch hundreds of feet just before sunset, where you loom large, and lonely.

The Postmodern Old West, or
The Precession of Cowboys and Indians

[1996]

I. COWBOYS, OR WALKING INTO THE PICTURE

The most breathtaking moment in the *Road Runner* cartoon show came when Wile E. Coyote set a trap for Road Runner. The trap poised on a mesa's edge was a billboard-like image extending the mesa's dead-end road into a different land-scape, so that the coyote's prey would crash through the paper image and fall to its death. But the indomitable bird ran straight into the picture and vanished up its road. Representation had become habitable space, and it was no coincidence that the landscape represented was the arid terrain of the Southwest. In much the same way, Ike Clanton escaped the Earp brothers' assault at the OK Corral in Tombstone, Arizona, by jumping inside the adjacent photography studio; and the events he had just survived made their own entry into the picture—into litera-ture, moving pictures, and TV. This habit of walking into pictures is the defining cultural habit of the American West, a habit that could be called identity-shifting, self-mythologizing, self-reflexive, simulationist, and a host of other words more often associated with the present moment. But if postmodernism had a birth-place, it was in the Old West.

In the 1970s and 1980s, as tourism sociologist Dean McCannell points out, roving herds of theorists—Umberto Eco, Jean Baudrillard, Fredric Jameson among them—invaded California, which they described as the capital of post-modernism, the place where the future had arrived. Had they spent as much time reading the region's history as they did staring out car windows and watching

TV, they would have found that theme parks and drive-by shootings, rogue cops and actor politicians, amnesia and identity-laundering were nothing new; they were in fact Western heritage, just as the toxic waste wars and technology booms bore a strong family resemblance to the previous century's Indian wars and gold rushes. And if this cowboy postmodernism had a mother, it was Jessie Benton Fremont. She played a willing Wile E. Coyote to her husband, John C. Fremont, who disappeared into the picture of the West she made, and a whole nation followed after him. Out of that picture a century later came a cowboy movie star president who transformed the whole nation into his vision of the Wild West: more weapons, more punishment, more mythology, less regulation, less social welfare, less memory (and another publicly adoring wife, Nancy Reagan, parenthetically pulling the hero's puppet strings). In that version of the West, past and present, identity is infinitely malleable, and history is indistinguishable from fiction.

Jessie Benton Fremont, by all accounts, would have preferred to be a man, and thereby an adventurer. Born in 1824 to a retiring southern belle and the powerful expansionist senator from the old Old West, the Missouri frontier, she was named after her paternal grandfather and grew up to become her father's confidante and political aide. Thomas Hart Benton himself saw her as his son and raised her much as though she were one. When she first realized how her gender would constrain her, she cut off her hair and refused the role; a few years later, at seventeen, she scandalized her relatives by cross-dressing in a military uniform at a family wedding. Finally, she settled for marrying the handsome nobody John Charles Fremont, and she and her father invented him as the son she should have been (a good proto-westerner, the illegitimate Fremont had already improved upon his father's name by adding the accent on the first syllable and the final *t* that made the name speak of mountains).

Thanks to his father-in-law's influence, Fremont received the command of the government's 1842 surveying expedition to the Rocky Mountains. Though the journey was of scientific and political significance, it was the literary quality of the report that made it a huge success. By all accounts, that literary flair was Jessie Fremont's. She got up from her childbed to ghostwrite for her neurasthenic husband, and she continued to write in his voice throughout his subsequent surveys and for the rest of their lives. The 1843 *Report on an Expedition of the Country Lying between the Missouri River and the Rocky Mountains* became a best-seller and a guidebook, and it made the man whose name was on the title page a national hero. Emerson complained about Fremont's narcissistic self-consciousness for all the descriptions of how he and his party looked, amid the romantic descriptions of scenery and thrilling accounts of adventure, but it may have been Jessie Fremont who saw it all as a picture. This pivotal first-person account of the West, this testament of manhood and authenticity, seems to have been the literary construct of a teenage girl who had stayed in the East.

Fremont's first expedition, the expedition of 1842, reached its climax with the ascent of what he called Fremont Peak in the Rockies. On Fremont Peak, he saw a bumblebee: "It was a strange place, the icy rock and the highest peak of the Rocky Mountains, for a lover of warm sunshine and flowers, and we pleased ourselves with the idea that he was the first of his species to cross the mountain barrier, a solitary pioneer to foretell the advance of civilization." The mountain and the bumblebee are both reinvented as portraits of the hero, a billion years of geology undone so that the man precedes the mountains; this utterly new place is only a mirror, and, layers upon layers, the man himself may be a fiction made up by a woman. It is clear the West is being invented, not even discovered, let alone encountered. As a text in which one finds in the landscape symbols and signs of oneself, Fremont's bumblebee incident has a place in symbolist literature; as documentary, it's more problematic. For the brave bee who is the author's double in this fiction of authenticity, literature, not life, is the ultimate destination: Fremont pays it fitting tribute by squishing it between the pages of a large book he happened to have with him.

One could wish that the West he concocted had been worthy of a greater philosopher—but Fremont was carrying out Baudrillard's agendas: "Henceforth it is the map that precedes the territory—PRECESSION OF SIMULACRA—it is the map that engenders the territory. . . . Simulation threatens the difference between 'true' and 'false,' between 'real' and 'imaginary.'" (The other West—the West of Native Americans as inhabitants rather than invaders, of an economy dependent on massive federal handouts rather than rugged individualism, of women and various others disqualified from cowboyhood, of a colossal military infrastructure in which further expansionism is rehearsed—has seldom appeared since, except in recent revisionist Western histories and photographs.)

It was this report and the military actions that followed that Americanized the Mexican West, opened up the land for mining, cattle grazing, military training, the crime and punishment industries, boasting, and forgetting—the characteristic activities of the American West. Before the Fremonts made the place literature, what lay beyond the Mississippi was little known to Yankees. Nobody was interviewing the Indians, and the trappers who knew it well were largely illiterate outsiders too; one of these illiterates, the Indian slayer Kit Carson, became Fremont's principal guide and was rewritten, by Jessie Fremont among others, into a national hero. Fremont and Carson have towns, streets, mountains, and rivers named after them. They became both the landscape they explored and the developments that effaced it (and in their wake came John Wayne Airport and Roy Rogers State Park). This opportunity to invent oneself, to enter into the new America as a fiction is what the West offered, and what its rootless amnesiac open spaces and society offer still: the self-made man as an artistic rather than merely economic possibility.

Such frontier heroes as Fremont and Carson were adored for their authenticity, for the physical courage and stamina that made their involvement in the blood-drenched exploration of the West possible, and for their encounters with the grit of real mountains and real prairies. Yet the details of their adventures and their characters were often fabricated. For the inhabitants of the Wild West they founded, there seems to have been no clear border between the world and its highly embroidered representation. Buffalo Bill (William Cody) and Wild Bill Hickok (James Butler Hickok), respectively a scout and buffalo hunter and a gunman and lawman, had been the subjects of laudatory fictions published in the East, and they collaborated with the mythmaking by lying extensively about their own lives afterward—or perhaps they had become true inhabitants of that murky borderland. They began in 1872 to reenact their adventures for audiences, helping to create a pageantlike docudrama that drew equally from circus, theater, and rodeo. This hybrid reached its apotheosis with the Wild West Show that Cody founded in 1882 with the pseudononymous Ned Buntline, who wrote more than a hundred novels about his partner. The circus, formerly a blend of the fabulous and the exotic, became a vehicle for presenting the celebrated characters, skills (shooting, roping, riding), and events of the West as entertainment. The West had already ceased to be a place and become a genre: it had become the Western.

In his autobiography, Cody wrote about fashion and fiction:

> At the last minute I decided to take along my buckskin suit. Something told me that some of the people I had met in New York might want to know just how a scout looked in his business clothes. . . . I was still wearing the wonderful over-coat that had been given me by the Grand Duke Alexis, and it was a source of continuous admiration among the officers, who pronounced it the most magnifi-cent garment of its kind in America. . . . In the papers the next morning I found that I had had adventures that up to that time I had never heard of. The next evening I had my first adventure in high society.

Cody was born in 1846, the year the United States began its war with Mexico for what is now the American Southwest, and died during the First World War; he began his career as a buffalo hunter and army scout and ended as a silent-movie producer. He is the crowning achievement of this proto–shape shift-ing, a prefigurative mix of Andy Warhol and Steven Seagal and Michael Eisner. There is now a Buffalo Bill Museum in Colorado, and, like the Gene Autry Museum in Los Angeles, it presents Western history and theater as though they were one—and in crucial respects they were. To comprehend the Wild West Show, imagine that Colin Powell toured the country in a theatrical production simulating the bombing of Baghdad, and that Saddam Hussein joined him occa-sionally for a command performance. The stars played themselves, and actors played the smaller parts. Enemies on the battlefield became co-stars of the circus, and Cody harbored an outlaw for a while who played himself—Gabriel Dumont of Canada's Riel Rebellion. For many of the most prominent characters of the West, crime, law enforcement, and entertainment were not distinct categories: Las Vegas already existed in spirit.

In the 1880s in Montana, some young outlaws were apprehended with saddlebags full of dime novels—they must have been copycat criminals, egged on by their reading. In his book *Spaghetti Westerns*, Christopher Frayling recounts, "Emmett Dalton, the last surviving member of the Dalton Gang specializing in great train robberies, actually collaborated on a book in 1937 (subsequently filmed) entitled *When the Daltons Rode*. This book told the story of how Emmett Dalton had died a romantic death at Coffeyville, Kansas, forty-five years previously." Wyatt Earp's sister-in-law Allie, married to Virgil Earp, tells of an occasion when Kate Holliday, the common-law wife of Doc Holliday, accidentally stumbled upon Earp's other identities, in the presence of Mattie, Wyatt Earp's wife:

> Kate had been leanin' against the closet door, her hand on the doorknob. As she flipped around, the door flew open. There was a bang and a clatter. Out of the closet tumbled a big suitcase, spewin' out on the floor some things that made my eyes pop out. Wigs and beards made of unravelled rope and sewn on black cloth masks, some false mustaches, a church deacon's frock coat, a checkered suit like drummers wear, a little bamboo cane—lots of things like that! Mattie gave a scairt little cry and fell on her knees in a hurry to gather all those things up.

Earp was a gambler, a criminal, and sometimes a Wells Fargo stagecoach guard; he and Doc Holliday used this Cindy Sherman–like collection of disguises to cover up that they were working both sides of the law.

After he and his brothers shot and were shot by a few rivals at the OK Corral, Wyatt Earp jumped town and dedicated himself to his own myth. He was always seeking someone to write his version of the facts about his two years in Tombstone; toward the end of his life, he served as a film consultant on Western movies. The love of his life was a San Francisco actress, and by the time he died in California in 1929, he had transformed himself from a petty criminal into the paradigmatic law-and-order marshal of American movies and, eventually, TV. Among his coffin bearers was Tom Mix, the most popular Western actor of his day; a few decades later, Henry Fonda would play Earp in a John Ford movie. Wyatt Earp had arrived in the pictures.

This is what Jim Jarmusch was trying to get at in his 1996 Western *Dead*

Man, in which Johnny Depp eventually becomes the notorious gunman he is initially mistaken for, as he wanders across a West where wanted posters bearing his likeness have preceded him—and the rock star Iggy Pop cross-dresses, in a calico-and-sunbonnet cameo role. For all the ethos of manliness, gender became as malleable as any other aspect of identity in the West, whose foundational document was Jessie Fremont's ventriloquism. In the 1870s, Calamity Jane was following George Armstrong Custer's Seventh Cavalry dressed as a man. Elizabeth Custer was wearing a wig made from her husband's golden ringlets. Custer himself was writing articles celebrating Wild Bill Hickok as the quintessential plainsman, and Calamity Jane made up a story that she had married Hickok; she claimed him as the father of a daughter eventually demonstrated to have been born four years after his death. Both Hickok and Buffalo Bill did stints with Custer's Seventh Cavalry at various times, but Hickok was shot in a bar in 1876 shortly after playing the part of himself in a three-act entertainment entitled *Scouts of the Prairie*, the same year that Custer and his cavalry were wiped out by the Oglala Sioux at Little Bighorn. In *Son of the Morning Star*, Evan S. Connell tells the tale of a much-married laundress for the Seventh Cavalry who was posthumously discovered, by her fellow female camp followers preparing her for burial, to be a man. (During the California Gold Rush, dances were often held in which some members of the all-male society took the part of, or dressed as, women; and Western newspapers of the era tell of same-sex couples of both genders.) The berdaches—the gay men who took on female roles in Plains Indian society—are another story; Crazy Horse, one of the Oglala leaders who creamed Custer, was said to have had a berdache wife.

Pictorially, the Old West existed in the interval between the development of wet-plate photography and the development of motion pictures and exists still in the timelessness of pictures and movies. Photography came of age with the settlement of the West, which became the first place to become widely known to the rest of the world through photographs. (Carleton Watkins's large-plate photographs of Yosemite, for example, were winning medals in Paris before more than a few hundred white people had ever seen the place, and Yosemite would become the great national shrine of nature as a work of art.) The Western photographers already knew what Foucault would preach, that knowledge was power: surveying the landscape was a military exercise, and places were often invaded so that they could be documented and measured. An information age had begun.

But the Western took place in the suspension of history. The Western is a conservative genre, intimating that cowboys and their environment of rough authenticity are how things have always been, or ought to have been, and that change is about to ruin both. Its sentiments echo still in conservative speeches claiming a Platonic steady state for the Heraclitan flux zones of family, culture, and nation. The nostalgia may be not for a past but for an impossible condition: the Western enshrines the self-conscious desire to be unself-consciously masculine, enshrines a condition in which masculinity has achieved the status of nature rather than culture. The only people who *had* been cowboys long enough to be traditional were the Mexicans and their indigenous ranch hands, and even gringo cowboys' accoutrements and skills—lassoes, the high-cantled saddles with saddle horns, cowboy boots—were borrowed from Spanish-speaking vaqueros (and even the word *vaquero* was anglicized, as *buckaroo*). But when movie cowboys—like the gunslingers of *The Magnificent Seven* (1960)—ride into Mexico, all they find are campesinos and a few inept bandits.

The great Kansas-bound cattle drives that form the basis for Texas Westerns like John Ford's Oedipal *Red River* (1948) took place in the brief years between 1866 and 1886, before the fences and trains reached Texas. The Western depended on the delicate balance between a wild space and a tame audience, between Texas plains and Chicago slaughterhouses, between the authenticity of cowboys and the insincerity of actors. The first narrative feature film is 1903's *The Great Train Robbery*, which was almost simultaneous with the events it fictionalized, but afterward technology appears largely as a threat in an ever more sophisticated Western cinema. In Sam Peckinpah's *The Wild Bunch* (1969), trains, cars, and automatic weapons are making it hard for traditionalist horse-riding thieves. In Clint Eastwood's *Unforgiven* (1992), the same sense that the spirit has gone out of the times prevails. Clint, as the protagonist, has hung up his guns, and everyone else except tired fellow retired gunman Morgan Freeman is despicable: the easterner who has come out to write about the bungling Duke of Death, the sadistic sheriff, the nearsighted would-be young gunman who idolizes the bloodshed of the past, the fat guy whose attack on a prostitute who giggled at his tiny dick sets the rest of the events into motion. It is an austere Western because it lacks the lush homoeroticism of almost all the movies in this genre, in which men represent Nature and women are the intrusive force of Culture come, like Huck's Aunt Sally, to civilize them ("We won't play culture to your nature" could be the rallying cry of Western feminism).

Late twentieth-century entertainers have reversed the trajectory of the frontier heroes, from acts to representations, from nature to culture. Ted Turner in Montana and Robert Redford in Colorado, Ronald Reagan in Santa Barbara, and costume maker Ralph Lauren in New Mexico celebrate their entertainment successes with the purchase of the ultimate reality, real estate. They become ranchers, and the lifestyle they impersonated becomes the one they take up in life (though rather than exiting the picture, they seem to be moving into an enlarged arena in which to carry out their cultural enactment of the nature and value of manliness and westernness). Buffalo Bill and Sitting Bull went from the landscape of the West into the theater of the Western. This reversal always reminds me of children's tales of toys like the Velveteen Rabbit and the puppet Pinocchio becoming flesh and blood: if they love you enough at the box office, you can become a real cowboy. After Fremont, what could be a more perfect precession of simulacra than the career of Clint Eastwood, who clambered up from playing in TV's *Rawhide* to the spaghetti Westerns of Sergio Leone to American Westerns to becoming a rancher, a landowner on a vast scale, and, for a while, the mayor of Carmel?

II. INDIANS, OR BREAKING OUT OF THE PICTURE

One of the most spectacular moves from the solid ground of the West into the nebulous genre of the Western was made by Sitting Bull, the great Hunkpapa chief who had been instrumental in wiping out Custer and his Seventh Cavalry. He became an actor who played himself. In 1884, Sitting Bull and his entourage exhibited themselves as "representations of wild life on the plains" in a New York City wax museum, already relics of the authentic only eight years after the Battle of Little Bighorn. He toured the West and then joined Buffalo Bill's Wild West Show with his entourage (and contractually retained the right to sell photographs of himself).

As a spectacle, Sitting Bull fit into this new West; as a speaker, he did not. In 1883, he had given a public address at an event commemorating the completion of the Northern Pacific Railroad, another commercial artery slicing up the West's open spaces and bleeding off its resources. Abandoning his text, he stood up and told the white audience that he hated all white people, that they were thieves and liars—but his army interpreter decided not to depart from the script and translated Sitting Bull's speech as a flowery welcome full of faux-Indian clichés. The audience applauded enthusiastically. A speech he gave in Philadelphia, this time about the end of fighting and the importance of education for his people, was "translated" as a lurid account of Little Bighorn. The inherent inadequacies of language so beloved of deconstruction had, in the case of Sitting Bull, become a political gap between signifier and signified that effectively silenced him. In his public speeches, Sitting Bull described a territory neither east nor west, but central: home, a complex, real place. His translators relocated it to the fictional zone of the Western, assimilating him into that authenticity they had to simulate.

Back on the Standing Rock Reservation in South Dakota during the heyday of the Ghost Dance cult and its bloody repression, Sitting Bull was shot down by the reservation police sent by the U.S. Army to capture him, a side note to the 1890 massacre at Wounded Knee. In the midst of the gunfight, the white horse Buffalo Bill had given him began to go through his circus tricks. In *Bury My Heart at Wounded Knee*, Dee Brown writes, "It seemed to those who watched that he was performing the Dance of the Ghosts. But as soon as the horse ceased his dancing and wandered away, the wild fighting resumed." Sitting Bull had exited the picture, but his horse was still performing on cue.

I claimed, in the first half of this essay, that postmodernism—as a cluster of simulacral precessions, self-conscious mythologizings, rootless identity manipulations, and erasures—was born in the Old West and that California is, rather than where the future has come to pass, a place where the regional past has borne strange international fruit. Those western emigrants turned actors, politicians, developers, and crooks created a mythology of the West so powerful it became a literary and cinematic genre that largely eclipses the factual history of the place, an inhabitable mythology with a large place for cowboys and a small one for Indians. When I think back to the Westerns of my childhood, it was the wagon train that functioned as the stable center of the movie, despite its invasive mobility; the Indians were, compositionally, invaders from outside the frame. Jane Tompkins writes in her marvelous treatise on the Western, *West of Everything*, that during her marathon of movie watching, "The Indians I expected did not appear. The ones I saw functioned as props, bits of local color, textural effects. As people they had no existence."

Western history is, in some respects, the history of the accretion of these distortions or fictions, and contemporary Native American political activity is often an attempt to break out of that history. Imagine Western history as an action movie—part *Cape Fear*, part *Home Alone*—in which a home is invaded by loveable gunmen who insist that the residents play all the lousy bit parts in an interminable drama or just shove them in the closet and play house themselves: the Native American land wars are attempts to take back part of the house, but the cultural wars are attempts to recast the characters or rewrite the drama. The sardonic artist Jimmie Durham revises it thus: "Nothing could be more central to American reality than the relationships between Americans and American Indians, yet those relationships are of course the most invisible and the most lied about. The lies are not simply a denial; they constitute a new world, the world in which American culture is located."

This new world of the United States was almost literally founded on appropriating indigenous identity: in 1773, the Sons of Liberty dressed up as Mohawks to stage the foundational gesture of revolt against England, the Boston Tea Party. Since then, playing Indian has been a popular occupation for children and, of late, for adults; and decorative motifs, from New Mexico license plates to Pendleton woolens to the ever popular chief's-head tattoo, draw from indigenous iconographies. For Native American culture to be infinitely appropriable, it must belong to everyone—and to no one in particular. This desire to possess has generated both the widespread belief that Native Americans have vanished and the concomitant problems of the visibility of contemporary Native people. The authenticity attributed to nativeness seems to be something everyone can impersonate; as cowboys are to American actors, so are Indians to—apparently everyone, including hordes of part-time wannabe Indians in Germany and Central Europe and New Age wannabes all over the United States. The Western's self-invention finds its final frontier, or final solution, in immigrants reinventing themselves as indigenous people, self-conscious simulators of an aesthetic of unself-conscious authenticity, happy inhabitants of a historical fiction.

Perhaps the conceptual reservation onto which Native Americans have been forced is called Art: like works of art, they are expected to exist either outside of time or in the past tense of classics and masterpieces, to be on exhibit, to be public property, to be seen and not heard, to be about the spiritual rather than the political, and to embody qualities to which everyone can aspire, whether they are the Czech and Slovak "Indians" in John Paskievich's 1996 documentary film *If Only I Were an Indian* or sports teams such as the Atlanta Braves, the Washington Redskins, the Kansas City Chiefs, the Chicago Blackhawks (to say nothing of Chevrolet Apaches, Jeep Cherokees, Pontiacs, and Winnebagos). As they have become more vocal—or audible—in recent decades, many native North Americans have worked to move out of or mock this conceptual museum. In the visual arts, Edgar Hachivi Heap of Birds, Jimmie Durham, James Luna, Zig Rising Buffalo Jackson, Hulleah J. Tsinhnahjinnie, and many others have taken on the politics of indigenous identity with humorous outrage.

One such battle against the museum was mounted by Pemina Yellow Bird, a Mandan woman appointed to the board of the North Dakota State Historical Society. After an incident in which two non-Indian men were apprehended with the shellac still drying on the skulls they had robbed from a local burial mound, she asked the state archaeologists where the recovered skulls were going:

> And they said, Well, we'll just put them in the vault with the others. The others? Yeah you want to see? So we went to the Heritage Center and down into

the basement where an armed guard was standing next to a vault. . . . They lead me into this warehouse-like room that was filled from the floor to the ceiling with boxes and boxes of remains of dead Indian people. And I said at that time—you know, I was just shocked, it knocked the wind out of me—Are these all Indian people? And they go, Yup, they're all Indians. The non-Indians get reburied, but we bring the Indians here for study.

Yellow Bird stood up at four board meetings to explain that the remains must be reburied, but, like Sitting Bull, she became inaudible when she became challenging: her remarks were ignored in the meetings themselves and were absent from the board minutes. It took five years of statewide Intertribal Reinterment Committee effort to achieve her goal.

The Smithsonian alone has the remains of more than eighteen thousand Native Americans in its collection, demonstrating yet again that Native Americans are considered artworks on the same order as their baskets. No matter how recent, indigenous burial sites were regarded as legitimate sites for archaeological digs until Congress passed the Native American Grave Protection and Repatriation Act of 1990. But the same year that legislation liberated Native American remains from museums, another law put live artists back in: that law mandates that no one may describe himself or herself as a Native American or Indian artist unless that individual is a registered member of a federally recognized tribe or is able to demonstrate a heritage of a quarter or more "Indian blood" (a definition that American Indian Movement activist Ward Churchill calls arithmetical genocide, since within a century no one will meet the genetic criterion, no matter what their cultural experience). No other ethnic group in the United States is thus certified—in somewhat the same way Old Masters paintings are authenticated or discredited. Punishment for unauthenticated artists or the exhibitors of their work can include up to fifteen years in prison or a million dollars in fines. Supposedly drafted to prevent imposters from cashing in on the Santa Fe art market, this law immediately caused several Oklahoma museums to close down and excluded uncooperative artists from many other arenas.

Jimmie Durham, for example, was scheduled to have a show at the nonprofit gallery American Indian Contemporary Arts in San Francisco, but the gallery faced closure or loss of funding, because its legal mandate is to show Native American artists and the part-Cherokee Durham, a prominent AIM activist in the 1970s, has declined to be certified by the federal government. The show was moved to another venue, and soon after, the artist Hulleah Tsinhnahjinnie made this law the subject of an installation at the San Francisco Art Institute, drawing an analogy between registration numbers and concentration camp numbers. Durham writes:

> To protect myself and the gallery from Congressional wrath, I hereby swear to the truth of the following statement: I am a full-blood contemporary artist, of the subgroup (or clan) called sculptors. I am not an American Indian, nor have I ever seen or sworn loyalty to India. I am not a "Native American," nor do I feel that "America" has a right to name me or un-name me. I have previously stated that I should be considered a mixed-blood: that is, I claim to be a male, but only one of my parents was male.

For a lot of tribes, the primary war nowadays is to prove that they exist; as extras from the Golden Age, they are assumed to have faded into the sunset along with the credits. Like Sandra Bullock in *The Net* (1995), a movie about a woman whose identity is electronically destroyed, or Vanessa Williams in *Eraser* (1996), the Schwarzenegger flop about the federal witness protection program, they do not officially exist; and without federal recognition of their existence, they cannot obtain the land rights and legal benefits owed to Native Americans. Proving they exist means coming up with a paper trail demonstrating cultural continuity, a peculiar demand to place upon people whose largely oral culture was violently disrupted and dislocated by the same government.

Proving that they exist to the general public can be equally challenging. Innumerable works of art mourn (or celebrate in a giddy whirl of melancholy) their vanishing: cultural monuments from *The Last of the Mohicans* (1826) to James Earle Fraser's sculpture *The End of the Trail* (1915, but still widely reproduced on postcards, belt buckles, and so forth) to *Dances with Wolves* (1991) wave them a fond but insistent farewell. Even the Northern California Karuk artist and story-teller Julian Lang embarked on a project about the nearby Mattole people under the impression that the Mattole were extinct—but learned better along the way. Thanks to the museum wall text accompanying an exhibition of Karl Bodmer's frontier watercolors of the 1830s, I myself believed that Mandans had been utterly wiped out by smallpox, until I met the Mandan artist Zig Jackson.

Ishi, much cherished as "the last Yahi" while more thriving California tribes were largely ignored, was exhibited at San Francisco's Panama Pacific International Exposition, along with *The End of the Trail*, and spent the last years of his life as exhibit-in-residence at a University of California museum in San Francisco, among Egyptian and Peruvian mummies and Indian bones. Performance artist James Luna critiqued Ishi's status when he put himself on display at the San Diego Museum of Man in 1986. Contemporary groups from the Ohlone of the San Francisco Bay Area to the Gabrielano of the Los Angeles Basin have been mourned as vanished tribes; and Edward Curtis's costumed portraits, in which he dressed up Native people in a multitribe pastiche of authenticity, haven't helped much either, insisting as they do that the only real Indian is a vanishing Indian. Tourists still sometimes get indignant about traditional dances performed by people in Reeboks.

Southern Sierra Miwok activist and Yosemite Park employee Jay Johnson told me the following story a few years ago:

> I think it was 1980, Julia and four of us on business for our tribe [seeking federal recognition in Washington] went to the Smithsonian and found the California museum exhibits, then Yosemite. . . . It had a little statement on the side, and it left off with "It's very sad today. There's no more Yosemite Indians." Period. I said, "Let's go down, talk to the people at the desk about this statement." So we went down there and this lady, she was at the desk, and I said, "Ma'am, about that diorama about Yosemite," and she says, "Oh, isn't that nice?" And I said, "It's nice, but there's an error in the statement," and she says, "Oh, no, there can't be. Every little word goes through channels and committees and what-not." And I says, "It's OK, but," I says, "it tells me that there are no more Yosemite Indians today." She says, "Well, that's true, it's very sad. But what-

ever's out there is true." So I say, "Well, I hate to disturb you, but I'm a Yosemite Indian, and we're here on business for our tribe." And she caught her breath and said, "Ohhh . . ."

Kit Carson finds a book that tells of feats he never did. Jay Johnson finds a museum display that tells him he has vanished long ago. In the simulacral West, cowboys expand, Indians contract.

Some tribes are fighting for federal recognition, others against appropriation in the representational wars. Many practitioners of New Age spirituality have been appropriating indigenous identities as though the world was their shopping mall and religious identity was no more than a costume to be tried on, mixed and matched, traded in and up. White people with bound braids and symbolic trinkets and animal names doing their own version of sweat lodge, drumming, vision quest, and sun dance ceremonies are rampant in the New Age and men's movements. In 1992, the Lakota Nations, the heirs to the victors of the Battle of Little Bighorn and the victims of Wounded Knee, issued a "Declaration of War against Exploiters of Lakota Spirituality." It read, in part, "The absurd public posturing of this scan-dalous assortment of pseudo-Indian charlatans, wannabes, commercial profiteers and cultists comprise a momentous obstacle in the struggle of traditional Lakota people for adequate public appraisal of the legitimate political, legal and spiritual needs of the real Lakota people." Like dressing up as Indians, religious appropria-tion threatens to homogenize, fictionalize, and commercialize an identity to the point where it can belong to everyone or no one, but not to anybody in particular. Confrontations with New Age people have attracted little outside attention, however. The Native newspaper *The Circle* reported that in 1993 indigenous activists caught up with Lynn Andrews, "a Beverly Hills housewife-turned-shaman," at a Los Angeles Whole Life Expo "and tried to convince her to admit that what she was writing about [in best-selling books such as *Jaguar Woman*] was fantasy, not Indian spirituality. Andrews is reportedly considering the pro-posal, but has not officially responded as she is negotiating a movie deal."

Indian gaming may be where many tribes are making themselves visible now. In a recently opened Pueblo casino just north of Santa Fe, Pueblo Indians are having their long-delayed revenge on the kin of Coronado, who blundered through the vicinity in the 1540s looking for the fictional Seven Cities of Cíbola. The casino is called Cities of Gold, after the jackpot Coronado never found, and poor Latinos get poorer there every night. It remains to be seen what the long-term results of the transformation of some of the poorest people in the country into some of the richest may be, but one of the early indications is counter-appropriation: back east, the Mashantucket Pequots, who operate the nation's most profitable casino, have just given the Hartford Ballet half a million dollars to stage an American version of the *Nutcracker* to be set not in their own Connecticut, but in Yosemite and Sequoia National Parks—as dizzy a tour de force of hybridization as anyone could imagine.

But the biggest wars are still over land, particularly over toxic and radioactive waste disposal on the land still held by Native Americans, wars to unload the excreta of technology upon the involuntary symbols of a pristine continent. (The same exemption from state regulation makes both dumping and gaming possible.) I participated in a Native American land war once. At stake was whether the U.S. government or the Western Shoshone Nation owns much of Nevada; the test case considered whether two Western Shoshone elders, the Dann sisters, had to pay federal grazing fees for running their livestock on the contested land.

The case went all the way to the U.S. Supreme Court and, because all the evidence was on the Shoshone side, the government was forced to make up a fictitious date of taking for the land it had forgotten to steal in the last century. In 1979, the courts decided that the land had been "taken" in 1872, though nothing resembling taking had actually happened that year, or any other, to the still largely unfenced and sparsely inhabited land, and no paperwork documents a transfer of land by any means. Transplanted elsewhere, the outrageousness of this historical revisionism resonates more strangely: imagine, if you will, that France claims Napoleon did conquer Russia and thereby asserts sovereignty over it in the present; or recall the occasions when Ronald Reagan cited events from the movies as historical fact. It is as though the courts asserted that Fess Parker and John Wayne beat the Mexicans at the Alamo.

The decision was economic: the federal government could afford to buy eastern Nevada for $26 million at 1872 prices (without interest), but not at late twentieth-century prices. The fact that it wasn't for sale didn't enter the calculations. The Dann sisters didn't respect the court's rulings, or its jurisdiction. So in 1992, the government hired cowboys from Utah to steal the sisters' cows from the contested land. I was one of the supporters at the Dann ranch the day of the first cattle raid, April 10, 1992, and though I missed the actual raid, a stalwart German supporter caught it all on videotape with Carrie Dann's camcorder (along with camcorders, walkie-talkies, faxes, computers, and radio-telephones played a part in the defense; information was the most powerful weapon in our nonviolent defense project). The raid took place in the morning. Carrie Dann single-handedly prevented the government men and the rent-a-buckaroos from loading her rounded-up cows into their cattle trucks by occupying the loading chute.

In the afternoon, we all watched it on TV with Carrie's humorous live narration. A few days later, I took the videotape to San Francisco and convinced a member of Paper Tiger TV to cut the footage into a short documentary. Within a couple of weeks, it was being screened in theaters (it opened in San Francisco as the short before Craig Baldwin's revisionist film O No Coronado!, which ends in the Coronado shopping plaza in Santa Fe), broadcast on public access TV, and distributed to activists. The Danns and their allies had become postmodern Westerners, living simultaneously in art and life, even if their version of history clashed with the cowboys' master narrative.

The Struggle of Dawning Intelligence

Creating, Revising, and Recognizing
Native American Monuments

〖1999〗

"The celebration of the past can easily be made to play politics, and monuments are linchpins of this process," writes Lucy Lippard, and nowhere is this more true than with monuments involving Native Americans. European Americans have long been fascinated with Native Americans, but not with their history, which often implicates early emigrants and undermines the heroic versions of history preserved in songs, school lessons—and monuments. In recent years, that history has been told more accurately and more audibly, with often turbulent results. In earlier versions, Native Americans either were the adversaries in a Manifest Destiny version of history or were outside history altogether, as timeless and infinitely appropriable totemic figures. Almost all Native American monuments commemorate Indian-European interaction rather than autonomous indigenous history, and only a handful of helpful or nonadversarial Indians—Squanto, Sacajawea—are remembered by name in public monuments. Coming to terms with that history has generated a new era of Indian wars, with iconography and words as the weapons this time around.

Earlier monuments are often merely evasive. On the coast of northernmost California, there is a National Historic Landmark plaque whose text names "Indian/Gunther Island" and asserts: "This site possesses national significance in commemorating the history of the United States of America." What the plaque fails to mention is the nature of that significance: on this island, formerly known as Tolowot, settlers axed to death all the women, children, old, and infirm of the Indian village while the men were out hunting. Others celebrate the "us" in the old "us/them" model of Euro-American/Native American history. The central plaza of Santa Fe, New Mexico, features a monument to those who died fighting "savage Indians" (although guerrilla reformists chiseled off the word *savage*); in front of one of its civic buildings is an obelisk commemorating Kit Carson, although it doesn't mention whether he's being commemorated as an expansionist scout or the scourge of the Navajo. Such monuments are predicated on an obsolete idea of who the public is: more and more Americans come from neither side of the historic "us/them," while if "us" now means the mainstream rather than an ethnicity, most Native Americans are participants in it to varying degrees.

San Francisco generated a lot of conflict when it tried to adjust one monument. The Pioneer Monument in San Francisco's Civic Center was dedicated on Thanksgiving Day 1894, less than half a century after California became part of the United States. The eight-hundred-ton piece, which serves as a statement about the Americanization of California, is a massive hunk of iconography, with thirty-seven bronze elements on five granite pedestals, including a forty-seven-foot-high central figure, four sculpture groupings on lower surrounding pedestals, commemorative names, bas-reliefs of representative events, medallions, and captions. Women, like Native Americans, have more often appeared as emblems than as individuals in public sculpture, and the Athena-like figure of Eureka standing atop the central structure along with a California grizzly is no exception. Two of the subsidiary sculpture groupings, allegories of commerce and agriculture represented as women, are standard-issue, too; although the artist, Frank Happersberger, was born in California, he learned his academic-classical clichés during years of study in Munich. The other two groupings are more specific and more interesting. One, captioned "In '49," shows a trio kneeling with picks and pans. The other grouping is where the trouble began.

Captioned "Early Days," it is meant to represent the peoples who lived in California before the Yankees. In the rear is a dashing vaquero; in the middle, a figure wearing a monk's habit and leaning over the figure of a prone Indian, who is in front. While the other two figures have upraised hands—the vaquero is energetically twirling a now-vanished lariat, the priest is chastising with upraised finger—the Indian's arms are draped resignedly across his body, as if to suggest that his space is contracting as that of the others is expanding. From left of center, it looks as if the vaquero and the priest are raising up invisible whips to lash the Indian. With his two feathers, braids, lanky body, and Roman nose, this representative Indian looks more like the Last of the Mohicans than like most Native Californians, and he is clearly an older cousin of James Earle Fraser's *The End of the Trail*, the famous sculpture of the downcast warrior slumped on his drooping horse that was first exhibited at San Francisco's Panama Pacific International Exposition of 1915 and now sits in Visalia, in central California. Happersberger's grouping represents the Spanish and Mexican eras, during which the Franciscan missions were built to convert—into Christians and laborers—the indigenous inhabitants of the coast. According to the San Francisco Municipal Report of 1893–1894, "The group of figures fronting the City Hall consists of a native over whom bends a Catholic priest, endeavoring to convey to the Indian some religious knowledge. On his face you may see the struggle of dawning intelligence."

The 1906 earthquake destroyed the City Hall that this first version faced, but the monument survived unmoved until a few years ago. It was slated to be relocated to accommodate the new public library when the San Francisco Arts Commission received a letter from Martina O'Dea, "on behalf of the American Indian Movement Confederation and the Native American and Indigenous people of the San Francisco Bay Area," early in 1995. "We request," she wrote, "the removal of a monument which symbolizes the humiliation, degradation, genocide and sorrow inflicted upon this country's indigenous people by a foreign invader, through religious persecution and ethnic prejudice." The Arts Commission, which administers such civic sculptures, decided instead to attach a plaque providing a contemporary interpretation of the grouping. An early draft stated, "In 1769, the missionaries first came to California with the intent of converting the state's 300,000 Native Americans to Christianity. With their efforts over in 1834, the missionaries left behind about 56,000 converts—and 150,000 dead. Half of the original Native American population had perished during this time from the whites' diseases, armed attacks, and mistreatment."

Although the draft text was intended to counter the image of oppression conveyed by the statue, it actually reinforced its message by linking indigenous and

Spanish/Mexican history with the "Early Days," as if the Spanish and the Mexicans had superseded the Indians before fading away themselves. Clearly neither group was imagined as part of the audience Happersberger addressed, the audience that identified with westward migration and a romanticized version of the Gold Rush. In representing the domination of Indians by the Spanish, the sculpture pitted against each other, then and now, two peoples who had both suffered in the Americanization of California—and presumed that neither would be its audience, though in the 1990s both are.

The proposed revision of the text prompted both the local Spanish consul and the Catholic archbishop to write indignant letters to the mayor. Their point was that the most brutal treatment and precipitous population decline of Native Californians came with the Gold Rush, not the mission era (although being less brutal than the Forty-Niners is a dubious distinction). Should the text appear, said Consul General Camilo Alonso-Vega, "many of us, including myself, would feel discriminated against and indelibly unwelcome at the very core of this city founded by Spaniards." Alonso-Vega missed the point that the statue had for a century made indigenous Americans feel those very things. Archbishop William J. Levada even suggested another interpretation of the grouping: "a Franciscan missionary directs the attention of a native American and a vaquero heavenward." Most of us who are not archbishops distrust authority more than did the citizens of 1894; an image of one man asserting such intensely bodily authority over another would appear ominous to many viewers even without historical contextualization.

Some suggested that the Pioneer Monument be replaced with other monuments: the premise of these proposed monuments was that the oppression was not sufficiently obvious and that the wrongs done to indigenous Americans *should* be represented, even more explicitly. One proposal called for a forty-ton stone block crushing an Indian, another for a Promethean figure chained to a rock. O'Dea's original complaint was that the sculpture grouping commemorated "the crimes committed against indigenous Americans," though she may have meant that it celebrates or sanitizes those crimes. She didn't want them forgotten, but rather remembered differently.

The whole ruckus was decried by local newspaper columnists and by State Librarian and historian Kevin Starr as "political correctness." The latter wrote, "How can San Francisco, or any city for that matter, hope to address its pressing problems, hope to achieve community, when an agency of government—for whatever perverse and distorted reasons—stigmatizes a culture and a religion with horrific charges of genocidal intent?" It is surprising that Starr ignored the many, many historical statements—albeit by Protestants—demonstrating genocidal desires and expectations; there was, for instance, California governor Peter Burnett's 1851 declaration to the new state legislature "that a war of extermination would continue to be waged until the Indian race should become extinct, and that it was beyond the power or wisdom of men to avert the inevitable destiny," which, like many similar statements, suggested that the war and the extinction were mysteriously inevitable and even more mysteriously unlinked.

Believing that Indians were vanishing, then and now, seems to have been wishful thinking, a wish for the circumstances under which monuments such as this could survive ideologically intact for a unified "us" untroubled and unenlarged by a "them" who had been safely relegated to the ahistorical realm of the emblematic. As emblems, they would be national ancestor-spirits rather than the ancestors of particular individuals with sometimes inconvenient political demands. It is this conveniently vague fading away, a disappearance for which no one bears responsibility, that is represented in the Pioneer Monument, as well as in such ideologically similar works as The End of the Trail and Edward Curtis's reconfigured photographs.

The text that was finally put on the bronze plaque in front of "Early Days" reads, in part, "At least 300,000 Native people—and perhaps far more—lived in California at the time of the first settlement in 1769. During contact with colonizers from Europe and the United States, the Native population of California was devastated by disease, malnutrition, and armed attacks. The most dramatic decline of the Native population occurred in the years following the discovery of gold in 1848." From a text that commented on the grouping, it has become a text that draws attention away from it, toward the Forty-Niners on the opposite side of the monument, and that also underscores the congratulatory tone of the whole ensemble. It concludes with the statement that, in 1990, the indigenous American population of the state was 236,078 (though it left out the fact that many of those are not Native Californians). Having weathered the reaction, the Arts Commission has permanently reoriented the meaning of the sculpture—has made it an artifact rather than an expression of public sentiment.

The San Francisco monument pitted two relatively disenfranchised groups against each other, but the conflict is more often between indigenous and dominant-culture values and interpretations, as with the new memorial to the Indians killed at the Battle of Little Bighorn in the summer of 1876. The history of this Montana site reflects changing federal attitudes: established in 1879 as a national cemetery for the soldiers of the U.S. Seventh Cavalry who died and were buried there, it became Custer Battlefield National Monument in 1940, and in 1991 was renamed Little Bighorn Battlefield National Monument in a law signed by President George H. W. Bush that also called for an additional monument at the site (a granite obelisk bearing the name of General Custer and his fallen troops having been erected long ago). As the official Little Bighorn Battlefield statement put it, "The law also stated that the memorial should provide visitors with a better understanding of the events leading up to the battle and encourage peace among people of all races." An advisory committee was formed, a public competition was held, and a ruckus ensued.

In 1997, the *Times* of London reported that "enraged critics say that erecting an Indian monument at Little Bighorn is akin to 'handing the Vietnam War memorial over to the Vietnamese.'" Another unnamed traditionalist told the western states' progressive newspaper *High Country News*, "It's like erecting a monument to the Mexicans killed at the Alamo." Philadelphia designers John R. Collins and Alison J. Towers's winning design for the monument is an earthwork, a circular berm with a northern aperture through which can be seen a grouping of three larger-than-life mounted Indians. It's an odd mix of contemporary siteworks, à la Maya Lin and Nancy Holt, and old-fashioned heroic representation. It provides both a place to gather and to think and something to look at—something for

everyone but those still fighting the Indians. As in the San Francisco case, governments have become more progressive than some of the governed.

In his 1995 book of photographs, *Sweet Medicine: Sites of Indian Massacres, Battlefields, and Treaties*, Drex Brooks portrays places important to indigenous history and culture across the continental United States. What is most startling is how many are unmarked. The site where King Philip and his Wampanoag war-
riors were massacred in Bristol County, Rhode Island, in 1675, for example, is only a stream in a thicket of young branches; and many others are likewise unaltered, unmarked landscapes. A massacre site in Mystic, Connecticut, is built up, but uncommemorated: the bland buildings and signs constitute an erasure of the past.

Monuments are reminders that something important happened somewhere and interpretations of its significance. The premise of monuments—that without such markers the history of a place would be lost—may be true for cultures whose memory is preserved in material forms and whose members do not remain long in one place—that is, for cultures such as that of the settlers and contemporary Euro-
Americans. Leslie Marmon Silko writes of the web of stories woven around every-
day life in her Laguna Pueblo community, stories that "carefully described key landmarks and locations of fresh water. Thus a deer-hunt story might also serve as a map. Lost travelers and lost piñon-nut gatherers have been saved by sighting a rock formation they recognize only because they once heard a hunting story describing this rock formation." She continues, "Indeed, stories are most frequently recalled as people are passing by a specific geographical feature or the exact location where a story took place. It is impossible to determine which came first, the incident or the geographical feature that begs to be brought alive in a story."

Anthropologist Keith Basso describes a similar relationship in the culture of the Western Apache, for whom natural places call forth stories, so that the landscape provides a practical and moral guide to the culture. Even allowing for the profound differences between tribes, the many accounts like this suggest a worldview in which oral tradition continually generates a network of stories that map and make intimately familiar a landscape in which, as Silko puts it, "the precise

date of the incident is often less important than the place." All of which suggests that bronze sculptures and granite obelisks with their inscriptions and emphasis on dates might be alien or redundant to such a tradition. In her essay in *Sweet Medicine*, however, historian Patricia Nelson Limerick argues that "Americans ought to know what acts of violence bought them their right to own land, build homes, use resources, and travel freely in North America. Americans ought to know what happened on the ground they stand on; they surely have some obligation to know where they are." Knowledge of such past violence, she says later, might save Americans from nostalgia for "a prettier time in the past." For Limerick, such monuments would speak most powerfully to the nonindigenous population. By these terms, putting up monuments is as significant a project as revising those that exist.

One European-style monument to insurgent indigenous history has long been in the works: the giant equestrian figure of Crazy Horse being carved into a mountain near Mount Rushmore. The brainchild of Boston-raised Korczak Ziolkowski, who assisted Gutzon Borglum in the carving of Mount Rushmore, the Crazy Horse memorial was begun half a century ago and, according to its web site, will be the biggest sculpture in the world when completed. It could be argued, however, that the European sculptural tradition within which this work fits and the massive blasting of the mountainside it requires celebrate the artist and the technology more than the dead leader, who refused to be photographed.

The continent is already densely populated with monuments—that is, sites of significance—recognized because of oral traditions, which means that those outside the traditions are often unable and or unwilling to see them. A case in point is Devils Tower National Monument, in northeastern Wyoming, where conflicting interpretations, or at least interests, led to a lawsuit. A steep and startling granite butte standing alone in the landscape, with ridges sweeping up to its flat crown, it was designated in 1906 as the first National Monument in the country (a National Monument is a national park named by presidential order rather than by an act of Congress). Devils Tower has been mainly a recreation destination during most of its subsequent history, but long before its absorption into the terrain of scenic tourism, it was a sacred site for several tribes in the region, including the

Lakota and the Kiowa (who call it Bear's Lodge, because of the story in which seven sisters fled their brother, who had become a bear; they were saved by a giant tree stump that rose from the ground with them on it: the butte we see today is scored by the bear's claw marks, and the sisters became seven bright stars in the night sky). Lakota leader Charlotte Black Elk recalls, "I grew up going to Devils Tower. As a kid with my family, we would pass ourselves off as tourists, initially. Back then, the park wasn't a high traffic place." The butte appeared in *Close Encounters of the Third Kind* as the site where the aliens landed, which, says Black Elk, caused tourism to increase significantly. So too did the growing popularity of rock climbing. In 1973, 312 climbers visited Devils Tower; now about 6,000 do so every year. Because of the popularity of rock climbing and the growing respect for Native American religious beliefs and rights, monument superintendent Deborah Ligget called for a voluntary moratorium on climbing every June, when Native Americans conduct ceremonies at Devils Tower.

The number of June climbers dropped dramatically when the moratorium was instituted in 1995; but Andy Petefish, who owned a climbing service, sued to have the ban declared illegal. Petefish and the Mountain States Legal Foundation, which represented him, argued that the voluntary ban was a violation of the First Amendment—that protecting Native American religious practices amounted to establishing a religion. Petefish, whose real motives seemed to be economic, asserted, "Climbing on Devils Tower is a religious experience for me. But when the rock gets crowded, I don't ask for my peace and quiet to be regulated. I just want equal treatment on public land." Since he wasn't prevented from climbing or guiding clients on the butte, he seemed to be suing to protest being made to feel that climbing there was inappropriate.

The same attitude has prevailed at many other sacred sites across the West, where protecting indigenous rights or respecting non-Western religious beliefs by limiting access to the land has been attacked as reverse discrimination, by non-Natives who assert that the pleasure of outdoor recreation and scenic views is equally a form of spiritual observance. Some of the friction arises because many contested sites are federal land; another problem is that natural sites are not visibly tied to specific cultural practices, as is the case with, say, churches. An interpreta-

tion dependent upon oral tradition is less distinct than one embodied in architecture and sculpture—it changes how people look rather than what people see.

Similar cultural clashes have arisen at Rainbow Bridge in Utah (sacred to Dine
[Navajo] people and already damaged by the flooding of nearby springs and petroglyphs caused by the Glen Canyon Dam); at Cave Rock in South Lake Tahoe
(sacred to the Washoe and popular with climbers); and at the Western Shoshone
sacred site at Rock Creek in northern Nevada's Landers County, whose officials
wanted to create a recreational reservoir that would put the site underwater
(with a lot of activist work, the county measure was recently defeated). As
Malcolm Margolin, a historian of Native California, said when discussing a sacred
spring in the San Joaquin Valley that was threatened, "I began to realize that for
them the religion, the religious experience was rooted in that particular place, in
the power and the beauty of that particular place, and if you destroy the place,
you destroy the religion."

Edgar Hachivi Heap of Birds has worked as a public artist for more than a dozen
years. All his public works have been temporary or permanent monuments to the
erased or invisible indigenous history of the chosen site. The pieces most often consist of short texts placed on objects from the existing vocabulary of public space—
billboards, bus signs, enameled metal signs like those used for traffic—which gives
them a neutral, official aesthetic. In the late 1980s, he completed *Native Hosts* for a
public art project at City Hall Park in New York. This work consisted of twelve
signs made by the city's Traffic Department, each of which said, "New York, today
your host is ___" and named one of the tribes that had lived or still lives in the
region. A few years later, in Seattle, he paid tribute to the city's original inhabitants and the homeless Indians on the streets today with an enameled metal sign in
Pioneer Square, next to and addressing the existing statue of Chief Seattle. One
side of *Day Night*, decorated with crosses and dollar signs, said, "Chief Seattle the
streets are our home"; the other, decorated with leafy splotches, said, "Far away
brothers and sisters we still remember you." Both these projects spoke to the presence, then and now, of displaced Native people in urban spaces. So did a third proj-

ect in San Jose, California, which used bus posters to critique the effects of the mission system—and, inevitably, offended the Catholic Church. "Who owns history?" another project asked point-blank, at a Pittsburgh, Pennsylvania, monument already commemorating "Anglo-Saxon supremacy in the United States."

Among Heap of Birds's more controversial projects were billboards commenting on the centennial of the 1889 Oklahoma land rush from which the "Sooner State" took its name; one had the text "Sooners run over Indian Nations, Apartheid?" with the word "Sooners" written backwards. In 1992, Heap of Birds recalled,

> All of the state of Oklahoma is Indian Territory. They changed the treaties and took the land away and gave it to the settlers and that's why they had the land run. So every April they have an incredible reenactment which goes throughout all the school system. All the grade school kids come to school and they have a little red wagon and they dress up like pioneers and they bring their sack lunch and they run across the school yard and put a stake in the ground and take away Indian land. . . . So I made a series of billboards that just try and turn the Sooners away and run them [in] the other direction . . . and just try to remark about this kind of practice of racism really. So we had the billboards up and then I made some t-shirts and then people started wearing them and then the day was coming when the city was going to have its big celebration, and then everyone said well let's have a protest march, so we made more t-shirts and then people marched from the Native American Center in Oklahoma City to the State Capitol and had a forum on the steps of the Capitol and followed the path of the billboards, so it was a very, very positive kind of way to bring people together and focus people on this other part of the history.

You could call Heap of Birds's works counter-monuments: they speak to excluded people of erased history; they revise, but they don't reconcile or conciliate.

The gestures of conciliation and recognition are due elsewhere. Those fighting to deny recognition of the presence of Native Americans then and now and the atrocities suffered are cultural Custers, caught up in a doomed assault on truth, justice, and even awakening government bureaucrats. But the conflicts they stirred up are not yet over.

The Garden of Merging Paths

[1995]

> You are in a maze of twisty little passages, all alike.
> Screen text from the early computer game Adventure

> Place your right (or left) hand on the right (or left)
> wall of green, and doggedly keep it there, in and out of
> dead ends, and you will finally get to the middle.
> Julian Barnes, on hedge mazes

In 1989, I went to a demonstration at United Technologies in San Jose, a company making fuel components for Trident II missiles, which carried nuclear warheads. The corporate headquarters was nothing special, just another glass-walled box with a Pizza Hut–style mansard roof, a parking lot full of late-model cars, and nobody in sight but security guards. It was in a business subdivision so new that much of the earth was still exposed, with raw compacted clay and gravel up to the curving suburban sidewalks; and there was a fruit orchard just behind the offices, where one of the protestors escaped when chased by a guard. This, the visible landscape of military technology, was bland, closed-off, a mask. There were other United Technologies landscapes. Some were even more invisible, or only potential: the military bases where the Trident missiles were stationed; the targets they were intended for in this, the late rococo phase of the cold war; and the workplaces where they were manufactured—we were at design and corporate headquarters. (Nuclear weapons are traditionally pork-barreled all over the country, so that almost every state has an economic interest in their perpetuation and no one is responsible for *making* weapons.)

Another United Technologies landscape was underground, that of the colossal fuel plume which was (and is) leaking toward the reservoir that holds most of

San Jose's drinking water. Although Silicon Valley's industries are often thought of as clean for their lack of industrial-era smokestacks and other such visible emblems of poisons, they are full of such high-tech toxins in the workplace and in storage tanks leaching underground into the water table.

The most visible UT landscape at the time of our protest was an ostentatious show of American painting, mostly landscapes, from the Manoogian Collection in Detroit, underwritten by this corporation which was destroying so many landscapes out of sight. The works in this show at San Francisco's M. H. de Young ranged from the Hudson River School of the 1830s to American impressionism at the turn of the century, mostly heroic and idyllic landscapes, images of glorious possibility and pleasant interlude. This was what UT chose as its public face.

Finding the landscape of Silicon Valley isn't as easy as getting lost among the subdivisions and freeway exits and industrial parks. When Langdon Winner wrote a profile of Silicon Valley a few years ago, he reached for the Winchester Mystery House as its emblem. It's an obvious one in a region whose other landmarks are scarce. The Stanford Linear Accelerator, cosponsored by the Atomic Energy Commission; Paramount's Great America amusement park, with its Top Gun military flight simulator ride; Moffet Air Field; the off-limits Blue Cube missile control center next to Lockheed (officially called Onizuka Air Force Base after one of the Challenger's victims); Mission Santa Clara—all contain something of the valley's character as well, but Mrs. Winchester's paranoiac maze in San Jose sums it up best.

Sarah Winchester moved west after she became the widow of the man whose repeating rifle was the definitive weapon in western expansion—"the gun that won the West." Frightened of the souls of the Native Americans killed by the Winchester repeating rifle, she sought spiritual advice and was told that as long as her house was being built, she was safe—and the result is the 160-room chaos of architecture that has been a local tourist attraction since 1922. The house had no overall plan, so that doors and staircases lead nowhere, windows open onto rooms added later, architectural details clash, and floor levels and design scales are inconsistent. Workers were kept busy twenty-four hours a day so that construction was always in process. Perhaps the house can be seen as a mad monument to mechanized capitalism. In the words of *Capital* itself: "If machinery be the most powerful means for increasing the productiveness of labour—i.e., for shortening the working time required in the production of a commodity, it becomes in the hands of capital the most powerful means for lengthening the working-day beyond all bounds set by human nature. It creates on the one hand, new conditions by which capital is enabled to give free scope to this its constant tendency and on the other hand, new motives with which to whet capital's appetite for the labour of others."

The invisible counterweight to the elaborate uselessness of this monument to wealth and fear is the ruthless efficiency of the rifle that paid for it: between the two of them—military technology and diversionary folly—the valley might begin to be defined. The rifle's pursuit of death in open, contestable space; the house's sequestering from death and the dead in sequestered interior space. The implications of Mrs. Winchester's acts are interesting: that guns do kill people; that technology does have a moral dimension; and that perhaps she could buy her way out of the implications, fend off the spirit world with unending consumption, build a literal nowhere in which she could become lost to the spirit world.

What other stories can provide a thread through the labyrinths of Silicon Valley? The problem of understanding it seems to be the inadequacy of its stories and images. There's the arcadian story, of paradise lately become limbo, of the world's greatest prune orchard paved over to become the world's greatest technology center; and there's the utopian one, of the glorious future opened up by technology, the old Crystal Palace–World's Fair rhetoric, which has become less credible for most people about most technologies. The two stories have some interesting things in common. The arcadian nostalgia of Wendell Berry or Jerry Mander has its counterpart in the feckless utopian enthusiasm of the *Wired* and *Mondo 2000* consumers for a brave new world of cyberspace and techno-wonders. Mander's *In the Absence of the Sacred* is among the most recent attempts to assess technological progress, but the book bogs down in a refusal to engage social issues (as well as in a romanticization of his own early years, in which the Great Depression becomes Edenic). Technology becomes an inevitable march toward consolidation, control, ecocide—a kind of Big Brother Godzilla. By making technology autonomous, rather than literally and historically a tool of power, Mander avoids most questions about the social forces that control the development and use of machines and the social changes that might detour us from the current trajectory. What begins as a radical critique ends as a refusal to engage the powers that be. In this, Mander is not much different from the more widespread enthusiasts for the new technologies, who also imagine technology as autonomous and also leave out any social analysis, except for happy projections of empowerment through information access. Both these arcadian and utopian analyses insist on a straight line, backward or forward toward the good; but in a maze, straight is the quickest route to immobility, and the route may call for lateral moves, shifting perspectives.

The maze becomes an inevitable metaphor for the moral tangles of technologies and social change; for the equivocal gains and losses; for arguments that can only lead deeper in, not outside the problem; for the impossibility of plunging straight forward or backing out altogether—that is, for simply embracing or rejecting the technologies and the visions of futures that accompany them. And the maze's image is echoed in the circuit boards and silicon chips, in the suburban sprawls of curving residential streets and industrial parks, of centerless towns that melt into each other, in the limited choices of computer games, perhaps in the rhetoric of technological progress that avoids social and teleological questions. Silicon Valley itself is an excellent check on the technophiles' enthusiasm, since the joyous liberation of the new technologies is so hard to find here, in a place known for its marathon work schedules, gridlock traffic, Superfund sites (twenty-nine, the greatest concentration of hazardous waste sites in the nation), divorce rate, drug consumption, episodes of violence, and lack of corporate philanthropy and organized labor.

Certainly the orderly grid of fruit trees is more appealing than the jumble of mismatched corporations and assembly sheds, and certainly the most familiar story about California, even about America, is of a paradise that fell sometime not long ago, the story Mander tells. But the paradise of the orchards is partial at best: they are themselves workplaces for immigrant and migrant laborers, whose poor working conditions and exposure to pesticides foreshadowed the sweatshops of microchip manufacture. And the first of these fruit trees came with the Spanish missionaries in 1777, who established Mission Santa Clara as a slave labor camp for the Ohlone and nearby indigenous people. (Santa Clara County is named after the mission and includes San Jose and the southern half of Silicon Valley; the northern half extends up along the San Francisco peninsula into San Mateo County. The term *valley* is something of a misnomer for this sprawl.)

When the missionaries came on their double mission for salvation and empire, the whole peninsula was a vast expanse of live oaks maintained by the Ohlone. As the explorer Sir George Vancouver wrote after a visit in 1792, "For almost twenty miles it could be compared to a park which had originally been planted with the true old English oak, the underwood . . . had the appearance of having been cleared away and had left the stately lords of the forest in complete possession of the soil, which was covered with luxuriant herbage and beautifully diversified with pleasing eminences and valleys." The planting of the orchards represents a reduction of a complex ecology into the monocultural grid of modern agriculture, and the transformation of a complex symbiosis with the land into the simpler piecework of agricultural labor for surplus and export. It may be that the orchards even have something in common with the Winchester repeating rifle as symbols of frontiers of conquest and rules of order. But they also represent sustenance and continuity, two things hard to condemn out of hand, and I have been told that the sight of the valley in bloom was exquisite.

By the 1820s, the slave population—which included members of tribes from farther away as well as locals—had begun to escape, raid their former prison, and liberate their comrades. One successful raider, Yoscolo, carried out many such missions until he was caught; his head was nailed to a post near the church as a disincentive to the remaining workers. This is the not very edifying early history of European civilization in Silicon Valley, and the anticolonial raiders here have their successors in contemporary Vietnamese gangs who steal vast quantities of silicon chips for the gray and black markets. Perhaps the missions, too, are proto-types of Silicon Valley, of information colonization. The neophytes, as the mission captives were called, were required to memorize and recite long lists of saints, prayers, and so forth, which they were unlikely to have understood; salvation was a matter of having the right information.

In between the missions and the corporations, a golden age is hard to find and a fall is hard to postulate. Leland Stanford, one of the Big Four railroad barons whose government-subsidized rail monopoly made him a millionaire many times over, founded Stanford University in 1885 as a memorial to his dead son. The pho-tographer Eadweard Muybridge invented high-speed stop-action photography here in 1877, often considered the crucial precursor of motion pictures, to confirm Stanford's belief that all a horse's feet were off the ground simultaneously at some point during a gallop. Around that time, the Bing cherry was bred here by Seth Lewelling, who named it after his Chinese cook—according to legend, in lieu of back wages. (It's worth remembering that the Silicon Valley region is now also a capital of genetic engineering, with giant Genentech headquartered in South San Francisco and Stanford University again deeply involved.)

Technological innovations continued in the region, including Philo T. Farnsworth's invention of the iconoscope tube, a crucial TV component, in the 1920s, when the valley had nearly 125,000 acres in orchards; Charles Litton's San Carlos labs, which did war work, laser research, and more; and the refinement of magnetic tape recording technology for Ampex and ABC soon after World War II. Moffet Air Field opened up in the 1930s and was for sixty years an impor-tant aviation research center. Silicon Valley environmentalist Ted Smith calls the place the greatest concentration of military-industrial sites in the country. Later, Stanford University became an ally of the electronics industry in much the way that nearby UC Berkeley took on nuclear weapons research and lab management; Stanford Research Park was built on university land in the early fifties as Stanford Industrial Park. Stanford electronics engineering students William Hewlett and David Packard invented the audio oscillator in 1938 and sold their first ones to Walt Disney for *Fantasia*. Long before Robert Noyce invented the integrated circuit—the silicon chip that gave the valley its name—military technology and entertainment technology were already aligned on parallel paths.

In 1958, the Santa Clara planning department published a report that jumbled its metaphors interestingly: "Santa Clara County is fighting a holding action in the cause of agricultural land reserves. We are a wagon train, besieged by the whooping Indians of urbanization, and waiting prayerfully for the US Cavalry." The cavalry had already arrived, in the form of defense contracts that supported much of the research and development in the technology field, a connection that doesn't fit with the image of the independent inventor or with the images of the planning department. The fruit orchards of Santa Clara, like the citrus groves of Orange County and the San Fernando Valley, are vestiges of a cleaner environment and lower property values. In a place such as Cupertino, with land prices up to a million dollars an acre, hanging onto farmland is difficult (though some farmers became wealthy enough by selling some of their land to cultivate the rest of it for pleasure). By the 1980s, more than four-fifths of the agricultural land had become industrial or suburban space, and only 8,000 acres of orchard stood, much of it between office buildings and clearly doomed. The peninsula and San Jose were developed with little more foresight than Mrs. Winchester's house.

In this, Silicon Valley is not unique but typical in contemporary America, a decentralized, diffused region: postindustrial, postcommunal, postrural, and posturban—postplace, but for the undeveloped western slopes and the undevelopable bay. As Langdon Winner writes, "Perhaps the most significant, enduring accomplishment of Silicon Valley is to have transcended itself, and fostered the creation of an ethereal reality, which exercises increasing influence over embodied, spatially bound varieties of social life. Here decisions are made and actions taken in ways that eliminate the need for physical presence in any particular place. Knowing where a person, building, neighborhood, town, or city is located no longer provides a reliable guide to understanding human relationships and institutions." As much as specific products—for the military, for business, and for entertainment, whatever that is—Silicon Valley seems to have generated prototypes of a more pervasive American future, one of dislocation. It has no center; rather than being a city radiating bedroom communities, which generates a coherent commute, it consists of myriad clusters of industry and housing, with commuters jamming in all directions at the beginning and end of every workday. As we discovered at protests there, Silicon Valley lacks centers that can function as social or political arenas.

I went to another demonstration at Lockheed Missiles and Space Corporation, the region's biggest employer and the prime contractor for Trident missiles, where there were no sidewalks, no focal points, no public spaces. In some sense, protest and community had been designed out of the place, and the workspace too had been suburbanized. Interestingly, many of the Silicon Valley corporations are based on "campuses," attractive, diffused, pseudodemocratic spaces that belie the traditional corporate structure within most of them, a design that originated with the not very parklike Xerox PARC. Diffuseness seems to have become an irreversible condition, in which both the consciousness and the place for consolidating individuals, for community, are virtually impossible. Suburbia represents an early triumph of such diffusion, and the new technologies often seem to further it. Suburbia is a landscape of privatized space, of the division of home from work, with the scenes of production both industrial and agricultural (and now informational) separated from those of consumption, a sequestering that has progressed with the shift from the public space of shopping streets to the private space of shopping malls.

There is the decentralization of anarchist direct democracy, in which power is everywhere; and the decentralization of postmodern control, in which power is transnational, virtual, in a gated community, not available at this time, in a holding company, incomprehensible, incognito—in a word, nowhere. Mrs. Winchester's house is also a maze whose center was nowhere, and here it is important to distinguish types of mazes as well. The original myth of a maze centers on the one Daedalus built at Crete to hide the monstrous result of Queen Pasiphaë's union with a bull, the Minotaur. Later mazes, such as those on the floors of many medieval churches, symbolically compress and reconstitute pilgrimage, and the maze functions not as a tangle in which to lose things but a mandala in which to find them (the artist Paul Windsor recently mocked this tradition with a giant sand painting at the San Francisco Art Commission Gallery, which merged Tibetan and Hopi mandalas with the microchip). These mazes often have only one route to the center. The maze at Crete and that of the Mystery House apparently have no center; as such, they are types of the new landscape of the suburb, the multinational, the subcontracted and subdivided, the faces of nowhere, in which it is impossible to get found.

Here it is important to distinguish the actual tools generated in Silicon Valley and its sister sites from the visions of their implementation. Computers and the information they manipulate are the means to many ends; in one of these, they are an end in themselves. In its most dematerialized state, Silicon Valley is a blueprint for a future: in this future, outside has disappeared, the maze has no exit. The world of information and communication online, much hailed as a technological advance, is also a social retreat accompanying a loss of the public and social space of the cities; a loss of the aesthetic, sensual, and nonhuman space of the country; a privatization of physical space; and a disembodiment of daily life. A central appeal cited for the new technologies is that their users will no longer have to leave home, and paeans accumulate lauding the convenience of being able to access libraries and entertainments via personal computers, which become less tools of engenderment than channels of consumption. This vision of disembodied anchorites connected to the world only by information and entertainment, mediated by the entities that control the flow, seems more nightmarish than idyllic. Postulated as a solution to gridlock, crime on the streets, the chronic sense of time's scarcity, it seems instead a means to avoid addressing such problems, a form of acquiescence.

There is another maze, another landscape, that has bearing on the tangle of Silicon Valley. The multimedia mazes resemble the maze of Jorge Luis Borges's "The Garden of Forking Paths," in which a Chinese assassin finds out the secret of his ancestor's chaotic novel and missing maze—the two are one.

Ts'ui Pen must have said once: I am withdrawing to write a book. And another time: I am withdrawing to construct a labyrinth. Every one imagined two works; to no one did it occur that the book and the maze were one and the same thing. Almost instantly I understood: "the garden of forking paths" was the chaotic novel; the phrase "the various futures (not to all)" suggested to me the forking in time, not in space. . . . In the work of Ts'ui Pen, all possible outcomes occur; each one is the point of departure for other forkings.

An extensive but finite number of forks can be represented on an interactive CD or laser disc, but they do not reproduce life, in which the unimaginable is often what comes next. The greatest tragedy of the new technologies may be their elimination of the incalculable—the coincidences and provocations and metaphors that in some literal sense "take us out of ourselves" and put us in relation to other things. To live inside a mechanical world is to live inside plotted possibility, what has already been imagined; and so the technologies that are supposed to open up the future instead narrow it. I am not arguing for existentialist freedom with this difference between inside and outside, only for an unquantifiable number of paths in the latter, a too predictable course in the former.

Much recent attention to the use of interactive media proposes that it makes passive viewing become active engagement. What is interesting about these products is that they map out a number of choices, but the choices are all preselected (and, with the rare exception of work by artists such as Lynn Hershman, the choices have little to do with meaningful decisions). That is, the user cannot do anything, go anywhere the creator has not gone before; as usual with computer programs, one must stay on the path and off the grass (by which analogy hackers do get off the path, a subversive success that keeps them in the park). We could chart the game as a series of forks in the road, in which each choice sets up another array of choices, but the sum total of choices have already been made. Thus, the audience becomes the user, a figure who resembles a rat in a conceptual version of a laboratory maze. The audience-user is not literally passive; he or she is engaged in making choices, but the choices do not necessarily represent freedom, nor this activity thinking. Participating is reduced to consuming. The ur-game, Pac-Man, made this apparent: the sole purpose of the Pac-Man icon, a disembodied head-mouth, was to devour what was in its path as it proceeded through a visible maze.

Perhaps what is most interesting about this form of interactivity is its resemblance to so many existing corridors of American life, in which a great many choices can be made, but all are ultimately choices to consume rather than to produce. About a decade ago, the 7–11 chain of convenience stores ran a series of television ads whose key phrase was, "Freedom of choice is what America is all about." The ads echoed a pervasive tendency in the culture to reduce freedom to the freedom to choose from a number of products, to the scope of the consumer's ability to consume. Perhaps it is not surprising that consumption should become the metaphor for democracy in a country that has long had little but representative democracy: that is, the ballot too is a kind of Garden of Forking Paths and not an open plain on which to roam and encounter. By the time the political process has reached the voting booth, all the real choices have been programmed in, and the voter becomes a consumer. Few genuine choices remain, and the act of voting becomes the act of acquiescence, an endorsement of the maze as an open field. The laboratory maze through which the rat moves is one metaphor for it. Another is supplied by the critic Norman M. Klein in an *Art issues* article on virtual reality: "VR is reverse Calvinism—predestination posing as free will. In that sense, VR may be as old as the Massachusetts Bay Colony, a new consumerist form of metaphysical redemption."

The real landscape of Silicon Valley seems wholly interior, not only in the metaphor of the maze and the terrain of offices and suburbs but also in the much promoted ideal of the user never leaving a well-wired home and in the goal of eliminating the world and reconstituting it as information. Again, what disappears here is the incalculable, this time as the world of the sensory and sensual, with all the surprises and dangers that accompany it. In all the hymns to information, little is said about the nature of that information or the ability to use it; one pictures the empty trucks of metaphor hurtling down that information highway. Thinking is an aesthetic occupation, a matter of perceiving relationships and resemblances between things on many levels that defeat computerization because they are aesthetic, not rationalistic; the sensual world is necessary to it as grounding and inspiration, and as parallel. Computers can reason, but they will never really imagine, because the incalculable of the body is forever beyond them, though it may be simulated with increasing complexity—toward what end?

Understanding works largely by means of metaphors and analogies—the incalculable relationships between bits of information—and the way those metaphors and analogies are drawn from the nonconstructed world. The most obvious examples are expressions: *stubborn as a mule, dumb as two sticks, pigheaded, dog breath, pussy, cock, cuckoo, horse sense, drones, worms, snakes in the grass, aping the gentry, bovine, donkey's years*. There are also shared (but fading) fables: the ant and the grasshopper, the tortoise and the hare, the dog in the manger, and a million coyote stories, which provide animal analogies for human dispositions, moralities, and fates. The microcosmic macrocosmic metaphors are particularly important, and they're most immediately obvious in geography metaphors: the foot of a mountain, the bowels of the earth, a river's mouth, the heart of the forest, tree limbs, even the soft shoulders of roads. (For a minor example, in *Tristes Tropiques*, Claude Lévi-Strauss compares speaking of his research to an unreceptive audience to dropping stones down a well, an analogy few would be likely to make nowadays.) The majority of figures of speech that make the abstract concrete and the abstruse imaginable are drawn from animals and organic spaces. It's the animal world that makes being human imaginable, and the spatial realm that makes activity and achievement describable—career plateaus, rough spots, marshy areas. And it's the image of the maze that's gotten me through all the aspects of Silicon Valley I've approached thus far, and the approach to a specific landscape in California that's made it possible to articulate some effects.

Computers are significant for their lack of metaphor: their processes don't resemble organic processes, and only the crudest analogies can be drawn. Instead, they provide imaginatively sterile terms that are projected back onto organic life; we can be made to resemble them more easily than they can be made to resemble us. (It's interesting that another machine-age invention, the superhighway, was used as the metaphor for information circulation systems and even more interesting that the information highway already has "gridlock.") I wonder if generations of being without contact with such undeveloped spaces and nonhuman beings will eventually diminish English into a kind of blanked-out newspeak, a machine language, which has already appeared as the shorthand on networks, the disembodied platitudes of electoral politics, and the starkly denatured language of inner-city rap with its license-plate number-letter combos, police codes, and so on.

All those metaphors are ways of navigating the way things span both difference and similarity; without metaphor, the world would seem threateningly amorphous, both identical with ourselves and utterly incomprehensible. The anthropological theorist Paul Shepard writes, "Humans intuitively see analogies between the concrete world out there and their own inner world. If they conceive the former as a chaos of anarchic forces or as dead and frozen, then so will they perceive their own bodies and society; so will they think and act on that assumption and vindicate their own ideas by altering the world to fit them." The loss of a relationship to the nonconstructed world is a loss of these metaphors. It is also loss of the larger territory of the senses, a vast and irreplaceable loss of pleasure and meaning.

Finally, even nowhere has its twin: everywhere. Silicon Valley has become a nowhere in the terms I have tried to lay out—an obliteration of place, an ultimate suburb, a maze in which wars are designed, diversions are generated, the individual disembodied. But the physical landscape of Silicon Valley is now everywhere, not only in the attempts to clone its success but in the spread of its products and its waste throughout the globe, the outside world being ravaged by the retreat to the interior.

If you imagine a computer not as an autonomous object but as a trail of processes and effects and residues, which leave their traces across a global environmental maze, then it is already everywhere. The clean rooms in which poorly paid chip makers were exposed to toxic chemicals are now subcontracted out in the Southwest, Oregon, and the third world, so there's a little of the valley there. The waste that was leaching through the once fecund earth of Silicon Valley is leaching still, and more of it is leaching around the globe. Some of the chemicals used to clean the chips have been peculiarly potent ozone-depleters (though most Silicon Valley firms have switched over to other compounds), so think of the upper atmosphere too; and the landfill where the packing and shipping material goes; and the electrical generating station your computer is plugged into and its energy sources (coal, hydropower, nuclear, geothermal, natural gas?); think of the networks it may be hooked into; think of the corporations whose pockets it lined—but don't picture pockets, the money is in imageless cyberspace—and the stock markets where their shares are traded; think of the forests the manuals are printed on; think of the store that sold it; think of where it'll be dumped when it's rendered obsolete, as all computers have been.

These are the tentacles, the winding corridors, the farthest reaches of Silicon Valley, and the hardest to imagine. It is the scene of the crime that has vaporized, and resisting an unlocatable and unimaginable crime is difficult. One of the principal challenges for environmentalists is making devastation that is subtle and remote seem urgent to people with less vivid imaginations. Another is finding a site at which to protest (which is why Greenpeace has largely relocated from actual sites to wherever the media can be found). And the ultimate problem of the landscape of Silicon Valley in its most abstruse, penetrating, and symbolic forms is that it is unimaginable.

Apple Computer, which is headquartered in six buildings, indistinguishable but for their security levels, on Infinity Loop in Cupertino, is a key landscape for Silicon Valley, one that apparently displaced real orchards. When I was there, the Olson orchard across Highway 280 in Sunnyvale was selling Bing and Queen Anne cherries, and Latino workers were cutting up apricots to dry. But a third of the orchard was bulldozed this past spring [1994] for housing, and the rest of the Olson orchard is on its way out. What does it mean, this rainbow-colored apple with the bite taken out of it, which appears everywhere on Apple computers and on the many commodities (mugs, key rings, t-shirts) Apple markets, this emblem that seems to sum up the Santa Clara Valley's change from agriculture to technology? It seems to have been appropriated to connote simplicity and wholesomeness, though apples aren't rainbow colored in anything but the sloppiest association of positive emblems; and the bite also recalls temptation in Eden: the emblem is denatured, reassuring, and threatening all at once. But more than that, it is forgettable, dead in the imagination, part of nowhere—it has been a decade since I last pondered the Apple logo, which has become part of a landscape of disassociation in which the apple image connotes neither sustenance nor metaphor, only a consumer choice, the fruit of the tree of information at the center of the garden of merging paths.

2

BORDERS AND CROSSERS

A Route in the Shape of a Question

[2004]

The incomparable writer-philosopher Walter Benjamin long imagined that his life could be drawn as a map, but never imagined that the map would come to an abrupt termination in Port Bou, Spain, in 1940. In 1939, when the dictator Francisco Franco declared an end to the Spanish Civil War, tens of thousands of refugees walked north over the Pyrenees, seeking shelter in France. They expected to be welcomed as defenders of democracy, but many were forced into camps. A year later, the tide had turned, and refugees from the Third Reich and the Vichy regime began trickling into Spain, seeking passage out of Europe altogether through Spanish or Portuguese ports. Benjamin, a Berlin Jew who had been living in Paris for many years, was one of them, and the tale of his walk from France to Spain has acquired something of the aura of a legend in the academic and intellectual circles where he matters most, for at the end of it he died.

A map of an altogether different sort fell into my hands when I went to Port Bou to retrace Benjamin's final walk. I had expected that my task would be an obscure one, but as soon as we arrived in the town, my companion and I found a kiosk by the little beach bearing maps of the region and an unfolded brochure on Benjamin and the monument to him that stands on the edge of town. The brochure contains a greatly reduced topographical map on which his final walk is marked with a thick orange line. There were other surprises. Most accounts say that he "walked across the Pyrenees," but by the time the Pyrenees meet the Mediterranean, they are only steep hills, not the mountains I had always pictured.

Port Bou and the nearest French town of Cerberes (Portbou and Cervera are the Spanish spellings) are separated by a range of hills and connected by a tunnel. The French trains run on a different gauge track than the Spanish, so each town represents the terminus of a foreign system. It would've taken us two trains and several hours to get from Port Bou, where we woke up, to Banyuls, the second-to-last French town on the Mediterranean, where Benjamin began his walk, so we gave up halfway and took a taxi from Cerberes. The young man who drove us was affably multilingual, chatting to us in French and broken English and asking directions in Catalonian of a gaunt old man rearranging the stones on one of the terraces of a vineyard. At our request, he took us up into the steep amphitheater of grape terraces behind the town and left us in what to him looked like the middle of nowhere. We wouldn't have minded walking there, but we weren't sure we could have found the right road out of town.

The Mediterranean was blue, the unripe grapes were the same green as the leaves of the vines, and the ground was covered with the same deep-brown shale that the terraces, culverts, and occasional huts were made from, a stone that broke up into flat tablets and shards. I'd never been anywhere remotely nearby, but it all looked strangely familiar, the terraced vineyards like a leaner, steeper version of Sonoma or Napa, the hillsides above like the coast north of San Francisco where I hike all the time, even down to the live oaks, rattlesnake grass, and fennel growing in the hills. After we climbed above the vineyards, we walked for a long time on a road, alone, except for the insects.

There were huge grasshoppers with the wingspans of dragonflies when they took to the air, and small ones whose scarlet wings made them look like butterflies, though they vanished into drabness again when they landed. And there were many species of butterflies, small white ones, a yellow one that folded its wings to look like a green leaf, and a pair of swallowtails that chased and courted each other in the breeze. My companion remarked that butterflies have four basic wing motions that occur in so random a sequence that predators cannot predict where they will be; their erraticness makes them elusive. I answered that this sounded like Benjamin, who in his work was a historian, a theorist, a lyrical writer, creating writing as uncategorizable as it is influential. Though his most famous essay is

"The Work of Art in the Age of Mechanical Reproduction," he devoted himself at far greater length to elucidating the meaning of Paris, labyrinths, cities, walks—a series of ideas that spiral around, double back, open into each other, metamorphose, and make endless connections, a map of the world drawn as much by poetic intuition as by rational analysis.

On his walk to Spain, he carried a heavy briefcase containing, he told his companions, a new manuscript more important than his life; and it was part of what made the walk so arduous for him that he had to stop one minute out of ten to catch his breath. There is a steep ascent up to the plateau between Banyuls and the slopes east of Cerberes, during which the route is due south. It then rises to loop around the ridgeline, which is also the international border. Finally, the route heads due east again along the south-facing slopes above Port Bou. The route looks like a giant inverted question mark, like the ones at the beginning of questions in Spanish. There's a Paul Auster novel, *City of Glass*, that Benjamin would have loved, in which one character takes walks across a city whose routes trace the outlines of letters of the alphabet and another character has to figure out what the walks spell; but he probably never knew that his last walk was in the form of a question.

Benjamin succeeded in leading a largely uneventful life until history at its most virulent intervened. Mostly he read, wrote, talked, and walked, activities that blurred together in his thinking, where the city was a magnificent labyrinthine mystery to be read by walking, a musing, meandering kind of walking. Though he had grown up in Germany when climbing mountains was so established a part of sentimental-romantic culture that he was photographed with an alpine background and alpenstock as a child, he was devotedly, unathletically urban in adulthood, nearsighted, with heart trouble, wandering his Paris labyrinths slowly. He was supremely unequipped for what even the foothill walk from France to Spain would require of him, though he was fortunate in his guide.

Lisa Fittko is one of the countless heroes who rise to confront disaster. Active against the Nazis, she had fled Germany years before and was living in Paris when the French government began sending foreigners, regardless of affiliation, into camps. As France surrendered and the Nazis moved south, Fittko, like Benjamin, like myriad Jews, foreigners, and resisters, fled south, looking for a way out of the noose. Fittko came to the southeast corner of France alone to look for escape routes and was given enormous assistance by the socialist mayor of Banyuls and, during the months she lived there, the townspeople. The mayor, Monsieur Azema, told her about a smuggler's route that had also been used by the communist General Enrique Lister in the Spanish Civil War. This was the route she was exploring for the first time when she guided Benjamin, a woman called Frau Gurland, and Gurland's teenage son over the mountains, turning back herself once she had gotten them to Spain and within easy reach of Port Bou. Over the next six months, she helped hundreds more escape along this route. She survived to flee to Cuba and then the United States [where she died in 2005, in her mid-nineties].

Perhaps because of the taxi ride, perhaps because of the roads and paths incised into the hills since 1940, perhaps because we had no fears other than the ferocious heat of midday, we found the route remarkably easy, so easy that we could have done their nine-hour route in three, until I made a navigational mistake. Thinking we were looking down at Cerberes, the southernmost French town, and had another ridgeline to ascend, I took us straight up a steep slope, where a couple of guys with chainsaws were cutting brush, a nasty hike through sharp stubs of bushes and piles of debris, until we hit the trail for the two-thousand-foot peak called Querroig on which stands a ruined tower. From there, I could see Cerberes and Port Bou, lying together like mirror images of each other, each with its small bay and huge train yard, and realized we had gone too far. Since we were most of the way there, we decided to go ahead and reach the summit. Thus it was that we were indeed tired when we walked down into Port Bou six and a half hours after we started.

For refugees in 1940, there was a labyrinth of international paperwork to wade through as well. Fittko, in her memoir *Escape over the Pyrenees*, recounts the nightmares of scrambling for money to buy exit visas and destination visas, fake papers and real ones, the appeals to consuls and smugglers and forgers, amid a constantly shifting set of opportunities, risks, and rules. Having survived the walk, Benjamin fell into one of those traps: though he had a U.S. visa issued in Marseilles and a

Spanish visa, he did not have a French exit visa, and in Port Bou the Spanish authorities told him he would be sent back. It was a tragedy of timing. When he left Marseilles, the regulation had not existed; a few weeks later, the regulation would have lapsed. That day, however, Benjamin saw no way out, though it's still unclear whether he died of a cerebral hemorrhage, took an accidental overdose of his heart medicine, or committed suicide. Though the nature of his death is unre-solved, it is certain that Benjamin died in Port Bou, in a hotel that no longer exists, on September 26, 1940, at age forty-eight. Moved by the tragedy, the authorities allowed his companions to continue their journey to Portugal.

They paid the first five years of rent on a grave for Benjamin and fled. Benjamin's remains were put into a common grave after the rent on his resting place expired. The death certificate, says Fittko, recorded the briefcase with "*unos papeles mas de contenido desconicido*"—"with papers of unknown content"—but case and manuscript vanished. In recent years, the town has begun to remember him, with the brochure I found, with a new grave (which is unlikely to contain his body), with a museum that is just a large room of photographs and photocopies (closed when we were there), and with a brilliant monument by the Israeli artist Dani Karavan. On the same steep slope as the cemetery, it consists of a long walled flight of stairs down toward the sea, a portion of it passing under the surface of the hillside. When you enter, the view through the slot of solid rusted steel the same color as the local stone frames a view of the blue ocean; when you look up, it shows pure sky.

It's acutely attuned to the tragedy of Benjamin and the tides of refugees pushed by violence and intolerance across borders then and now. For neither the sea nor the sky is an attainable place—both are only beautiful beyonds. And when you descend, you find that a thick slab of clear plexiglass bars your way before you fall into the ocean. Etched on it, in several languages, are words of Benjamin's: "It is more arduous to honor the memory of the nameless than that of the renowned. Historical construction is devoted to the memory of the nameless." Benjamin doesn't need a memorial in Port Bou, for his real memorial is his influence on writers ranging from Susan Sontag to Mike Davis, his presence on college read-ing lists across the North American and European continents, and his books, still being read. If he deserves one, it's for his commitment to what Karavan singled out in his monument, "the memory of the nameless."

For me, there's always been a question mark inscribed across Europe, one that asks what that culture would have looked like without the persecutions and exterminations of the Second World War, a Europe with six million more Jews and their descendants, along with dissidents, Gypsies, and the other exterminated. For the Europe Benjamin came from is as vanished as he is; many of his friends—Theodor Adorno, Hannah Arendt, many other poets, scientists, philosophers, painters—were more successful and got to the United States, never to return. Many more went to Israel in the years and decades since, a country whose intolerances are all too clear a mirror of the intolerances of the left-behind lands. In Europe, towns from Salonika, Greece, to Krakow, Poland, lack the Jews who were central to their cultural life. In France, Jewish emigration to Israel has nearly doubled of late, perhaps in response to a new wave of anti-Semitism. I remember hearing a decade earlier that the four thousand Jews who lived in Ireland in 1904, the Ireland memorialized in James Joyce's *Ulysses*, with its Benjaminian wanderer Leopold Bloom, had become two thousand.

Meanwhile, the debates on allowing Turkey into the European Union have made apparent what was implicit: that the EU can also be conceived of as a Christian union, despite its Jews and Muslims; and Italy, Poland, and some other member nations argued in May that it should be so. The week we walked, the World Court ruled that much of the fence across the Palestinian West Bank was illegal. In Arizona, vigilantes patrol the U.S.-Mexican border. In Tijuana, a new border fence and station are going up. And the United Nations counts seventeen million refugees and displaced people in the world, a considerable portion hoping for sanctuary in Europe, Christian or otherwise. At the beginning of our hike, our taxi driver told us that he got calls sometimes from refugees seeking rides across the border. He always refused, he added.

Benjamin was extraordinary in his life. But in his death, he was ordinary, another refugee denied refuge. On his empty grave, another line of his is written, from his last work: "There is no document of civilization which is not at the same time a document of barbarism."

Thirty-Nine Steps Across
the Border and Back

⟦2005⟧

I

In the United States, or at least in my part of it, the Border means the U.S.-Mexican border, not the other one we share with Canada. That's one semantic oddity located somewhere in the nebulous borderlands, like monotheism, mono-marginality, perhaps. God, not the gods; the Border, not the borders.

II

In the 1984 indy punk-rock movie *Repo Man*, set in Southern California, there's a character driving around in a Chevy Malibu with a trunkful of lethally radioactive aliens, nonhumans from outer space. I failed to understand much of the movie because I thought the trunk contained undocumented immigrants—Mexicans or Central Americans who maybe picked up some radiation at a border military base, like Yuma Proving Grounds, where depleted uranium armaments were tested. After all, trunks of cars are one of the places *coyotes*—smugglers—hide people attempting to cross the border illegally. It's a telling linguistic overlap, this migra-tion of meaning back and forth from outer space and outside national boundaries, an other-ization of neighbors and people who aren't even always from there but from here, when here was there. The border, the aliens, the makings of a theology.

Still, my friend Guillermo, who is from Mexico City but has been in the

United States most of his adult life, has a penchant for collecting glow-in-the-dark outer-space trinkets, of which there is a copious supply. A few of them conflate the two kinds of aliens: bug-eyed monsters in sombreros. Was there ever a fifties horror movie in which the flying saucer disgorged mariachi bands? You'd think so.

III

That is the unspeakable background to this premise that the border is some kind of great natural division and brown people are some kind of outer-space creatures who belong on the other side of it. That and the war Mexico never forgot and the United States can never quite remember, the 1846–1848 war Thoreau went to jail to oppose but U.S. history books hardly mention, the one whereby Mexico was cut in half and the United States was increased by a third, to become its current sea-to-shining-sea self, the war some Latinos reference when they say, "We didn't cross the border, the border crossed us." The border is also a migrant. Texas had already been taken, but New Mexico, southern Colorado, Arizona, Utah, Nevada, and California were added to the spoils pile of Yankee expansion. Its arbitrariness is everywhere; in the existence of two Californias, Alta and Baja; in tribes such as the Tohono O'odham, whose homeland (like that of the Mohawks on the other, lowercase border) is on both sides. The border is a strictly western phenomenon, going from the Gulf of Mexico to the Pacific, from Texas to California, from Brownsville-Matamoros to Tijuana–San Diego. Everywhere north of it, the influence of Mexico is evident, down to the outfits cowboys wear and the food everyone eats and the Spanish place names for the cities, rivers, and land forms, the mesas, arroyos, and canyons. The influence of the people who are not supposed to be here is so everywhere that they are perhaps in some way the dominant culture already, before they become a majority, as they will in a few decades.

In California, the Mexican-American War began as the Bear Flag Revolt on June 16, 1846, when some trigger-happy Yankees in California illegally started a little shooting in the beautiful Spanish-style plaza in Sonoma, where General Mariano Vallejo was in charge of the northern half of Alta California. The U.S. anxiety to grab Mexican territory was so powerful that these Americans wouldn't know for months that President James Polk had declared war on Mexico much farther southeast, though the two wars would become two fronts of one war. The actions of the Americans in Sonoma carried all the moral authority of a convenience store holdup, and the bear on the flag they raised was so poorly drawn that Californios—the non-Native Spanish-speaking citizens— thought they were flying an image of a pig. (It became the California state flag, but the California grizzly it represented was hunted into extinction over the next several decades.) Lieutenant John C. Fremont of the U.S. Army came to the aid of the Americans, various North Bay Californios were killed or taken hostage, and the squabble joined the war being fought in other scattered locales across the West.

The war that began in Texas in 1846 was a more serious business, and a third front opened up when the U.S. Army landed in Veracruz and invaded Mexico City. More soldiers died of disease than of combat in this war, and, like the Gulf War, it was largely won by the superior technology of the U.S. forces. Mexicans still annually commemorate *los niños heroes*, the teenage military cadets who fought bravely, and mostly died, defending the capital. But the U.S. military record in this war is made up more of squabbles, insubordination, and desertions. The people wading and swimming across the Rio Grande then were U.S. soldiers seeking more civilized conditions than the U.S. Army camp. The first aggressive border patrol was instituted to stop this leak of U.S. troops to Mexico; Major General Zachary Taylor gave orders to shoot all deserters. Keep those deserters in mind; they will return in the twenty-first century.

I went to the sesquicentennial celebration of the Bear Flag Revolt on June 16, 1996. It was during the heyday of Governor Pete Wilson's demonization of Latino immigrants and, by extension, Latinos generally, not long after Proposition 187 attempted to deny basic services—education and health care, including emergency medical care—to undocumented immigrants. Few remember now, when terrorists so neatly occupy the bogeyman niche vacated by communists, the many other groups who were cast in that role, most particularly immigrants (and, in fact, terrorists—if you ignore Timothy McVeigh and all the abortion-clinic shooters—and immigrants share the basic status of Outsider or, if you prefer, Alien, so that anti-terrorism rhetoric has continued to focus on the border—particularly on the Border, even though some of the September 11 terrorists came over the Canadian border and none over the other one). Proposition 187 explained away California's sagging economy by blaming it on illegal immigrants, who allegedly were siphoning off social services without paying taxes, though in fact it was more the other way round: they were failing to collect major social services— unemployment, disability, social security—while working hard, sometimes under the table, sometimes with taxes, which they would never file to recoup, taken out of wages. Then, too, those who pushed the notion that they were stealing jobs never looked very carefully at how many gringos were hoping to break into dishwashing and strawberry-picking careers.

Anyway, the sesquicentennial celebration in Sonoma Plaza was beautifully staged. The parade celebrating it seemed to consist almost entirely of white people, including adult men in the Davy Crockett outfits of their youth, toting rifles. A group of young Latinos protesting the celebration—which was by no means merely a commemoration—arrived in the plaza first, before the parade, so that the Yankees had to take the plaza all over again, with a certain amount of conflict, or at least anxiety. Governor Wilson, whom the great émigré artist Enrique Chagoya once depicted as a cannibal in an Aztec codex, spoke, and the Latino kids shouted and drummed while he did so. "I don't know *what* they're so angry about," an elderly lady clucked to her husband, so I told them. He said to me, at this celebration of the seizure of Mexico's northern half, "Young lady, California was never part of Mexico. You should go to college and study some history."

VI

Thus the border, which is not so much a line drawn in the sand of the desert but in the imagination, a line across which memory may not travel, empathy may be confiscated, truth held up indefinitely, meaning lost in translation. The West is cast as nature, not culture, which is part of why we do not believe we have to remember anything that happened here. If the border is natural, it must not have a history, since despite the realm called *natural history*, we consider those two terms to describe exclusionary territories. It is its naturalness that is its justification, in a nation that has long cast itself as nature against European culture, which required forgetting the displacement and devastation of Native Americans, an easy omission for all the nativist groups opposed to immigrants, at least since the Irish began to arrive in quantity after the Great Potato Famine of the 1840s. It may have been their homeland, but it was our Eden; we were Adam and Eve, they were just a trailer for another movie. And the defense of nature has become another semiautomatic weapon in the arsenal of exclusion.

VII

Some might consider the fact that fences are unnatural a slight problem here, a little blight on the landscape or at least on the ideology of nature wielded on the border's northern side. To put up a fence is to suggest difference when there is none (though there will be), and to draw a border is much the same thing. Paradise means a walled garden, and when Adam and Eve are expelled from Eden, its walls first appear in the narrative, because they matter only from outside. Adam and Eve are the first refugees, the fig leaves the first canceled passports, Paradise the first immigration-restricted country. And of course the Angel with the Flaming

Sword is a Border Patrol agent, like the ones with their flaming guns and night-vision goggles who kill people in California, in the stepped-up Border Patrol program called Operation Gatekeeper. In recent years, the wall, the guard, and the gate have become increasingly popular devices for maintaining difference, the difference between the garden and the world. They show up on every scale, from the domestic to the national front, and though usually seen separately, it makes sense to look at them together. Whatever is inside the wall, past the gate, protected by the guard is imagined as some version of Paradise, but Paradise only so long as its separateness is protected. Which means that Paradise is a violent place.

On the smallest scale, these dividers are nothing more than incongruous little garden ornaments I noticed on a recent visit to the highlands of West Hollywood and then started to notice in affluent zones everywhere. In the more plush parts of Southern California, every house has a garden in front of it, a garden that seems to be a sort of no-man's-land, since nobody but the gardener ever diverges from the driveway to tread upon it. It provides a certain buffer of private property between the house and the street, and it proclaims, in lawn and bougainvillea, a certain pastoral attainment and affluence. In the midst of each one is a little medallion on a steel stick promising some security company's "armed response." A flaming sword for every Paradise, and an armed response for every garden (or perhaps the medallions are more like fruit of the Tree of Knowledge of Good and Evil, as long as we're going to allegoricize).

Visually, these medallions are akin to the fire extinguishers, bathroom signs, and so forth one is not supposed to notice as part of the wall furnishings of museums. Symbolically, they proclaim the same message as the garden, albeit to a different audience: that the goods herein are both coveted and secured. Politically, these gardens seem to be constructed for two distinct audiences: those who are meant to admire the plants and ignore the medallion and those to whom the medallion speaks; the former being a majority audience of friends, neighbors, and those who belong, the latter being those who do not belong (and seldom show up, making them something of an imaginary audience). To a third audience—to me, anyway—the medallion and the garden cancel each other out: what kind of serenity can a garden promising armed guards provide?

Anti-immigration rhetoric portrays the entire United States as a kind of garden and imagines the border as intrinsic a part of the terrain as mountains, rivers, forests. Too, the border has become, like the flag, a kind of sacred object in the cult of nationhood. Often described as an object or a fact rather than a concept, the border is nothing more than a line on a map drawn by war and only occasionally imposed on the actual landscape. It can be imagined as a kind of blueprint for a largely unbuilt public art work, like a three-thousand-mile Christo Running Fence with just a few chunks completed in places like Tijuana/San Diego. It exists largely as a line running through the national imagination now. Sometimes the map is the territory, or at least fuels the territorial imperative. But since there is no border, armed response is supposed to keep people out of our garden.

As James Baldwin once remarked, "If I am not who you think I am, then you are not who you think you are either."

VIII

In fact, putting a fence across nature has been pretty actively destroying it in one respect: Operation Gatekeeper, which intensified security in urban areas, forced more and more people to cross the border in remote places. In defecating, littering, making fires, and otherwise messing around in fragile desert territory, they have created unfortunate environmental impacts, as have the government's all-terrain vehicles sent out to hunt them. A lot of immigrants began to die in the desert, too, hundreds every year, and the hunts became in part search and rescue missions, hydrating and cooling down the undocumented, who were dying of heat and dehydration. In Arizona, however, vigilantes began joining the hunt with considerably less empathy than some of the Border Patrol.

In his novella *Heart of Darkness*, Joseph Conrad depicts his Kurtz living with human skulls as ornaments outside the house deep upriver. If the United States is to be pictured as a garden out of which the aliens must be kept, imagine it with skulls and skeletons and mummies, not garden gnomes or pink flamingos, as its lawn ornaments. Along with those death-threat lawn plaques and angels with flaming swords. A very crowded garden, withal, not crowded with immigrants but with props and weapons to guard the boundaries of empathy and imagination.

IX

The fantasy of the nationalist garden wall emerged in 1998 as Amendment A, a Sierra Club ballot measure, which for a while that spring threatened to fracture the organization and even the environmental movement. The measure stated that restricting immigration was key to protecting the domestic environment. It implied that immigrants were to blame for the deterioration of the environment, as though those huddled masses were rushing out to buy jet skis and ten-acre Colorado ranchettes, as though sheer numbers alone, rather than habits of consumption and corporate practices, were responsible for degradation of the U.S. environment. It reeked of American isolationism—the idea that our garden could be preserved no matter what went on outside its walls, though many ecological issues are transnational: migratory birds, drifting pollutants, changing weather—and it implied that we live in a garden and they do not.

Amendment A was meant to be a kind of garden medallion to be read by politicians as well as potential intruders. It harked back to the unattractive origins of one part of the environmental movement, the Save the Redwoods League. Historian Gray Brechin recently unearthed the organization's turn-of-the-century origins in a eugenicist linkage of preserving native species with preserving "native"—that is, white Protestant old immigrant—culture and majority. Saving the environment is usually imagined as being inherently moral and apolitical, but neither condition is necessary: think of the greenness of the Nazis postulating their forests as a nationalist landscape and their mountains as an Aryan zone. Hate and suspicion are not uncommon garden crops.

Amendment A was signed by nature romantics rather than central players in the Sierra Club's environmental work, by the (Canadian) nature writer Farley Mowat, by ecoreactionary Dave Foreman, by neon-sunset-photography superstar Galen Rowell; it was opposed by most of the club's past and present leadership.

Entertainingly enough, San Francisco's Political Ecology Group demonstrated that Amendment A had been introduced by people who were themselves largely outsiders to the club, which is to say that the club itself could be imagined as a kind of garden of shared beliefs that had been invaded by hostile raiders seeking to transform its nature. (As one of their tactics, supporters of Amendment A urged members of anti-immigration and population-control groups to join the Sierra Club en masse to vote for the measure.) Fortunately the proposal lost, but it left in its wake this renewed vision of the United States as a garden that could be sequestered from the world. The winning alternate amendment proposed that drawing such lines between nations and people would alienate important allies in the battle over the real issues.

X

Having been blamed for every other sin under the sun, immigrants were now to be scapegoated for our environmental problems as well. By the time the Sierra Club's membership had voted down Amendment A, a lot of participants were embittered, and the environmental movement was tarnished in the eyes of many onlookers. The 1990s had seen the rise of the environmental justice movement, which addresses environmental racism—who gets poisoned by dumps and incinerators, among other things—but the mainstream environmental movement is not always so good at the racial politics within its own priorities and assumptions. The very white-collar premise that nature is where you go for recreation belies the possibility that some people toil in nature or on its agricultural edges and would rather do something less rugged on the weekend.

Still, this is a long way from the politics of the anti-immigration activists who attempted an openly hostile takeover of the Sierra Club in the spring of 2004, with three candidates for the March board elections looking to form a majority with some of the more dubious current board members, and with various outside organizations—some clearly racist and white supremacist—encouraging their members to join the club and sway the vote. (That the name of the Sierra Club is half

Spanish, a souvenir of when California was part of Mexico or Spain, recalls a history no one in these debates seems to have examined, or perhaps the exclusionary British term *club* trumps it.) "Without a doubt, the Sierra Club is the subject of a hostile takeover attempt by forces allied with . . . a variety of right-wing extremists. By taking advantage of the welcoming grassroots democratic structure of the Sierra Club, they hope to use the credibility of the Club as a cover to advance their own extremist views," said the Southern Poverty Law Center in a warning letter.

The three candidates were Frank Morris, David Pimentel, and Richard Lamm. A former Colorado governor, Lamm is a longtime board member of the Federation for American Immigration Reform (FAIR), which receives funding from the pro-eugenics and "race betterment" Pioneer Fund. Lamm, who has apparently spent little time in Switzerland, has said, "America is increasingly becoming, day by day, a bilingual country, yet there is not a bilingual country in the world that lives in peace with itself." He once projected a fantasy near future in which "the rash of firebombings throughout the Southwest and the three-month siege of downtown San Diego in 1998 were all led by second-generation Hispanics, the children of immigrants." He spoke in 1984 about the elderly having a "duty to die," and he believes in rationing medical care. The garden is the pretty metaphor employed by anti-immigration activists; the more ferociously paranoid imagination of characters like Lamm picture the nation instead as a lifeboat with limited supplies, which is why you have to clobber the fingers of those swimmers clinging to the boat. Only perhaps it was their boat, but the fact of their being tossed in the ocean had been obliterated; or perhaps they are the ones who row and bail and keep the boat going. Nevertheless, their fingers were being clobbered.

XI

The vision of a homogenous place overrun by disruptive, destructive outsiders is a better picture of the Sierra Club under siege than the United States in relation to immigration. Outside groups such as the National Immigration Alert List encouraged their members to join the club to force it to endorse an issue it had rejected six years before and so perhaps permanently warp its identity and image. Further, most candidates for a seat on the club's board are active longtime members, but the three outsiders seemed to have become members specifically to stage the nonprofit equiv- alent of a hostile corporate takeover. This was underscored by their filing, and then petulantly dropping, a lawsuit against the club, various club personnel, and three other board candidates (including veteran club activist Phil Berry and civil rights activist Morris Dees, who had called attention to their links to racist groups).

Thirteen past presidents of the Sierra Club came out in opposition to the coup; eleven of them issued a statement that included these remarks: "These out- siders' desire is to capture the majority of seats so as to move their personal agenda, without regard to the wishes or knowledge of the members and support- ers of the Sierra Club, and to use the funds and other resources of the Club to those ends. . . . We believe that the crisis facing the Club is real and can well be fatal, destroying the vision of John Muir, and the work and contributions of hun- dreds of thousands of volunteer activists who have built this organization." (Of course, John Muir was a racist, too—he said some pretty astounding things about Native Americans—but that's another story, and era.)

A lot of leftists have already written off the 112-year-old Sierra Club, and though I've occasionally thought that its slogan could be that of Earth First!— "No compromise in the defense of Mother Earth"—without the "No," it remains what it has been for so many decades: the flagship of the environmental movement, dealing with everything from clear-cutting and global warming to endangered species and water pollution. Discrediting it would drain credit and potency away from much of the movement. And it seems that the goal of these anti-immigration activists has little or nothing to do with the protection of the environment. After all, the links between immigration and environmental trouble are sketchy at best.

XII

During the 1990s, the border was always talked about as though it were a tangi- ble landform, a divinely ordained difference. I grew up with a clear picture of the

Iron Curtain, too, since it was spoken of as though it were as coherent an artifact as the Berlin Wall. But the Berlin Wall was made of concrete, while the Iron Curtain was not made out of metal, despite the vision I'd had of a continental Cyclone fence. Like the U.S.-Mexican border, it was a political idea enforced by a variety of structures, technologies, and people with guns.

The spring of Amendment A, I actually spent several days on the border, or rather in the place where the border is supposed to be: along the lower canyons of the Rio Grande, where the left bank is named Texas and the right bank is Chihuahua. The river, which divides nothing at all on its long run through New Mexico, has been an international boundary since the signing of the Treaty of Guadalupe Hidalgo ended the U.S. territorial war on Mexico 150 years ago and transferred a million square miles of Mexico to this country. Yet rivers are capricious, and this one has a habit of throwing out oxbows that put some bewildered farmers and their land in a new country. So in the 1960s, the border was designated as the deepest part of the river during the years of the survey, regardless of where the river should go afterward. Which means that the phantom river of thirty years ago is now the international border—not the most solid object for nationalism to rest upon. After all those years of fiery rhetoric about the border, it was strange to float down the place it was supposed to be and find nothing but water, rock, and prickly pears. The possibility that the Border didn't exist was a stunning one.

As our raft floated downstream, crossing songbirds and cattle seemed indifferent to the idea that the Chihuahuan desert was really two countries. The slow river along the banks of which all this life clustered and bloomed was not a boundary but an oasis where the toxins from American agriculture and Juarez maquiladoras mixed indiscriminately. Not quite a Berlin Wall, even if you're not a swallow or a cactus wren.

Borders don't exist in nature. I learned that again in northern Canada, up where British Columbia meets the Northwest Territories. I was traveling by raft again, and the ornithologist with us would get up at dawn to identify, band, and free the songbirds that she caught in her mist nets. She liked to point out that a lot of them wintered in the tropics of Central America, and so conservation efforts needed to be transnational. Canada's remotest wilderness was not a place apart; it was intimately tied to the tropics. Weather, toxins, species all move without regard to borders, which is one of the reasons why environmental politics don't work as nationalist politics. Though on the Rio Grande I was once again with Canadians, who simply didn't grasp the dangers and resonances of this border.

XIII

There were, of course, people to enforce the concept of the border and to profit from it: during my ten-day rafting trip, I saw what appeared to be a drug smuggler, a picturesque old man with a heavily laden burro; was confronted by a Mexican army commandante and his machine-gun–carrying soldiers; and on the last day met an armed Immigration and Naturalization officer who was there to patrol that stretch of river, which even livestock crossed regularly. Like the front yards of Angelenos, the international border is usually just an expanse with a few threats and armed-response guards scattered along it. But the conceptual line running down the river didn't mark a garden off from the world; the river was instead a different kind of garden, an oasis around which flourished birds and plants that couldn't have survived elsewhere in the arid desert spreading far in all directions. And birds and seeds and air pollution emigrated across the river without passports; contaminants from upriver agriculture, sewage, and industry flowed down it without visas. Amendment A, it seemed to me there, was wishful thinking, a fantasy that spaces could be truly sequestered, could have happy fates independent of the unhappiness all around. Which is not to deny that environmental devastation and crime are bad things. They are unquestionably bad. The questions are all about the way they are imagined and addressed.

XIV

When the Mexican army with their machine guns arrived at Hot Springs Rapid, two of the river guides and several passengers were drinking wine in the hot spring and hooting out lurid speculations about the guides' anatomy. The commander and his three stolid Mayan-faced soldiers were first seen by someone napping in a tent, who did little more than hope it was a bad dream; the second to see them went to tell the trip leader in the springs; and I must have been the third. My primitive Spanish regressed further under the circumstances, but I figured that being female, fully dressed, and impressed with the gravity of the situation made me the best person around to take on the job of soothing diplomatic liaison. (The one Spanish speaker in the group was off hunting red-eared slider turtles, unsuccessfully—"*el buscar las tortugas*," I said, or something to that effect, and my interrogator laughed.) We were camped on the Mexican side of the river, of course, on one of the few spots where a road leads all the way to the river— twelve miles down a long canyon from the nearest ranch. The road was used periodically by people coming to bathe in the springs.

I never ascertained why the Mexican army had arrived—whether we were interrupting their bathing schedule, or whether it had something to do with the old man and the burro we'd seen the day before, who fit the bill for a drug smuggler. It seemed unlikely to be a routine patrol, in this remote place bordered by cliffs. I did ascertain that the commander, who seemed to be in a good if unrelenting mood, preferred "*la costa—Acapulco y Puerto Vallarta*" to "*el desierto*" and wouldn't mind being transferred soon. I was just trying to put in a good word for the desert, though I myself live on "*la costa*," as he had seen when he inspected my papers, when the trip leader came along and found out that he didn't want to stay for a drink.

The Canadians were horrifically clueless about where they were; they regarded the desert with all its dangers, both intrinsic and manufactured—dehydration, flash floods, rattlesnakes, scorpions, drug dealers and other armed desperados, intensely toxic water—as some sort of underequipped version of Club Med. Only an older man who had spent time in Africa comprehended the possibilities of the situation; he and I seemed to be on one trip, the rest of the crew on another, down a pleasantly meaningless river I couldn't recognize as the borderlands Rio Grande, let alone what it is called from its right bank, the more ominous Rio Bravo, the ferocious river. (Of course, the right bank is nowise different from the left bank farther upstream, where it divides, for example, West Albuquerque from Albuquerque proper: my aunt and uncle cross it every day to babysit grandchildren.)

XV

On the last day of my journey down the river, a long parade of goats trotting by the dusty riverbank made me think of Ezekiel Hernandez, who lived and died not far upriver, in Redford, Texas. His story seemed at last to make the ominous ambience of the border real to the people I was traveling with. A high school senior and a U.S. citizen, Hernandez was herding his goats near the river one evening when he was shot in the back by U.S. Marines wearing camouflage and night-vision goggles. They claimed that he had threatened them with his .22 rifle, which he apparently carried for rattlesnakes (and because he was a West Texan—even the fisherman I saw on the Rio Grande had six-guns on either camo-clad hip). The circumstances, however, make it seem unlikely that he ever even saw the marines. Who knows why they shot him, except that he looked like a Mexican, a stranger in the garden?

Hernandez's story reads like a pastoral eclogue—not one of Theocritus's cheerful Greek ones, but Virgil's sad pastorals, where Arcadia is always under siege, and where shepherds are the principal spokesmen for a vision of tranquility in the deterritorialized pastures. Sometimes their songs are of Daphnis, the ideal shepherd who died in the fifth eclogue. The men with arms win the battles, but those with the shepherd's crook win the war of representation, as Cain and Abel demonstrate.

What is so peculiar about these new wars of meaning in the American West is that the imagery is so rustic, full of appeals to the beauty of the mountains and the fields. But the dead young goatherds are on the other side, not of the border, but of the cult. We have reversed Virgil's terms, or perhaps Virgil himself distinguished between the eclogues' Arcadia and the georgic Paradise. After all, it was Cain who was the gardener. (Along these lines, one can trace the moral reversal of

Jews becoming Israelis as that of nomads becoming gardeners; since goats walk and crops don't, agriculture requires territoriality in ways that pastoral nomadism does not. Or note that country boy Timothy McVeigh used a truckload of fertilizer to blow up the Oklahoma Federal Building.) Gardens are portrayed as serene spaces, but perhaps it is time for the guards to be incorporated into the iconography of gardens.

XVI

Borders don't exist in nature, but they can be made. In San Diego and Tijuana shortly after the devastating 2003 October fires, friends pointed out to me how a single bioregion had sharply diverged because of distinct human practices. On the Baja side, the resources to put out fires never really existed, the fire cycle had never been seriously interrupted, and so the colossal fuel loads that would incinerate so much around San Diego had never accumulated. Besides, Mexicans are less interested in moving into locations remote from their fellows. The upshot is not only that they don't have such devastating fires but that they tend not to have mansions in canyons and on mountaintops for which firefighters must risk their lives and the state squander its funds. Sometimes the ecology is better preserved south of the border than north of it. Consider the case of the nearly extinct Sonoran pronghorn on the Arizona-Sonora border. About ten times as many survive on the Mexican side, while on the U.S. side, they're pretty much confined to the Barry Goldwater Bombing Range—not the healthiest habitat for the last couple dozen of their kind in the United States. I traveled there too, amid signs warning of live ordnance and the sound of distant bombing operations.

XVII

And back and forth across the Tijuana–San Diego border, where you can head south without fanfare but get stuck in endless traffic and searches and screenings on the route north. Part of the border there is made out of old slabs of metal from the first Gulf War, an ugly literal iron curtain, but the new border wall is elegant and visually perforated though equally impassable. When you cross into Mexico, nothing changes, because you're still in the same territory, and everything changes, because you're in a whole other cosmology and economy.

XVIII

The takeover of the Sierra Club would have succeeded only if the invaders had convinced people to believe again that the border marks a coherent environmental divide. The official idea is that immigrants are bad for the environment, but you can reframe that a couple of dozen ways. One is to point out that we don't need help being bad for the environment. The United States consumes the world's resources in huge disproportion to its percentage of the global population, and most of us work overtime to do our bit for global warming. (My mother got caught up in the same arguments the last time the immigration issue roiled the Sierra Club waters and exclaimed to me, "But what if they come here and live like us?" to which the only possible reply was, "What if we stay here and live like us?") If you care about the environment, there are more relevant issues you might choose to take up before immigration. But if you care about stopping immigration, the environment is a touchstone of conventional goodness, or at least of liberalism, you can hide behind.

The poor nonwhite immigrants who are the real targets of this campaign are generally building and cleaning those big houses in remote places and mowing the lawns and fueling up the snowmobiles, but they tend not to own them, or to make the decision to delist an endangered species, or to defund the Superfund cleanup program, or to lower emissions standards. (We elect people to do that, actually.) In fact, if sprawl and resource consumption are the immediate threats posed by population growth, then the new immigrants, who live frugally, densely, and often rely on public transport, are a rebuke to the suburban majority in the United States.

XIX

The fantasy that the United States can be sealed off from the world like a walled garden in a slum overlooks dozens of other inconvenient facts, such as the role of our country, with tools such as agricultural dumping and the World Bank, in making those other nations slummier; or the fact that they too have their gardens and we too have our slums. (Sometimes it's the destruction of their gardens that set them on the immigrants' path in the first place—certainly that's the case with the Mexican farmers bankrupted by NAFTA, the North American Free Trade Agreement.) But it's also dismaying because setting gardens apart is how the conservation movement began, back at the turn of the twentieth century, when it was far more closely affiliated with racist, nativist, and eugenicist movements. Behind the early national parks and wilderness areas was the idea of scenery segregation—that it was enough to save the most beautiful and biotically lush places, a few dozen or hundred square miles at a time.

XX

The implication of setting one piece apart is that the rest of the environment is put up for grabs, and into the 1960s the Sierra Club's basic strategy was doing exactly that. They fought a nuclear power plant in California's Nipomo Dunes, but agreed that it was okay to put one in Diablo Canyon instead. Club activists such as David Brower eventually came to regret that they had secured protection of Utah's Dinosaur National Monument from damming by letting Glen Canyon Dam go forward. Now most environmentalists are against big dams and nuclear power, so that the debates are about policy, not just geography.

Back then, Rachel Carson had only recently brought the bad news about pesticides—that they didn't stay put but moved through the environment into both wild places and our own bodies—and with that, it began to become clear that you couldn't just defend places. You had to address practices; you had to recognize systems; you had to understand that, in John Muir's famous aphorism, "When we try to pick out anything by itself, we find it hitched to everything else in the universe." When he said that, of course, he wasn't imagining plastic detritus being ingested by seabirds in the center of the Pacific Ocean or polar bears beyond the industrialized world becoming hermaphroditic from chemical contamination. But we can.

More and more things come under the purview of environmentalism these days, from what we eat to where our chemicals end up. Immigration, unless it's part of a larger conversation about consumption, birth rates, reproductive rights, trade, international economic policy, sprawl, and dozens of other issues, isn't really one of them. It seems instead that environmentalism is a cloak of virtue in which anti-immigration activists are attempting to wrap themselves. But they're better looked at naked.

XXI

And those portrayed as invaders are in fact maintaining the garden. Throughout this century, various bracero programs have brought in Mexicans to do the work citizens don't want—namely, to toil in the garden, not only the gardens of the wealthy, but the agricultural fields. Despite all the rhetoric depicting immigrants as assailants of the economy, the vast agricultural economy of California and much of the rest of the country is propped up by farmworkers from south of the border, documented or not (including many fleeing the post-NAFTA economic collapse of small farms, brought about by the sale of cheap U.S. corn in Mexico; NAFTA opened the borders to goods but not people). Think Virgil, think wetback georgics.

And the desire to secure cheap labor has created an alternative boundary around some of these agricultural gardens, ones that the workers cannot get out of. In 1990, a Southern California flower grower was given a small jail sentence and fined for enslaving undocumented Zapotec Indian immigrants from Mexico (and fear of the Border Patrol keeps many undocumented inhabitants of the South-west not as outsiders but as insiders, afraid to leave the house or the private property boundaries of the farm they work on, garden captives). It is part of the murderous poetry of these garden wars: slaves on a flower farm. Who thought, picking up a dozen roses for love's sake, that one person's bed of roses was another's wall of thorns?

XXII

"A people who would begin by burning the fences and let the forests stand!" exclaimed Thoreau. America was founded on a vision of abundance, enough to go around for all. The relatively open immigration policies of past eras are based on this assumption, as was the Homestead Act, which gave away western land to anyone willing to work it—a vision of privatized land but universal ownership that would've put everyone inside some garden or other. On a smaller scale, city parks were founded on the interlocking beliefs that nature was uplifting, that open space was democratic, that it was possible and even important for all members of society to find literal common ground.

The great irony of Central Park in its early years was that public money and democratic rhetoric were used to make a place most notable for its concessions to the rich, who promenaded there in carriages, while the poor took to private pleasure gardens where less aristocratic pleasures such as drinking beer and dancing the polka were acceptable. As Elizabeth Blackmar and Ray Rosenzweig write in their magisterial history of the place: "The issue of democratic access to the park has also been raised by the increasing number of homeless New Yorkers. Poor people—from the 'squatters' of the 1850s to the 'tramps' of the 1870s and 1890s to the Hooverville residents of the 1930s—have always turned to the park land for shelter. . . . The growing visibility of homeless people in Central Park posed in the starkest terms the contradiction between Americans' commitment to democratic public space and their acquiescence in vast disparities of wealth and power."

XXIII

This is the same park from which Michael Bloomberg, the Republican mayor of New York, banned activists in August 2004 during the Republican National Convention, saying that they would be bad for the grass if they gathered on the Great Meadow, as a million antinuclear activists had done some twenty-two years before. New York, in this scenario, became pristine nature to be protected. Despite the overwhelmingly Democratic majority in New York, the media reassured viewers that the anti-Bush contingent was made up of "outsiders." One of them carried a photograph of his son, Jésus A. Suarez, who had died in Iraq, on a pink sign labeled *Bush lied, my son died (and 1000s more)*, and his face was filled with an unabashed infinite sorrow. One of the peculiarities of the current war is that the economic draft brought in thousands of young people who were not citizens; those who died fighting the "war on terror" were given retroactive citizenship. In death, but only in death, did these young Mexicans, Salvadorans, and Guatemalans become Americans. One could rearrange the old Western saying about Indians to go something like, "The only naturalized immigrant is a dead immigrant."

XXIV

But when I flew east for the New York event, the airline screened the film *The Day After Tomorrow*, a movie in which global warming convulses the Northern Hemisphere with a boomerang cold snap that buries and freezes most of the United States and Europe so fast that millions freeze like popsicles. In the most interesting scene in the movie, groups of gringos wade across the Rio Grande carrying luggage, trying to flee the ecological destruction of El Norte, while the Mexican border patrol tries to keep them out. Finally, in return for a blanket forgiveness of Latin American debt, the Yankees are welcomed in, and the Dick-Cheney-look-alike president admits that the United States has been wrong in its environmental and social policy and vows to try to do better. The Yankee refugees waded across like the U.S. Army deserters of 1846–1848 whom no one on the north side of the border remembers.

XXV

After the Southwest was seized from Mexico, when the gringos from the East began settling the American West, they came to terms with deserts—or didn't, for a fair number of them died in the terrible crossings of the salt flats west of the Great Salt Lake, the great Nevada sinks into which the rivers vanish, and, most famously, Death Valley. What does it mean that once again the deserts are for dying in, under similar circumstances, despite the existence of railroads and high-ways and refrigeration and air conditioning and airplanes and interstate water-works? What do these twenty-first-century reenactments say about the first time these gringos waded, these wanderers died?

XXVI

In August of 2004, a life-size statue of Jesus Christ was found in the Rio Grande, near Eagle Pass, Texas. Border Patrol agents spotted it from the air and thought it was a body, Jesus as an unsuccessful border crosser, a dead alien. They launched a rescue attempt and retrieved the statue, which no one subsequently claimed as lost property. It was regarded by Catholics in the area as a message from God. On the south side of the border, in Piedras Negro, the statue was regarded as the Christ for the undocumented. "He's telling us he's alive and he is here with us," Veronica de la Pena told a newspaper. "He's trying to tell us that there is hope."

XXVII

Thirty-nine steps across the border; where do we go from here?

Nonconforming Uses

Teddy Cruz on Both Sides of the Border

〖2006〗

Somewhere, somehow, decisions were made for us in the United States about how we would live, work, travel, and socialize, the decisions institutionalized as the very architecture and geography of our everyday lives. What were they thinking, those mid-century designers who divided up the world on so many scales as if fearful of mingling, whether it's the mingling of public and private, work and home, rich and poor, or old and young? Who insisted we should keep building houses for a middle-class nuclear family that is less and less common, rather than flexible spaces to accommodate solo dwellers, single parents, extended families, and communities whose ties soften the bounds between public and private? Who privileged the car so much that the parking lot, driveway, and garage have almost replaced human-scale architectural façades; who let cars eat up public space and public life? Who forgot to build anything for the service sector, even though those workers more than anyone keep a city running?

In recent years, radical architects have begun to question and jettison those decisions. This route hasn't always resulted in high-profile projects, but it has opened up broad possibilities, a more significant if less visible achievement. At its most provocative, this opening up is a series of challenges to borders and categories, and its most inspired practitioner might be architect Teddy Cruz. That he is based in San Diego is no coincidence, for that city's southern edge is divided from Tijuana, Mexico, only by the most trafficked border crossing in the world, an ever more militarized line between the first world and the third, between chaotic exuberance and beige reticence; and for him Latin America supplies a lexicon of alternative practices from which the United States could learn.

He says of his fellow architects, "We are just working to insert our refined high aesthetic into an invisible city that has been shaped by developers, economists, and politicians. This invisible city is made of height limitations, setbacks [the rules about how far back from the property line you can build], zoning regulation that is very discriminatory. So what came to be my interest is what I call urbanism beyond the property line." Cruz would like to knit back together the fragmented places that result from a lack of collaboration between urban planners and architects and to spur a level of social engagement that he thinks is absent in most American cities. To do this, architects have to cross the property line and venture into public space, and then cross still another divide. This latter divide he calls the "the gap between social responsibility and artistic experimentation."

One cloudy Sunday, he drives me in a friend's scruffy Miata, the one whose trunkful of blueprints looks like contraband, to his newest work in San Diego. We wind through the city's central green space, Balboa Park, to the museum complex at its heart. A supreme expression of the enthusiastic mix of Mission Revival and Alhambra fantasia that characterized much prewar California architecture, its buildings form a hollow square with, of course, parking at its center. But much of the parking lot is now occupied by Cruz's pavilion for InSite, the transborder biennale also taking place in Tijuana. The work of installing two tractor-trailer beds and building a tented structure and AstroTurf lounge area was relatively easy; getting permission to do so was not. But breaking rules and opening borders are what Cruz's work is about. "We closed a parking lot—one of the most sacred parking lots in the city," he says with satisfaction and amusement. "That was the achievement."

Cruz is no fan of the way parking lots dominate the American built environment. The reconquest of space for unfettered human interaction might be what he's after. Or the reinvention of the whole urban fabric. He's modest but hardly unambitious. A professor at Woodbury College in downtown San Diego, he was recently hired away by the University of California, San Diego. His longtime collaborators in his architecture firm, estudio Teddy Cruz, moved on to other opportunities at the same time, so his own life is a project under construction these days. At forty-three, Cruz is dapper, sturdily built but somehow slight, perhaps from nervous energy, elliptical in his rapid speech, passionate in his enthusiasms, and usually running late. Somehow, as we traverse both sides of the border this Sunday, I begin to feel like Alice being rushed along by the White Rabbit, though the rabbit in this case is not so white. Born and raised in Guatemala City and brought to San Diego at age twenty by his stepfather, Cruz has been here contend-ing ever since with suburbia, sprawl, real estate booms, the border, and other con-tingencies of contemporary California.

The crowded, chaotic richness and poverty of Guatemala City instilled in him a permanent enthusiasm for density of both buildings and activities. The father-less son of the proprietor of a fashionable nightclub, he grew up middle-class in the bustle of a third world city, graduated from high school, and planned to become a doctor until a fellow student took him to see a corpse dissected. Squeamish, he backed off from the plan. An aptitude test established architecture as an alterna-tive. But what decided the matter for him was the sight of a fourth-year architec-ture student sitting at his desk at a window, drawing and nursing a cup of coffee as rain fell outside. "I don't know, I just liked the idea of having this relationship to the paper and the adventure of imagining the spaces. That was the first image that captured me."

As he was studying architecture, his mother, already opposed to the govern-ment's growing brutality, got caught storing weapons for rebels in her basement, went to jail, and then emigrated to the United States, where she married a Yankee and brought her offspring over. Cruz moved as soon as he got his BA in architec-ture, leaving the overstimulation of Guatemala City for the anomie of the brand-new San Diego suburb of Mira Mesa. At first he loved it, and for a year he stayed there, studying English. "I was moving from downtown Guatemala, a place full of smog, an overpopulated old neighborhood, into this incredibly pristine, clean, homogenous kind of place. I saw that it was incredibly ordered; I thought that it was very nice." The new uncle he was staying with warned him not to go down-town where danger lay, but boredom set in, and he began to explore. "I think it was incremental, this dissatisfaction with suburbia, with lack of social complexity.

In retrospect, every time I wanted go out, I couldn't move, and the distances were huge to get to places. It can get to you, that relentless kind of sameness."

He began working in architecture in San Diego in 1984, won his first award in 1986, went back and got a couple more degrees in architecture, spent a year in Florence. After taking another degree from Harvard's Graduate School of Design, he was awarded the Rome Prize and spent another year in Italy (another place that has provided him with alternative models of public space and life). Somewhere in there, he got married and had a daughter, now eighteen; eventually got divorced; started his own practice; and began to teach. He also got married again, to the landscape architect Kate Roe, and had two more daughters, now nine and four. He founded estudio Teddy Cruz in 1993, and in 1994 began the LA/LA (Latin America/Los Angeles) Studio for students from all over Latin America at SCI-Arc, the Southern California Institute for Architecture. It was in those years that he began to find his focus—and his dissent.

It came in part from his conflicted experience of Latin America. "I wonder," he muses, "if having grown up in Guatemala makes you like a socialist or a kind of Marxist by default because you are surrounded by so much stuff—by an intense sort of realism." His mother's opinion was even more dour: she "wanted us out of there in such disgust with the institutions, and she used to talk about how she hated seeing the archbishop parading in a Mercedes-Benz in the middle of the favelas [impoverished neighborhoods]." As a student in Guatemala City, he re-calls, "I was put off by the fact that this school of architecture saw social respon-sibility as the boxing of people in these awful buildings, very sterile." Years later, when he went back, "somebody in the audience got up and said, 'Oh, it's easy for you to show these artsy images, when in reality the problem here is poverty.'" If the Guatemalan architects fell into a utilitarian gloom, the Yankees suffered from an aesthetic drive so pure that it didn't serve people at all. In the end, he had to start from scratch, looking not just at what could be built but at how to reinvent the conditions in which architects work.

The conventional media for architects are buildings and building materials, but Cruz's are ideas, images, and conversations with students, developers, colleagues, and citizens—so his greatest influence may be impossible to trace. Though he can take credit for a few dozen innovative structures in Southern California, he can take far more for tearing down old conventions and charting new ways of thinking. His PowerPoint presentations are things of beauty, zooming from maps of the world to details of children at play, combining computer-generated images, architectural models, his lush collages, photographs of buildings, streets, and aerial views. They leave crowds exhilarated and ready to change the world. It's not a misnomer to call Cruz an architect—after all, there are enough buildings out there that he has authored. But his most important function may be as a visionary, an exhortatory voice.

Another of his innovations is to focus on traditionally overlooked people and spaces. When he delivered the prestigious James Stirling Memorial Lecture at the Canadian Centre for Architecture in Montreal in 2004, he declared,

> At the time when these mega projects of redevelopment are becoming the basis for the skyrocketing of the real estate market in many city centers across the United States, creating a formidable economic bubble of land speculation, practically no one is asking where the cook, janitor, service maid, bus-boy, nanny, gardener and many of the thousands of immigrants crossing the border(s) to fulfill the demand for such jobs will live, and what kinds of rents and housing markets will be available to them. Well, they live in the inner city. It is not a coincidence, then, that the territory that continues to be ignored is the inner city.

He has designed for these sectors repeatedly and is currently in discussion about a project to create a day-laborer center in San Francisco ("day labor" being the current term for the mostly undocumented painters, builders, landscapers, and other mostly Latino workers who line up each morning at informally designated sites in cities across the country, waiting for employers to pick them).

He is also interested in working with the in-between spaces and no-man's-lands that cities generate, the empty space that surrounds each design for a site, and the niches too minor for architectural glory. "Nonconforming uses" is the planning-codespeak for projects that violate the zoning code, and it's a phrase Cruz is so fond of that, he tells me, he "was proposing to change the Coalition of

New Urbanists" to the "Coalition of Nonconforming Urbanists." The New Urbanists are a bugbear of his, because what began as a radical project to bring public and pedestrian space, mixed uses, and classes back to cities and towns has too often settled into a dressing-up of middle-class housing with more density and some commerce, but no room—again—for the poor and no real transformations in social life. Cruz cherishes human interactions, and none of his designs or critiques overlooks how people actually inhabit buildings and spaces.

At his parking-lot transgression for InSite in Balboa Park, Cruz is delighted that some teenagers broke in after hours to hang out in the pavilion, without damaging anything; their desire to use the space was a real measure of success to him. He proposes that rather than measure density by the number of dwellings or residents per square block, we measure it by the number of interactions—the more the better. With goals like this, the solutions stop looking like ordinary architecture. From the pavilion, we head to San Diego's Gaslight District, which is supposed to be the center of a great downtown revival—meaning, mostly, that its grid has filled up with chain stores, restaurants, and high-rise condos. Cruz complains that such projects "are ironically importing into city centers the very suburban project of privatization, homogenization, and 'theming' accompanied by 'loftlike' high-end housing, stadiums, and the official corporate franchises." He thinks it's great that the middle class is coming back to cities, but terrible that in doing so they make these centers less citylike.

We drive around and around looking for parking, closer to publicly financed, corporately named Qualcomm Stadium than to the Gaslight District. Strangely, there is no parking nor any people—the area by the stadium feels deserted. Or almost no people. We pass a woman wearing headphones and waving a giant sign advertising condos—a common sight in this real estate boomtown. Back and forth she swings this placard, selling a downtown that isn't a downtown in crucial ways, bored and alone on her corner near the stadium, her sign promising dream homes, her face reporting alienation. The green space in front of the stadium that was supposed to be a public park has been surrounded by fencing and annexed by the sports corporations, Cruz points out, another wall he is indignant about. Near it, we find a place to dump the Miata.

Many of the downtown condos, he tells me, are second homes, meaning that they are often empty. The emptiness of affluence annoys him, and one of his plans is a series of drawings showing how "a McMansion can be turned into three houses"—that is, how ostentatious waste and selfishness could be retrofitted for ordinary people and more environmentally reasonable living. "Well," he says, "if we were really to look at the factors, the conditions that have transformed the last forty years, could we anticipate that in the next forty years the third and fourth forces, immigrations, will be equally transformative?" Clearly, he hopes so.

He said on local television not long ago, "I could be in the center right now of one of those new communities in Del Mar and, just viscerally, when I'm in the middle of that place, I just . . . feel completely sad. Twenty minutes later, I'm in the middle of Tijuana. I feel a lot more charged. . . . I cannot help but want to escape that kind of sterility in San Diego and then embrace this, what you might call chaos." Chaos, as in a lot going on and a lot of kinds of people present—as in social density.

We leave the car to walk into a parking structure where the work of another InSite artist, Aernout Mik, is installed, a huge screen in the sepulchral gloom of the garage showing a video that mixes footage of subdivisions seen from above—San Diego—with images of a fictionalized version of Tijuana's pharmacies. Cruz finds it amusing that the place that was once a magnet for the illicit is now a mecca for people looking for cheap but legal drugs; the pharmacies that line Avenida de la Revolución are temples—mirrors multiply the carefully arranged piles of toothpaste, drugs, and toiletries into a confusion of abundance, and employees in white doctors' jackets solicit customers at the open front.

The sight of the pharmacies whets our appetite for something livelier than this abandoned zone, and so we drive south on I-5 to another parking lot—this one a short walk from the militarized carnival zone that is the border. And with that, all the rules are about to change, which is part of why Cruz brings people across so often. There you can see difference, see the innovativeness born out of poverty and its sometimes exuberant results.

To enter Mexico is easy; there are no delays, no checks, no armed officials sorting out who may enter or who may not. You walk up a long ramp lined with vendors and keep going, until the down ramp spits you out into a pedestrian plaza circled by makeshift buildings. Women and children approach, selling crafts—my pale presence is a magnet for them, Teddy ruefully notes—but we walk on to the city center, down streets as gleaming and theatrical as in Dutch artist Mik's parking-garage video. Somehow the very texture changes when you leave San Diego for Tijuana. There's more color and more people, even the texture of sidewalks and streets is different—more potholes and irregularities, a veneer of dust and grime that tints the energy and the vividness of this other world.

Cruz decides on a detour, and suddenly we leave behind the gringo-commodities zone to join a mostly Mexican crowd. Men and women, walking in a large group, are chanting angrily and carrying placards we cannot read from behind. They march down the middle of the street, and cars and trucks in the one remaining lane honk in solidarity. Street and sidewalk are crowded and bustling. We follow the protestors for blocks, and at an intersection lined with onlookers and vendors of cut fruit, Teddy asks one of the participants what's going on. It's a demonstration against the Tijuana mayor's decision to eliminate the unofficial transit network, the Blanco y Azul buses that transport workers around the city and its sprawling periphery of slums and sweatshops. For Cruz, this is a sign of the Americanization of the place, the insistence on official monopolies and the banning of the unofficial options, whether they work or not.

It's the improvised solutions to poverty that he seeks out among the slums and favelas of Latin America, starting with Tijuana, and he admits that it's easy to romanticize poverty rather than admire the poor, whose solutions are often creative, subversive, and environmentally sound—Tijuana does much to recycle the discarded materials of San Diego. On an earlier tour, he took me to see the small houses salvaged from San Diego as an alternative to demolition, homes that had themselves emigrated across the border. Whole structures have been imported to Mexico and resituated, often on raised metal scaffolds so that the first story becomes the second. The improvised architecture of Tijuana delights him, the homes built piecemeal and the retaining walls made out of tires, the squats and guerrilla housing that Mexico, with a very different attitude toward real estate rights, often allows to become neighborhoods of legitimate homeowners.

We saw La Mona, the five-story statue that dominates one poor barrio—a voluptuous, naked, plaster-white woman that is not a public monument like the more prim Statue of Liberty but a private home, built by Armando Muñoz in this zone of no zoning codes. Kids running in the dust of the unpaved roads, power lines with dozens of lines spliced into them, houses in vivid lavenders and oranges and lime greens, laundry on the line, and stray dogs are fixtures in this barrio. Just past it is the international border, the new fence being put in, a row of deceptively open-looking, off-white vertical strips that look less brutal but are also more forbidding than the corrugated metal landing pads from the Gulf War that were erected in the early 1990s (a recycling suggesting that this too is a war zone). In his presentations, Cruz often shows a picture of Colonia Libertad, this border neighborhood, in the early 1970s, fenceless, with a little boy flying a kite on the undeveloped U.S. side of the line. The border has grown steadily more massive and more militarized over the past two decades. It didn't used to be such a big deal.

On the Mexican side, homes push all the way up to the fence—"zero setback," Teddy likes to say, adapting zoning language to the layout of international relations. Such shifts in scale are a big part of his language and worldview; he is as interested in the borders that govern the single-family home as those that divide two nations on one continent. Tijuana "crashes against this wall. It's almost like the wall becomes a dam that keeps the intensity of this chaos from contaminating the picturesque order of San Diego. . . . It's a whole country leaning against the other." But he goes on to explain that there's more than physical distance at stake: "I'm talking about an attitude toward the everyday, toward the space, toward the way that we use the space, toward ritual, toward the relationship to the other." Not the utilitarian architecture he encountered in school in Guatemala City, but the vernacular, improvisational responses and networks that could do much for more affluent realms.

The ever more militarized border makes San Diego in his terms, "the world's largest gated community." Though the United States likes to consider Mexico a corrupting influence, it's the Mexican city serving the United States that is regarded as shameful, weird, and not quite part of its own country, while the booming U.S. city abutted up against it calls itself "America's Finest City." That's part of the great paradox of the border. Another is the abrupt line where two worlds meet—or rather where one world presses forward and the other shrinks back. Even the ecology has become different on each side. And yet there are countless ways it doesn't divide anything. Mexicans emigrate north with or without papers; Americans who work in San Diego have moved south to buy affordable waterfront homes on the other side, an American dream no longer in America; California as a whole becomes more and more Latino, with Latinos due to become the majority population in the next decade; and by some accounts 40 percent of the San Diego workforce lives south of the border. Tiendas selling Mexican washtubs and other goods show up in San Diego, while U.S. chain restaurants spread in Tijuana. It's a dam that builds up pressure without truly stopping the flow, a line that does and doesn't divide.

This reading of the border lets Cruz think about the two great forces of globalization and privatization in relation to everyday life. Globalization as the influx of human beings from other cultures to the United States and as the export of dubious U.S. models of architecture, urban (and suburban) design, and consumption; the spread of chains; and the concomitant erosion of local culture. Privatization as the spatial and psychological withdrawal from the public sphere and the collective good that accompanies an ideology of individualism and free enterprise. And perhaps a counter to privatization in the reinvigorated sense of public life and public space that sometimes comes with Latino immigrants.

And though Cruz is interested in what the United States could learn from Latin America, it's clear that Latin America and much of the rest of the world are learning from the United States—there's an elite development in China that he points to in dismay, an exact replica of an Orange County suburban tract, with lawns, boxy stucco houses fronted by garages and driveways, and curvy streets. And then there is the subdivision in Tijuana we went to look at one day, a strange grid of miniaturized single-family homes plopped like a carpet on a rolling landscape. Each home had a driveway out front, but there was not enough room for them to be freestanding; instead they pressed against each other in long rows. "The first image is that of a cemetery, these small mausoleums," he remarks. "This is not that different from San Diego, in that sense."

For him, the Tijuana subdivision redeemed itself through the quick customization of each home, painted different colors, with wrought iron safety gates or ornaments added, with small businesses and built additions, so that they began to diverge into something more varied and more expressive—in other words, the dwellers became informal collaborators with the architects, a step he welcomes. Such customization also happens in non-Latino American neighborhoods, he agrees; it is more because this is where his roots are that he comes back again and again to the world south of the border—that and the fact that what the United States is getting from Mexico and from Latinos is highly politicized now.

From the bus protest, we go on to wander through a mercado, a cluster of small open shops under one barnlike roof. People arrange flowers at one stand, hover over kitchenwares at another. We sidle down the narrow aisle of a taqueria, past men carrying five-gallon water jugs on their shoulders, to a bend in the labyrinth. Teddy points out the altar to the Virgin of Guadalupe built into the wall, with candles, plastic flowers, and AstroTurf, and then we turn past an old man hanging his cap on the nail in the raw wood wall rising from the countertop at which he was eating his Sunday lunch. At the entrance, we come to a fruit seller with small egg-shaped fruit Cruz has rarely seen, he tells me, since his youth in Guatemala; and he buys a few, which he will eventually hand to a beggar kid in the plaza on our way to the border, having realized that this taste of the past isn't going to be exportable.

It has become time to return to America's Finest City, and so we reverse our route, walking through Avenida de la Revolución and the flagstone plaza to cross the bridge over the many lanes of traffic so we can join the line to enter the United States, a line that is alarmingly long this Sunday afternoon. An hour later, we've moved perhaps a hundred yards, and we're sitting on a bus stuck in the massive traffic jam at the border. We had jumped on the bus hoping it would move faster than the thousand or so pedestrians winding away out of sight on the sidewalk, inhaling the bus fumes, and mostly ignoring the peddlers of lamps and churros and other trinkets. Surrounding us at the back of the bus are blue-collar shoppers, women with bright fingernails, squirming children, and, amassed around their ankles, full plastic shopping bags. A black man sits imperturbably with sunglasses on in the dim bus. These are not the people who have rediscovered the city, the people for whom downtowns are being redeveloped, nor are they suburbanites. They are the people who never left the urban zones, the service-economy workers who keep everything running and yet remain largely invisible to most architects and urbanists—which is why Cruz is preoccupied with them in his work, though on this ride he's more concerned with getting home to fulfill a promise to drive one of his daughters somewhere. And he is indignant both that so many are stuck at this border this afternoon and that the border has been built with a disregard for the needs of people with lives on both sides.

This is one of those in-between zones that preoccupy him. As he says, "The immigrants bring with them their sociocultural attitudes and sensibilities regarding the use of domestic and public space as well as the natural landscape. In these neighborhoods, multi-generational households of extended families shape their own programs of use. . . . Alleys, setbacks, driveways, and other 'wasted' infrastructures and leftover spaces are appropriated and utilized as the community sees fit." Or, as his friend and fan, the urban critic Mike Davis, has written, "Immigrant homeowners are indeed community heroes. . . . Latino immigrants are confronted with a labyrinth of laws, regulations and prejudices that frustrate, even criminalize, their attempts to build vibrant neighborhoods. Their worst enemies include conventional zoning and building codes (abetted by mortgage lending practices) that afford every loophole to developers who airdrop oversized, 'instant-slum' apartment complexes into formerly single-family neighborhoods, but prevent homeowners themselves from adding legal additions to accommodate relatives or renters."

But just across the border in San Ysidro, Cruz has found his ideal collaborators. There, in a low-income community that's 89 percent Latino immigrants, Andrea Skorepa directs Casa Familiar, an organization whose low-key approach to community service disguises its radical aims, which are Cruz's aims as well: to break through the rules that prevent the creation of an urbanism that truly serves the public good. Cruz has designed two projects for Casa that will be built in the next few years. One is titled Living Rooms at the Border. It takes a piece of land with an unused church zoned for three units and carefully arrays on it twelve affordable housing units, a community center (the converted church), offices for Casa in the church's attic, and a garden that can accommodate street markets and kiosks. "In a place where current regulation allows only one use," he crows, "we propose five different uses that support each other. This suggests a model of social sustainability for San Diego, one that conveys density not as bulk but as social choreography." For both architect and patron, it's an exciting opportunity to prove that breaking the zoning codes can be for the best. Another one of Cruz's core beliefs is that if architects are going to achieve anything of social distinction, they will have to become developers' collaborators or developers themselves, rather than hirelings brought in after a project's parameters are laid out. Casa Familiar has provided his first opportunity to work exactly as he believes architects should.

After seeing Cruz present the project, San Francisco landscape architect and city activist Jeffrey Miller commented that Cruz is designing spaces similar in some ways to the old courtyard housing projects that failed in the inner city, and that if this one works, it will be as much because the Latino residents inhabit that space differently as because the scale is far more humane.

"What sets Teddy apart," says the distinguished New York architect and critic Michael Sorkin, "is his quest to realize the social through the beautiful."

He's an exceptionally talented architect who devotes himself to projects for people for whom most "artistic" practitioners show little interest. Teddy, on the other hand, is not simply politically dedicated, but he is able to produce tremendous innovations from the very exigencies with which he deals. The work is not about foisting some arcane and incomprehensible aesthetic on unsuspecting subjects but about finding the measure of beauty in the actual circumstances of their lives and situations and in responding with authentic sensitivity to the particulars of site and need. The work is not "popular" in the sense of some phony channeling of the ineffable wisdom of the people but in the sense of offering a genuinely artistic collaboration with no compromise on either side. This is incredibly empowering. His vision is strong for being flexible, for a certain panache for hybridity that never lapses into surreality or parody, and for being squarely rooted in a still-lively set of modernist formal traditions that are globally shared. Marvelous things can happen at the intersection of modernity and conscience. . . . What's exciting about Teddy is both the fierceness of his talent and its youth, the fact that none of us know what he'll be doing in ten years' time.

Living Rooms at the Border is part of a larger scheme by Casa Familiar, spearheaded by Skorepa and architect David Flores, to create a community that works. The day after our detour through Tijuana, I went down to talk to Flores and Skorepa, who work out of offices in a low-slung, shady house and speak with passion of the long, slow process of transformation they have set into place—not the utter transformation of the whole fabric of a city section, but a few catalytic interventions into how it works and how people might perceive it. Toward this end, they've been trying to formalize the paths people use to navigate this hamlet of about forty-five thousand people, asking homeowners to set back their fences so that safe walkways with benches and lights can be built apart from automotive spaces—a radical reorganization of public and private, organizing meetings where people can talk about what they want the place they live to be like.

San Ysidro is an immigrant community. Skorepa says, "One thing that identifies our community as more Latino than Chicano—the Latinos here say hello to you, teenage kids say hello; when you're walking down the street, they greet you." People are still pedestrian, though they're increasingly reluctant to let their kids run free—but a system of jitney buses runs through the community, since nearly half the households are without cars. They are also seeking to get density ordinances waived so that people can build (or legalize the already built) second and third units on their property. "San Ysidro," Flores tells me, "was the only community in San Diego to say, 'We don't have a problem with density: our houses are full of cousins, aunts, grandparents, anyway.'" If these and their other innovations work, Skorepa, Flores, and Cruz can make a case for relaxing or revising zoning codes throughout the vast expanse of San Diego (if not for abolishing them altogether; some of the wildly precarious cinderblock houses of Tijuana serve as reminders that municipal codes serve a purpose). Skorepa and Flores share Sorkin's enthusiasm for Cruz, speaking of him as the visionary they had been waiting for.

Around the corner from Living Rooms on the Border, on a triangular parcel with two large trees, recently acquired by Casa Familiar, will go Cruz's second prototype of an alternative urbanism, Senior Gardens—Housing with Childcare. The structure addresses two often overlooked facts: that seniors frequently care for their grandchildren and need spaces that accommodate the young, and that the young and old have in common a need for secure spaces for socializing, playing, and walking—safe from cars and from crime. Twenty housing units will open onto a communal garden promenade, with frontages that can either be opened up for informal socializing or closed down for privacy. A childcare facility can be used by both seniors and children and adapted at times to other community uses. The archetypal architect is supposed to aspire to build something grandiose, a big civic or cultural institution, an airport, or, these days, an upscale flagship store; but Cruz's quixotic ambition is evident in these small housing projects for society's most vulnerable in an overlooked border barrio.

The projects grew in part out of a series of community meetings about how spaces could be designed and how they are designed. For community members who were not familiar with the language of planning, moveable three-dimensional models were set up so they could see how many ways a given space could be used to open up or close down access, accommodate many or few. Cruz and Skorepa were delighted when one old woman from Guadalajara, Mexico, exclaimed in surprise about a classic suburban structure, "This house is selfish!" Their designs look toward how spaces can be less selfish and more sociable. These two projects will house perhaps a hundred to a hundred and twenty people, but architect and developer see them as prototypes to argue for another urbanism, one that opens up how we live. It's a beginning.

3

TROUBLE BELOW

Mining, Water, and Nuclear Waste

The Price of Gold, the Value of Water

〚2000〛

When you tour the museums of the California Gold Rush, you see picturesque sepia-toned photographs of the men who made a killing in the mines. But if you want to know who picked up the bill, look in a mirror. The profits were quickly spent, but the costs are still rolling in, both as an inventory of what we lost and an assessment of what still needs cleaning up.

By 1857, California gold miners had extracted 24.3 million ounces of the metal, but they left behind more than ten times as much mercury, along with devastated forests, slopes, and streams. Today, there's a new gold rush underway on the other side of the Sierra Nevada, and it too is racking up huge bills for the public, bills that will be coming due for centuries to come, bills that we will pay in taxes for restoration, and bills that can never be paid, for pure water, cultural survival, wildlife, and wilderness. All the gold that multinational mining corporations are taking out of the country won't buy back an extinct trout species or a pristine aquifer. When you tour the museums of the Gold Country, as the Sierra Nevada foothills are still called, you see children dressing up in historical costumes and playing at panning for gold—but it might be more educational for them to play at testing for clean water, imitating mercury-poisoning madness, reading a corporate prospectus, or conducting a wildlife survey. More educational, but less fun—and there's nothing romantic about the current gold rush in Nevada (unless you like multinationals and heavy machinery), which might be why we hear so little about it.

In most parts of the American West, frontier families came to turn places—

often someone else's places—into homes. But miners came to grab and get out, and they laid waste to their surroundings with gleeful abandon (for example, in *Roughing It*, Mark Twain's book about his mining years, he recalls how he accidentally started a colossal forest fire at Lake Tahoe, watched it burn as entertainment, and then picked up and moved on without a backward glance). Tens of thousands of miners stormed the Sierra Nevada foothills with picks, shovels, and rifles, an army of mostly young men making war on the earth itself for its hidden gold. For the Native inhabitants of the Mother Lode region, whose sustenance depended on an intact ecology, the Gold Rush was Armageddon. At Coloma State Historical Park, on the site where, in January 1848, James Marshall found the few flakes that started the rush, a museum wall text says, "For most Nisenan [the local tribe], the Gold Rush meant death from disease or violence. For the survivors, it spelled the quick destruction of their culture and habitat." Marshall himself, a nearby text states, "was temporarily driven from Coloma because he tried to prevent a massacre of local Indians." In the twenty years after the Gold Rush began, the indigenous population of California declined by four-fifths.

In 1853, an Indian agent in El Dorado County reported:

They formerly subsisted on game, fish, acorns, etc. but it is now impossible for them to make a living by hunting or fishing, for nearly all the game has been driven from the mining region or has been killed by the thousands of our people who now occupy the once quiet home of these children of the forest. The rivers or tributaries of the Sacramento formerly were clear as crystal and abounded with the finest salmon and other fish. . . . But the miners have turned the streams from their beds and conveyed the water to the dry diggings and after being used until it is so thick with mud that it will scarcely run it returns to its natural channel and with it the soil from a thousand hills, which has driven [out] almost every kind of fish.

Salmon historian Michael Black reports that the mighty Sacramento River had its last healthy spring salmon run in 1852, and fish runs died out altogether in some rivers during the Gold Rush. Even the mostly boosterish Gold Country museums acknowledge that the Gold Rush was an atrocity for the local environment and those whose lives were intertwined with it.

At the museum of the Mariposa Historical Society near Yosemite, hand-lettered texts record that a miner panning in a stream could work about a cubic yard of earth a day. Greed and a constantly diminishing ratio of gold to ore prompted new technologies that allowed more and more earth to be worked over with less labor and thus made lower-grade deposits worth working. As the technologies became more elaborate, the capital costs increased, and the era of the miner as rugged individualist rapidly gave way to the era of corporate operations and distant investors. If mining was a war on the earth, the heavy artillery arrived when hydraulic mining was invented in the early 1850s. Its high-pressure water cannons allowed mining operations to wash away gravel, earth, hillsides, whole landscapes at a hitherto unimaginable rate. To bring the water and generate the pressure, vast quantities of water were diverted from river and stream beds into flumes and pipes and stored in wooden dams—and the construction of both flumes and dams called for more and more timber. By 1855, a total of 4,493 miles of canals ran through the Gold Country.

A wilderness had been turned into an outdoor factory; rivers into washing machines, conveyor belts, and drains; hills into holes; forests into plumbing supplies. The only part of the landscape these miners valued was being sent out as bars of bullion, and what they didn't value they were turning into sludge and desolation. Hydraulic mining, reports John McPhee, sent 13 billion tons of the Sierra Nevada downstream. Of this, 1.146 billion tons washed into the San Francisco Bay, diminishing its wetlands and raising its floor. The rivers en route rose far more dramatically. The Sacramento rose an average of 7 feet. The town of Marysville, which once sat securely above the Yuba and Feather rivers, began to build levees that rose higher than the housetops, as the rivers rose higher than the streets, but in 1875 a torrent of toxic mud buried the town. The Yuba was at one point 110 feet above its original bed and is still 65 feet higher than it was in 1849. Mine tailings were burying the rich farmland of the Sacramento Valley—about

270,000 acres were severely damaged, 40,000 destroyed—and it was farmers who fought back.

In a momentous decision, hydraulic mining was outlawed by Judge Alonzo Sawyer on January 7, 1884, in response to the farmers' lawsuit. It was the first time American courts had ruled that the general welfare outweighed individual profiteering, the first environmental victory in American legal history.

The men who profited are all long dead, but we're still paying for their Gold Rush. No one took much account of the mercury used in gold mining, but about 7,600 tons of it—243.2 million ounces, if you describe it in the same language used for gold—entered California's lakes, streams, rivers, and the San Francisco Bay just from the mining in the central Mother Lode, and it's still there. Sean Garvey, executive director of the South Yuba River Citizens League, told me that gold mining "is the single most destructive event that's happened in the Sierra Nevada ever. There's no other environmental degradation that even comes close: not logging, not road building, not extirpation of species. Almost all the environmental issues we deal with are in some way related to the impact of hydraulic mining 140 years ago, whether it be flooding, a clean water supply, Superfund sites, airborne toxins." He told me of the enormous problems with mercury and arsenic, of the thousands of hydraulic mining sites that "used to be forest land here that no longer grow any type of vegetation" and increase flooding because they can't hold the water of storms and snowmelt, of the dilemma of dams that keep mercury from moving downstream but turn it from inert to methylated mercury, which readily enters the food chain. The Gold Rush is still poisoning the Golden State.

Until recently, gold was the measure of value for all other things, perhaps because it is exceedingly stable and relatively scarce. Gold was money, and money in its material form was gold, the fulcrum between the concrete world of things and the abstraction that is the exchange value of things. Gold was an anchor for national economies, the basis for their currency. Until 1933, higher-denomination U.S. coins were still made of gold (while paper money was originally just a receipt for governmental gold and silver, a receipt that could be exchanged for the metal on demand). In the early 1970s, the United States went off the gold standard, the system that based monetary value on gold reserves, and now none of the world's major economies are tied to the gold still sitting in vaults. The *Economist* calls these national stockpiles the "spent fuel of an obsolete monetary system." Older financiers still think of gold as money, but younger ones recognize that it is no longer a good investment.

The scramble by nations such as Australia and Britain to sell off much of their gold reserves has contributed to the rapid decline in gold prices in recent years. This decline has the benefit of curtailing some mining operations and the detriment of bankrupting some companies before they've cleaned up their mess. Unlike most other extractive-industry products such as oil, gold has little practical use: of the 4,000 tons used worldwide each year, about 85 percent goes into jewelry. About four-fifths of all the gold ever mined is still around, in bank vaults, home stashes, and jewelry stores (by volume, this is not much; all the gold ever mined, an estimated 125,000 tons, would form a sixty-foot cube; 90 percent of that gold has been mined since 1848). How do you weigh gold against a whole landscape? The quantities of gold extracted from the Sierra during the Gold Rush are diminutive compared to the splendor of a four-hundred-mile expanse of pristine mountain range containing grizzlies, elk, antelope, spring-run salmon—all gone from that part of the world now—and downslope, clear fast-flowing rivers, a big clean bay full of wetlands, aquatic life, edible fish. Even if you could put a price on this, you couldn't put one on the dozens of small Indian nations who had woven the places and creatures into marvelous stories, names, and local knowledge, the richest legacy of people who didn't much prize material culture, who had no use for gold, and who were devastated and sometimes annihilated by the Gold Rush. It is all this that was being traded in for gold then and, on the other side of the Sierra Nevada, is still being traded in now. There is no more classic tale of the benefit of the few at the expense of the many.

The California Gold Rush wasn't an anomaly; it was the beginning of modern large-scale gold mining, which is still going on. In America's new gold boom in Nevada, the dimensions are staggering. As the California Gold Rush tapered off, miners began to move across the Sierra into Nevada. Only Virginia City's Comstock Lode is remembered now, but there were gold and silver mines across the state, with the usual effects. The indigenous inhabitants were displaced and slaughtered, and the native food sources—fish, game, and piñon pines—were devastated. To feed the smelters of Eureka in central Nevada, all the piñon and juniper for fifty miles were cut down by 1878. Nowadays, Nevada produces nearly 10 percent of the world's gold and three-quarters of the nation's. This new gold rush began slowly when geologists located the Carlin Trend—a fifty-by-five-mile belt across northeastern Nevada's Humboldt Basin bearing "invisible gold," gold in particles too small to be seen. The first big new open-pit mines came in 1965, but it was the rise of gold prices in the 1980s (after decades of price regulation) and the invention of cyanide heap-leaching that made mining such low-grade ore profitable. Higher-grade ore is still refined in roasters and mills, but the low-grade stuff is leached outdoors. In this method, pulverized ore is heaped up in huge sloping mounds atop a plastic liner, and cyanide solution is poured through it. The solution carries much of the gold with it as it runs off, and the gold is extracted from the poisonous solution.

Gold is now mined on a scale none of those men in the sepia-tone photographs could have imagined, from ore far more low-grade than they could have considered worthwhile. The Mary Harrison mine, which opened in 1853 in Coulterville, near Yosemite, yielded about one-third to one-half an ounce of gold per ton. In 1997, the Toronto-based Barrick Corporation's Betze/Post mine, in the center of the Carlin Trend, mined 159 million tons of rock and earth to produce 1.6 million ounces of gold—about a hundredth of an ounce per ton. Its pit is now 1,600 feet deep, a mile wide, and a mile and a half long. Nevada anti-mining activist Chris Sewell points out the irony that "invisible gold" leads to mines that can be seen from space, with 350-foot-high leach heaps covering as much as three hundred acres along with the colossal pits.

The modern history of gold mining is about these technologies that have made it profitable to go after lower and lower grades of ore. From hydraulic mining then to cyanide heap-leach mining now, more and more land and water are disrupted and polluted for every ounce of gold. Today's mining is intensely toxic: cyanide is so deadly that a teaspoon of 2 percent solution will kill a human being, and some cyanide remains inside the mine tailings. In earlier years, the cyanide-laced water was left to break down in open ponds, where waterfowl would sometimes land and die; nowadays, mines are obligated to net over such poison ponds. Because much of the ore contains other heavy metals, excavating it, breaking it up and watering it, or making it accessible to rain and other natural water sources make it a potent contaminant. Often ore contains sulfur, an element that forms sulfuric acid when exposed to air and water. Sulfuric acid thus formed is called acid mine drainage: it draws the heavy metals—including arsenic, antimony, lead, mercury—out with it into the environment. At the Yerington pit, for example, a toxic plume is moving toward the Yerington Paiute Reservation well field, but the corporation that created the impending catastrophe has gone bankrupt. The Paiutes are working on getting Superfund designation for the site. One way to describe modern gold mines is to say that they are displacing earth and water on a gargantuan scale and producing and dispersing toxins in smaller quantities, with gold a proportionally minute by-product of this disruption.

Water is being sacrificed for gold in Nevada's gold rush, as it was in California's—but in Nevada water is being both contaminated and used up. Though Nevada is the driest state in the union, the slender Humboldt River meanders nearly four hundred miles west from its beginnings in the northeast corner of the state. Springs and mountain streams feed the river, and the region is blessed with huge aquifers not far below the surface of the earth—but eighteen of the large mines in the Humboldt region are working below this water table. To do so, they "dewater" the mine site, by pumping out the underground water at stunning rates—the Betze/Post mine alone has pumped more than half a million acre-feet, and the Lone Tree mine northeast of Winnemucca pumps an amount equal to about 14 percent of the Humboldt's annual flow. Groundwater, remarks water historian Mark Reisner, "is as nonrenewable as oil." A deficit of 5 million acre-feet is being created in the Humboldt Basin, 1.6 trillion gallons, the equivalent of twenty-five years of the river's annual flow. Some of this water is pumped into the Humboldt River, where it's generating higher streamflow and wetter wetlands before it leaves the region for good. Some of it is being used to irrigate alfalfa fields. Some is used to process the ore, which contaminates it with cyanide, acids, and heavy metals. Some of it is "recharged"—put back into the ground—but it will not necessarily be the same pure water that was pumped out, nor will it necessarily go back where it came from.

Nevada hydrologist and Great Basin Mine Watch director Tom Myers estimates that the water table around each mine is being drawn down more than a thousand feet, with localized "cones of depression"—deep subterranean dry areas. When the mines stop pumping out the water, some water will be drawn back to these dry areas to fill up the mine pits to the water table, creating a whole string of deep dead lakes, including the two largest artificial lakes wholly in Nevada. Local springs, streams, and parts of the Humboldt River may dry up. The water table will be radically rearranged. Nobody knows exactly what will happen: Myers's models allow for various scenarios, none of them pretty. I asked Myers why most of the anti-mining activists are working in places like Washington and Montana, when most of the gold mining is in Nevada. "Nobody moves to northern Nevada for the scenery," he said. "You and I know how beautiful it is, but the public doesn't."

Few writers and artists have celebrated the Great Basin the way they have extolled sandstone canyons and mesas, and maybe that's why so much of it is still unpopulated and unprotected. It is a gorgeous, austere stretch of country, with great seas of fragrant sagebrush and grass sweeping up to juniper and piñon at higher elevations. The mountains in this basin-and-range country conceal marvelous clefts and canyons where streams make small oases of wild rose, cottonwood, aspen, and willow; where butterflies, songbirds, and the endangered—but unlisted—sage grouse can be found. Another endangered subspecies, the Lahontan cutthroat trout, lives in the Humboldt River (and in two other rivers, though in the Carson and Truckee rivers it has interbred with introduced trout species). Pronghorn still range in the more remote places—but mining is doing in those more remote places, too.

More than 350,000 acres of roadless Forest Service land vanished in Nevada between 1985 and 1997, largely because of mining and prospecting roads; and the figures for vanishing land controlled by the Bureau of Land Management are probably greater, but no one has calculated them. Mining is devouring Nevada, and the state is getting very little in return: twelve thousand jobs and a 1 percent tax on the gross (about 25 percent of the gross is profit). Most of the profits go out of state, or out of the country. Of course, the question of whose land it really is has yet to be settled.

One oft-neglected fact about the California Gold Rush is that it took place on land that still legally belonged to its resident tribes. One of the issues in Nevada's gold rush region is that the Western Shoshone, whose homeland it is, have never ceded their land to the U.S. government or accepted the payment for it that the United States tried to force on them anyway (and the payment of $40 or so million is pure peanuts compared to the quantities of gold being taken from the region every year, as were the diminutive payments California Indians received for their land long after the Gold Rush). In southern Crescent Valley, Nevada, a huge new mine has opened up, Cortez Gold's Pipeline Deposit mine. For thousands of years in this area, there had been nothing but sagebrush grassland and open space, through which any creature might move freely; and even a few years back, when I worked as a land rights activist with the Western Shoshone, it was open space threatened by nothing worse than a few cows. Now its expanse is dominated by steep slopes of waste rock piles and fenced-off cyanide leach heaps, thousands of feet long and hundreds high, mounds that mean an equally large hole exists nearby. Black pipes lead into the distance, where a grid of rectangular recharge ponds gleams—the mine pumps about 13,000 gallons per minute to get under the water table.

The recharge isn't working the way it's supposed to. The water that does sink back into the ground will have changed in quality as it filters through soil on its way, and much of it is spreading into the valley instead, making it unnaturally green—and turning the family cemetery of the Danns, an extended family of Western Shoshones who have been living in the valley for generations, into spongy marsh. Traditional Western Shoshones have been fighting to get their land back throughout most of the twentieth century. But mining means that not merely the ownership but the very survival of the land is now at stake. In earlier times, whatever the land's legal status, it was still there, full of life; but it is now being bled dry, dug up, and depleted of its wildlife.

I asked Carrie Dann, a traditional Shoshone elder, about the mining in Crescent Valley, and she said, with an outrage unblunted by five years of living with the Pipeline mine and thirty years of living with the smaller Cortez mine nearer her home:

> Mining is against our culture, is against our spiritual ways. They're pumping all the life out of the earth. It's not humane, it's not right. It'll be being paid for by children who's not even here yet. To me, to pump water like that for the sake of gold . . . why not keep the water clean so people can drink? The gold mining that destroyed California with the mercury was on the surface, but what's happening now is underground. How do you control that? How do you deal with underground contamination? Are they going to tell me that they're going to control underground water contamination when we can't clean above-ground contamination?
>
> To me water is a gift of life.

If gold has been prized because it is the most inert element, changeless and incorruptible, water is prized for the opposite reason—its fluidity, mobility, changeability that make it a necessity and a metaphor for life itself. To value gold over water is to value economy over ecology, that which can be locked up over that which connects all things. The oldest story I know about gold is really about gold and water, and I thought of it when Chris Sewell, who heads the Western Shoshone Defense Project, took me to look at the recharge ponds and the acid mine drainage of the shut-down Buckhorn mine, just over the mountains behind the Danns' home. A few newly bulldozed embankments were all that kept the acid out of beautiful Willow Creek, which runs between the two sides of the mine. A scientist had told Chris that when the acid was still running down the mining road into the stream, the road was full of dead earthworms, and the stream was dying.

King Midas, says Ovid, was "delighted with the misfortune which had befallen him," until even the water he tried to drink turned to gold as it touched his lips. Parched with thirst and surrounded by gold, he begged the god Bacchus to take back his gift. Bacchus sent him to a sacred spring to "wash away his crime" and recover his ability to drink, to touch, to live. Afterward, Midas hated riches and dwelt in the forest. Midas is also the name of a tiny town just up the road from the huge Twin Creeks mine—the mine that, when it proposed putting a huge tailings pile over the site of the 1911 Shoshone Mike massacre, assured Western Shoshones that those tailings would "protect the site in perpetuity." Twin Creeks was pressured into putting its waste elsewhere, but many other archaeological and sacred sites have been erased or desecrated by mining.

I went on a tour of Barrick's Betze/Post mine—the largest gold mine in North America, third largest in the world—and was amazed how much the pit had grown since 1992, when I had seen it last. I was equally amazed that Barrick's young tour guide told me and the leathery, upbeat Texas retirees who made up the tour group that "the first inhabitants of the Elko area were fur trappers in 1828." Another tour guide showed us one of those steep embankments in which large-scale gold mining specializes and told us that the faint flush of green there meant that the landscape had been restored to its natural condition. Before the mine, biologists had noted an active lek, or sage grouse dancing ground, on the site. More than a hundred of the imperiled birds would gather there then; now the sage grouse are gone. One day the creek disappeared too: Maggie Creek, which runs past the mines of Barrick and Newmont corporations, vanished into a sinkhole mining had created; it had to be revived with sandbags that kept it out of the new rupture in the water table.

Back in the Mother Lode country on the other side of the Sierra Nevada, I joined activists from around the world at Project Underground's 1999 conference on the impacts of gold mining around the world; and their reports put California and Nevada into context, with stories of both horror and hope. The conference was held near the Malakoff Diggings. The largest of California's hydraulic mining sites, Malakoff's hollowed-out hillside still looks like a fresh wound of bare red earth more than a century later. It was owned by the North Bloomfield Gravel Mining Company, the defendant in the lawsuit brought by farmers that ended hydraulic mining in 1884.

At the conference, there were new stories of triumphs over gold mining's environmental devastation. The Okanagan Highlands Alliance, based in eastern Washington, had just benefited from a decision almost as radical as the ban on hydraulic mining: for the first time, the government had reinterpreted the infamous, anachronistic 1872 Mining Act in the environment's favor. Basically, the law provides for a five-acre mill site per mining claim. Modern mining takes up far more room—so Battle Mountain Gold Corporation's permits for Buckhorn Mountain were denied on the grounds that the mill site exceeded the permitted size. If the decision holds up, a lot of new gold mines could be denied permits. The Okanagan Highlands Alliance started bottling Buckhorn water and labeling it with their slogan—"Pure Water Is More Precious Than Gold"—as a publicity tool, and they pointed out this was literally true: it would take Battle Mountain Gold two thousand gallons of water to produce an ounce of gold, which was then worth about $270, whereas the water itself was worth $1,500 bottled. The nearby Colville Indian Reservation, whose anti-mining activists had been involved in fighting Battle Mountain, had already banned hard rock mining on their lands. Battle Mountain Gold is itself named after the north-central Nevada town whose name commemorates a miner-Shoshone confrontation; the corporation is still at work in Nevada despite its defeat in Washington State.

Not all the stories were uplifting. The world's first cyanide heap-leach mine, Pegasus Gold Corporation's Zortman-Landusky mine in eastern Montana, opened in 1979, was fined $37 million for violating the Clean Water Act with acid mine drainage and cyanide contamination in 1996. The company moved to expand the mine to 1,192 acres anyway, was fined again in 1997 for stream contamination, and went bankrupt in 1998. That left the state to pick up the tab for a cleanup that will cost tens of millions and still won't create pure water or restore Spirit Mountain, which is now just a pile of poisonous powder. Aimee Boulanger from the Mineral Policy Center told me that cyanide was coming out of the taps of the residents of the Fort Belknap Reservation, next to the mine; and Rose Main, a

White Clay Assinboine from that reservation, told me about dry wells and contaminated creeks, concluding, "Our worst nightmares have come true. And now
we're living in them." The mined land had originally been part of the reservation,
but when gold was discovered there in the 1890s, the boundaries were redrawn
and the first wave of miners came in. Thanks to this disaster and many like it in
Montana, Montanans recently voted to implement legislation that bans cyanide
heap-leach mining.

Perhaps people in Montana value scenery and ecology more than corporate
profits and temporary jobs, but Nevada is still in thrall to the mining industry
("mining works for Nevada" says the industry bumper sticker a Reno activist friend
of mine rearranged to read, "Nevada works for mining"). Gold miners have almost
always been mobile, rootless people; the mines punish most those who are rooted
and committed, unable or unwilling to move on once the damage has been done. So
from British Columbia to Venezuela, from the Philippines to Indonesia, gold is being
extracted from the earth for the international market—and locals, along with the
birds, the fish, and the water, are being left to deal with the consequences.

Carrie Dann once said that everyone who buys gold jewelry should get to deal
with the consequences, too—such as the tailings it took to produce that much
gold. Ever since, I've pictured a truck driver ringing the doorbell of a home to say
something like, "Ma'am, about that new wristwatch: would you like your sev-
enty-nine tons on the front lawn or the back? You'll want to keep the kids and the
dog off them 'cause of the acid and arsenic." Gold mining is like all the other environmental dilemmas, distilled into an essence. It's about prizing what can be pock-
eted and possessed versus cherishing those phenomena whose value is inseparable
from their location and their role in larger systems. It's about systems that measure and exalt immediate profit for the few versus those that benefit the many over
the millennia. It's about two kinds of tangibility: the figures in a stock report or a
dividend versus the water that seeps up from springs, flows over rocks and down
slopes to nourish—everything. Gold used to be the more tangible of the two
goods, but gold going out of the country or being locked up in vaults now seems
less tangible than even the remotest stream in which trout swim, sage grouse
splash, pronghorn drink.

Meanwhile Back at the Ranch

〔2004〕

In July 2004, the Feds handed down to Nevada the state's bitterest defeat and sweetest victory in ages: the former, a termination of thousands of years of Western Shoshone history; the latter, a reprieve from an apocalyptic future as the world's biggest—and maybe dumbest—nuclear waste dump. In one three-day period, Nevada's past was canceled while its future was salvaged. But this Indian war and these nuclear politics are just part of a panoply of glaringly weird things going on in the state; there's a gold rush, a water war, and vast military operations, just for starters, and all of them are ecological bad news.

Nevada's invisibility may be as alarming as the apocalyptic dimensions of its plight. The state is a truly peculiar place, a hole in public consciousness. Where else could you set off a thousand nuclear bombs unhindered—from 1951 to 1991, at the Nevada Test Site—while even most antinuclear activists were arguing about nuclear war as a terrible possibility rather than as an ongoing regional catastrophe? Once nuclear testing went underground in 1963, and American babies stopped having fallout-induced radioactive milk teeth, Nevada fell off the map, even as the nuke-a-month program continued unimpeded for almost three more decades.

WESTERN SHOSHONE SHOWDOWN

Across the United States, the contemporary Indian wars are invisible in part because most non–Native Americans believe that all such wars happened in the picturesque past, in part because they're fought by other means, in part because the mainstream media don't give a damn. One of the most egregious wars has been the ongoing battle between the Western Shoshone and the federal government for title to most of Nevada. It began in 1848, when the U.S. government claimed the Southwest from Mexico; heated up in the post–World War II era, when the Shoshone went to court to protect their rights; and may have ended July 7, 2004, when President George W. Bush signed into law the Western Shoshone Distribution Bill.

That bill dishes out money the government set aside a few decades ago as payment for much of eastern and southern Nevada. The area had looked so worthless to the bureaucrats of the nineteenth century that they drew up a treaty letting the Western Shoshone, unlike most indigenous nations, retain title to their lands. The bureaucrats of the twentieth century, desperate to reverse this misstep, realized that the best way to seize title to Nevada was to pretend that the government had already taken the land at some point in the past—back when it was more affordable. Of course, you have to overlook the fact that, as Western Shoshone bumper stickers say of their homeland, "Newe Sogobia is not for sale." The price set was $26 million, or 15 cents an acre, a discount price even for the 1870s. (With interest, the sum to be disbursed is now $145 million.)

Reasonably enough, the Western Shoshone point out that they never offered their land for sale, and many of them refuse to take the money. The disbursement was made against their strenuous opposition. (Others believe that $30,000 per person is the best they'll ever get and are willing to settle up.) The case matters in part because Western Shoshone "traditionalists" have strenuously opposed mining, military operations—20 percent of all military-controlled land in the United States is in Nevada—and nuclear activities on their land. Though environmentalists sometimes decry their cattle-grazing as destructive to the desert, the Shoshone look like far better stewards of Nevada's arid lands than the federal government ever has been. They have deep roots in the past and are interested in the long-term future of the place. Then there's the simple matter of justice: the Western Shoshone are being stripped of their birthright and their rights just as surely as any Palestinian on the wrong side of Israel's Great Wall of Intolerance or the Iraqis whose resources have been redistributed to various American corporations.

The corporations reaping twenty-first-century profits from the great Shoshone land grab, and already engaged in a gold rush in the heartland of Shoshone territory, aren't even American in most cases. The 1872 Mining Act allows virtually anyone to acquire public land for pennies in order to mine it; the Toronto-based Barrick Corporation, for instance, paid less than $10,000 for land containing an estimated $8 billion in gold. Unfortunately, we're not talking about the gold nuggets often seen in pretty engravings of the Forty-Niners. Barrick and the other megacorporations are mining microscopic gold, dispersed throughout the subterranean rock along the Carlin Trend in northeastern Nevada, enough gold to make the state the world's third most productive gold mining region.

To get microscopic gold, you dig up huge hunks of the landscape, pulverize them, and then run a cyanide solution through the resultant heaps, which pulls the gold out. It takes about a hundred tons of ore to produce an ounce of gold. Grinding up the bedrock releases other heavy metals in the ground, which is why Nevada—with less than 1 percent of the nation's population—was, until a court changed the measurement standards in 2001, tops in the release of toxic substances. Its annual half billion tons of toxics amount to 10 percent of the nation's total, and a soaring 88.7 percent of U.S. mercury releases, to say nothing of the cyanide, which at least is an organic compound that breaks down under the right circumstances. Mercury is forever.

WATER WARS

The environmental price of gold is pretty high, and that's not even counting groundwater. But groundwater counts too. Much of the Carlin Trend gold is underneath the water table, so the mines, here in this arid state, pump out vast quantities of groundwater and discard it. They are, in other words, mining water as well as gold; and as demonstrated by recent attempts around the world to privatize water—by Bechtel in Bolivia, for example—pure water is getting more and more valuable. The elderly Western Shoshone activist and mystic Corbin Harney had a vision about water scarcity long ago and has made it a focus of his work ever since. In Nevada's gold rush districts, water is being contaminated or dispersed into nearby waterways, where it will run away, never to return. According to Great Basin Mine Watch, Nevada mines wasted enough water in 2001 to serve a city of half a million people.

It takes thousands of years to recharge an aquifer. To drain one, or even drop the water table, creates "drawdown," the drying up of surface waters that would otherwise feed agriculture, rural communities, and wildlife. That's one of the reasons why environmentalists and rural citizens are up in arms about the latest plans to suck out the water under White Pine, Lincoln, and Nye counties, as well as that under rural Clark County for the benefit of urban Clark County (aka Las Vegas). This conflict is already being compared to the water war between Los Angeles and the Owens Valley, immortalized in Roman Polanski's movie *Chinatown*. What Polanski's movie didn't show was the dry lake bed breeding dust storms and the habitat drying up, as part of the ecological disaster that Los Angeles lawns and car washes demanded (and which Mono Lake activists have partially reversed in recent years).

Currently, Las Vegas gets most of its water from the Colorado River. In 1900, the city's population was in the single digits; it had made it only to about half a million when I started swinging through in the 1980s to protest the nuclear testing taking place sixty miles to the north. The city now has 1.4 million people, almost two-thirds of the state's population, and five thousand new Vegans arrive every month—which is why the entire Nevada congressional delegation is behind the water grab. That's where the votes are.

Even the usually environmentally respectable Senator Harry Reid so strongly supports a bill to start building the two-hundred-mile Lincoln-to-Vegas pipeline that he's threatening to attach it to some larger piece of legislation that is bound to pass. "They have enough water for the existing population," says Jan Gilbert, a longtime state activist. "They don't for this explosive growth."

Pat Mulroy, general manager of the Southern Nevada Water Authority, struck a different note when she said, "The notion that we have a finite supply of water, and when that finite supply is gone you stop growing, is in the past." Welcome to Nevada, driest state in the union, where water is infinite; where you

can wait until the late twentieth century to make things happen in the nineteenth century; where gold is cheap; and where the future is radioactively bright.
Or was. Not all the news is bad.

REPEALING THE APOCALYPSE

Once again, it was the water that was the problem, only this time it wasn't a
shortage. Yucca Mountain, it turned out, was all wet, and a truly lunatic place to
put seventy-seven thousand tons of high-level nuclear waste.

The government created the nuclear power industry with a promise to reactor
operators that the essential crisis of the industry—the dangerous, exceedingly
long-lived waste it produces—would be taken off their hands. In all the subsequent decades of nuclear power production, spent fuel rods have been piling up in
"cooling ponds" onsite, while the operators waited for the government to make
good on its promise to get rid of the stuff (mostly located in the population-heavy,
resource-light East). Three New England reactors are already suing the government for failing to come up with a dump.

For more than two decades, the Department of Energy (DOE) has done everything it can to create one of the most scientifically dubious dump sites imaginable,
at Yucca Mountain, about ninety miles north of Vegas, on the northern edges of
the Nevada Test Site, where all those nuclear bombs were detonated (and will be
again if Bush has his way).

The initial plan was to compare sites in three western states and choose the
safest one, but two of the states—Texas and Washington—had the political clout
to get out of the competition. So the "comparative study" never studied any place
but Yucca Mountain, and yet the longer it was studied, the less suitable it
seemed, even for the mandated ten thousand years it was supposed to keep us and
the waste apart (forget the quarter million years the stuff would actually remain
dangerous). Somehow, this never seemed to stop plans from proceeding. For a lot
of geologists, the fact that Yucca Mountain had, in geological terms, recent vol-

canic activity and has very contemporary seismic activity might have been grounds enough for doubt. But the DOE officials just kept lowering the standards, fudging the data, firing the dissenters, while spending nearly $100 billion to try to make it happen—the cost of a nice, short foreign war these days.

Nevada itself has fine activists who have stood up to some of the atrocities, and the state itself has vociferously fought the federal plan to make it into what might have been the world's largest nuclear waste dump. And for now, this time, on this issue, they won, which is no mean feat. Early on, the Yucca Mountain plan was nicknamed the "Screw Nevada" bill, and the feckless plans to send the stuff across the country from the mostly eastern nuclear reactors is popularly known as "Mobile Chernobyl."

Easterners imagine that the Wile E. Coyote landscape of Nevada means true inert dryness; the *New York Times* has seldom been able to resist deploying the adjectives *sterile, empty, barren,* and *useless* in any description of the place. But underneath it is a surprisingly high water table that could rise further in a changed climate, and flowing through the mountain's billion fissures is rainfall that leaches out the chemicals in the rock, making a brew capable of eating through almost any metal, including pretty much every metal proposed for nuclear waste containment.

Originally, the rock itself was supposed to isolate the stuff. When it turned out that wet Yucca Mountain was uniquely unsuited for the task, the idea was that the metal containers would isolate the waste. When it turned out that the leaching would eat the containers away, the plan switched to little titanium umbrellas on top of each cask—so we'd gone from protection by the thick mantle of the earth to parasols in a couple of decades of study. And they call it science.

The state's Nuclear Projects Office (which means anti-dump) geologist, Steve Frischman, told me long ago that they had picked ten thousand years as the period during which the waste must be isolated because you can at least pretend to estimate geological and climate changes over ten millennia; beyond that, it's the utter unknown—Nevada could be a rainforest; its ancient lake beds could refill; and God knows who's going to look after the stuff then. The Western Shoshone?

Among the more surreal aspects of the whole Yucca Project have been the many schemes to create warning labels for the waste that would make sense to unknown civilizations of the deep future.

But surprisingly, on July 9, 2004, two days after Bush signed the Western Shoshone Distribution Bill, a federal appeals court ruled that the standards for Yucca Mountain were wrong, that the Environmental Protection Agency should have accepted a ruling by the National Academy of Sciences setting the safety standard not at ten thousand years but at the point of peak radiation—which could be three hundred thousand years away, long after the metal containment casks have corroded into irrelevancy. As Joe Egan, an attorney for the state of Nevada, told the *Las Vegas Sun*, this means that "the department will have to apply a standard that all their own evidence says they can't meet."

This ruling, which could mean the death of the Yucca Mountain nuclear waste dump, is startlingly good news for Nevada. Scientists have always said that Yucca Mountain was a disaster in the making, even leaving aside those 50 million Americans who live within half a mile of the shipment routes on which the Yucca-bound nuclear waste would travel for decades to come, or the estimated ninety to five hundred accidents of unknown scale that statistics suggest would take place en route over the years. (Who needs terrorist dirty bombs when our own tax dollars can supply them?)

When you consider the human rights abuses, the squandering of resources for the benefit of the few, and the lunatic decisions being made for the long-term future of the state, the war in Iraq looks a little like a decoy from troubles at home, or a parallel universe with all the same ingredients. Except that there's almost no opposition to Nevada's impending catastrophes—outside Nevada. But you can bring back other perspectives from Iraq too. One is that Goliath doesn't always win: the David of local activists and the Nevada state government has been fighting Yucca for decades, and Goliath lost this round. Another is that if you're tenacious enough, what looks like defeat can change—and the Western Shoshone have patience and commitment on their side.

Poison Pictures

[2003]

Manufactured Landscapes: The Photographs of Edward Burtynsky, by Lori Pauli, with essays by Mark Haworth-Booth and Kenneth Baker and an interview by Michael Torosian (New Haven: National Gallery of Canada in association with Yale University Press, 2003), 160 pp., 64 full-page images.

Edward Burtynsky's photographs are large, and colorful, and mostly ravishing, despite their subjects. They show seldom-seen industrial landscapes, the places from which resources come to us and to which they go when we're done with them: mines, oil fields, refineries, quarries, dumps. These places look inhuman, for their scale and for their poisons and hazards, but they're the landscapes on which most human beings now depend. It may be that industrial civilization is predicated on blindness and alienation, on not knowing that sweatshops or copper mines make your pleasant first world urban/suburban existence possible, for that knowledge would at the least make that existence less pleasant. Certainly most people nowadays would be hard-pressed to say where their water comes from or their garbage goes to, let alone their tungsten or their oil tankers. Burtynsky photographs those places with an eye to their aesthetic power.

"Although he understands that modern technologies can have devastating effects on the earth and its ecosystems, he believes that it would be hypocritical of him to use his photographs as a diatribe against industry," writes Lori Pauli in one of the essays in *Manufactured Landscapes: The Photographs of Edward Burtynsky*. But such a statement seems predicated on an old model, in which to be politically engaged you had to foreground your own outrage, engagement, virtue (and certainly ostentatious display of appropriate emotion is part of many performances on all sides of the political spectrum). Facts themselves are political, since just to circulate the suppressed and obscured ones is a radical act. That, for example, an EPA official resigned because under Bush he wasn't allowed to enforce air quality regulations that would save far more lives than were lost on September 11, and that depleted-uranium armaments pose a threat to the health of U.S. troops as well as Iraqis are stories that subvert the status quo and thus don't get heard much. Environmental facts can be loaded, and Burtynsky's certainly are: foremost among them that the industrial civilization we have created, from its marble façades to the contents of its gas tanks, depends for its existence on this inhuman scale of desolation and poison that remains out of sight. That he chooses to pay attention to these places is already an engagement, and the questions a photographer raises may be more profound than the answers the medium permits.

An earlier generation of environmentalist landscape photographers concentrated on ideal landscapes that in the end came to seem irrelevant, places that were fine because they had nothing to do with us, though these images were, and to a lesser extent still are, useful for conservation politics. In the past quarter century, most photographers have concentrated on some version of the social landscape, on inhabited wildernesses; dystopias; comic, disastrous, and mystic engagements with place, land, and nature. The three essays in *Manufactured Landscapes* do what essays in handsome books about artists usually try to do: establish the subject's place in the grand narrative of the history of art.

But the Canadian Burtynsky is more interesting for his divergences than his heritage. He tells of the incident that launched his current work, a wrong turn that took him to the mining wasteland of Frackville, Pennsylvania, where "in that entire horizon there was nothing virgin. It totally destabilized me. I thought, is this earth? I had never seen anything transformed on this scale. The pictures I took in Frackville sat as contacts for almost a year. I kept looking at them and then I realized, this is what I have to do. All the things we inhabit, and all the things we possess, the material world that we surround ourselves with, all comes from nature." And this is what nature looks like when we wring our material world out of it: luridly red-orange rivers of water saturated with oxidized iron at a nickel quarry, a tire dump whose millions of black donuts become canyons and crevasses and mountains.

Among Burtynsky's most interesting subjects are marble and granite quarries, the voids in the unseen landscape from which buildings, particularly civic and corporate ones, are extracted (the critic Lucy Lippard often refers to these as the holes left in rural places to create urban erections). These are vertiginous, precarious terrains in which human beings and even their stoneworking machines are tiny. The geometry of architecture is already present in the horizontal and vertical lines and ledges carved into the walls and amphitheaters of stone. The stone is almost monochromatic, but the red and orange equipment in Carrara or a jade-green lake at the bottom of a Vermont quarry and a few yellow aspens on a ledge midway up give scale and relief to the monotony. They also magnify the Piranesi-like terror of these cliffs and abysses.

The photographer whom Burtynsky most resembles is Californian Richard Misrach, who also makes breathtaking large color images of overlooked and sequestered places. Military sites in the desert Southwest have been Misrach's definitive subject, from the abandoned Enola Gay bunker and sheds in Utah to the ammunition-storage berms, bombing ranges, and radioactive landscapes of Nevada. A dozen or more years ago, this work was greeted with outrage for "aestheticizing evil"; viewers seemed to blame Misrach for the challenges that sublime and fascinating evils pose. Misrach was always more interested in testing this kind of tension, and his work differs from Burtynsky's in its interest in conceptual and philosophical questions—notably the photographic representation of what can't be seen—and in its tendency to end up more often with images that have the skies and spaciousness of traditional landscape. The culture seems to have become more sophisticated about the beauty/virtue schisms since Misrach's bombscapes, but Burtynsky isn't interested in pushing the contradictions and the politics of representation in the same way. He's a more straightforward documentarian, though his work is hardly in the documentary mode, at least not in the mode in which a certain aesthetic and emotional remove—including a remove from the sensuality of the world—is part of the equipment. For Burtynsky's

images are beautiful, or rather, like Misrach's, sublime, of the same visually compelling order as forest fires, wartime ruins, floods, and other spectacles.

Nowhere are they more so than in his shipbreaking images. These, mostly
made in Chittagong, Bangladesh, show the half-dismantled hulks of cargo ships
and oil tankers on beaches, huge fragments over which men scramble like ants
(apparently, though this is nowhere evident in the images, dismantling them with
little more than blowtorches). Often taken in raking light or fog, these photographs depict colossal shards standing up at intervals from dramatic foreground to
deep background, the most conventionally landscapelike of Burtynsky's images
(though some also show a façade that fills the image area and approaches abstraction). They are reports back from an unseen world—who in the first world ever
thought much about oil tanker recycling?—in which our daily lives are embedded. But they seem almost allegorical, antlike men fragmenting the colossi that are
the only relief to that vast, flat expanse.

And, like Misrach, Burtynsky cares about his subject matter, even though
he's no advocate. This concern sets him apart from the other photographer he
resembles, the much lionized Andreas Gursky (like Burtynsky, born in 1955).
Gursky specializes in huge prints in which antlike human beings seem to inhabit a
world—of arena concerts, ski areas, the tiered balconies of hotel lobbies—that
we mostly do know (though he too photographed a landfill), and whose alienating
and inhuman scale and overabundance we know better through his images. But
Gursky is, comparatively, a formalist, interested in digital manipulation and questions of scale and representation. His commitment is not to the subject.

Burtynsky is starting to approach something that photography could have
pursued all along, and maybe did once or twice in the era of the *Life* photo essay:
an inspection of systems rather than places. His oil fields, oil refineries, tire dumps,
oil pipelines, and dismantled tankers begin to get at the cycle of oil, nasty at every
turn even without politics and wars. They aren't presented that way in the book,
but they accrue that way in the imagination. A truly ecological photography
might pursue something along those lines, tracing the life of a commodity from
extraction to disposal (Burtynsky's pale uranium mine site with its dead trees
invites this line of investigation, raising as it does the specter of bombs and power

plants and nuclear waste disposal). Or it might address what photography has mostly been unwilling to acknowledge: so toxic is the medium itself that Kodak in Rochester—not far from Burtynsky's Ontario home—is New York State's number one polluter, cranking out in a typical year 2.5 million pounds of airborne methylene chloride as well as enough dioxin to cause more than half a billion cancer deaths. This could be why a really thoughtful photographer, in Pauli's words, "believes that it would be hypocritical . . . to use his photographs as a diatribe against industry."

4

REACHING FOR THE SKY

Excavating the Sky

〚2000〛

"Don't show the sky unless the sky has something to say."
Eliot Porter, quoted by David Brower

I. A COLUMN OF CLOUD BY DAY

Here the sky is changing, all the time, every day, demanding attention lest one get caught in a lightning storm but rewarding that attention with the unpredictable magnificence of what light, space, and water vapor can do. This summer, the rains periodically reach a tropical intensity, and lately tall feathery cirrus clouds have been coming in among the cumulus like eagles among sheep. The cirrus reach upward, making palpable the heights of the sky, while the cumulus scatter across its breadth as though floating on an invisible plateau more level and far wider than the New Mexico prairie from which I watch. At the end of the day, some of the clouds become dark against a luminous sky, others pale against the night; and as darkness deepens, they become obscured regions, *caelum incognita*, in the map of the stars.

A few days ago, when strangely beautiful, individual gray clouds floated beneath the soft gray sky after a deluge, I began to think that the sky is the consciousness of landscape. Landscape is generally thought of as being about land, and the earth is solid matter that changes only slowly, imperceptibly. But light and weather hourly give it new aspects, new moods: the tentative, fleeting radiances of dawn and dusk; the flat, objective glare of shadowless midday; the ambiguity of days when scattered clouds drag shadows across the terrain, storms not brewing but brooding. The light and weather of the sky give landscape its temperament even more compellingly than facial expression and posture convey a person's disposition. And the sky isn't just a reflection of mood but a creator of one, as anyone exalted by a storm's ferocity or made joyous by sunshine after rain knows. Beaumont Newhall writes of walking out in the desert while waiting to be sent to war in 1944: "Somehow the sky seems important in moments like that. And it did seem an optimistic sky—not because of its blanket of clouds, but because of the quality of them."

Photographers know that a place is utterly transformed by its light, that everything earthly depends on the sky for what, after all, is called atmosphere; desert dwellers know that not just aesthetics but life itself depends on the sky, on its light, on its cooling darkness, and on its rain. In the arid West, the sky determines everything. The desert bares itself, submits to a sky so turbulent and glorious that it is a place of revelation and awe. If the earth is the record of what has happened, the sky is the realm of portents and prophesies, from the practical stuff of incoming weather to the apparitions of deities and omens. Yahweh, the wrathful God of the Old Testament's desert-dwelling Hebrews, was originally a Semitic storm god—"a traveling deity who was everyplace and therefore not bound by location"—according to Paul Shepard. This origin is evident in his association with light, with high places, and with celestial phenomena, from the rainbow as postdiluvian promise to the psalm that says, "He shall come down like rain." In the dichotomies that structure much Western thinking, the sky is aligned with the mind and the masculine, while the earth is associated with the body and the feminine.

The horizon, the boundary between earth and heaven, gives most Western landscapes orientation and limits, a balance between above and below, consciousness and incarnation. When Frederick Sommer photographed landscape entirely below the horizon, making the southwestern terrain into a repeating pattern of stone, saguaro, and shrubbery, the image was disorientingly radical. Since then, it has become more common to make such subhorizon scapes and easier to read them. However common in photographic history, pictures of sky without earth are likewise still disorienting—they have no apparent location, and location is one of the things we're used to getting from landscape photography. Clouds without land have often been seen as pure subjectivity, as in Alfred Stieglitz's famous 1920s photographs of them, which he and his interpreters have usually regarded as abstract art. "These series are not meteorological records of the movements of the clouds, nor are they documents of the sky on a particular day; they are instead totally artificial constructions which mirror, not the passage of real time, but the change and flux of Stieglitz's subjective state," write Sarah Greenough and Juan Hamilton in the text for a Stieglitz retrospective, as though the clouds had surrendered their biospheric functions for aesthetic toil, as though photographs must be either documents or expressions.

Richard Misrach's photographs of the cloudless, horizonless sky insist on being both, and their place-name titles unfurl history across a sky that is usually the home of the immortal and the ephemeral. They could be considered photographs of that most elusive and elementary photographic subject, time itself. One could ask questions about the distance light travels to reach the film and information travels before it fades into unrecognizability or flares up into revelation. There are other questions about the time it takes the imagination to travel from rapture to analysis, beauty to politics. Clouds drift, stars rotate, and sometimes the shortest distance between two places leaves out the most important sites.

II. A PILLAR OF FIRE BY NIGHT

Stars are made of flaming gases, but constellations are made of stories. Stars are the things themselves, constellations the way we connect those things to each other and ourselves through words, names, stories. Every culture has read constellations into the night sky, perhaps because we remember things and beings by their names; and calling people, places, things by name is how we establish a relationship to them at best, claim them as property at worst. Constellations connect the stars to each other, but in a way that no longer speaks of stars but of animals, goddesses, and heroes. Constellations are an essential metaphorical construct—or one might say that metaphor is an art of making constellations, of constellating. A constellation is made by drawing imaginary lines between stars to make a picture of something other than stars; a metaphor draws analogies between disparate things, finding a common ground for them that makes each look different. As Aristotle explains it in the *Poetics*, "A metaphor is a word with some other meaning which is transferred either from genus to species, or from species to genus, or from one species to another, or used by analogy. . . . For example, to cast seed is to sow, but there is no special word for the casting of rays by the sun; yet this is to the sunlight as sowing is to seed, and therefore it has been said of the sun that it is 'sowing its divine rays.'" The acts of the sower and the sun are linked in this metaphor, which suggests the life-generating force of sunlight and perhaps the way the celestial calendar dictates the agriculturalist's routine. Writing of Walter Benjamin, Hannah Arendt notes, "Metaphors are the means by which the oneness of the world is poetically brought about."

In a wonderful extended metaphor from the thriller *Smilla's Sense of Snow*, the protagonist sees a chest x-ray as a photograph of the cosmos: "The rib bones are the closed ellipses of the planets, with their focus in the sternum, the breastbone, the white center of the photograph. The lungs are the gray shadows of the Milky Way against the black leaden shield of space. The heart's dark contour is the cloud of ashes from the burned-out sun. The intestines' hazy hyperboles are the disconnected asteroids, the vagabonds of space, the scattered cosmic dust." Metaphor means the body can look like the heavens, and constellations fill the heavens with bodies (for the ancients, these metaphors became so entrenched that a comet moving through the pudenda of a constellation foretold an increase in moral laxity). Seven stars slightly west of due north conjoined make something wholly different than stars, a dipper, and the dipper makes the sky navigable — but it also makes the sky offer up a metaphysical drink and a recognizable earthly object. Runaway slaves called the constellation "the drinking gourd" and followed it north. Farther west, the Zuni also saw it as a drinking gourd, but the Hopi saw it as a "star thrower," the Northern Paiute and Western Shoshone as a rabbit net, the Chumash as seven boys who became wild geese, the Isleta Pueblo as a cradle, and the Tohono O'odham as a cactus-gathering hook. The same stars can make up entirely different maps.

The night sky is a clock, a compass, and a calendar for those who know how to read it. Wristwatches and calendars measure a cyclical time abstracted from the movements of the heavenly bodies that still describe its intervals: the earth's daily rotation and its yearly orbit of the sun. Once, though, the heavens themselves were the timepieces people needed to read. Three thousand years ago, Hesiod advised his farmer brother, "When Orion and Sirius are come to the middle of the sky, and the rosy-fingered Dawn confronts Arcturus, then Perses, cut off all your grapes and bring them home with you." Orion was huntsman for Artemis, the moon goddess; he was seen as forever chasing the seven Pleiades across the sky, in a sky that was an anthology, an inventory of myth. Agriculturalists had particular need of annual calendars or calendrical knowledge such as Hesiod describes, and in some places the landscape itself marked the seasons. Pueblo Indians in the Southwest sometimes used the formations of their local horizon to mark the agricultural year. As the sun moved from south to north through spring, each notch or peak from which it rose marked a time at or near part of the preparing and planting. Time and space were correlated; the movement of celestial bodies marked the passage of time, and the largely cyclical nature of time was borne out by the reliable repetition of these movements. That is to say, the sky was once a repository of important information as well as cultural lore; looking at it was a necessary pleasure. Standing stones, pyramids, medicine wheels, and other structures around the world bear witness to the ceremonial importance of tracking the movements in the sky, and a few artists—notably Nancy Holt and James Turrell— have built new observational structures in our time. Celestial observation requires a kind of triangulation of three pieces of information: time, observer's earthly location, and observed heavenly body. You could say that the three form a constellation of knowledge.

That earthly places—rainforests, wetlands, prairies—are disappearing is commonly bemoaned, but the sky is disappearing too. Ecologically speaking, the ozone layer is thinning, and so we are losing our atmospheric protection from the cosmos; but aesthetically speaking, thicker and thicker layers of humanly produced stuff intervene between us and that cosmos. We spend more and more time under roofs and surrounded by walls, whether in cars or buildings, and less and less time in night's true darkness, unmitigated by artificial light. The light pollution generated by cities makes it hard to see more than a few of the brightest stars in many places, and smog taints the colors of the sky by day (and gives Los Angeles its blood-red sunsets). In a national park last summer, I heard an astronomer who was pointing out the constellations assert that the sky is the most important place to save, because it is available to everyone, visible to prisoners and urbanites as well as outdoorspeople. Who looks at it nowadays? A century and a half ago, John Ruskin wrote, "It is a strange thing how little in general people know about the sky"—strange because the sky is ubiquitous.

> The noblest scenes of this earth can be seen and known but by few; it is not intended that man should live always in the midst of them, he injures them by his presence, he ceases to feel them if he be always with them; but the sky is for all: bright as it is, it is not "too bright, nor good, for human nature's daily food"; it is fitted in all its functions for the perpetual comfort and exalting of the heart, for soothing it and purifying it from its dross and dust. Sometimes gentle, sometimes capricious, sometimes awful; almost human in its passions, almost spiritual in its tenderness, almost divine in its infinity.

Ruskin was writing about the sky in the course of mounting his massive defense of J. M. W. Turner, who often had the sky dominate and even overwhelm his paintings and made the sublimity of power, vastness, emptiness, and light as evident as they ever have been. But even when the sky is visible, it is no longer readable to most people, not as a collection of stories, a clock, or a compass. A man tells me that the U.S. Navy has stopped teaching celestial navigation because satellite geopositioning devices have at last, after millennia of skygazing, made knowing the stars unnecessary to knowing where you are, unless the batteries run out.

III. STARRY MESSENGER

In the spring of 1609, Galileo Galilei improved upon the telescope that a Flemish inventor had presented to the world the previous year; it was the first vision-expanding machine, though the camera would probably become the most influential. The first telescope Galileo made he gave to the Senate of Venice, after demonstrating how the device could be used to see the approach of enemy ships far earlier than ever before. The second telescope he made he kept and aimed at the heavens to see what had never been seen before. In January 1610, he looked through it at Jupiter and saw "that beside the planet there were three starlets, small indeed, but very bright." They appeared in various arrays on one or the other side of Jupiter, and he realized that they were satellites orbiting the larger body. In *The Starry Messenger*, his report on what he saw through his telescope, he described "four planets swiftly revolving about Jupiter at differing distances and periods, and known to no one before the author recently perceived them and decided that they should be named the Medicean Stars," or Siderea Medicea. In fact, he had at first named them the Siderea Cosmica, but the patron he sought to flatter, Cosimo de Medici, duke of Tuscany, preferred that his whole dynasty be commemorated by the name.

Galileo's sighting and naming of Jupiter's moons represent many kinds of rupture with the past. The most often observed is that his discoveries confirmed the Copernican, or heliocentric, interpretation of the universe and undermined the Aristotelian, or terracentric, view. The perfection of the nine crystal spheres orbiting the earth was undone by these celestial bodies orbiting around other bodies, and they complicated the elaborate charts of the movements of the heavenly bodies worked out by astronomers. Galileo is often presented as a Prometheus in revolt against tyranny, but, though he subverted traditional knowledge, he flattered contemporary power with his act of naming. He seems almost a prefiguration of the military-industrial-academic complex, with his recognition of the military uses of the telescope and his courting of favor—and tenure—in both Venice and Tuscany.

Another rupture is between stars and constellations, information and stories. Before the telescope, astronomers saw what everyone else saw, and it was their perseverance in observing and skill in interpretation that set them apart from others who craned their necks skyward. After the telescope, the sky began to fill with objects that had no place in culture, that were accessible only to specialists, and that outreached the ability of culture to assimilate new objects into existing patterns. That is to say, since Galileo's time, many new stars have been sighted and named, but there have been no new constellations. The very reason he could propose naming Jupiter's moons after his patron was because they did not belong to the culture at large as part of its experience; that he thought it fitting to name a heavenly body after a mortal makes his discovery akin to the encounters and namings taking place on the other side of the world—makes it colonialism, albeit of a very metaphysical sort. It was the first inkling that the sky itself could become a specialist's preserve and a political territory, and it spread history's linear time to the heavens. Galileo's names never caught on. Instead, what had staying power was the astronomer Johannes Kepler's facetious suggestion that the moons be named after Jupiter's sexual conquests—a suggestion that was revived in the nineteenth century: Io, Europa, Callisto, and Ganymede are the names of Jupiter's four largest moons, and they are collectively referred to as the Galilean satellites.

Galileo invented the telescope during the turbulence of the Reformation, and, as we all learned in school, the Reformation was in part about allowing people to read and interpret the Bible directly. It might have marked the beginning of a rise in literacy with fine democratic side effects—but other forms of reading were beginning their decline, at least in Europe: reading the sky, the weather, tracks and footprints, iconographies, plants. As Michel Foucault notes in *The Order of Things*, constellations of meaning linked by metaphor were being replaced by expanding galaxies of information. Calendars and clocks proliferated, making direct observations less necessary and knowledge less accessible to the unequipped (though the Vatican in Galileo's time and afterward employed astronomers to calculate the correct dates for holy days, just as earlier Muslim astronomers had used their art to calculate the exact direction of Mecca and the correct times for daily prayers). Galileo first saw an eclipse of one of the moons of Jupiter in 1612. He realized that the rapidity and predictability of the event meant that it could be used to calculate time, and thus place, far more precisely than ever before. A traveler with a table of the eclipses, a telescope, and an accurate timekeeping device could note the time of an eclipse of one of Jupiter's moons, compare it to the time at which it would happen in the locale of the table, and calculate his distance from that locality. That is, he (or, rarely, she) could calculate longitude. Galileo negotiated with the great colonizers of his day, the Dutch and the Spanish, to perfect this system, but it wasn't until the end of the seventeenth century that the eclipse of Jupiter's moons could be used to calculate earthly locations. People who had access to the new astronomy could cease being local without becoming lost: they could go farther with confidence, and they did.

IV. WESTERN LONGITUDES

"The streams were timbered with the long-leaved cottonwood and red willow; and during the afternoon a species of onion was very abundant. I obtained here an immersion of the first satellite of Jupiter, which corresponding very nearly with the chronometer, placed us in longitude 106 47' 25". The latitude, by observation, was 41 37' 16"; elevation above the sea, 7,800 feet; and distance from St. Vrain's fort, 147 miles." Two hundred years after Galileo, this relationship between celestial knowledge and colonial power persisted, as this August 2, 1843, extract from John C. Fremont's journal demonstrates. The chronometer, transit telescope, compass, sextant, barometer—and a lot of guns—allowed "the Pathfinder" and his men to map the American West and the West that was not yet America for scientific, military, and commercial purposes. The famous geological surveys of the 1860s and 1870s would follow in their wake, equipped with one further device of conquest: the camera. Though in his heyday the technology was not yet adequate to the circumstances, Fremont attempted to photograph the land as well; on Fremont's third expedition, the Sephardic Jewish daguerreotypist Solomon Nunes Carvalho became the first to photograph extensively in what would become the American West. Fremont was a superb surveyor, an insubordinate soldier, and a great romanticizer, and he named some of the major features of the West—the Great Basin, the Humboldt River, the Golden Gate—and confirmed the Spanish name of the Sierra Nevada over the English one.

Surveying the land was a military operation reaffirming the relationship between knowledge and power. Knowing the lay of the land was preparatory to seizing and settling it; being able to read the stars was necessary to write a new meaning on the earth below with names, guns, and laws. On May 23, 1844, while returning from a trespassing foray into Mexican California, Fremont ruminated, "From the Dalles to the point where we turned across the Sierra Nevada, near 1,000 miles, we heard Indian names, and the greater part of the distance none; from Nueva Helvetica [Sacramento] to las Vegas de Santa Clara, about 1,000 more, all were Spanish; from the Mississippi to the Pacific, French and American or English were intermixed; and this prevalence of names indicates the national character of the first explorers." The names of the stars make clear that Greek and Arab astronomers established much of the knowledge of the night sky for Europe; the constellations are named after Greek gods and heroes. But the surface of the American West is named after Native American observations and events, Spanish saints, and American men and their whims. In Greek mythology, Narcissus and Hyacinth became flowers; Orion and Cassiopeia became constellations. Like ancient heroes, the prominent men of the nineteenth century were at least in name becoming plants, mountains, towns, and rivers. But most often the names led and lead only to a sense of land as real estate, a businessman's landscape with only occasional odd moments of poetry and reversions to a more profound sense of place. The names on the land often obliterated the original names as part of the act of conquest, replacing them with names that contribute nothing to the place beyond distinguishing it from other places.

There is a great incongruity in the names of men upon the land, for these rogues and bureaucrats are too recent and prosaic to convey the benediction of saints, heroes, gods. Instead of the certainties of mythology, they convey—to those who know the history of the names—turbulence, economics, ambition, and brutality. In Europe, white people are indigenous, and they are often named after places. Some Anglo-Americans were named Winchester after the English cathedral town, and so were some eastern U.S. towns, but the western towns—there are twenty-one Winchesters in the United States—are often named after the men who bore that place-name, including two towns honoring the inventor of the Winchester repeating rifle, "the gun that won the West." Winchester itself comes from a pre-Celtic word and a Latin suffix, -chester, meaning a walled town, and the word is at least twelve centuries old. When places are named after men and not the other way around, people become more real and permanent than land. As Robert Frost once observed, "The land was ours before we were the land's."

But even these names tell stories to those who listen. Maps are narratives that sprawl in all directions. Reno was a Civil War general (not the Reno of the Battle of Little Bighorn), but the city of Reno is surrounded by Washoe County, and the Washoes are an indigenous nation. To the south is Fremont's scout, Indian fighter Kit Carson, in the form of Carson City, Carson Pass, and the Carson River; but passing through Reno on its journey north from Lake Tahoe is the Truckee River, named after the Paiute chief whose son, Winnemucca, gave his name to a town farther east and near the Humboldt River. Yet farther up the Humboldt is Battle Mountain, whose name recalls what George R. Stewart said in his book on American place-names: "Massacre Rocks and Battle Mountain tell their stories to him who knows the language—that where Indians killed whites, it was a massacre; but where whites killed Indians it was a battle." And the Humboldt River was named by Fremont, who, guided by Carson, explored and mapped the West for American expansion and who named Pyramid Lake, the destination of the Truckee River. Like so many American names, it harked back to an Old World often known only through books and pictures. Fremont had not been to Egypt, but he thought the steep stone island near the lake's eastern shore looked like the pyramid of Cheops, so Egypt is now memorialized in Nevada. The whole state might have been named Washoe, but Congress insisted on Nevada, which means "snowy" in Spanish and was taken from the mostly Californian Sierra Nevada, named by the Spanish and reaffirmed by Fremont. The lack of Spanish names beyond the Sierra Nevada testifies to the limits of the Spaniards' travels.

V. WEIGHING THE NAMES

What does it mean to name something, and what to know the names? To name something is to presume to know it or to make it into something knowable, to identify what can be known or to presume that it takes no getting to know. The

West was claimed, named, and settled with too much haste for naming to be any-thing but a sticking on of handy labels. Names have power: in Hebrew tradition, the name of God was unspeakable; and in Tibetan Buddhism, the names of God are all but infinite. In fairy tales and myths, to call someone by name is to have power over him or her—think of Rumpelstiltskin. Names have weight. They influence how we read a place, how we see the stars, how we estimate each other: Mr. Bernstein is looked at very differently than Mr. Big Eagle.

There are styles in naming that can be read across the map of this country. The Indians usually named descriptively and never commemorated a person, though sometimes an event or a deity. The Spanish often described and obses-sively sanctified; Mormons invented themselves as the new Israelites and ex-ported the Old Testament to Zion, Jordan, Moab, and a host of other places in Utah; and non-Mormon whites saw the devil a lot, from Devils Tower National Monument in Wyoming to Devils Postpile National Monument in the eastern Sierra. Fremont recorded of one midwestern locale, "The Indian name of the lake is Mini-wakan, the Enchanted Water; converted by the whites into Devil's Lake." Euro-Americans often used indigenous language decoratively, for its sound, so that the meaning of the word or its place of origin no longer mattered. *Minnesota* means "muddy water," but romantics soon made "muddy" into "cloudy," until the place became "the land of sky-blue water"; Sequoia was a Cherokee chief in the Southeast whose name was appended to the giant trees and then the California national park; the word *Yosemite* means something very different than the namers of the valley, and then the park, intended.

Perhaps the awkwardness and arrogance of some place-names come merely from their recentness; they are still more redolent of the namers than of the places themselves. But time will sand their edges and erase their paternity. Some people relish the sounds of the names for their own sake, as did Stephen Vincent Benet in his famous "American Names":

> I have fallen in love with American names,
> The sharp ones that never get fat,
> The snakeskin-titles of mining claims,

The plumed war-bonnet of Medicine Hat,
Tucson and Deadwood and Lost Mule Flat.

This is the poem that ends:

Bury my heart at Wounded Knee.

This pleasure of names flared up again in country music during its classic era, when countless songs suggested that though you couldn't count on love, you could count on geography and lovingly reeled off the names of lost homes yearned for, destinations not yet reached, stops along railroad lines and highways. The popular song "Route 66" does the same; with its litany of names, it made the road a major tourist attraction. Names structure the landscape as surely as buildings and roads do. They can be pointers and blinders, billboards and graves, though often descriptions and commemorations eventually become true proper names— after the general was forgotten, Reno came to mean only the "biggest little city in the world."

An English place-name dictionary begins, "Most place-names today are what could be termed 'linguistic fossils.' Although they originated as living units of speech, coined by our distant ancestors as descriptions of places in terms of their topography, appearance, situation, use, ownership, or other association, most have become, in the course of time, mere labels, no longer possessing a clear linguistic meaning. This is perhaps not surprising when one considers that most place-names are a thousand years old or more." One might say that rather than possessing no clear linguistic meaning, they mean nothing but themselves; the descriptions have become proper nouns united with that which they describe. During the heyday of American naming, Ralph Waldo Emerson took up the subject of names, saying, "The poets made all the words and therefore language is the archives of history, and, if we must say it, a sort of tomb of the Muses. Language is fossil poetry. As the limestone of the continent consists of infinite masses of shells of animalcules, so language is made up of images or tropes, which now, in their secondary use, have long ceased to remind us of their poetic origin." It is too soon to forget the original names or the acts of naming that sought to reinvent this place as something else, too soon for the shells of the animalcules to lose their echo and fossilize.

In places whose inhabitants have been there longer than memory, the names are laid thick upon the land, with the intimacy of the local. In Ireland, I once went on a ten-mile walk that took me from Ballydehob past the Bownuknockane River where it enters Roaringwater Bay; past Knockroe, Knockaphukeen, the Dawnu-knockane, Coosane, Ballybane, Barnaghgeehy; across Letterlicky Bridge; across the Durrus, Hollyhill, Cappanaloha to Bantry Bay. Of these Irish names I know only that *Knock* means hill, and this density of naming means that the place was inhabited by intensely local people, people who had reason to distinguish each hill, each small region, for navigation and conversation. The anthropologist and essayist Richard K. Nelson writes of traveling in a sealskin boat along the arctic coast of Alaska and hearing one of his walrus-hunting hosts and guides begin to name the places they passed: "Nullagvik, Pauktugvik, Milliktagvik, Avgumman, Aquisaq, Inmaurat. For a few he offered translations: Quilamittagvik: 'Place to Hunt Ducks with Ivory Bolas,' Mitqutailat: 'Arctic Terns,' Nannugvik: 'Place to Hunt Polar Bears,' Inuktuyuk: 'Man-Eater,' a spring hunting-camp used by those willing to overlook its ominous name." Nelson imagines

the entire North American continent in a time before living memory—this enormous sprawl of land, sheathed and cloaked and brilliantly arrayed with names. Names covering the terrain like an unbroken forest. Names that wove people profoundly into the landscape, and that infused landscape profoundly into the people who were its inhabitants. . . . I imagined how these names had dwindled with the deaths of elders, beginning five hundred years ago; a steady impoverishment of names, as the Europeans spread west, knowing too little of the land and its people to realize what was being lost. Many parts of the conti-nent were plundered of their names, left desolate, emptied of mind and memory and meaning. But all is not lost. Many Native American names survive, others are now being recorded, and some are finding their rightful places on maps.

He mentions Denali, which means "the High One" in Koyukon, a more apt name than McKinley for the highest mountain on the continent.

Monument Valley is a formalist name, drawing attention to the aesthetics of the place, the way the abruptly rising buttes stand like pillars or pedestals, articulating the depth of space and perspective that makes the place so spectacular. Since ordinary monuments commemorate something other than themselves, this name makes the place a monument to nothing but monumentality. The individual rock formations have names that are clearly imported: along with the famous Mittens, there's an Elephant Rock and a Camel Rock, though neither of those beasts has been native to this continent since the last ice age. But Monument Valley has another name. A Navajo medicine person, Mike Mitchell, says,

> Monument Valley's Navajo name is *Tse Bii'Nidzisigai* (White Rocks Inside). The story is that the valley is where "Rocks Are Pointing Upward" (*Tsenidee-zhazhaii*). Before that it was called White Rocks Inside. As they tell the story there used to be monsters out there. The monsters were the enemies of the Navajo and used to be somewhere in White Rocks Inside. There are Holy People who live there now and they say that important Holy Way ceremonial stories were originally formed there. The valley is protected. . . . Now for some, the valley's purpose is sightseeing. For others, its purpose is to produce good minds and good thoughts, and hogans are built here and there.

The place looks different under this name. Tse Bii'Nidzisigai is clearly a place where people lived and history unfolded long before John Wayne scowled across its distance for John Ford's movie camera, a place that tells us there is more there than we can know.

VI. LOOKS LIKE

When it comes to naming, clouds pose a different, almost an opposite, challenge than that posed by constellations. While constellations are unchanging over millennia, so that they can be collectively named and assimilated into the culture, clouds are evanescent, changeable. They function something like Rorschach blots, suggesting private resemblances that individuals can read to themselves. (In the

1960s, the comic strip *Peanuts* had a recurrent episode in which Charlie Brown and Linus displayed their personalities through cloud interpretation; Charlie always saw the simple and obvious, Linus the elaborate and arcane.) For something to be named, it must have a distinct and durable identity, but clouds appear, metamorphose, and vanish too quickly. Only storms with the force or speed to do permanent damage are named, at least since 1938, when meteorologists began to give them women's names, beginning with A and moving through the alphabet each season. Probably something about Euro-American gender politics could be found in the idea of storms labeled with women's first names sweeping over mountains given men's last names (though as I write, Hurricane Dennis is menacing the Carolina coast—about fifteen years ago the meteorological authorities decided to give men's as well as women's names to storms).

Because clouds themselves cannot be named, nomenclatural passion has focused instead on classifying and naming their standard formations. Though knowledge of the weather had previously been the province of shepherds and sailors, meteorologists latinized the formations: a cirrus, for example, is "a form of cloud, generally at a high elevation, presenting the appearance of divergent filaments or wisps, often resembling a curl or lock of hair or wool. Particular varieties are known as cat's or mare's tails," says the *Oxford English Dictionary*. *Cirrus* is a word that itself means "a curl-like tuft, fringe or filament." Like Linnean plant names, the cloud names create a metaphorical structure: an information tree. There are four principal forms, according to this system—cumulus, stratus, cirrus, and nimbus—meaning, in English, heap, layer, curl of hair, and rain; and these can be classified in various groups according to altitude. Further names describe cloud types that do not fit into these four groups, a category of the uncategorizable, suggesting something about the amorphousness of clouds and the tenaciousness of the desire to order the world through language and representation—and not the language of mare's tails that relies on metaphor and resemblance, but the language of science in which the stories and analogies are hidden in a dead language. Clouds and cloud terminology are an acute and comic form of the pervasive gap between words and things, between the particulars of experience and the universals of classification.

At workshops for more than twenty years, Richard Misrach has been presenting an exercise in which the participants are invited to write down their interpretations of a photograph that has been given three different titles—for example, a Charles Sheeler industrialmodernist photograph that is first introduced to them as "Industry," then as "Five Hundred Tons of Airborne Pollutants a Year," then as "Untitled." Each title inflects the image differently, tells the viewer what to look for, what to ignore. "Untitled," Misrach remarks, always means art, high and disassociated. Names are one of the most important and overlooked sites of visual art, guiding people as powerfully as placenames do. Titles are hypnotic suggestions, operating instructions, associational links, pedigrees, home addresses, credentials, and disclaimers. They constellate a work of art: the title changes the way the image is seen, and the two together describe something in the outside world, whether a place, person, event, idea, or value, differently than either alone. Titles undermine the idea that most visual art is purely visual.

Think how different Robert Motherwell's abstractexpressionist paintings would look were they not titled *Homage to the Spanish Civil War* or how Barnett Newman's *Stations of the Cross* would look without a title that refers not only to sequentiality but to suffering and impending apotheosis. Andy Warhol took the opposite tack, with titles that offered to siphon the lifeblood of content away: *Lavender Disaster* and *Saturday Disaster* pick at the scabs of formalism while seeming to follow in James Abbott McNeill Whistler's footsteps—for the painting commonly known as *Whistler's Mother* is in fact titled *Arrangement in Grey and Black No. 1: The Artist's Mother*, a title requesting that viewers give more weight to composition than to content. On the other hand, Robert Rauschenberg's famous *Erased de Kooning* is entirely dependent on its title to reveal the act behind the faintly inscribed piece of paper and thus give the piece its iconoclastic impact. Conceptual artists had fun with titles, making them either amusingly literal— Mel Bochner's *Three Drymounted Photographs and One Diagram*, Ed Ruscha's *Every Building on Sunset Strip*—or aggressively, mockingly instructive—John Baldessari's painting titled and inscribed *Everything Is Purged from This Painting but Art. No Ideas Have Entered This Work.* Titles tell us that this is not a janitor but a king we are looking at; that this landscape that could be anywhere is in fact somewhere history took place; that this still life was documented on a particular date.

Titles are operating instructions, telling us how the artist would like the work used, in what direction he or she imagines it can take us, and "Untitled" is as different from "Five Hundred Tons of Airborne Pollutants" as Monument Valley is different from Tse Bii' Nidzisigai. In recent decades, curators and photo-historians have been trying to make the photographers of the U.S. Geological Surveys of the 1870s into artists and their photographs into art. Theirs is an act not unlike Misrach's exercise with the Sheeler photograph; they ask us to look at each picture not as, for example, "rock formation suggesting the validity of the catastrophic theory of geology" or "suitable place to bring the railroad through," but as "untitled." Though they are indeed often beautiful photographs taken by men with great visual acuity, to look at them this way is to forget that the camera, like the telescope, has many uses. Galileo's first telescope was an instrument of political power; it was his second that was dedicated to celestial observation. The cameras of the U.S. Geological Surveys were instruments of national power, just as aerial photography was during World War II and satellite imaging often is nowadays.

VIII. THE SLOWNESS OF LIGHT

The titles on Richard Misrach's celestial photographs ask you to come back to earth, tugging against the boundless sublimity the visual matter itself offers, tethering it to earthly problems of meaning and political history. All these histories of names are part of his continuing investigation of both the formal vocabularies of landscape and photography and the political grammar of the American West. One could say of these photographs what Robert Rosenblum said of Mark Rothko's radiant field paintings: "And ultimately, the basic configuration of Rothko's abstract paintings finds its source in the great Romantics: in Turner, who similarly achieved the dissolution of all matter into a silent, mystical luminosity; in Friedrich, who also placed the spectator before an abyss that provoked ultimate questions whose answers, without traditional religious faith and imagery, remained as uncertain as the questions themselves." These photographs look like color field paintings, abstract expressionism, Turner's skies, like painting with its claims to the subjective and the expressive, but as photographs they also can claim the documentary status Stieglitz disavowed in his photographs of clouds. Traditionally, abstract and sublime art invites the viewer to remain indefinitely in the realm of the beautiful, the visual, the emotional. The titles on these yank viewers over to the territories of conceptual and political art. Together, image and title draw up their own constellations—relationships between celestial and earthly names, between eternity and the exact time, between language and visual representation, and, as ever in Misrach's work, between beauty and politics. This time, the questions are about place and politics too.

Landscape is both a composition and a subject. As the former, it is usually a picture of land and sky, organized by a horizon line and further organized by foreground, middle ground, and distance. As a subject, it is about nature, space, location, and other organic and inorganic elements of the physical world as well as about the desires and associations particular places call forth. Throughout much of the history of European and then American landscape, landscape was supposed to be an apolitical genre, a refuge from strife and humanity, a place apart. But in the American West, the wars were always over land until they became wars against the land waged by bombing, dumping, damming, and developing; and it is necessary here to remember that land can mean homeland, battlefield, nation, territory, and real estate. Because the history of a place is largely invisible, representing the visible landscape often ignores history in favor of aesthetics. One of the alternatives is to make works that are landscapes in content but not in form.

Misrach has made some of the most swooningly lovely landscape photographs of the American West, even if they do contain bombs, fires, floods, and ruins. But he has gone on to photograph dead animals and bomb craters below the horizon; bullet-riddled *Playboy* magazine pages from a target range near the Nevada Test Site; paintings that give a sense of the daydreams and hoardings, the cultural aspirations and brutalities of the western places where they now hang; diurnal clouds without a horizon; and now color fields—the cloudless sky—and night skies of clouds and stars. In the relatively recent *Desert Cantos* series titled *The Playboys* and *The Paintings*, he lets representations stand in for the history of their places, for the Europeanization and conquest that are relatively subtle in the landscape itself. That the paintings are indoor phenomena though they represent landscape, that *The Playboys* are photographs of photographs, begins to open up further questions about documentary and photography: Is a photograph of a representa-tion documentary? What are we looking at when we look at a photograph of a two-dimensional object, since photography is usually used to portray vanishing-point perspective, dimensionality, depth? What about the unclouded sky, which is the opposite of a two-dimensional object, since it is profoundly dimensional but without tangible objects? Can you have documentary photographs without a solid subject, save the color the image shows? What part of a place do you need to show in order to depict the place, since you can never show more than parts? I wrote of Misrach's work once before that it is "so lavishly, engagingly visual that it doesn't occur to most viewers that their principal subject is more often than not what remains unseen. He may luxuriate in the visibly beautiful, but he hardly en-courages us to trust our eyes alone." He himself writes, "I wanted to deconstruct the conventions of landscape, I wanted to deconstruct the premises of the camera premised on one-point Renaissance perspective. All three cantos in this sky book are premised on a defiance of the implicit and authoritative dictates of the camera that I have been mindlessly heeding for years. Like the telescope, the camera cre-ates what we can see."

What can we see in these photographs? They portray the sky as too eternal, too mutable, and too ubiquitous to supply very specific information about time and place (though the visibility of Polaris, the North Star, and the curves the con-stellations draw as they rotate indicate something about latitude and duration to those who know how to read them). The titles attach the specificity of locale, cul-ture, language to these ethereal color fields and starlight drawings, turning these sublime images into records of two histories: the travels and nocturnal vigils of the artist and the naming of the sky and the American West. The sky is a blankness, a meditation room of sorts; works in this tradition tend to invite contemplation of the sublime, the void, the pure visual experience. This is their beauty.

But these particular beautiful pictures have titles that are instructions to think about specifics of geography, history, biography, and politics. I remember a tray of bees in a natural history museum in the Rockies, each dusty insect impaled on a pin, with a tiny label floating above indicating where and when the bee was captured. Though the bees all looked alike, the labels made them into a calendar and map of the region and, perhaps, of some entomologist's peregrinations. Similarly, these photographs are specimens of the sky impaled on language, on the words of location and the numbers of temporality. There is an awkwardness, a disjuncture between title and image; and just as the sky is an open space that invites contemplation of beauty and possibility, so the disparity between title and image is an open space to be contemplated. Here the title can be a set of instructions the viewer can choose to disobey, because when instructions don't fit our expectations they become noticeable, and what is noticeable can be resisted. The sky is visible here, and so too in a sense is the mechanism of titles nudging the viewer toward one or another interpretation. Among the invisible displays offered by these gloriously visual artworks are the rules of photographic and linguistic representation.

One could imagine the images as a deck of cards that could be laid out according to aesthetics, geography, chronology, or by types of place-names—Biblical, violent, historical, indigenous, descriptive, personal names. Misrach himself has called them a "dysfunctional journal." The British artist Richard Long has been "documenting" his walks in the landscape for decades with photographs of landscapes accompanied by texts revealing some scant information: how far he went, how many hours or days, what his starting point and destination were. The images do not show a walk, which is, after all, hardly representable in static media; they show unpopulated landscapes in which the text or title invites us to imagine a walk that had duration, location, direction. The texts work like the labels on the bees, like place-names, constellation names, asking us to visualize something that is not visible. Similarly these titles tell us two things the photographs do not quite show: the date of the artist's presence in places whose names were their attractions, and the duration of nocturnal vigils as the camera made its slow exposures. A diary of sorts is contained in the titles, not a confessional one but an austere one that, like Long's texts, gives a few spare facts about an act and its location (and makes clear how much artmaking is about selecting what to leave out as well as selecting what to include).

This series is also a journal that has an odd reciprocity with Fremont's record of traversing an unmapped West, locating latitude and longitude by astronomy and giving coordinates, times, and place-names all together in a kind of constellation whose points are geographical and astronomical location, personal and celestial time, and cultural imposition. These works draw up the same constellations on the open field of exploration, but for the sake of looking back at the project of inventing the American West that Fremont and his peers began. They examine what is constructed by language and what cannot be represented by language. Sometimes the location was clearly chosen to draw out humorous or peculiar relations between celestial and earthly sites, as with "Venus Seen from Virgin Valley." The conjunction between time, place, and celestial body observed no longer calculates the exact location of a place, as it did for Fremont, but stumbles toward some inexact coordinates: of the relationship between words and images, between the beauty of experience and the information of history, between time and place, between two crucial parts of landscape—sky and location—when the land itself is absent. Stars are made of flaming gas, but constellations are made of stories. These works ask us what stories—and whose stories—have been inscribed on our experiences and what has been erased, overlooked, forgotten. And they ask us if we want stories when we have beauty, if we need meaning when we have pleasure. If names are fossilized language, these pictures perform a paradoxical act: looking skyward to excavate those fossils.

Drawing the Constellations

⟦2004⟧

The stars we are given. The constellations we make. That is to say, stars exist in the cosmos, but constellations are the imaginary lines we draw between them, the readings we give the sky, the stories we tell. We come to see the stars arranged as constellations, and as constellations they orient us, they give us something to navigate by, both for traveling across the earth and for telling stories, these bears and scorpions and centaurs and seated queens with their appointed places and seasons. Imagine the lines drawn between stars as roads themselves, as routes for the imagination to travel.

A metaphor is in another way a line drawn between two things, a mapping of the world by affinities and patterns, which is to say that a constellation is a metaphor for a metaphor. And the word *metaphor* in the original Greek means to transport something. So metaphors are, like constellations, navigational tools to travel by. They let us enter a world of resemblances and kinships, in which we can approach the unknown through the known, the abstract through the concrete, the remote through what comes to hand. They measure the route from here to there. The body of the beloved is a landscape, but landscape is also a body; each is traveled in terms of the other, and thus the world is knit together, with those constellating lines of imagination. Aristotle observed, "A good metaphor implies an intuitive perception of the similarity in dissimilars." So metaphors are an erotic force binding together the disparate things of this earth, the language of love, the mapping of relationship, though they do not need to be literal language: "shoulder of a road" is a phrase, but a photograph of a road and of a shoulder can convey the same resemblance, make the same relationship.

The Western Apache, writes anthropologist Keith Basso, understand automobiles in terms of the human body. When cars arrived in their culture, there were
no words for the inner workings, and so the mechanically inclined men called the
various working parts hearts, lungs, and other things, bringing the car to life not
just through language but through the resemblances that language maps. A battery is a heart, and when headlights become eyes, the possibility of a blind car
arises (and we forget the metaphor built into the head of headlights, for our own
language not only coins but buries in familiarity this imagistic language of constellations: think of the trove of buried coins in this sentence).

An engine does not become biological in this constellating, nor does a heart
become mechanical, but a route has been traced that connects the machine and the
body. They are still themselves, but the world has been knit a little more tightly
together, a path has been trod. A lowrider brings a car to life another way, by
making it into a shrine, a coffin, a chapel, a social arena, and a canvas, turning a corporate product into personal and communal expression, connecting a new technology to old cultural practices, and linking together many things. We are constantly
drawing the world together in terms of resemblances and recastings, and the job
of artists is to draw the lines anew to startle us, wake us up, see the secret route
there or where we've always been. Same stars, different constellations.

This is different from definition, for a definition endeavors to draw things
apart, to draw lines that divide one from another: an insect is not an arachnid, a
star is not a heart. But metaphor, this art of drawing constellations, draws them
together. A battery *is* a heart. A lowrider car is a chapel with the sacred heart
painted on it. A bed is a labyrinth in which you must find your way to the dark
center. They are themselves and lovers, and perhaps like love this metaphorization
lets them become more deeply themselves. A labyrinth has at its center the
Minotaur that came of the Cretan queen's copulation with a sacred bull. The
Minotaur was the Greek mind/body problem—we have the urges of animals
and yet have intellects—but this might not be a problem for an imagination that
accepts the lines drawn to constellate things rather than to divide them.

The Cretan labyrinth was made to lose things in, notably the monster offspring of that union; but the Christian labyrinth was made to find things in,

notably the route to salvation. Thus the former has many paths, the latter only one, going, with meanders, delays, and turnarounds, to the center. The labyrinth in which the lines we draw between things become tangled, become a network of connections to get lost in. Getting lost, a necessary mode of finding things, the journey into the unknown known as questing. And perhaps, with the arrival at the center, the discovery of not the right answers but the right questions. Childbed, deathbed, marriage bed, dreamspace, cave, camera, cavern, chambered heart. Daedalus builds the Cretan labyrinth like an elaborate riddle in which to hide the Minotaur; when he is stuck in it himself, he escapes on wings of wax and fallen feathers, a route out that is not an answer to the intricacies of the labyrinth but a simple question about larger forces.

The desire to go home that is a desire to be whole, to know where you are, to be the point of intersection of all the lines drawn through all the stars, to be the constellation-maker and the center of the world, that center called love. To awaken from sleep, to rest from awakening, to tame the animal, to let the soul go wild, to shelter in darkness and blaze with light, to cease to speak and be perfectly understood.

In Meridel Rubenstein's photographic image "Home," four disparate things are stacked and ordered by their visual resemblance, a concavity that cups and gathers and cherishes and invites in. Or perhaps not disparate things, but things whose definitions would not automatically connect them in this four-starred constellation about yearning and destination, which travels from the cosmos to the lover's loins, which refuses to let the distinctions between the advanced technology of the Very Large Array satellite dish, the animal craft of the swallow's nest on the porch, the natural forces behind the sacred salt lake of the Zuni mean more than the affinities, to let the stars signify more than the constellation drawn by the artist. More than a metaphor, which links two things, this links four, and thereby implies that more could be linked, that the world could be navigated by this finding of patterns of form and desire. That refuses the distinction between landscape and body, between animal and human, traditional and technological, to find the affinities between them, as the center of the labyrinth is the point at which all the paths arrive.

Hugging the Shadows

[2004]

For the longest time, my friend Val has had a passage from Martin Luther King Jr. tacked to her e-mails: "Darkness cannot drive out darkness; only light can do that. Hate cannot drive out hate; only love can do that. Hate multiplies hate, violence multiplies violence, and toughness multiplies toughness in a descending spiral of destruction." I agree with the meaning, but the metaphor bothers me every time, because why should a man who was called Negro and then black, who was wringing justice from a society dominated by people called white, endorse the old metaphorical Manichaeism of light and darkness? Yet this denigration of darkness is a common phenomenon.

Bill Clinton, whom Toni Morrison famously called our first black president, wrote in his autobiography about the scales of our psyche, saying, "If they go too far toward hopefulness, we can become naïve and unrealistic. If the scales tilt too far the other way, we can get consumed by paranoia and hatred. In the South, the dark side of the scales has always been the bigger problem." Clinton returned to the metaphor when he preached against the second President Bush with the New Testament line about "seeing through a glass, darkly." Has anyone ever made a metaphor out of snow blindness, an experience admittedly not much available to the writers of the New Testament?

Another e-mail yielded a Jungian analysis of Bush, arguing instead that he is out of touch with his shadow, "those parts of the personality rejected by the ego," and adds, "Until one is conscious of the shadow, one continues to project this rejected self onto others." Thus it is that the war on terror, which sought "to eliminate evil from the world," claims the simple binaries that begin with "you're either with us or against us." Such simple oppositions disguise what Christian and Muslim fundamentalists have in common and that violence bears a compelling resemblance to violence, whether it is termed terrorism or the war on terrorism. Differences are not necessarily opposites, and manufactured oppositions are often disguises for interdependences and affinities.

Metaphors matter. They make tangible the abstractions with which we must wrestle. They describe the resemblances and differences by which we navigate our lives and thoughts. I published a book recently called *Hope in the Dark*, which the inattentive routinely call "Hope in Dark Times." Dark times, like dark ages, are gloomy, harsh, dangerous, depressing, when the good stuff has fled. But the darkness I was after was another thing entirely. This wasn't hope despite the dark; darkness was the ground and condition of that hope, drawn from a line of Virginia Woolf's: "The future is dark, which is on the whole, the best thing the future can be, I think." For Woolf, the future was dark because it was unknowable. Hope in the dark is hope in the future, in its constant ability to surprise you, its expansiveness beyond the bounds of the imaginable. That dark has the richness of night, of dreams, of passion, of surrender to boundless mystery and possibility that shrink out of reach in the light, as do the stars. Other writers have found complexity in the dark. John Berger wrote recently, "In war the dark is on nobody's side, in love the dark confirms that we are together."

Another writer, Joseph Conrad, called his most famous novella *Heart of Darkness*, but in it he plays with light and dark like a master of shadow-puppets, sometimes inverting his own ingrained Victorian racism. Early in the novella, the narrator, Marlow, famously describes his childhood passion for the blank spots on maps, which still existed then. "I would put my finger on it, and say, When I grow up I will go there." And so he went to the Congo. "True, by this time it was not a blank space any more. It had got filled since my boyhood with rivers and lakes and names. It had ceased to be a blank space of delightful mystery—a white patch for a boy to dream gloriously over. It had become a place of darkness." Here the white spaces are, like Woolf's darkness, the spaces of potentiality, but Conrad's African darkness is a complicated thing. Marlow has already said of

England, "And this also has been one of the dark places of the earth." The Congo he goes to is "the heart of darkness," but that is because imperialism has indulged the savagest urges of the imperialists come to carry out the ivory trade (and, of course, "exterminate the brutes"). The white bones of elephants and skulls of native victims are the key emblems at the heart of white men's darkness.

Conrad's era had imperial maps, cartographers filling in what colonialism claimed, but our own time has its maps too, including the spectacular satellite images of the world at night, the ones where the electrical light of western Europe, the eastern United States, Japan, and the crest of Brazil glare white in a beautiful nocturne of deep blue land and black sea, letting us see literally the dark places of the earth and the light ones. Africa is once again a dark continent, with little energy consumption, and one's eyes can bathe in the beautiful darkness too of the Andes and Amazon, Siberia, Greenland, Canada's far north, and much of interior Australia—which is to say, the lightly inhabited and often still-indigenous places of the earth, the ones that have thus far escaped dense populations and industrialization (though the darkness in North Korea is about poverty). The map tells us directly about the amount of light emitted at night, the glare that eliminates the stars from view, and about the dusky blue velvet places beyond. It gives us a less direct sense of where energy consumption and population clusters are greatest, and it's in the white places of the earth, where many people together light up the night, that some of our largest catastrophes are being prepared, including the ozone thinning that has made the sun more pernicious than before to the pale-skinned.

New Mexico has banned excess light pollution. The state passed a bill in 1999 banning powerful and sky-directed night lights, counting the darkness of night as one of its natural resources. There, unless you're in one of the few real metropolises, you can see the Milky Way, which showed up in San Francisco only during the velvety darkness of the blackout brought on by the 1989 Loma Prieta quake. And the 2003 blackout across the Northeast revised that unnerving night map; the area from New York to Toronto fell off the nocturnal map, returned to the darkness of untrammeled night. I don't know what happened in the sky that night, but I know that in the great blackout of 1977, the Milky Way presided over Manhattan for the first time in perhaps a century.

Ursula K. LeGuin once noted, "To light a candle is to cast a shadow." Conversely, it's in the dark that faint light shines, starlight, candlelight, fireflies, the bioluminescence of the sea. I don't want to reverse the binaries, to make darkness good and light problematic. I want a language and an imagination where they are not enemies but perhaps dance partners, whirling each other around this globe that spends half its time away from the sun in night. I want people to remember how photography works, the medium that depends on perfect darkness within the camera to capture the image, for an image of boundless light would be purely black, an exposure in perfect darkness would show just the white of unexposed paper. The visible world depends on both.

Justice by Moonlight

⟦2003⟧

There might have been as many as four hundred activists, marching toward the ChevronTexaco refinery in Richmond, California, on September 9, 2003. When we got there, the Richmond police had arrived ahead of us and had done what we had planned to do: blockade the refinery gate through which Iraqi crude was brought in by gasoline trucks. Those of us who were willing to be arrested linked arms and sat down anyway in a single line across the wide street, twenty-two people in front of that gate choosing civil disobedience as a way to state our outrage. Outrage about the arrival of Iraqi oil in the United States, about the role of ChevronTexaco in profiting from this war, about the environmental impact of a fossil fuel economy, about the war itself, about the transnational corporations whose profits seemed to have much to do with the motives for that war, about a world run by and for those corporations.

We were acting both globally, as one of hundreds of actions around the world in solidarity with activists who had gone to Cancun to oppose the World Trade Organization's fifth ministerial meeting, and locally, in solidarity with the people of Richmond. Richmond isn't how most people picture the San Francisco Bay Area: ChevronTexaco's pipelines, smokestacks, and storage tanks dominate the city, whose poor, mostly nonwhite citizens are periodically confined to their houses or sent to the hospital by leaked fumes from the huge refinery. The march included community members and community activists, three Catholic priests, white-haired peace activists, environmentalists, and a lot of young radicals connected to the organization that had called the action, Direct Action to Stop the

War, which had also orchestrated the twenty-thousand-person shutdown of San Francisco's Financial District when the bombing began in Iraq the previous March.

Because ChevronTexaco refines stolen Iraqi oil, we were able to address the linkages between local environmental justice issues, global corporate pillage, and the ongoing war in Iraq. The profits from Iraqi oil go to the "rebuilding of Iraq"— aka Halliburton and Bechtel. It's all connected in the ugliest possible way, long chains of profit and violence and pollutants stretching around the globe, from the toxic fumes in Richmond to the ruins of Iraq. So we sat down in solidarity with the rest of the world, the organic world, the small world, the local world, the rural world, the indigenous world, the diverse world, the democratic world facing off against the WTO. Ahead of us in the east, as day turned into night, the full moon rose from a bank of glowing clouds into a clear sky. Mars shone.

I had spent the summer traveling around the West, a journey made out of beautiful summer evenings sitting with friends watching day turn to night. Sitting still at ChevronTexaco for two hours was the culmination of that summer. Sometimes you go to an action to demand peace, to speak up for the connectedness of all things. Sometimes peace is not a demand but a realization, and it felt like a strange triumph to sit there with the priests, the punk kids, the locals, as sunlight behind us became moonlight ahead. It was as beautiful as any evening in the Rockies or the Eastern Sierra, and in that stark industrial space the sky was just as wide.

Whenever I turned around, I saw that the ranks of cops were growing— eventually there were a hundred of them at our backs, the first solid row only a few steps behind us, shifting weight from armored leg to armored leg, explosives strapped to their bodies, holding clubs, holding canister rifles that could shoot tear gas, rubber bullets, beanbags, and various other "sublethal" projectiles that can cause blindness, broken bones, severe wounds—and death. When the war broke out, the Oakland police had used these weapons to injure more than sixty activists, longshore workers, and journalists at a peaceful picket to protest weapons shipments from the docks. But the Richmond police never budged that September day. And we held our line too. Kids with faces masked in bandannas—

a group known as the "black bloc," who've gotten an outrageous reputation for property destruction—walked down the line, tenderly kneeling and offering to feed us blockaders from plates of rice and beans.

Maybe what's so important to me about my summer evenings under the open sky is being out in the wide world, not just moving busily through it from one place to another, not doing what most of us in the industrialized world do most of the time, looking through a window or remaining in our boxes, but sitting with nothing between me and heaven and everything else on earth. Open to the world and the world open to me, under the same sky in which the moon had already risen over Iraq, over Cancun. Everything is connected, and that's the nightmare of how Chevron is choking kids here and benefiting from wars there and thinning the skies above. Everything is connected, and that's the dream we dreamed under as day turned to night and we sat down under the Richmond sky to link up with sister demonstrations around the world.

That week in Cancun, a huge gathering of activists came together from around the world, led by Mexican campesinos, who are among those hardest hit by free trade since NAFTA, the North American Free Trade Agreement, went into effect in 1994 and flooded Mexico with cheap industrial-agriculture corn. Activists, nongovernmental organizations, and third world countries formed unprecedented alliances in Cancun. The developing nations, led by Brazil, China, and India—which alone represent nearly half the world's people—together could stand up to the developed world and its devastating economic proposals. The talks collapsed amid ecstatic celebration. It was an extraordinary victory for activism, for democracy, for farmers, for the poor, for the power of nonviolence over the violent institutions seeking to rule the world.

Sometimes we're called antiglobalization activists or anticorporate globaliza-tion activists, but the right term might be global justice advocates. After all, to defend the local against the corporate domination of the globe, we've formed alliances that are themselves global, slender skeins of ideas, of words, of plans, of hopes spread by Internet and encounter, beautiful networks of indigenous elders and Korean farmers and Swaziland officials and punky black bloc kids, and this delicate net first pulled down the literal steel fences erected to protect the free-trade advocates from the free people and then pulled down the whole meeting.

There's a lot of Japanese poetry about moon-viewing, and I wrote to my friends that moon-viewing with a platoon of heavily armed potential adversaries behind one's back could be a whole new subgenre. One of them wrote back that it wasn't so new and recalled a few Japanese poems: "I remember one in which the poet looks at a full summer moon (over a river, I seem to recall), and thinks of people far away who, he's heard, have just suffered from a flood and are starving, and he knows they are looking at it also. The last line is on the order of 'Ah, the people of Nara are watching too: this summer moon.' " He concluded, "Moon-gazing is the nicest kind of globalization."

5

LANDSCAPES OF RESISTANCE AND REPRESSION

Fragments of the Future

The FTAA in Miami

〚2003〛

The future was being modeled on both sides of the massive steel fence erected around the Intercontinental Hotel in downtown Miami last Thursday. Inside, delegates from every nation in the Western Hemisphere but Cuba watered down some portions of the Free Trade Area of the Americas (FTAA) agreement and postponed deciding on others, in an attempt to prevent a failure as stark as that of the World Trade Organization (WTO) ministerial meeting in Cancun two months before. Outside, an army of twenty-five hundred police in full armor used a broad arsenal of weapons against thousands of demonstrators and their constitutional rights. "Not every day do you get teargassed, pepper-sprayed, and hit in the face," said Starhawk, a prominent figure in the global anticapitalism movement, who experienced all three Thursday.

Since the Seattle surprise of 1999, it has become standard procedure to erect a miniature police state around globalization summits, and it's hard not to read these rights-free zones as prefigurations of what full-blown corporate globalization might bring. After all, this form of globalization would essentially suspend local, regional, and national rights of self-determination over labor, environmental, and agricultural conditions in the name of the dubious benefits of the free market, benefits that would be enforced by unaccountable transnational authorities acting primarily to protect the rights of capital. At a labor forum held the day before the major actions in Miami, Dave Bevard, a laid-off union metalworker, referred to this new world order as "government of the corporations, by the corporations, for the corporations."

The corporate agenda of the North American Free Trade Agreement

(NAFTA) and related globalization treaties is demonstrated most famously by the case of MTBE, a gasoline additive that causes severe damage to human health and the environment. When California phased it out, the Canadian corporation Methanex filed a lawsuit demanding nearly a billion dollars in compensation from the U.S. government for profits lost because of the ban. Under NAFTA rules, corporations have an absolute right to profit, and local laws must not interfere. Poisoning the well is no longer a crime; stopping the free flow of poison is.

The FTAA, modeled after NAFTA, was originally intended to create a borderless trade zone that would encompass the whole hemisphere (except, of course, Cuba). That globalization is an economic disaster for many existing industries is so apparent that, while paying lip service to a borderless economy, both presidents Clinton and Bush have attempted to protect the U.S. steel industry from cheap foreign imports, though neither has done anything about the export of former union jobs to the maquiladoras of Mexico (and now those jobs are fleeing Mexico for yet cheaper venues in the infamous "race to the bottom," while more and more white-collar U.S. jobs, from programming to data processing, are also being exported).

And it's a fact that even the richest nations—the United States and the European Union—won't live up to their own rhetoric of capitalism without borders, which trips up the globalization agendas they pursue. Both maintain high agricultural subsidies that undermine the ability of poorer nations to generate export-crop income or in some cases—as with corn in Mexico—even to compete successfully domestically. NAFTA, which will be a decade old this New Year's, devastated hundreds of thousands of Mexican subsistence farmers. Florida's citrus industry would be undermined by tariff-free Brazilian imports, and small Kentucky tobacco farmers are going out of business because of imports of the crop from the developing world. The question now is not whether globalized commodities are profitable but who profits, and the answer is usually the already rich, while the rest get poorer.

The Clinton administration genuinely believed in the corporate internationalism that the word *globalization* stands for, and the FTAA talks were first launched by Clinton nine years ago. If there's one thing to be grateful to the Bush junta for, it's their commitment to a narrowly defined national self-interest that makes their pursuit of globalization pretty indistinguishable from old-fashioned colonialism and thereby less inviting: you open your borders to our products and principles, perhaps after a little arm-twisting, and then we'll pretty much do whatever we want. This is much the same screw-the-world-community policy that made Bush and Co. disregard the U.N. Security Council and world opinion to pursue the current war in Iraq with only a few allies. The solution to the collapse in Cancun and stalemate in Miami will be pursuit of a similarly splintering agenda—bilateral trade agreements, mostly with nations the United States can bully. As the WTO was collapsing, the United States was already turning to the FTAA, and as it becomes evident that the FTAA will likely flop, the Bush administration has stepped up its pursuit of bilateral trade agreements with nations in Latin America, southern Africa, and elsewhere.

Cancun was a watershed victory because more than twenty nations in the global south, led by Brazil, stood up to the United States and the European Union, urged on by the activists and nongovernmental organizations (NGOs) who were part of the continuum of conversation there. In Miami, there was no such continuum and no exhilarating victory, but there is room enough for those who oppose corporate globalization to continue resisting it. The FTAA conference dissolved a day early, having achieved only what has been dubbed "FTAA lite." This version allows member nations to withdraw from specific aspects of the FTAA agreement and otherwise weakens its impact. Brazil, the economic giant in the south, had objected to two provisions: protection of foreign investment and intellectual property rules. FTAA lite let Brazil win on those fronts. As Lori Wallach of Public Citizen put it, "All that was agreed was to scale back the FTAA's scope and punt all of the hard decisions to an undefined future venue so as to not make Miami the Waterloo of the FTAA."

THE WAR AT HOME

It's popular to say that corporate globalization is war by other means, but what went down in Miami during the FTAA skipped the part about other means. And though it was most directly—thanks to clubs, pellet guns, rubber bullets, tear gas, pepper spray, and other weapons—an assault on the bodies of protestors, it was primarily an assault against the right of the people peaceably to assemble and other First Amendment guarantees, a dramatic example of how hallowed American rights are being dismantled in the name of the war on terrorism.

For months beforehand, Police Chief John Timoney—engineer of the coup against constitutional rights at the 2000 Republican National Convention when he headed Philadelphia's police force—had portrayed protestors as terrorists and the gathering in Miami as a siege of the city. Much of the money for militarizing Miami came, appropriately enough, from an $8.5 million rider tacked onto the $87 million spending bill for the war in Iraq. Miami will pay directly, however, both in revenue lost from shutting the city down and, presumably, in activists' lawsuits for police brutality and civil rights violations.

Perhaps the silliest example of the paranoiac reaction to the arrival of protestors was the removal of all coconuts from downtown Miami palm trees, lest activists throw them at the authorities—whether such attacks would have come after first shaking or scaling the trees was not made clear. The city also apparently removed every outdoor trash can from downtown; second-guessing terrorists is an exercise whose creativity knows no bounds.

One of the most explicit ways the FTAA policing was modeled after the "war on terror" abroad was the police decision to "embed" reporters. While a number of reporters—looking dorky in their borrowed helmets—joined the Miami cops, protestors invited the press to join the other side as well, and many did. (Some got teargassed and reported on it.)

Many activists in the streets said that one of the functions of this Miami police mobilization was to adjust the American public to the militarization of public space and public life, to a John Ashcroft–style America. It may also have been an attempt to condition police to functioning as a military force against the civil society they're supposed to serve. The city of Miami and a few nearby communities passed emergency laws banning basic civil liberties such as the right of assembly, laws that could easily be challenged—but not before the FTAA was over. Activists were already talking about what kind of police state will take hold of

Manhattan during the Republican convention next year. And civil libertarians are taking note of the way dissent of every kind is being reconfigured as terrorism.

THE WAR OF THE POSSIBLE WORLDS

Thursday, November 20, was like a day out of the science fiction movies I grew up on, the ones where the world we know is in ruins and guerrilla war rages in the rubble. Central Miami had been totally shut down. Stores and offices were closed, nothing was being bought or sold, no one was driving, the Metromover elevated rail system was locked up, few went to work that day. The FTAA negotiators from thirty-four nations of the Western Hemisphere were sequestered in the tower of the Intercontinental Hotel, and occasionally I'd see some of the hotel people, tiny on the roof of that skyscraper, watching the turbulence below. We must have looked like ants. Helicopters droned overhead, reportedly using high-tech surveillance equipment to pinpoint activists for arrest or assault by ground forces.

Thursday morning, the city was abandoned but for those twenty-five hundred cops and an approximately equivalent number of activists. We've seen the world Miami was that day in movies that range from *The Terminator* to *Tank Girl* to Terry Gilliam's *Brazil*. Maybe the earliest and most somber version can be found in H. G. Wells's *The Time Machine*, in which humanity has diverged into two species: the bestial subterranean Morlocks who prey on the pretty lamblike Eloi. We had moments of being Tank Girl and moments of being lambs to the slaughter. Friday afternoon, Eddie Yuen, who's written about the antiglobalization movement since Seattle, commented to me that at these antiglobalization summits, "There are laboratories of dissent and laboratories of repression, and right now the laboratories of repression are dominant."

The police—except for a squadron of bare-kneed bicycle cops—were in full riot gear: black helmets with visors; black body armor that protected limbs, crotches, and torso; combat boots. All seemed to carry long wooden clubs, and many had the rifles that fire "sublethal" rubber bullets, beanbags, and other projectiles capable of causing severe injury—and even death. Four years before, in Seattle, I had seen the dystopian future: it was a Darth Vader cop guarding the ruins of a shattered Star-bucks. Now there were twenty-five hundred of them, and they weren't guarding, they were marching. As environmental activist and pagan author Starhawk com-mented, "It wasn't the worst I've ever seen, compared to Israel and Palestine, and Genoa [where Italian police engaged in bloody assault and torture against three hun-dred thousand activists come to protest the G8 summit in the summer of 2001]. But there was a quality of sheer brute calculated fascism that's hard to equal."

Some activists were picked off or hassled long before they got to the site of the early morning demonstration. More police were waiting for us when we got there, ranks of cops, two or three thick, blocking off streets, clubs clutched ready for action. Periodically they would move in and herd us in yet another direction, and they never let us get near the steel fence that steelworkers shouting against the FTAA had marched past the afternoon before. Sometimes they would come out clubbing and shooting. Local television claimed that activists threw smoke bombs at the police, but what they videotaped was activists lobbing back the tear gas canisters that had been fired at us.

At midmorning, when it looked like they might surround us and engage in wholesale arrests, I escorted a noncitizen out of the last possible exit from the scene. Another member of our group, a professor with a bandage around his head—he'd been clubbed from behind and bled profusely—joined us, and we stayed on the sidelines until the permitted march of perhaps ten thousand union members came by at noon on its way through the abandoned city and then back to the safety zone of a rented arena.

As the unions dispersed, the violence resurfaced. Puffs of tear gas rose up from the crowd in the distance. The helicopters roared overhead, the only machine sound on that day when cars had been shut out of the central city, except for the occasional police vans and buses bringing reinforcements or hauling away the arrested. What looked like an amphibious tank rolled around in front of the steel fence. Snatch squads moved into the crowd to seize individuals. A few vul-tures had circled the skyscrapers in the morning, and by mid-afternoon there must have been fifty of them, a flock of black carrion-eaters soaring sometimes above, sometimes below the level of the helicopters.

The police rushed the crowd again, becoming so violent that the activists splintered into small groups fleeing north into Overtown, an African American neighborhood of lush vacant lots, boarded-up buildings, affable people out on the streets, and evident destitution. Sirens screamed past us, and small groups were pounced upon or hunted farther from downtown. My group was carrying a number of huge puppets that had been used in the morning's procession. Weary, we came to a stop under a row of street trees, where we wouldn't be so visible to the helicopters hovering low for surveillance. Just this kind of hiding and being hunted made it clear that what was going on was warfare of a sort. This day, more than a hundred would be injured, twelve hospitalized, and more than two hundred arrested.

Later that night, people would be pulled out of their cars at gunpoint or stopped on the street for no particular reason—not just the young but ministers, middle-aged NGO workers, anyone and everyone. And the next day, more than fifty activists were arrested in a peaceful vigil outside the jail, where many of the previously arrested languished. "They were surrounded by riot police and ordered to disperse," reported organizers. "As they did, police opened fire and blocked the streets, preventing many from leaving. We are now receiving reports from people being released or calling from jail that there is excessive brutality, sexual assault and torture going on inside. People of color, queer and transgender prisoners are particularly being targeted." Sunday, many of those arrested were released.

The visionary slogan of the antiglobalization movement is "Another world is possible." This time around, some of the steelworkers had the slogan emblazoned across the backs of their royal-blue union t-shirts. What we don't talk about so much is that many worlds are possible, and some of them are hell.

FRAGMENTS

Seattle in 1999 has become a genesis story in which the revolution began as Eden. There were tens of thousands of us blockading the WTO, the story goes, and we were all as one: "turtles and teamsters" is the cliché. Actually, there were about fifty thousand in the big labor-organized parade, and ten thousand or less—few union members among them—shut down the streets around the WTO meeting on November 30, 1999. The various groups coexisted nicely, but few articulated a profound common ground for us all (though the globalization issue has pushed activists from labor to the Sierra Club to develop a broader analysis and to reach for broader coalitions).

After the "black bloc" of young anarchist activists first made its presence known by smashing up the windows of Niketown, Starbucks, and a few other downtown Seattle corporate entities, some of those who supported the blockade sparked internal squabbles when they decried the property destruction. The Seattle police were brutal, attacking activists, passersby, nearby neighborhoods, and even an older woman on the way to her chemotherapy appointment. Seattle was no Eden but a miracle all the same, and a huge surprise for the world—both that direct action could be so effective and that globalization was not going to go forward unimpeded. Four years later, the tank of corporate capitalism that seemed to be inexorably advancing on the world is idling its engines or going in circles, and it could yet end up in a ditch.

Cancun was another miracle, notable for the fluid circulation of passion and politics between the developing nations that stood up to the United States and the European Union; the NGO activists, who were both inside at the ministerial meeting and outside in the streets; and the street activists, who included Yucatán and Korean farmers and a fair representation of the rest of the world, from Canada to Africa. As in Seattle, the activists stiffened the resolve of the poor nations, and the poor nations stood up for themselves against the agendas of the rich ones.

The street activists in Miami were overwhelmingly white Americans, and there was no such porousness: the Intercontinental Hotel was for all intents and purposes hermetically sealed. NGOs had no role in the FTAA talks or even access to the hotel. AFL-CIO President John J. Sweeney went to visit the Convergence Center, the warehouse north of downtown where the direct action was organized and decried the police violence (which never targeted the union people). But the protests felt fragmentary: beforehand, the direct action contingent had had to negotiate long and hard to get the unions—who acted as if they owned the day—to consent to even letting the direct action supporters demonstrate on the same day. Though we joined the labor march, they didn't join us, and the teach-ins held at the Doubletree Hotel and other venues around town seemed to separate out more circumspect activists from the stuff in the street.

Uprisings, protest, civil disobedience—the stuff in the street—still matter, even though they don't change the world every time. Sometimes it's just an exercise of democracy and bravado, exercise in the sense of maintaining the strength and ability to intervene at a time when it will count. A month ago, Bolivians in the streets and roads of their own nation forced the resignation of their millionaire president, who was trying to export the impoverished nation's resources. An insurgent spirit and direct action are radicalizing Bolivia, Argentina, Brazil, Ecuador, and Venezuela. The surprise in Miami isn't that so little was agreed to but, with the revolt against neoliberalism well underway in South America, that anything was.

Jailbirds I Have Loved

[2004]

About a month ago, I planned to commit civil disobedience in New York—there were some Republicans in town for their national convention, as you may remember—but circumstances beyond my control put me a few hundred miles farther north at the crucial moment, so I did the next best thing: stopped at Walden Pond on my way back to Manhattan. *Walden*—the book, not the pond—turns 150 this year, but the people at the pond that hot August day were paying more homage to cool water than to cultural history. Most of the swimmers seemed to be locals for whom the site was part of their familiar landscape, not outlanders like us paying homage to the pond and the guy who cultivated beans and contrary thoughts by its side from 1845 to 1847. It wasn't what I expected: the trees shrouded everything up to the water's edge; a secondary thoroughfare full of commuters ran very nearby, so that after paying to park in a large lot, you had to dodge speeding commuter vehicles. I didn't mind that it had become a social or a suburban place, for Thoreau, in his legendary sojourn at the pond, never intended to be remote from society for long and reported on the train speeding by his retreat.

If it was a retreat. In one of the most resonant passages in his book, he enumerates among his many visitors "runaway slaves with plantation manners, who listened from time to time, like the fox in the fable, as if they heard the hounds a-baying on their track, and looked at me beseechingly, as much as to say,—'Oh Christian, will you send me back?' One real runaway slave, among the rest, whom I helped to forward toward the north star." Politics came tramping through those woods, which were never far from Concord, where his mother and sister housed runaway slaves, or from the conflicts of the era. During his time spent at Walden, Thoreau became an outspoken antiwar activist and tax resister, spent that famous night in jail, and on January 26, 1848, he delivered as a talk at the Concord Lyceum the great American landmark "Civil Disobedience."

I did wonder a little about which Thoreau the sesquicentennial of Walden events and reprints was commemorating. The pond is now Walden Pond State Reservation, a 411-acre reserve, with lifeguards on duty that day; but Thoreau is still unreserved and unsafe in his writings, advocating that "when . . . a whole country is unjustly overrun and conquered by a foreign army, and subjected to military law, I think it is not too soon for honest men to rebel and revolutionize." Homages to Thoreau sometimes seem to have domesticated him first, as have the avalanches of books of nature quotes taken from his longer writings. Those passages leave out the dangerous Thoreau, the one who went around suggesting that the abolition of the government might be a good thing and defending John Brown, who was already in jail for taking up arms against slavery.

Of course, Thoreau is no longer dangerous in the sense that he was in 1849, the year "Civil Disobedience" was first published. That transcript of the earlier talk, given soon after he was resident at Walden, inveighs against slavery and the 1846–1848 war with Mexico (whereby we acquired that nation's northern half, now known as the American Southwest). Slavery is ended, and the long-ago war on Mexico is concluded. But he is still dangerous as a man who cared more about justice than law and saw that the two were not uncommonly in conflict. He was the man who argued that voting was not enough, that any cooperation with an unjust government was complicity in that injustice; the one who still shames me for paying taxes during wartime; the voice that declares, "I say, break the law. Let your life be a counter-friction to stop the machine. What I have to do is to see, at any rate, that I do not lend myself to the wrong which I condemn."

People in public and private argued about whether demonstrating in New York against Bush and the war was strategic for the election or whether it would feed into portrayals of progressives as dangerous fringe elements. Within the argument that we should have stayed home was a larger argument about whether political demonstrations and civil disobedience are largely media stunts or whether they're moral acts taken to change the world with less of an eye to press coverage.

We should always, especially when it is difficult, exercise our freedoms of speech and assembly, and I mean the word *exercise*. Rights are like muscles: they atrophy and aren't there when you need them if you don't use them. The First Amendment is in trouble not just because of U.S. Attorney General John Ashcroft and the USA Patriot Act, but because of a pall of self-censorship—some have spoken up with great courage, but many have been silenced not only by the acts of the authorities but by the prison of their own fear. Still, if people could stand up to Pinochet, if the Mothers of the Plaza de Mayo could march in Buenos Aires during the time of the generals, if people could speak up in Prague in the 1980s, we can here, far more than we do. An atmosphere of repression exists specifically because people don't speak up against it. When you speak up, you are not repressed—you might be suppressed or punished, but you have freed yourself. Too, a tyranny can rise more easily by shutting up a thousand people than a million, and that's a reason to stand up and speak out.

Thoreau was more optimistic, writing, "I know this well, that if one thousand, if one hundred, if ten men whom I could name—if ten honest men only,—ay, if one honest man in this State of Massachusetts, ceasing to hold slaves, were actually to withdraw from this copartnership, and be locked up in the county jail therefore, it would be the abolition of slavery in America. For it matters not how small the beginning may seem to be."

The National Lawyers Guild, in its report titled "The Assault on Free Speech, Public Assembly, and Dissent," has been more pessimistic of late. "The facts assembled in the following pages attest to the pathology of a government so frightened of its own citizens that it classifies them as probable enemies," the report's introduction begins. It's a statement that might answer quite a different question about the war on terror: why have the soldiers in Iraq been so underequipped for their war, while the Miami police last November at the Free Trade Area of the Americas meeting and the New York police at the Republican convention were able to draw on endless new technologies and resources? "The abuses have been so aggressive that rights of free assembly and free speech guaranteed by the First Amendment of the United States Constitution are simply no longer available to the citizens of this country," states the preface of the Lawyers Guild report.

Those rights are indeed under assault, but they are not unavailable for those willing to take the risks or pay the costs. "No, you can't have my rights, I'm still using them," said a sign one woman carried in that long, passionate, stymied August 29 march against the war, George Bush, the Republican Party, and its 2004 convention at Madison Square Garden, up Seventh Avenue to Madison Square Garden and then to—wherever—not to Central Park, since the city's Republican mayor claimed that democracy was bad for the grass.

Being afraid of how the media would represent us was just part of a larger landscape of fear I met with on the East Coast. "Don't get arrested," acquaintances told me over and over, as though getting arrested was some road of no return, as though going to a demonstration with half a million others was a terrible risk even for those of us who won't ever want security clearances.

Certainly, the mayor, the New York police, and the attorney general had done everything they could to discourage people from coming. As had the media. One of the worst problems facing democracy in America is that a free press, while not entirely eradicated, has gone underground, on the Internet and in the small magazines. The mainstream media have generally taken up and run with the allegations the Bush administration uses to justify putting the First Amendment in mothballs and staging preemptive strikes against potential exercisers of free speech and assembly.

Exercising your rights, by these accounts, was pretty much tantamount to terrorism. ABC News reported that the New York Police Department was tracking "56 potentially dangerous people . . . the anarchist groups which disrupted the W.T.O. conference in Seattle in 1999." The FBI "interviewed"—or, in the words of civil rights advocates, "intimidated"—activists across the country who "the government believed were plotting to firebomb media vehicles at the Democratic National Convention," a rather improbable crime for people committed to public actions and nonviolent principles. After the Republican convention, the *New*

York Times reported that "five years ago in Seattle, for example, there was wide-spread arson" and then spoke admiringly of New York City's reign of repression, stating that "Starbucks survived, the streets were not ablaze, and the police did not wipe acid from their faces."

I saw the widespread arson in Seattle. It consisted of one mostly empty dumpster with feeble flames contesting with the northwestern drizzle. Nor was there ever evidence that anyone planned to set the streets ablaze or assault fellow human beings in such a vicious manner, as the *Times* insinuated (with the implication that if those crimes did not happen, credit must go to law enforcement). Still beat your wife? No? Thank the police. Seattle was constantly referenced as a moment of criminal violence. In fact, it was one of the great moments of civil disobedience in American history. Ten thousand or so people, in concert with protests from India to Iceland, took an oppositional step beyond the big march that was vocally opposed to the World Trade Organization's summit downtown. They sat down in intersections all around the WTO meeting and shut it down as it was supposed to begin. The Seattle police had not anticipated this and went berserk afterward with clubs, tear gas, and enough violence against activists and scads of passersby to keep a lot of class action suits afloat for a long time.

"On the tear gas–shrouded streets of Seattle," reported the *L.A. Times* back then, "the unruly forces of democracy collided with the elite world of trade policy. And when the meeting ended in failure on Friday, the elitists had lost and the debate had changed forever." It was a world-changing moment, the golden dawn of a so-far not-so-rosy new millennium. But there wasn't any activist violence against living beings. (Some "black bloc" kids did do a little downtown window smashing and spray-painting and stirred up an interesting side debate about whether property damage alone constitutes violence.) The year 1999 was the otherwise uncommemorated 150th anniversary of the publication of "Civil Disobedience," though, come to think of it, ten thousand anarchists and environmentalists standing up against giving the world away to corporations is perhaps the most apt anniversary event that eco-anarchist Henry David could have dreamed of.

The police and the media willfully, if not consciously, mistake what kind of danger civil disobedients pose. Martin Luther King Jr., that reader of Thoreau and great advocate of nonviolent civil disobedience, was a dangerous man in his time, because he posed a threat to the status quo, and it was for that reason that the FBI followed him and many hated him. Like Thoreau, he went to jail; like Thoreau, he posed no physical danger to anyone. But to admit that activists can be dangers to the status quo is to admit first that there is a status quo, second that the status quo may be an unjust and unjustifiable thing, and third that it can indeed be changed, by passionate people and nonviolent means. Better to portray activists as criminals and the status quo as the natural order—and celebrate revolutionaries only long after their causes are won and their voices are softened by time, or misrepresentation, for Thoreau and King are still dangerous men to those who pay attention to their words. And so for my own as-yet unassimilated generation of activists, the fiction of a violent past has been manufactured, just as the fiction of spitting in returning soldiers' faces was fabricated to damn the activists who opposed the war in Vietnam.

In 1999, civil disobedients in this country changed the world by bringing the conversation about globalization to the first world and joining the movements that brought the WTO into its state of stalemate. Exercising your rights doesn't always achieve something so remarkable, but the exercise is important anyway. Rights are only valuable if they are used. My heroine from that recent spell of First Amendment wrestling matches in New York is a fellow San Franciscan, the sister of a friend, June Brashares, who along with many other members of Code Pink got into the Republican convention (in her case, she thinks it was her fake pearls, along with a nice blue suit, that got her through security). "I wanted to get inside to show some of that dissent that was not being shown," she told me. "I'm very much in opposition to the war in Iraq. The lives that have been destroyed and the people that have been killed—I care very much about those things."

She stood up during Bush's acceptance speech to unfurl a banner that said, "Bush lies, people die." June is very polite and didn't interrupt the president, and she would have left if asked, but she was immediately tackled by burly security guards just for holding up dissenting words. And so, as she was dragged away, she shouted the words on her confiscated banner, though she was drowned out by the nearby party loyalists attempting to mask her voice by chanting, "Four more years." That ruckus was so loud that it rattled the president, who paused, looked cranky, and lost his place. June says of the many taped versions of the president's speech she watched, "He's got this frozen moment like the Pet Goat moment [Bush's famous paralysis, while reading to Florida schoolchildren, upon being told of the planes crashing into the World Trade Center towers] and looks to the side and kinda smiles and goes to go on, and then he stumbles. It made a lot of activists really happy, it made their night watching him drone on and on and then seeing this protest." Some television stations showed the disruption clearly, some did not. Thoreau said, "I say, break the law. Let your life be a counter-friction to stop the machine." She did. We should. And could.

Still.

Making It Home

Travels outside the Fear Economy

〚2005〛

In the final words of my 1994 book *Savage Dreams*, I claimed the Nevada Test Site as home—"This time I was only going back," I wrote about leaving the site, "because I was already home." To claim this place where a thousand nuclear bombs have been exploded as home was to embrace the generosity of the desert's light and space and of the community gathered there, and to assume responsibility for the legacies of the Indian and nuclear wars that will never come to something as simple as an end. This question of what home is comes up for me again and again in this era of real estate obsession, of *Dwell* and *Nest* magazines, and of abandonment or loss of any larger sense of belonging.

Even the word *home* is treacherous in this country's iron age of homeland security and homelessness. The first term implies that the nation is a home, but only by imagining everything beyond those bounds as dangerous, alien, and ominous. As we have learned during all those orange and chartreuse and maroon alerts, security is invoked only as the other face of insecurity, the threats that are supposed to make us close our doors and borders to strangers, to difference, to negotiation, to trust and hope. Homelessness is at the other end of the scale: it references the domestic interior that, thanks to our homeland economics, is denied to many people nowadays.

Somewhere in between, something is missing. The answer might be about being at home in the world, an answer that immediately questions homeland security, with its portrayal of everything outside a neatly defined home as a threat, and also questions homelessness, for these people are out in a harsh world that is

adamantly not home, made unwelcoming by the retreat from any embrace of common good and civil society. The retreat is spurred by the twin forces of privatization and what I now think of as the fear economy, the governmentally produced
fears—cold wars, terrorisms—that make for a more docile populace (and the government policies that have made the world genuinely less safe). Docile people are
less bold about challenging authority or otherwise venturing into the public
realm, a nice spur to the privatization that affects not only resources and rules but
psyches. It is the abandonment of this public sphere that has left the corpse of
democracy to be gnawed by the CEOs who are now also our federal government.

The forester and poet Gary Snyder likes to say that the most radical thing you
can do is to stay home. This implies a fine bioregional localness—but not as local
as the interior of your home. Rather, I think he means home as a foundation from
which to venture, a ground to stand on so that you can stand for something; and
home as a sense of community, of knowledge, of belonging through commitment
rather than only privilege. And this implies what it might mean to be at home in
the world, to have what for nomads is a winter camp—a familiar place to come
back to, but in part so that you can venture out and broaden your horizons, make
your peace with the world, embrace difference.

And here I think the literal public sphere—streets, subways, plazas, libraries,
post offices—matters as the staging ground for the imagined public sphere, the
arena in which people think about politics and public life and feel a sense of
embeddedness in it as both beneficiaries and caretakers. I think about this sense of
home in my own city as I cross paths constantly with people who live in a different sense of the same place—the undocumented immigrants who know the
Mission District, the construction sites, and the routes to their villages in
Mexico; the African American kids who often have hardly been out of the city at
all, even to the hills and beaches immediately across the Golden Gate, but have a
careful social map of their peers across the city. But they live in part in public.

I think about it too as I encounter the more suburbanized of my fellow citizens, who believe in home as what you have a mortgage on, with the rest of the
world beyond the bounds of that own secured homeland, these neighbors who
seem to leave their houses only to get into their cars to go to places they know—

perhaps know from other cities, the Starbucks and Walgreens that make every-where into nowhere nowadays. Nothing on earth is sadder than their rummage sales, where they sell off the Ikea and Pottery Barn trappings they will replace at the next stop in this world, which for them must seem so much like an infinite air-port without exits, familiar to the point of endless repetition but hardly home in any more passionate or particular sense. In the affluent world, you are never really at home but also are never really away, for the homogenizing forces of global capi-tal bring the familiar lattes and logo products to the far corners of the globe.

In the Bay Area, one of our more annoying Silicon Valley billionaires recently announced plans to build a 72,000-square-foot home that will essentially be a city made for one man and his family, but an impoverished city, empty of encounters, limited by their own imaginations. Kierkegaard once announced that thieves and the rich have in common that they live in hiding, and in this regard you can see that in some ways the rich are poorer than the ordinary citizens who don't fear to mingle with strangers and therefore own their cities or towns—who are at home in the world. Some of the less affluent children of suburbia embrace my city whole-heartedly, the kids living with lots of roommates who hold their cell phone conver-sations and smoke their cigarettes on the front steps, do their homework in cafés, and barrel around on bikes.

When I wrote about walking, I learned that one version of home is everything you can walk to. Thus I, with my few hundred square feet of rented space, can also claim a thousand-acre park that ends at the Pacific with a beach full of seabirds; four or five movie theaters; hundreds of restaurants, bars, and cafés; a big public library; way too many tattoo parlors; a fine collection of monuments, views, promenades, and more.

The Latinoization of the United States poses the interesting question of whether Latinos will urbanize us with a more dynamic life on the street before we suburbanize them—both forces are at work in the Southwest. Here is where we see that infrastructure is not enough, for different communities can privatize or socialize the same spaces; you can't design civil society, though you can design civil society's habitat out of existence.

An urban activist recently said to me, apropos of something else, "But they don't make kids with legs anymore," speaking of how the kids in the immigrant Latino community where she has spent her life don't walk around much anymore, kept inside both by television and by their parents' fears. I fear what will become of a generation kept under house arrest: Who will they be without the education in adventure, unfamiliarity, straying and finding the way back, damming creeks and climbing trees that was practically a birthright for most American kids (except the urban ones who had their own turf of tramlines and vacant lots)? How will they care about an environment they have barely encountered—for, after all, so many naturalists and environmentalists began by turning over logs to look at insects, by wandering the hills, by finding their way into a world in which human beings were not alone? How will these kids be at home in a world they have hardly visited?

There are no grand solutions, only everyday practices of paying attention, of valuing difference and the openness that comes with some risk, of rethinking home, and of refusing to be afraid.

Mirror in the Street

[2004]

Nineteenth-century Paris was often compared to a wilderness by its poets and writers. They sensed that the city had somehow become so vast, so magical and unpredictable, that one could wander it as though it were not made by human beings and reason, but rather had sprung up with all the mystery and intricacy of a jungle. And the feral city was perceived as a pleasure, at least for those bold and free enough to venture into its byways and dangers. Alexandre Dumas wrote about "Les Mohicans du Paris," and many saw themselves as explorers.

Before gas lighting, European cities had been as dark as a forest at night—darker than much of the countryside, for the buildings blocked starlight and moonlight—and predators roamed the byways, pouncing on unsuspecting stragglers. You dressed down or hired a torchbearer and guards, or both. Or you stayed home—if you had one. In the mid-twentieth century, the great German-Jewish cultural theorist and Parisian Walter Benjamin wrote again and again of Paris as a labyrinth, a forest, a mystery, and a joy. He once reminisced, "I saw sunset and dawn, but between the two I found myself a shelter. Only those for whom poverty or vice turns the city into a landscape in which they stray from dark till sunrise know it in a way denied to me."

In recent years, American cities have become a wilderness of another sort. The homeless live in our built environment as though they are not the species for which it was built. Doorways are their caves, boxes their beds of boughs, fountains their pools, sidewalks their porches and dining rooms. Like backpackers and nomads, they must carry their goods with them in bags or shopping carts. Like jackals and buzzards, they live by scavenging the leftovers of more privileged predators. They roam exposed to the elements, mapping the small routes of daily survival—the recycling center where cans and bottles turn into cash; the places that serve free food, offer social services, or allow congregation. The homeless live in the city as though it were a wilderness: not a wilderness of symbiosis, of beauty, of complexity, in the way hunter-gatherers might live in a landscape too well-known to be a wilderness, but a wilderness that is not safe, not reliable, not made for them. It is the wilderness into which Old Testament exiles were driven. It's the world we've made of late.

But it is not they who have become savages in the wild city. We have. They are there because we—the we who elected Ronald Reagan, who chose to vote for the tax cuts that meant drastic social services cuts, who allowed the New Deal and the Great Society to be canceled, the we who looked the other way or did not resist hard enough—decided to create this wilderness for them. I remember that twenty years ago, when the huge army of the homeless was first being turned out into American cities, a writer expressed shock that this wealthiest nation had become like Brazil or India, a place where the affluent stepped over the dying on their way to the opera. I thought of this recently when friends from suburbia came to town and I guided them around my familiar haunts. They were shocked and a little alarmed by the homeless, and I realized I'd grown accustomed to people living on the street. I was not afraid of them and tried to give them back, in conversation and body language, a little of the dignity that had been stripped from them. But I was also troublingly accustomed to a society in which people suffer, overdose, go mad, and die in the streets.

Perhaps my friends were frightened by the homeless because the sight of dirty, deranged people was so unfamiliar to them. Or maybe they couldn't distinguish between suffering and danger, and the homeless are often portrayed as dangerous. In all my years of walking the city streets, often alone, often at night, I've never been menaced by an evidently homeless person (as opposed to, say, careening luxury cars). Some of them become landmarks: the older man in the wide felt hat who was always on the park bench when I went running, seeming more like a country squire than a desperado; the sad woman sitting cross-legged on the same corner near city hall for years, day and night, rocking back and forth and holding a stuffed animal amid all her tattered belongings.

The homeless may indeed be a danger, but only to our idea of ourselves. They represent how deranged, how desperate, and how dirty human beings can become, something that most of us would rather not know. They represent how wide the spectrum of human nature is and how fragile our own civility is—though many of them are among the most polite and gracious people I encounter every day. Some of them seem to be homeless because they lack the initiative and cunning to survive in a world where security—long-term employment, unions, blue-collar jobs, affordable housing—is vanishing and we must all fend for ourselves, not just by working but by calculating, by planning, by competing, by abandoning and reinventing our sense of self. They are anachronisms, the people who might have done well in stable jobs that no longer exist, and when I give them food or money, they say, "God bless you," a lot of them, an old-fashioned response.

In parts of Asia, beggars are necessary to society because they allow others to honor their obligation to give. The Buddhist monks of southeast Asia, for example, take a vow not to deal with money and allow nonmonks to receive the spiritual benefit of giving: poverty and spirituality have a long acquaintance. Gavin Newsom, the restaurateur-businessman who is now San Francisco's mayor, built his career by beating up on the homeless (though he has since somewhat redeemed himself). John Burton, who represents San Francisco in the state Senate, was disgusted enough to fight back. "St. Francis was a beggar," said the signs he put up on the streets, and "Jesus gave alms to the poor."

In cities around the country, the homeless are most often treated primarily as an eyesore for others. Policies often focus on moving them away or making them invisible, as if they were a problem of aesthetics, not ethics, as if our comfort, not theirs, were all that is at stake. The homeless also signify that the distribution of wealth in this wealthiest society the world has ever known is itself an atrocity against humanity as well as against the environment, for the armies of the homeless were produced in large degree by decisions made by the affluent. Their decisions to defund mental health programs and dump the patients, to turn basic human needs for housing and health care into speculative commodities whose upward spiral has enriched the few and burdened the many, were decisions to break the social contract and try to buy their way out of it.

More and more often, the wealthy try to buy replacements for a functioning society—armed guards and gated communities in place of social justice, bottled water and expensive cancer cures in place of unpolluted resources, private schools in place of the good public education that was once a backbone of this nation, the stock market in place of social security. From Franklin Delano Roosevelt through at least Richard Nixon (who was considering universal health care and passed the Clean Water and Clean Air acts), the United States became more of a society, a place that recognized interdependence and obligation toward each other. From Ronald Reagan's presidency on, we have dismantled that social contract. The homeless are frightening because they are a mirror: in their fear, in the uncertainty of their predicament, in their hunger, in their desperation, we see that we have gone feral.

Liberation Conspiracies

〖2005〗

Bury the Chains: Prophets and Rebels in the Fight to Free an Empire's Slaves, by Adam Hochschild (Boston: Houghton Mifflin, 2005), 480 pp.

LABYRINTHS

Mark Lombardi's art consists of colossal drawings of networks of power, connecting politicians, capitalists, and corporations into intricate maps, like medieval cosmology or Kabbalah diagrams, whose huge arcs and circles linking the small handwritten names are as visually beautiful as they are politically daunting. His most famous work was about the BCCI (Bank of Credit and Commerce International, also known as the Bank of Crooks and Criminals) banking scandal. It linked up the bin Laden and Bush families long before the film *Fahrenheit 9/11*, even before the 2000 election and Bush's illegitimate apotheosis as president.

New York critic Frances Richard wrote of this work:

Lombardi's drawings—which map in elegantly visual terms the secret deals and suspect associations of financiers, politicians, corporations, and governments— dictate that the more densely lines ray out from a given node, the more deeply that figure is embroiled in the tale Lombardi tells. . . . The drawing is done on pale beige paper, in pencil. It follows a time-line, with dates arrayed across three horizontal tiers. These in turn support arcs denoting personal and corporate alliances, the whole comprising a skeletal resume of George W. Bush's career in the oil business. In other words, the drawing, like all Lombardi's work, is a post-Conceptual reinvention of history painting.

After September 11, 2001, the FBI visited the Whitney Museum to examine Lombardi's drawings for clues they might yield about the conspiracy that gave rise to the catastrophe.

Lombardi committed suicide in March 2000, for complex reasons, but it's easy to imagine him as a character in a Jorge Luis Borges story dying of Borgesian reasons, for Lombardi's drawings recall Borges's library of Babel, his Garden of Forking Paths, the Zohar, Zeno's paradox, or the Pascal aphorism that Borges loved, "The universe is a sphere whose center is everywhere and circumference is nowhere." Borges's parables and stories are attempts to grasp the infinite complexity of the world, and his version of Lombardi would have died of despair of ever approximating the reach and intricacy of these networks.

Lombardi's work is often regarded as evidence of sinister conspiracies by people who assume that "they" are thus linked up but "we" are not. We are, actually, at least when we try to achieve anything political. Politics *is* networks, rhizomes, roots, webs, to use a few of the popular metaphors from the increasingly popular studies of complexity. A more cheerful Lombardi might have charted the links that connect Naomi Klein, the Argentina Horizontalidad populist movements against neoliberalism, the Zapatistas, the Yucatán campesinos who opposed the WTO in Cancun in 2003, the internationalistas who joined them, the U.S. campus-based anti-sweatshop movement, the Sierra Club, Arundhati Roy, anti-Monsanto agriculturalists in India and Europe, on to Nigerian activists now shutting the operations of Chevron (based in San Francisco) and San Francisco activists against Bechtel Corporation (also based here), which links us back to the Bolivian activists who beat Bechtel a few years ago. (Thanks to the Internet, speaking of networks, the global justice movement has been able to link causes and confrontations into an unprecedented meta-community able to act in concert internationally.)

In fact, right-wing think tanks are probably lining up these affiliations and solidarities right now and portraying them as a conspiracy, as they have before. That's the rule of thumb: when we talk, it's a network; when they talk, it's a conspiracy. The sinister thing about Lombardi's BCCI drawing isn't that all these people, banks, and governments are linked up, but that they're linked up to screw you, me, and the world. That is to say, it's complexity that makes the drawing itself overwhelming, but intent that makes the denizens of the drawing scary.

AWAKENINGS AND COINCIDENCES

One can imagine the characters of Adam Hochschild's wonderful new history, *Bury the Chains: Prophets and Rebels in the Fight to Free an Empire's Slaves*, as they might have been drawn by Lombardi, such is the complexity of the network Hochschild depicts while tracing the British antislavery movement from Quakers in London to slave rebellions in the Caribbean, from the 1780s when the move-ment began to the final, long-delayed abolition of slavery in the British Empire on August 1, 1838. The book is both a gripping history of a particular movement and a beautiful embodiment of the erratic, unlikely ways movements unfold—an unfolding that consists of multiple kinds of linkages. If Lombardi's is post-concep-tualist history painting, Hochschild's book is likewise a kind of post–Great Man history writing, one with crowds, coincidences, and ocean currents looming up behind the key activists he delineates.*

*Of course, one can play with this, as Rachel Cohen does in her 2004 book *A Chance Meeting: Intertwined Lives of American Writers and Artists, 1854–1967*, which traces meetings and friendships as a game of telephone, a baton pass, in which X meets Y who meets Z—and thus she travels from Henry James during the Civil War to Robert Lowell during the Vietnam War. You can make this game slightly senseless—for example, in 1872, the photographer Eadweard Muybridge twice met with the human rights activist and novelist Helen Hunt Jackson, who was an intimate friend of Emily Dickinson, who corresponded with the abolitionist Thomas Wentworth Higginson, the white commander of a black regiment in the Civil War, and go onward through Higginson's brother-in-law Ellerly Channing, a close friend of Thoreau, or through his contact with antislavery terrorist John Brown to the abolitionists Frederick Douglass and William Lloyd Garrison, who visited Clarkson in 1846, shortly before his death.
    Or you could steer Higginson, the friend of Dickinson, who was the friend of Jackson, for-ward to his friendship with the California writer Jack London, who was a socialist but a social

One kind of linkage is coincidence. Another is friendship and the affinities of interests and emotions on which friendships are based. *Bury the Chains* begins, in

---

Darwinist, and through London reach anarchist poet Kenneth Rexroth, who got to San Francisco in the 1920s, attended poetry readings at the socialist Jack London Club here, and undoubtedly knew writers who knew London, and was a mentor to younger poets who still live here, like Michael McClure, and from there go in all kinds of directions—Bob Dylan, Jim Morrison, or, well, me. I'm friends with McClure and once received a cherry-flavored Lifesaver from Philip Whalen, who was, along with McClure and two other guys I've met, among the six poets who read that famous October evening in 1955 when Allen Ginsberg debuted "Howl" and Rexroth officiated. For that matter, I once talked to Elmer Stanley, an old Native American whose great-grandmother had met James Savage (after whom my book about nuclear bombs and indigenous nations, *Savage Dreams*, is named), who had been part of the U.S. Army seizing California from Mexico and its indigenous owners. That army was led by Fremont, with whom Savage was connected through Fremont's famous scout Kit Carson, and since Fremont's father-in-law, Senator Thomas Hart Benton, was a protégé of Thomas Jefferson, thus goes the conversation on land and aboriginal rights back to its roots with that slaveowning founding father. . . . But since the Englishman Muybridge—despite his un-American respectfulness toward Chinese and Native Americans in that era—shared few values and interests with either the abolitionists or the Beats, this is truly only a string of coincidences, the six degrees of separation between you and Idi Amin or Britney Spears. None of these examples I have given describes the starry points of a new constellation as the words Coleridge, Clarkson, Toussaint L'Ouverture begin to, as a new definition of humanness began to take shape.

This mapping, this construction of family trees, could be played with books rather than persons: reading *Bury the Chains*, I found myself going to Holmes's Coleridge biography and Kenneth Johnston's life of the young Wordsworth, but also to Peter Linebaugh and Marcus Rediker's magnificent *The Many-Headed Hydra: Sailors, Slaves, Commoners, and the Hidden History of the Revolutionary Atlantic*, books that cover the same period of time in varying ways, overlapping like habitats for different species.

And perhaps I should use the smallness of the U.S. progressive intelligentsia as justification while confessing that I live in the same town as Hochschild and share an editor with him—the remarkable Tom Engelhardt, who brought us together for dinner last year. It was, in fact, an early excerpt from *Bury the Chains* published on Tom's online news service, Tomdispatch.com, that excited me about the book and made me interested in reviewing it. Of course, it would be easy to trace a line through Tom, who edits Eduardo Galeano and Ariel Dorfman to . . . But I must stop, before we go the way of Lombardi.

fact, with two remarkable series of coincidences that deliver up as their results two of the principal activists against slavery. Granville Sharp was the youngest of eight siblings who played music together and shared an evangelical piety. King George III believed that Sharp had the best voice in England. His brother, William Sharp, the king's physician, provided free medical care to the London poor. Jonathan Strong, a slave whose owner had pistol-whipped him viciously about the head and then thrown him out on the street to die, came for treatment. Granville happened to be visiting that morning, and the brothers got Strong into a hospital. After his months of convalescence, they found him a job with a pharmacist. One day on the streets of London, his owner encountered his former property healthy and fit, seized Strong, and sold him to a Jamaican plantation owner, arranging for him to be jailed until he could be shipped to the West Indies. The Sharp brothers intervened and managed to free him. "With this case," writes Hochschild, "the thirty-two-year-old Granville Sharp became by default the leading defender of blacks in London, and indeed one of the few people in all of England to speak out against slavery. And speak he would, vehemently, for nearly half a century. The fight against slavery quickly became his dominating passion."

Only one coincidence, the meeting with Strong, made Sharp an activist. But the string of events that brought the most pivotal activist into being was far stranger and more Lombardian. An antislavery activist, Olaudah Equiano, a former slave from what is now Nigeria via Barbados and Virginia, whose autobiography later had a huge impact on the movement, saw a letter in the *Morning Chronicle and London Advertiser* on March 18, 1783, which recounted a case involving the British slave ship *Zong*. Equiano called on Sharp, and Sharp made the case a minor cause célèbre. It was an insurance case, on the face of it. The insurers challenged the claim of the *Zong*'s captain that he had ordered 133 African captives thrown overboard alive in the mid-Atlantic because the ship's drinking water was running out. Jettisoning slaves insured as cargo would have led to compensation under those circumstances.

Human rights were never a consideration in the case. But the chief mate, afflicted with pangs of conscience, testified that there had been plenty of water. The murders took place to collect insurance on slaves who were sick and dying and therefore would not be marketable commodities when they reached land. The court found in favor of the captain and the ship's investors. Sharp then wrote indignant letters to several prominent clergymen, who mentioned the case in their sermons and writings.

The case of the Zong was far from over, and as the concerns it raised migrated onward throughout England, linkages began to build that would spark a potent antislavery movement. One Church of England clergyman who took up the case was Dr. Peter Peckard, who soon after became vice-chancellor of Cambridge University. When it was his turn to set the subject for the school's prestigious annual Latin composition prize, he chose *Anne liceat invitos in servitutem dare?*— "Is it lawful to make slaves of others against their will?" It was by no means a particularly likely choice. The Church of England's Society for the Propagation of the Gospel in Foreign Parts, governed in part by divinity professors from Oxford and Cambridge, derived significant revenues from Codrington, one of the biggest Barbados plantations. The place relied on branding, whipping, murdering, and constant terror to maintain an intensity of labor that worked the slaves to death. Slavery was outside the moral universe that even those propagating the gospel concerned themselves with, as Hochschild points out; the former slave trader who wrote "Amazing Grace" worried about all sorts of minor sins long before he noticed that slavery might be a problem.

A scholarship student, Thomas Clarkson, won the 1785 Cambridge Latin Prize after devoting two months to researching and writing about slavery. But the winning mattered little, except that it drew attention to the essay and its writer, who would publish it in English as an antislavery tract. The publisher Clarkson found was a Quaker who introduced him to the few others, also Quakers, who not only believed that slavery should be abolished but were willing to work for the great unlikelihood that someday it might be.

This chain of encounters and awakenings steered Clarkson away from a religious career into a passionate championing of the rights and humanity of the slaves in the British Empire. He quickly became the most effective activist the movement would have, one who gave over the rest of his life—nearly half a century—to the cause. Writing, investigating, talking, riding tens of thousands of miles on horse-back, he recruited, inspired, and connected the recruited and inspired into a move-ment. The Quakers, who had organized a little earlier to abolish slavery, had long needed a mainstream Anglican champion. In Clarkson, they found a superb one, in close sympathy with them; he was by the end a Quaker in all but name.

Some activists are born into their disposition and vocation, but many of the most passionate lead ordinary lives until some injustice or atrocity strikes them like lightning and they are reborn dedicated. Clarkson was such an activist, and, like Saint Paul on the way to Damascus, he even had a transformative moment: riding to London, he got off his horse and sat down "disconsolate on the turf by the road-side and held my horse. Here a thought came into my mind, that if the contents of the Essay were true, it was time some person should see these calamities to their end."

With luck and dedication, he became that person. His movements and con-tacts among slave-ship doctors as well as theologians, in Liverpool as well as London, amount to a network whose complexity is comparable to some of Lombardi's diagrams. Like most high-profile activists, he had a committee behind him—nine Quakers, Granville Sharp, and another Anglican—with whom he founded what was almost unprecedented then though common now, a nongovern-mental organization, an NGO. (He also circulated the famous diagram of slaves packed into the hull of a ship that his Quaker colleagues published as a poster—a diagram still widely known and one of the great visual icons of inhumanity of all time.)

At various moments during the antislavery campaigns, there were widespread petitions to Parliament, at a time when petitioning was one of the few rights avail-able to ordinary citizens; sugar boycotts, since sugar was the principal West Indies slave product; gatherings of local antislavery groups and sympathetic

Parliamentarians—all the accoutrements, as Hochschild points out, of later human rights movements. Chief among the sympathetic Parliamentarians was the wealthy, pious William Wilberforce, who did not support labor organizing and other extensions of rights and powers to the underclasses but devoutly opposed slavery. (In the interim, he argued, the whipping of slaves should not be abolished, but rather should be done only at night: some compromise is strategic, whereas some—like the Democrats looking for a nicer version of the war—is moral compromise.) Timid and conventional, Wilberforce made an odd pairing with the radical, far-ranging Clarkson, but they remained friends for life.

Compromise ran all through this movement, or rather through some of its members, while others were ardent revolutionists, eager to see all the rights of man—and, when women took over leadership in the 1820s, of women—granted. In this movement and any other, the utility of compromise is an arguable point (or one can argue instead for a kind of symbiosis of unbending activists and back-room-dealing ones, whereby the revolutionists extend the argument and make the reformers look reasonable—which is how the Sierra Club often looks at groups like Earth First!—and, in due time, even revolutionists come to look reasonable, as abolitionists did once they had won).

For example, the movement long campaigned against the slave trade rather than against the existence of slavery itself in the British Empire, on the grounds that it was a more winnable battle—and it was. (British sugar plantations were so energetically murderous that they required constant replenishment of the slave population from Africa, which is why it looked as though British slavery, unlike slavery in the United States, could be undone simply by closing down the maritime trade in human beings—that is, the supply of fresh slaves.) The struggle against the slave trade was won in 1807, but the abolition of slavery took more than another quarter century and even then limped forward with a six-year interim period in which the slaves' labor was somehow to further compensate their masters, who had already been compensated in cash for loss of ownership of their fellow human beings. The most radical antislavery activist, Elizabeth Heyrick, had long before suggested that it was the slaves who were due compensation for their lives and labor. Still, the antislavery movement kept its eyes on the prize, clear that it was more important to free the slaves by any means necessary than to punish slavery's perpetrators.

Clarkson and his colleagues built a network consciously and conscientiously, recognizing that in doing so they were laying the foundations for the undoing of slavery. It stretched from the vast numbers of ordinary citizens who signed petitions and followed boycotts to the sympathetic witnesses who brought information back from Africa for what were, in essence, the first official human rights hearings in history, to the slaves themselves who turned up in London to testify or rose up in the Caribbean. (One of the things that distinguished the British abolition movement from the American was the fierce, effective slave revolts that terrified slaveholders and played a role on the road to abolition.) More fortuitous, or fortunate, or mysterious is the string of coincidences that brought the *Zong* to trial, the trial to Equiano's attention, Equiano into friendship with Sharp, Sharp to write to Peckard, Peckard to set the Latin prize topic as slavery, and Clarkson to be as inspired in his Latin as passionate in his conscience. It's one of those for-want-of-a-nail conundrums: how would it have come about had any element been absent?

FRIENDSHIPS AND ATMOSPHERES

Clarkson shows up on the periphery of other histories and other networks. In the 1790s, he moved to England's Lake District and became close friends with a poet who had also written a gold-medal-winning composition on slavery at Cambridge, this time an ode in Greek in 1792: the Romantic poet Samuel Taylor Coleridge. Clarkson's wife became Dorothy Wordsworth's close friend and key correspondent, and with this leap from the advancement of human rights to the advancement of British poetry, Hochschild bumps into a dizzyingly broad network of radical ideas stretching from the French Revolution to the vast slave revolution against the French in Haiti.

At that moment, some sense of what it means to be human was shifting, and the antislavery movement was part of that shift, as was the Romantic movement, with its cultivation of introspective awareness and its enthusiasm for liberation and revolution. Clarkson turns up briefly in Richard Holmes's Coleridge biography as someone who supported Coleridge in the depths of his opium addiction, while Wilberforce was close friends with Wordsworth's kindest uncle. Wordsworth himself wrote a sonnet to Toussaint L'Ouverture, who led the Haitian slave uprising, and William Blake and J. M. W. Turner both addressed slavery in their visual art (the moral if not the aesthetic ancestors of Lombardi). Others, such as the Wedgwood family, link the antislavery and poetry movements while branching into the sciences, the invention of photography, and beyond.

Hochschild's account of all this is certainly testimony not only to the smallness of Britain's intelligentsia then but also to the largeness of ideas about human freedom that were moving through and then beyond these networks, the ideas and passions that constitute the atmosphere of an age. Of all the networks he deals with, this one made up of ideas and ethical stirrings is the most important and the most nebulous. The changed spirit and beliefs that link these people are explicable up to a point and then ultimately mysterious. Why is it that suddenly slavery, which had existed in one form or another throughout history, became urgently intolerable not only to the slaves but to privileged people an ocean away from most of the suffering in Africa and the Americas? What made the Zong's first mate testify against his captain about the murder of those slaves? What made a Cambridge student abandon his career in the church and give his life over to a cause? What made tens or hundreds of thousands of anonymous Britons give up sugar and take up letter-writing and committee meetings? The networks can be traced, but the stirrings remain mysterious.

Without popular opinion at least periodically rising to meet them, Clarkson and the Quakers would have been just eccentrics and historical footnotes, the rebellious slaves a sad side story, rather than begetters of a new era. *Bury the Chains* quotes Wilberforce as writing in his diary, "How popular Abolition is, just now! God can turn the hearts of men." But it's clear that it was other men and women, uprisings and revolts, books and pamphlets that did the turning, that the change was mysterious, magnetic, or catalytic, but far from divine.

In both Britain and the United States, women who became involved in the anti-slavery movement began to question the enslavement of their gender, and so goes another long trajectory of links and steps in the expansive history of human rights these past two centuries. I have been reading another book lately, my friend Susan Schwartzenberg's *Becoming Citizens: Family Life and the Politics of Disability*. The book traces a group of Seattle-area mothers from the birth of their mentally disabled children to the discovery that their children were denied access to public education to those mothers' engenderment of an educational rights movement. That movement, with interim victories in Washington State, culminated in the 1975 IDEA—Individuals with Disabilities Education Act—some decades after these women decided to change the world to make room in it for children like theirs, and not quite two centuries after those nine Quakers and Clarkson met to launch a human rights movement. The two stories are akin, with initial private moments of realization, the building of public associations and communities, and eventually the overhauling of society. *Bury the Chains* is a kind of template for how the world gets changed, sometimes, for the better. Hochschild's book, like his *King Leopold's Ghost* before it, often reads like an exciting novel, as one character chases another, or an idea, or a ballot issue across the years. But it pauses periodically to take in the larger landscape of change; its original subtitle was *The First International Human Rights Movement*.

The book begins with a kind of trumpet cry:

To understand how momentous was this beginning, we must picture a world in which the vast majority of people are prisoners. Most of them have known no other way of life. They are not free to live or go where they want. . . . They die young. They are not chained or bound most of the time, but they are in bondage, part of a global economy based on forced labor. Such a world would, of course, be unthinkable today. But that was the world—our world—just two centuries ago, and to most people then, it was unthinkable that it could ever be otherwise. At the end of the eighteenth century, well over three quarters of all people alive were in bondage of one kind or another, not the captivity of striped prison uniforms, but of various systems of slavery or serfdom.

Midway through his story, Hochschild halts the narrative to cast about for a reason why the British should have been so much readier than, say, the French to oppose literal slavery. Here, he lands upon the essential enslavement of sailors in both the British Navy and its merchant marine, with their press gangs, beatings, kidnappings, horrific conditions, and high mortality, which kept the empire whole and the slave trade going. But why should empathy have been extended from sailors to slaves? The answer would make this into another, more speculative book.

The book that Hochschild gives us is valuable instead for its magnificent portrait of how activism works—by coincidences, friendships, patience, and stubbornness, by carefully built networks and belief systems that change slowly or suddenly like climate or the weather. There is the protracted timeline of change: a preliminary state in which almost no one cares about slaves; another moment when it seems that everyone in England does; moments during the Napoleonic wars when everyone, except a few diehards, is apparently too frightened—more by their own government than by threats from abroad—to say anything about slavery at all; and then decades more to go until a final victory. There are interim victories. There are moments of despair. Most of all, there are people giving over their lives to a battle that turns out to take more than a lifetime for most of them. And then there are the arguments over how the history will be written—Wilberforce's sons tried to write Clarkson out of it, and succeeded until 1989, when biographer Ellen Gibson Wilson revived his stature as the pivotal figure in the antislavery movement.

You can think of the nuclear freeze movement, which in 1982 had a million proponents gathered on its behalf in New York's Central Park, though few of those stuck with it long enough to realize the "peace dividend" that the collapse of the Soviet empire was supposed to spawn, or to push further the opportunities for disarmament that arose. The current bout of nuclear proliferation can be blamed in part on Bush, but it can also be traced to those who expected a three-year struggle rather than a sixty-year one; any eventual victories will be owed in large part to the dedicated minority of activists who have not been realistic, have not gone home, have not succeeded yet—but might. Or think of the movement against apartheid, which, like the antislavery movement two centuries before, combined the nonviolent and the violent, governmental and citizen action, domestic and foreign action, boycotts and educational campaigns to dismantle, piece by piece, slowly, with setbacks, a racist regime (but which, with the moderation that made victory possible, though far less of a victory, never dismantled the extreme financial injustices some call economic apartheid). That story, however, is still unfinished. So, for the record, is the global history of slavery. And what was once the British and Foreign Anti-Slavery Society, founded in 1839 to continue the good work after the signal victory of the year before, is still active as Anti-Slavery International, based in Thomas Clarkson House in London.

Sontag and Tsunami

[2004]

The news of Susan Sontag's death arrived as a single sentence spoken in the open-ing moments of a radio news program Tuesday morning, and then the program returned to what had been the main story since the day after Christmas: the tsu-nami and the death toll, then in the tens of thousands, that would continue to rise. It was strange to weigh these two incidents of mortality against each other. Though for some people it would be considered insensitive or even irreverent to do so, one of the things to be appreciated about Sontag, I think, is that she considered everything a proper occasion for more thinking, more analyzing, more writing.

I knew her very slightly: in the spring of 2003, she had invited me to visit her at home, in her apartment with a view of sky, river, and the back ends of rooftop gargoyles, and I visited a few times. It was an invitation to enter the republic of literature as she saw it; one of the things clear through all her work is that she was not interested merely in writing, but in tending and cultivating a literature-based public sphere in which ideas and principles mattered. It was a romantic idea, but not an unrealistic one—since, after all, she realized it. Sontag used her tremendous visibility to enter the political realm directly, going to Bosnia, taking stands on the Vietnam and Yugoslav wars, serving as American president of PEN, berating the Israelis as she accepted an award from them, defending Salman Rushdie in partic-ular and free speech and human rights in general.

The BBC set up a tribute web site immediately, and a man who had been prompted by *On Photography* to go back and finish college at age forty-eight wrote in, as did a man who had been inspired to direct *Romeo and Juliet* in Beirut by

Sontag's production of *Waiting for Godot* in the ruins of Sarajevo. Admirers from Vancouver to Gdansk to Taipei posted comments, as did a number of sneering detractors, some still bitter about her post–September 11 comments. Only God is right about everything, which is why we are fortunate that God speaks so seldom. It is not important whether or not Sontag was always right in her conclusions, only that she was right in raising the issues that she did—for the most useful position is the one that prompts people to test an idea and perhaps think for themselves by disagreeing. After all, on key subjects from communism to photography, she eventually disagreed with her earlier self. What she said when writing about the Jewish mystic Simone Weil can be said of her own outspoken writing as well: "An idea which is a distortion may have a greater intellectual thrust than the truth; it may better serve the needs of the spirit."

Sontag has achieved the immortality of people whose work reaches far beyond them in time and space, not one that means death does not matter, only that part of her is still here for us—a truth born out immediately by the way her comments on photography and representation allow us to continue navigating the world and examine the terms in which it is delivered to us.

In the disaster around the Indian Ocean, you read of people searching among scores of bodies for the body of their child or spouse; you see photographs of the search. One photograph shows untidy rows of dead children who mostly look like they are sleeping, save for the randomness with which they are naked or clothed; and in a corner a woman in a brilliant blue sari, head thrown back, bangle-adorned brown arms clasped to her temples, is contorted with sorrow. People were searching for their own children, for their own dead, among the many dead, for the tragedy that was personal amid the enormity; and anyone who believed that poverty or high levels of infant mortality loosen the bonds of parent to child got over it reading these shattering stories of people who wished they had died with or instead of their children. Photographs are being taken, have been taken, of many of the dead, so that the families can identify them on bulletin boards and web sites. Never has photography been more personal or more public. The photographs serve, as photography always does, to make us feel present, to make visible, imaginable what has happened. They serve empathy as much as understanding.

When the Loma Prieta earthquake struck the San Francisco Bay Area on October 17, 1989, it killed sixty people; but for many of the rest of us, the disaster seemed strangely reassuring. It was an assertion that nature was not so small and diminished as it sometimes seemed that fall when global warming was first entering the public imagination. Nature was more powerful than our plans and impositions. That disaster was not like a war; it was instead like a truce, perhaps like that famous Christmas morning in the First World War when soldiers on both sides stopped fighting. The region's tremendous engines of producing and consuming stopped; people didn't go to work; businesses were shut; the Bay Bridge was out of commission for months; and some of the elevated freeways were gone for good. People localized themselves in the here-and-now that certain disasters bring in their wake, staying home, talking to the people they loved, letting go of discontent, long-term plans, and distant travel.

This thousand-times-larger Indonesian earthquake was not like a truce but like a war, and for a while the death count hovered near what the estimated Iraqi death count is in our current war, and then it rose higher. The tsunami has been treated as an occasion that demands that we should know as much as possible, see as much as possible, feel as much as possible, give as much as possible. You can look at the superabundant photographs of those scenes of devastation, those bodies contorted with grief and loss, and extrapolate from them that the assault on Fallujah must have left orphans with the same blank, stunned looks on their faces, mothers without children contorted with the same unbearable grief, must have shattered homes, families, lives, hopes with the same kind of physical force. To realize this is to realize how much imagery—or its lack—shapes our response to both disasters. When our military has created the catastrophe, we are not allowed to see so much, not encouraged to empathize or to attempt to assuage it with charitable contributions—though those contributions are made anyway: the day the tsunami struck, the U.S. peace group Code Pink sent a delegation to Iraq with $600,000 in donations for the people of Fallujah.

The Iraq War has been a strangely unseen war, or rather a war in which conventional and uncontroversial images are the standard fare—lots of pictures of us, few of them, images of blown-up military vehicles and uninhabited Iraqi ruins, but not in this country the images of the injured and the dead civilians we have been producing in such prodigious numbers, nothing like the images of the tsunami. But it has also been a war of images. There was the staged toppling of the statue of Saddam Hussein as our invasion ended. There was the crisis opened up by the leaked photographs of Abu Ghraib torture (which Sontag wrote about in one of her last published pieces, "Regarding the Torture of Others"), and more recently the American soldier shooting a wounded man in a mosque in Fallujah. And there are the videotapes of guerrillas beheading their captives in what seemed to be media stunts of a sort. We know that Al Jazeera shows radically different images of this war and of the Israeli-Palestinian war, a difference both generated by and reinforcing the different views on those conflicts. Even Europeans see more graphic images of such civilian casualties.

You can remember the ways this war has been kept invisible, so out of range of our potential for empathy or outrage that even photographs of the returning coffins of American soldiers were banned—until the web site The Memory Hole obtained and distributed them against the Pentagon's wishes. The *San Francisco Chronicle* ran a gallery of pictures of all the U.S. dead nine months ago when the casualty figure was 556 and maintains that gallery of what is now 1,347 dead. The yearbook of images is a reminder of another gallery of images, the portraits of the victims of September 11, which the *New York Times* ran, along with sentimental biographies; and before that, the forlorn flyers posted in Manhattan by family members looking for the missing, who almost all turned out to be the dead. Now those kinds of missing-person flyers have been posted on walls in Thailand, but the photographs on the Thai web site are of the dead, mutilated by the force of the water.

You can say in some ways that what has happened in Iraq is a tsunami that swept ten thousand miles from the epicenter of an earthquake in Washington, D.C., an earthquake in policy and principle that has devastated countless lives and environments and cities far away—and near at hand, where friends and families of dead soldiers also grieve, and tens of thousands of those kids sent abroad to carry out a venal foreign policy are maimed in body and spirit. You can add up the numbers we spent to achieve all this devastation like that of the tsunami, the more than $150 billion it cost us to make this suffering and devastation. You can compare that price to the tiny offering of money Bush made to tsunami relief efforts, when he was forced to interrupt his Texas vacation—first $15 million, then $35 million (approximately the cost of his inauguration), and then, under shaming pressure, $350 million. You can understand the harnessing of the forces of nature— aerodynamics, chemistry, atomic fission—as means of making war more like natural disaster in its indifference, its scale, its ruination. But never natural.

One of the challenges of a natural disaster is that there is no one to blame, to allow us to make the shift from the difficulty of grief that is a kind of love to the ease of scorn or loathing that is a kind of hatred. Some polemicists have already moved to castigate governments, perhaps as a way of moving away from the uncertain, uneasy realm of such vast suffering that is in many ways natural, suffering that can be mitigated and sometimes prevented but not banned or outlawed. The economics that kept these countries from having warning systems and pushed the poor into living on the perilous coastal edge are part of the disaster, but no government generated or even foresaw this earthquake with, says my local paper, the force of 2 million atomic bombs the size of the one dropped on Hiroshima. The fault on which it occurred was thought to be inactive.

Thus politics plays a small role in this disaster, which is therefore not entirely natural, but not nearly as unnatural as drought- and war-induced famine, as anything having to do with the weather nowadays, like the four hurricanes to hit Florida in 2004. Not even like the 1985 earthquake in Mexico, where shoddy building codes, shoddy enforcement of those codes, and governmental indifference and incompetence had everything to do with the thousands who died; not like last year's earthquake in Bam, Iran, where old buildings collapsed so that one can say that it was the humanly created structures and not the earth itself that inflicted such mortality; not even like the cyclones that killed half a million Bangladeshis in 1970, 140,000 in 1991—colossal catastrophes that journalists and commentators seem to have forgotten as they frame the scale of this event as unprecedented. As so many images press us to feel and respond to this disaster, other unseen disasters come to mind, notably this year's displacement of Chinese and Indian farmers and villagers by the rising water of huge dam projects.

Sontag wrote beautifully about the images that we see, particularly those of suffering and of war. Now I wish she had said more about what we don't see, about how photographs must be weighed against the obliviousness they dispel as well as against the callousness they might generate, the exploitation they might cause, and the perils of interpretation. In her most recent book, *Regarding the Pain of Others*, Sontag writes, "Being a spectator of calamities taking place in another country is a quintessential modern experience, the cumulative offering by more than a century and a half's worth of those professional, specialized tourists known as journalists. Wars are now also living room sights and sounds." And then she took up her old argument, from *On Photography*, that there should be an "ecology of images" to keep "compassion, stretched to its limits," from "going numb." She argues with her former self, "There isn't going to be an ecology of images. No Committee of Guardians is going to ration horror, to keep fresh its ability to shock." But the images of Abu Ghraib were shocking anyway, and the images of the tsunami are harrowing.

What is now most striking about Sontag's argument is that it is not so much about photography but about compassion, an emotion and an ethic that photographs can awaken or undermine. Elsewhere in *Regarding the Pain of Others*, she writes, "Compassion is an unstable emotion. It needs to be translated into action, or it withers. The question is what to do with the feelings that have been aroused, the knowledge that has been communicated. People don't become inured to what they are shown—if that's the right way to describe what happens—because of the quantity of images dumped on them. It is passivity that dulls feeling."

We can act to deal with the consequences of the earthquake and tsunami, but the disaster was only faintly political in the economics and indifference that settled the poor along the coast. The relief will be very political, in who gives how much, and to whom it is given, but the event itself transcends politics, the realm of things we cause and can work to prevent. We cannot wish that human beings were not subject to the forces of nature, including the mortality that is so central a part of our own nature. We cannot wish that the seas dry up, that the waves grow still, that the tectonic plates cease to exist, that nature ceases to be beyond our abilities to predict and control. But the terms of that nature include such catastrophe and such suffering, which leaves us with sorrow as not a problem to be solved but a fact. And it leaves us with compassion as the work we will never finish.

6

GARDENS AND WILDERNESSES

Every Corner Is Alive

Eliot Porter as an Environmentalist and an Artist

〚2001〛

BEHIND THE EYES

"As I became interested in photography in the realm of nature, I began to appreciate the complexity of the relationships that drew my attention," wrote Eliot Porter. Complexity is a good foundational word for this artist whose work synthesized many sources and quietly broke many rules, whose greatest influence—an influence that has yet to be measured—was outside the art world. Porter may be one of the major environmentalists of the twentieth century, not because of his years on the board of the Sierra Club but because of his contribution to public awareness and imagination of the natural world.

When his first book, *In Wildness Is the Preservation of the World*, appeared in November 1962, it came as a revelation. Nothing like it had been seen before, and though the subject was ancient, the technology that allowed him to represent it so dazzlingly was new. Porter was one of the pioneers of color photography, and his editor, Sierra Club executive director David Brower, enlisted new printing technology to attain an unprecedented level of color fidelity and sharpness of reproduction. The essayist Guy Davenport wrote that the book "cannot be categorized: it is so distinguished among books of photography, among anthologies, among art books, that its transcendence is superlative." A later reviewer recalled, "A kind of revolution was under way, for with the publication of this supremely well-crafted book, conservation ceased to be a boring chapter on agriculture in fifth grade textbooks, or the province of such as bird watchers." Despite its $25 cover price, it became a best-seller in the San Francisco Bay Area and did well across the country. When a cheaper version was published in 1967, it became the best-selling trade paperback of the year. Porter's 1963 book *The Place No One Knew: Glen Canyon on the Colorado*, a counterpoint to his first, was similarly successful and influential. It is impossible to see what those images looked like when they first appeared, precisely because of their success.

There are two kinds of artistic success. One makes an artist's work distinctive and recognizable to a large public in his or her time and afterward—Picasso might be a case in point. The greater success is more paradoxical: the work becomes so compelling that it eventually becomes how we see and imagine, rather than what we look at. Invisible most of the time, such art may look obvious or even hackneyed when we catch sight of it. Such success generates imitations not only by other artists but throughout the culture: the ubiquitous photography in advertisements, calendars, and posters imitating the color aesthetic Porter founded may tell hikers and tourists what to look for in the natural world, and thus they may experience his aesthetic as nature rather than art. Color demanded different compositions and called attention to different aspects of the natural world than did black and white photography.

Porter's work came into the world as the product of an individual talent and became a genre, nature photography, in which thousands of professionals and amateurs toil (though most of them value beauty more and truth less than Porter did). His photographs have become how we look at the natural world, what we look for and value in it, what the public often tries to photograph, and what a whole genre of photography imitates. Porter's pictures of nature look, so to speak, "natural" now, and this is the greatest cultural success any ideology or aesthetic can have. We now live in a world Porter helped to invent. It is because his pictures exist behind our eyes that it is sometimes hard to see the Porters in front of one's eyes for what they were and are. Thus, understanding Porter's photography means understanding the world in which it first appeared and the aesthetic and environmental effects it has had since.

Sierra Club executive director David Brower chose to publish *In Wildness* in the centennial year of Henry David Thoreau's death; each of Porter's images was paired with a passage from Thoreau. But 1962 had plenty of history of its own. In September of that year, Rachel Carson's *Silent Spring* was published, and this indictment of the pesticide industry quickly became a controversy and a best-seller. In October, President John Kennedy announced that the Soviet Union had placed nuclear missiles in Cuba and that the United States would attack unless they were removed: the world came closer to an all-out nuclear war than at any time before or since. "The very existence of mankind is in the balance," the secretary-general of the United Nations declared. This context must have prepared the ground for the reception of *In Wildness Is the Preservation of the World*, which appeared in November. At the end of World War II, the revelations of the atomic bomb and the concentration camps had begun to erode faith in leaders, scientists, and the rhetoric of progress; and as the fifties wore on, that faith continued to crumble. *Silent Spring* and the Cuban missile crisis were only the crescendos of events that had long been building, and *In Wildness* may have succeeded in part as a response to these circumstances.

In the late 1950s and early 1960s, fear of a possible nuclear war was coupled with fear of what preparing for one entailed. The 1959 discovery that, in many parts of the country, milk—both bovine and human—was contaminated by fallout from atomic testing led to a national outcry. That what ought to be the most natural and nurturing thing in the world contained gene-altering, cancer-causing, manmade substances meant that nature was no longer a certainty beyond the reach of science and politics, and it meant that the government was generating biological contamination in the name of political protection. Similarly disastrous pesticide spraying campaigns in the nation's national forests had already provoked an uproar by the late 1950s (and Porter was among those decrying their abuse, with letters to his local newspaper). Science and politics had invaded the private realm of biology, reproduction, and health as never before. Carson wrote of pesticides,

"Their presence casts a shadow that is no less ominous because it is formless and obscure, no less frightening because it is simply impossible to predict the effects of lifetime exposure." The world faced a new kind of fear, of nature itself altered, of mutations, extinctions, contaminations that had never before been imagined. Porter wrote in a 1961 letter, "Conservation has rather suddenly become a major issue in the country—that is more people in higher and more influential places are aware of its importance and willing to do something about it."

Pesticides and radiation were only part of the strange cocktail that fueled what gets called "the sixties." In November 1961, Women Strike for Peace, the most effective of the early antinuclear groups, was launched with a nationwide protest that in many ways prefigured the feminist revolution. In 1962, the civil rights movement was supercharged, the United Farm Workers was founded, and Students for a Democratic Society (SDS) held its first national convention. The voiceless were acquiring voices, and with them they were questioning the legitimacy of those in power and the worldview they promulgated. Some of those with voices were speaking up for nature and wilderness with an urgency never before heard. During the late 1950s and early 1960s, the epochal Wilderness Bill was being debated alongside pesticide and radiation issues: nature in its remotest reaches and most intimate details was at stake. It is in this context that the small American conservation movement became the broad-based environmental movement, and Porter played a role in its broadening.

The ecological truth *Silent Spring* tells as a nightmare—that everything is connected, so that our chemical sins will follow us down the decades and the waterways—is what *In Wildness* depicts as a beatific vision. Carson's book addressed a very specific history, that of the development of new toxins during World War II and their application afterward to civilian uses; and she wrote about their effects on birds, on roadside foliage, on the human body, and on the vast ecosystems within which these entities exist. "The world of systemic insecticides," she wrote, "is a weird world . . . where the enchanted forest of the fairy tales has become the poisonous forest in which an insect that chews a leaf or sucks the sap of a plant is doomed. It is a world where . . . a bee may carry poisonous nectar back to its hive and presently produce poisonous honey." Porter's book showed the forest still enchanted, outside historical time and within the cyclical time of the seasons (the photographs had earlier appeared in an exhibition titled *The Seasons*, and the images are sequenced to depict spring, summer, fall, and winter). Only one image, of a mud swallow's nest built against raw planks, showed traces of human presence at all, and that presence is slight and benign.

The year before, Wallace Stegner had coined the term "the geography of hope," countering the argument that wilderness preservation served elites with the assertion that wilderness could be a place in which everyone could locate their hopefulness even if few actually entered it. The Sierra Club's Exhibit Format photography books could be, as environmental historian Stephen Fox points out, a way to bring the wilderness to the people rather than the other way round, to show them the geography of hope and create a kind of virtual access without impact. *In Wildness* was in many ways a hopeful book, an intimate portrait of an apparently undamaged world of streams, blackberries, moths, saplings—and a later Porter book would be titled *Baja California and the Geography of Hope*. These photographic books were in some sense documents, but in another, equally important sense, they were promises: not only did they confirm the existence of what they depicted, but they also showed what the future could hold—and it is a mark of profound change that the best hope for the future in the time of these books was for a future that resembled an untrammeled past, that industrial civilization yearned for Eden rather than the New Jerusalem.

Despite its lyrical celebration of the timeless and nonhuman, Porter's first book was widely recognized as a political book. Environmentalism is about what is worth protecting, as well as what threatens it; politics is ultimately about what we value and fear—and *In Wildness* spoke directly of these things. In a review of the 1967 edition, *Sports Illustrated* proclaimed, "Hundreds of books and articles have been written urging private citizens to do something ('Write your Congressman, now!') about the destruction of the nation's natural beauties, but the most persuasive volume of all contained not a word of impassioned argument, not a single polemic."

In fact, it did contain a few words of impassioned argument—at the end of his introduction, Joseph Wood Krutch stated, "If those who believe in progress and define it as they do continue to have their way it will soon be impossible either to test [Thoreau's] theory that Nature is the only proper context of human life or that in such a context we may ultimately learn the 'higher laws.' One important function of a book like this will have been performed if it persuades those who open it that some remnant of the beauties it calls to our attention is worth preserving." Out of these last two subtly wrought sentences comes an avalanche of assertions: that progress as conventionally imagined was devastating the natural world, perhaps irreversibly; that nature is a necessary but imperiled moral authority; that Porter portrays not only nature itself but also its moral authority; that the purpose of Porter's book may be to help rally citizens to preserve this nature; that photographs of blackberries, birds, and streams can be politically and philosophically persuasive because love of nature can be inculcated through beauty; and that such love can lead to political action on its behalf.

Modernity had placed its faith in science, culture, and progress. A kind of Rousseauist antimodernism that would be central both to the counterculture and to the environmental movement put its faith in nature, usually nature as an ideal of how things were before various interventions: before human contact, before the industrial revolution, before Euro-Americans, before chemical contaminations—an Edenic ideal. Krutch, who had had a distinguished career as a literary critic before he left the East Coast intelligentsia for Arizona and nature writing, embodies this shift—"an exile from modernism," curator John Rohrback has called him, cast out of the city into the garden. Krutch was a major ally of Porter, and Porter supplied Americans with one definition of what that nature worth preserving was (it is seldom acknowledged that that definition was made possible by a technologically advanced and aesthetically sophisticated art; such an acknowledgment would have greatly complicated the arguments).

In his next book, Porter depicted a place that had been as pristine as anything shown in *In Wildness,* or perhaps more so, but that by the time of publication had been lost or at least hidden: the labyrinthine canyonlands drowned by the Glen Canyon Dam. The Sierra Club had done an earlier book, in 1955, titled *This Is Dinosaur,* which campaigned against putting a dam in Dinosaur National Monument. *The Place No One Knew,* like *This Is Dinosaur,* was a crusade against a dam.

Porter portrayed Glen Canyon as a gallery of stone walls in reds, browns, and

grays and of gravel-and-mud floors through which water flowed, occasionally interspersed with images of foliage and, much more rarely, the sky. Some found it claustrophobic and longed for more conventional distant views. This book was much
more radical than *In Wildness*—radical formally, in its compositions; radical politically, in the directness of its advocacy; and radical conceptually, in its depiction of
a vast place facing an imminent doom that would have been unimaginable only a
century before. Most beautiful images, particularly photographs, and most particularly landscape photographs, are invitations of a sort; but this one was the opposite: a survey of what could no longer be encountered, a portrait of the condemned
before the execution, "the geography of doom." The beautiful images were inflected
by information from outside the frame: all this was being drowned. As environmental writer and photographer Stephen Trimble wrote about Glen Canyon:

> When I explored the Colorado Plateau, I carried Eliot's pictures in my head, and
> tried to let them guide my eye and then inspire me to see the same places and col-
> ors in my own way. My greatest sorrow is not having seen Glen Canyon. . . . It
> makes me sick at heart to look at the reservoir that drowned and destroyed the
> heart of the landscape that is my spiritual home. *The Place No One Knew: Glen
> Canyon on the Colorado* is the best book title of the second half of the 20th
> Century—and my first and best entry point into the lost basilica of my personal
> religion.

Elsewhere Trimble wrote, "The message was clear: go out into the land, stand up
for it, fight its destruction—you lose forever when you fail to know the land well
enough to speak for it."

FLOW AND CONVERGENCE

Many sources converge in the complex body of mature work, and that work arrived
in a world that was ready to receive it only after Porter, color photography processes,
and public awareness had evolved far beyond where they were when he began pho-

tographing in 1937, the year he turned thirty-six. Among the factors feeding Porter's vision were a socially conscious family, whose influence contributed to his lifelong support of human rights and environmental causes; a boyhood passion for the natural world; an involvement with photography from late childhood on; a medical and scientific education that gave him the skills to develop color photography technology; the inherited funds that allowed him to stand apart from fashions and pressures; and a sense of himself as an artist, dating from Alfred Stieglitz's recognition of his work at the end of the 1930s. In his training as a doctor and biomedical researcher, Porter refined his understanding of biology, chemistry, and laboratory work, which would stand him in good stead as a nature photographer, an environmentalist, and an innovator of color photography processes. "I did not consider those years wasted," he told a group of students. "Without those experiences it would be impossible to predict what course my life would have taken, least of all that it would be in photography. In retrospect, from my experience it appears highly desirable to order one's life in accord with inner yearnings no matter how impractical."

His grounding in both art and science is evident in statements such as this: "During my career as a photographer I discovered that color was essential to my pursuit of beauty in nature. I believe that when photographers reject the significance of color, they are denying one of our most precious biological attributes— color vision—that we share with relatively few other animal species." The statement moves from beauty to biology, aesthetics to science, as though it were the most natural thing in the world; and for Porter it evidently was, though few others could or would deploy biology in arguing art. This mix made him something of a maverick or a misfit in mainstream photography circles—even the landscapists didn't ground their work in science as he did. As a photographer, he engaged with evidence of natural processes, biodiversity, the meeting of multiple systems, with growth, decay, and entropy. Book designer Eleanor Caponigro recalled:

> Over the many years that I worked with him I became more and more aware of this complex composite of a man who was an extremely sensitive, articulate, visual artist and who was a scientist and a naturalist. He was a doctor. So you'd be looking at photographs and they would have their own aesthetic beauty, and—it

came up often in the Antarctica book—he'd say, "But this is how this rift is formed, by these two land masses coming across. And this particular lichen occurs in this particular setup. And these are the dry valleys and the desiccated seals and this is how this happened and this is what happens when an iceberg rolls over and it's absorbed . . ." You know, so he was fascinated by all of that, and I think that's what drew him to photography instead of a different visual medium, because it solved, or it satisfied, this quality of scientific exploration for him.

One aspect of his life Porter himself seldom spoke of in his books and lectures was his political views outside of environmental issues, but his archives portray him as an engaged citizen, informed about and involved in the activities of his government locally, nationally, and internationally. (In this, too, he has much in common with Thoreau, who is best known for his writing about nature but who took a strong stance on slavery, the Mexican-American War, and other issues of the time.) In 1924, while hopping freight trains in the West, Porter joined the IWW—the Industrial Workers of the World, better known as the Wobblies. Though he must have been influenced by the fact that IWW members were less likely to be rolled by brakemen, his act reveals an awareness and sympathy with radicals perhaps not common among Harvard students from wealthy families. His tax records portray him as a staunch supporter of human rights and progressive causes: the American Civil Liberties Union was the one organization that he donated to year after year throughout his life, and in the 1930s he gave small sums to support the Republican side of the Spanish Civil War and the National Committee for the Defense of Political Prisoners. Documents in his archives show that he was concerned about pesticides long before *Silent Spring* appeared, along with logging, grazing on public lands, and other subjects that environmental activists have since taken up. Later, he would write to politicians and newspapers repeatedly about the war in Vietnam and the Watergate crisis, both of which outraged him; he also took an interest in Native American issues long before most of the non-Native public was aware that there were any. Though his principles involved him with many questions of the day, his passion and his talent were dedicated to environmental causes, particularly wildlife and wilderness.

In 1939, Porter showed his bird photographs to Rachel Carson's editor, Paul Brooks, who was then the head of Houghton Mifflin. Brooks shared Porter's enthusiasm for natural phenomena—but not for the bird photographs. He told the artist that they would be far more valuable if they were in color. Thanks to this prodding, Porter became a pioneer of color photography. Eleven years later, he approached Brooks again, only to be told that his jewel-like bird images would be too expensive to publish in color and would have a limited audience anyway. Fortunately, Porter garnered support from other quarters, including the Museum of Modern Art's David McAlpin, Ansel and Virginia Adams (who strove to find Porter a publisher early on), and Beaumont and Nancy Newhall. Even so, he toiled imperturbably with little public recognition for more than twenty years after resuming photography, and neither the lack of attention during those years nor the avalanche of attention afterward seems to have swayed his sense of purpose.

The gist of those twenty years is familiar: Porter continued to photograph birds in the spring and summer and other subjects the rest of the year. When his wife, Aline, said that this other work was evocative of Thoreau's writing, he began to read Thoreau with growing enthusiasm and to make pictures "of comparable sensibility . . . and for which I hoped to find a compatible description by Thoreau." Like his bird photographs, his Thoreau photographs were admired and rejected by New York and Boston publishers. The story of his twenty years in the wilderness usually ends with his meeting with David Brower, and Porter himself let it be thought that it wasn't until his meeting with the Sierra Club director that he began to put his photography to political uses. In fact, he had already been using it to lobby years before. In 1958, he wrote to his middle son, Stephen, "The enclosed clipping is a letter I wrote to the paper about the Wilderness Bill which I hope very much will pass in the next Congress. To influence this legislation I made up an album of photographs of wildlife pictures showing what would be saved by the bill and sent them to [nature writer Joseph Wood] Krutch who agreed to write a short text to go with them. We will then send the whole work to the Senate committee that is considering the bill in hopes that it will influence them to recommend its passage." Whether the album was ever assembled and sent out is not known, but it demonstrates that by the 1950s Porter was linking his art not only to science and literature but to politics, with hope of influencing outcomes.

When *In Wildness* appeared, it was a convergence of childhood wonder, modernist art photography, breakthrough color photography technology, scientific interest and acumen, and political awareness, a convergence that would continue and evolve through the subsequent books and years. Porter's most significant contributions are his ability to use aesthetic means for political ends and his success in doing so. "Photography is a strong tool, a propaganda device, and a weapon for the defense of the environment. . . . Photographs are believed more than words; thus they can be used persuasively to show people, who have never taken the trouble to look, what is there. They can point out beauties and relationships not previously believed or suspected to exist."

DR. PORTER AND MR. BROWER

In David Brower and the Sierra Club, Porter met a man and an organization that had put the aesthetic to political use in a way no other environmental group had. In 1939, long before Brower had become the club's executive director, Ansel Adams had published *Sierra Nevada: The John Muir Trail* and sent it to Harold Ickes, secretary of the interior, to lobby—successfully—for the creation of Kings Canyon National Park and the expansion of Sequoia National Park. A Californian who spent much time in the Sierra Nevada and a board member of the club from 1934 to 1971, Adams was far more deeply tied to the club than the easterner Porter would ever be. It was another of Adams's books that opened the door for Porter. Brower had published *This Is the American Earth* in 1960; its black and white photographs were mostly by Adams, and its Whitmanesque text by Nancy Newhall. Rather like the 1955 *The Family of Man*, this landscape photography book was more rhapsody than documentary survey, and it was a respectable financial success. Edgar Wayburn, who was the club's president from 1961 to 1964, recalled that *This Is the American Earth* "changed Dave's whole way of looking at the conservation movement. He saw what a book could do." It was the first of the

Exhibit Format books the club would publish, books that would introduce many Americans both to fine art photography and to their public lands. A few subsequent Exhibit Format books likewise lobbied for the protection of threatened places, though, like *This Is the American Earth* and *In Wildness*, most were less specific in their political aims.

Brower himself came out of publishing and publicity, and he naturally gravitated toward books—and later, newspaper ads and films—as a means of educating the public and advocating for conservation issues. A brilliant mountain climber and mercurial personality, he more than anyone changed the club from a small regional outdoors society that did a little lobbying to the preeminent environmental organization of the 1960s. His book projects sometimes made money for the Sierra Club; more reliably, they brought in members and raised awareness. The club had 7,000 members in 1952; 16,500 in 1961; 24,000 by 1964; and 55,000 by 1967 (in mid-2000, membership stood at 636,302). But by the mid-1960s, the publications program had begun to lose money, not raise it. As Stephen Fox recounted in his history of the American environmental movement,

> The conspicuous success of *Wildness* concealed the more typical commercial failure of other books in the series. Brower, believing the books a triumph in conservation, if not financial, terms, disregarded the warnings of his directors and plowed more money into the program. Once he asked the Publications Committee . . . for permission to go ahead with an Exhibit Format book. Turned down, he imperturbably replied: "But I've already spent $10,000 on it." Such collisions delayed the execution of contracts and the payment of royalties, poisoning relations between Brower and some of his most prominent authors, including Porter, Krutch, and Loren Eiseley. . . . From 1964 onward, the books program lost an average of $60,000 a year.

Brower and the Sierra Club published Porter's *Summer Island: Penobscot Country*, a portrait of his family's island in Maine, in 1966; *Baja California and the Geography of Hope*, with an extended essay by Joseph Wood Krutch, in 1967; and *Galapagos: The Flow of Wildness* in 1968. Though the books were not always related to immediate conservation objectives, they were often orchestrated to complement the campaigns Brower was working on. In his history of the Sierra Club, Michael P. Cohen points out that *The Place Nobody Knew* is a corollary to the "Should we also flood the Sistine Chapel so they can get closer to the ceiling?" ad, just as the Galapagos book was linked to Brower's infamous advertisement proposing the whole planet as "Earth National Park." The Galapagos book also helped to feed the turbulent controversies swirling around Brower by the late 1960s, when Porter was a member of the board of directors.

Porter had been elected to the board in 1965 and served two terms during the great years of transition in the Sierra Club. In the 1950s, the club had been fairly active in organizing outings and expeditions, less so in fighting environmental battles, and little involved in such battles outside California. Then, the club took no stand on development and technology as such, only on their implementation in particularly beautiful or ecologically sensitive places. The Sierra Club essentially told the U.S. government that even though it opposed a dam in Dinosaur, it would not oppose one in Glen Canyon—and then the club found out too late what beauty the latter canyon of the Colorado held. Glen Canyon was not described as ecologically important but as aesthetically irreplaceable. In the 1960s, the club began to oppose many kinds of pesticide and herbicide use; and by the 1970s, nuclear power and other major technologies were called into question: it had moved from preserving isolated places to protecting pervasive systems.

Porter was an outsider in the club, whose directors were then mostly Californians, longtime members of the organization, and, more often than not, participants in its outings; he brought with him an independence from the club's traditional ties and limitations. Several board members of the 1960s had been great mountaineers in the days when the Sierra Club was a major force in American mountaineering, and many had ties not only within the club but within more powerful institutions in California—there were engineers, chemists, physicists, and executives involved with enterprises the club would later target. "The idea of playing hardball with big corporations—Standard Oil or PG&E and what have you—was a jarring thing to them," remembered board member Phil Berry.

With Diablo Canyon nuclear power plant, the drama of Dinosaur and Glen

Canyon was repeated. The builder was Pacific Gas & Electric, the same company that benefits from hydropower from Hetch Hetchy Dam inside Yosemite National Park, the early twentieth-century dam that John Muir strove so hard to prevent and that first made the club into a forceful political organization (and first threatened to split it, as members became divided over the relative merits of development and preservation). In 1963, members of the club discovered that PG&E was planning to build a plant at Nipomo Dunes on the central California coast, a site that had often been recommended for park status. After the club's executive committee voted to try to preserve the dunes, board president Will Siri privately negotiated to have the plant moved to Diablo Canyon. Once again, too late, Sierra Club activists discovered that Diablo Canyon was too important to trade off. Many board members, including Adams, argued that if the club had agreed to support the Diablo siting, then they had an obligation to stick by the agreement. Porter thought differently. As Berry puts it, the uncompromising stand advocated by board member Martin Litton "was most eloquently stated, really, by Eliot Porter. Eliot said at that infamous September '68 board meeting, that the Sierra Club should never be a party to a convention that lessens wilderness. That's the truth. We shouldn't be. I think we gained strength from the mess of Diablo."

Porter himself said in a letter published in the *Sierra Club Bulletin*, "Every acre that is lost diminishes our stake in the future. That is why a compromise is always a losing game. The wildness that we have set as our task to protect is finite, but the appetite of the developers is infinite." Litton managed to get a bare majority to vote to withdraw support and begin fighting against Diablo Canyon. Porter's stand on this action was his most high-profile act during his six years on the board. To Porter, Diablo was biologically important as well as scenic, just as his Galapagos book was about evolution, Darwin, and imperiled biodiversity as well as exotic fauna and scenery. (The club lost the Diablo fight, and by the 1980s, the antinuclear movement had taken over the job of protesting the nuclear power plant there, which was built with many cost overruns, huge errors, and unanswered questions about safety.)

At least since the battle over Hetch Hetchy, early in the twentieth century, the Sierra Club had experienced a lot of internal dissent about tactics and mission, but the battles during the sixties were far more heated than their predecessors. Like the controversy over Diablo Canyon, the controversy over the publications program threatened to tear the club apart in the late 1960s. Board conservative Alex Hildebrand later accused Porter of a conflict of interest for voting to support the lavish publications program, a charge Porter vehemently denied. Brower, Porter, and some of the others on the board saw the publications as having far-reaching, if indirect, effects, in promoting environmental awareness and raising the club's profile. Others saw the program—particularly the picture books—as a drain of time and money and believed that publications should be far more closely tied to specific campaigns and specifically endangered American places. Adams— who had mixed feelings about color photography anyway—was opposed to the lavishness and political indirectness of the publications program and to David Brower's direction in those years.

Porter's Galapagos book, which he had been thinking about since the early 1960s, joined Diablo as one of the conflicts that came to a head in 1968. "There was a great deal of opposition to the proposal within the board of directors," recalled Porter of the Galapagos project, "on the grounds that the islands were outside the continental United States, which, it was felt, put them outside the legitimate conservation concerns of the club; so the idea was rejected." Then-president Edgar Wayburn argued that "other projects have higher conservation priority; for example a Mount McKinley book could make or break a great national park."

Porter shared Brower's sense that the club and the American conservation movement should expand to begin working globally, and he was passionate about the threats to the unique species and ecosystem of the Galapagos. Brower reintroduced the project more successfully later. "The publications committee of the Sierra Club had at last agreed to finance an expedition to the Galapagos Islands," Porter wrote. However, he added, "before it left, our party reached an almost unimaginable size." Porter's son and daughter-in-law and Brower and his son Kenneth had joined it, along with various other individuals playing roles of varying necessity. Eventually growing impatient with continual delays in publication, Porter in 1966 approached Harper and Row about publishing the book, but it remained with the Sierra Club and grew into an unwieldy two-volume set whose publication costs, like the expense of the expedition, became enormous.

By 1968, as Cohen recounted, "Adams argued that Brower would not accept a position subordinate to the Club and demonstrated his thesis by detailing what he called the 'Galapagos Book venture,' wherein Brower flagrantly disregarded decisions of the Publications and Executive committees." Brower's waywardness pleased no one. As Porter recalled, "During a board meeting at the Sierra Club camp in 1968, Brower proudly presented me with the first copy off the press of *Galapagos: The Flow of Wildness.* . . . My initial delight was soon dampened, however, by the discovery that my name appeared nowhere on either volume other than as photographer. . . . When I asked Brower why my name was not on either volume, he said it was because there were so many contributors that no one could be named. I was so shaken and speechless I left the meeting." Despite this, reviewers and readers recognized it as Porter's book.

Porter would vote to keep Brower on the board of directors anyway, but the vote was ten to five against, and Brower left the job—but not the club—in 1969. He founded Friends of the Earth and continued working to protect wilderness, nationally and globally. Porter served out his second term and, to his relief and cha-grin, was not nominated to a third. He continued to support the club's objectives, served on the New Mexico Nature Conservancy board and on the Chairman's Council of the Natural Resources Defense Council, gave images as donations and for reproduction to environmental organizations (and Planned Parenthood), and continued to donate money to a wide variety of causes. And his books continued to be published, primarily by E. P. Dutton, which in 1972 finally put out the bird book that had inspired him to take up color photography more than thirty years before.

Porter himself roamed farther afield, completing books on Antarctica, Iceland, Egypt, Greece, Africa (with Peter Matthiessen), and China, as well as continuing to photograph North American places and phenomena. Many of the images made abroad incorporated evidence of human culture and portrayed human beings, as the American work generally did not. Perhaps it is that people were integrated into their landscapes in those places in a way they seldom are in the restless, rootless United States (though that process of integration has created some of the world's oldest environmental degradation in overgrazed Greece and topsoil-exhausted China). The African and Antarctic books were particularly concerned with environmental issues, though questions of extinction and habitat were present in most. From a modest initial definition of nature as birds and details of the New England landscape, Porter's photography grew into a global picture of natural systems and human participation—often benign—in those systems. His work seemed to evolve as the environmental movement did, from protecting specific species and places to rethinking the human place in the world, a world reimagined as a system of interconnected systems rather than a collection of discrete objects.

Porter remained a scientist as well as an environmentalist. When James Gleick's book *Chaos: Making a New Science* came out in 1987, Porter read it with excitement and, with the help of his assistant Janet Russek, organized his own book around its themes, *Nature's Chaos*, for which Gleick wrote an introduction. Porter was struck by the way the new scientific ideas seemed to describe nature as he had been attempting to describe it with his camera—for chaos theory might better be called complexity theory: it describes the intricate patternings, interpenetrations, and repercussions of natural processes. For this last book—which would be published posthumously in 1990—Porter collected existing images that suggested patterning, conjunctions of forces that overlapped and affected each other. In some ways, these had always been his themes.

AN ECOLOGICAL AESTHETIC

Perhaps the central question about Porter's work is about the relationship between science, aesthetics, and environmental politics. His brother, the painter and critic Fairfield Porter, wrote in a 1960 review of the color photographs: "There is no subject and background, every corner is alive," and this suggests what an ecological aesthetic might look like. The statement resembles Barry Commoner's 1971 declaration of the first principle of ecology, "Everything is connected to everything else," which ecofeminist Carolyn Merchant revised in 1981 as "All parts of a system have equal value." Merchant expanded, "Ecology assigns equal importance to all organic and inorganic components in the structure of an ecosystem. Healthy air, water, and soil—the abiotic components of the system—are as essential as the entire diverse range of biotic parts—plants, animals, and bacteria and fungi. Without each element in the structure, the system as a whole cannot function properly." A century before, John Muir had stated this with less science: "When we try to pick out anything in the universe, we find it connected to everything else." Porter's most distinctive compositions are the close-ups in which the frame is filled with life and with stuff. Rather than portraits that isolate a single phenomenon, they function something like samples from the web of inter-related phenomena.

This close-up scale emphasizes the ordinary over the extraordinary. Plate 17 in *The Place No One Knew* is titled "Near Balanced Rock Canyon"; Balanced Rock is a landmark, an outstanding and unusual feature of the landscape visible from a distance. But Porter's medium close-up shows large, river-rounded rocks on a rock surface, the small rocks mostly grayish, the bedrock on which they lie more yellow, a quotidian scene near the unseen exceptional one. Of course, this image was made to be seen in context, with other, more spectacular images of the rocks and water of Glen Canyon, and this serial approach changes the expectations for each photograph: they need not each be prima ballerinas, each straining for the spectacular, but a corps de ballet, fleshing out the overall picture. But plate 17 also suggests that ordinary rocks are important enough, that we can love a place for its blackberries or its stream ripples, not just for its peaks, waterfalls, or charismatic macrofauna. All parts have equal value. These images make it clear why Porter was willing to fight for Diablo Canyon, a beautiful, pristine, but unexceptional landscape.

Working in close-up, Porter was as often calling attention to that which we overlook as to that which we don't encounter because of its remoteness. He came near to stating a credo when he wrote, "Much is missed if we have eyes only for the bright colors. Nature should be viewed without distinction. . . . She makes no choice herself; everything that happens has equal significance. Nothing can be dispensed with. This is a common mistake that many people make: they think that half of nature can be destroyed—the uncomfortable half—while still retaining the acceptable and the pleasing side." Porter came of age artistically at a time when a radical shift was taking place in the way Americans understood and managed nature. In the late nineteenth through the mid-twentieth centuries, predators and rodents were often depicted as "nuisance species," to be eradicated so that the useful species—game and domestic animals—might flourish. Conservationists were evolving into ecologists as they came to understand that it is generally impossible to preserve a species or a place apart from the complex systems of which it is part. In his overall pictures, Porter comes as close as any artist has to portraying ecology.

"Every corner is alive" suggests another important aspect of Porter's characteristic close-ups. Landscape photography generally depicts open space, usually defined by a horizon line, with the camera looking forward, much as a standing or striding human being might. It depicts, most often, an anthropomorphic space—anthropomorphic because its central subject *is* space, space that can be entered at least in imagination. Too, it often shows things at such a distance that the entities themselves—the grass or trees or rocks—cannot be subjects, only compositional elements. The implication of many classic landscape photographs (and the paintings from which they derive) is that such space is, in some sense, empty, waiting to be inhabited. This evolves, of course, from the way landscape painting itself evolved out of anthropocentric painting: the banditti or the Madonna got smaller, and the landscape behind the drama got more complex, until eventually the actors left the stage—but the landscape was still composed as a stage, as scenery. And scenery's principal function was its ability to serve as a backdrop, to describe habitable space. Porter, on the other hand, often photographed flat surfaces up close—the surface of the earth, a stone, or a tree trunk—and with subtle tonal ranges. He looked directly at his subject, which was matter itself, rather than across or through it to space. There is very little empty space in his images and thus little or no room in which to place oneself imaginatively. The scale is not theatrical, or at least not anthropocentrically so.

He once remarked, "Don't show the sky unless the sky has something to say." This seems to propose that the sky should be a subject in its own right, rather than a provider of orienting horizon lines and inhabitable space above the surface of the earth. His extensive series of photographs of clouds bear this out by suggesting that clouds should be seen on their own terms, as scientific and aesthetic phenomena, not simply as part of a landscape scene. In fact, there are very few *scenes* in Porter's work. If the image is not a close-up, the camera may be tilted down or up to show things on their own terms, rather than as background to habitable space. And Porter's favorite view is straight ahead, into an impenetrable thicket of saplings. If landscape photography has an empty center, in Porter's work nature itself fills that center, whether with leaves, stones, creatures, or clouds: nature, not humanity, is the true inhabitant of Porter's places. This is not landscape photography, but nature photography, a wholly new genre, which Porter founded. If it has an ancestor, that ancestor is still-life painting and photography, though before Adams and Porter, still-life subject matter was nearly always domestic items, indoors, stuff that could be set up for the studio easel or camera— fruit, flowers, household objects, instruments, food, not wild stuff in its own place and on its own terms.

As Caponigro noted, Porter was motivated as much by ecological as by aesthetic aspects of a phenomenon. It may be that he liked lichen so much not only because it had wonderful color range and texture, but also because it represented a unique symbiosis between a fungus and a mold, making its home on the seemingly inhospitable faces of rocks. Many of his pictures are meeting grounds between various forces and beings. It seems likely that, in the absence of a color photographic tradition to learn from, Porter learned from painting, and the painting of the 1940s and 1950s was mostly abstract. In his flat-to-the-picture-plane images, Porter seems to have learned from abstract expressionism, and some of his rock-face pictures are impossible to look at without believing that he had been influenced by the movement. Abstract expressionism likewise emphasized what in Jackson Pollock's work was sometimes called "all-overness," and in the others later on "color-field painting." The composition in other of Porter's photographs shows the strong influence of the great modernist photographers, though he adapted what he learned from them to color and to a very different kind of involvement with his subject matter. Porter rejected much of high modernism's philosophy in the way he tied his work to science, politics, and literature, but he never quarreled with its strategies and aesthetics.

WILDERNESS AND STRATEGY

In some ways, the golden age of the Sierra Club publication program seems to parallel the golden age of American landscape painting in the second half of the nineteenth century, when the American West was celebrated in paintings by Albert Bierstadt, Frederic Church, and Thomas Moran and in photographs by Carleton Watkins, Eadweard Muybridge, William Henry Jackson, and others. In that time, it was the West that was terra incognita to the majority; in the 1960s, it was the remaining remote places east and west. Both were eras in which the American public discovered their terrain through artistic representation, and in both cases American landscape was seen as the stage on which no actors had yet entered, as virgin wilderness before the first efflorescence of civilization. Thomas Cole had written that "the most distinctive, and perhaps the most impressive, characteristic of American scenery is its wildness. It is the most distinctive, because in civilized Europe, the primitive features of scenery have long since been destroyed or modified." For Cole, American landscape was a stage on which the principal acts had yet to take place, and this idea of wilderness as a place before people, as a place as yet affected by nothing but natural forces, has been powerful ever since. Wilderness, as Wallace Stegner wrote of it in 1960 in the letter that coined the term "the geography of hope," meant a place apart from civilization, a place where humans had not yet and should not arrive on stage.

Since that era, much has been written to revise this idea, most significantly by acknowledging that Native Americans spent millennia in places Euro-Americans dubbed virginal, and that the supposed pristine condition had been much affected by the Native presence—and sometimes damaged by their absence. Out of the imagination of wilderness and the ignorance of indigenous presence came a false dichotomy: a wholly nonhuman nature and a wholly unnatural humanity. The latter was seen as a threat, meaning that the former had to be protected as a place apart. William Cronon has written, "The critique of modernity that is one of environmentalism's most important contributions to the moral and political discourse of our time more often than not appeals, explicitly or implicitly, to wilderness as the standard against which to measure the failings of our human world. Wilderness is the natural, unfallen antithesis of an unnatural civilization that has lost its soul." Now that the critique of modernity is accomplished, we have entered upon the critique of wilderness—not of places themselves, but of the way they are described, administrated, and imagined.

One of the ironies of Porter's career is that he did much to give "the wilderness idea" a face, but that face exists not so much in the images he made as in the way people perceive them. *In Wildness* was seen—and successfully deployed—as a book in defense of wilderness. Most of the congressional representatives and senators to whom Brower sent it called it *In Wilderness* in their thank-you notes. In fact, most of the phenomena it portrays might readily be seen on the near fringes of civilization—by a small-town New England schoolchild taking a detour through the woods on the way home, for example, or by Thoreau on the outskirts of long-settled Concord. The creatures are small—caterpillars, moths, songbirds; the bodies of water are brooks, not rivers; the trees are maples, not bristlecones. The photographs could have been used equally to justify development, in that the flora and fauna they show could and do survive on the fringes of developed areas. In 1962, simply depicting the quiet splendors of the natural world was a powerful argument, in part because it had never been made as Porter made it. Success would wear out this argument's impact, setting a different task for a later generation of environmentally concerned photographers.

There are no human traces in *The Place No One Knew*, though the region abounds with petroglyphs and ruins and is partially within the huge Navajo-Hopi reservation. Rainbow Bridge, which the Sierra Club fought for as a great natural phenomenon whose setting would be damaged by the Glen Canyon Dam, has more recently been fought for as a sacred site by five Indian tribes in the area. But the book seems to postulate Glen Canyon as an untouched place and the dam as the first devastating human trace that would be left on it. Now, wilderness can be seen as a useful fiction, a fiction constructed by John Muir and his heirs and deployed to keep places from being destroyed by resource extraction and whole-sale development. In more recent years, it has become equally valuable to understand the ways that human presences can do other than destroy, the way that wild places can be a homeland, not an exotic other. The wilderness idea may be specific to an immigrant industrial society. Porter and most of us have no trouble seeing traditional peasant and indigenous cultures with their biodegradable, bioregional, often handmade artifacts as part of their landscape; in his Baja book, he depicted a few religious sites amid the plants and rocks (and focused on Mexican churches in another book). Among one of Porter's most memorable later images is one of an apple tree, leafless, bearing withered golden fruit, on his Tesuque, New Mexico, property, an image of nature, but hardly of wilderness.

As Porter got older and went farther afield, more and more human traces began to appear: in his Iceland book, for example, there are abandoned houses nestled into treeless slopes and weathered by the same forces as their surroundings. In his work from Egypt and Greece, the stone buildings are treated much as the stone of Glen Canyon was—which is to say that if Glen Canyon's nature was seen as art, this art is seen as nature in its materials, its erosion, its sense of place (and one could argue that excluding human traces from Glen Canyon was necessary to postulate nature itself as art, so that Glen Canyon becomes a gallery being drowned—thus was Brower able to compare it to the Sistine Chapel—and proposing it as art made a very different argument than, say, proposing it as habitat). In Porter's work from China and Africa, people appear as part of the place, and the majority of the photographs show people. How to show contemporary Americans as part of their landscape is a problem that subsequent generations took on: one could almost trace a history from the discordance of tourists, nudists, and developers in the 1960s and 1970s to more recent photographs—by Barbara Bosworth, Mark Klett, Robert Dawson, among others—that show more complex, ambiguous, and sometimes even symbiotic relationships with the land.

Working on the scale of book sequences, rather than individual images, Porter can be thought of as creating a portrait of a place out of myriad details. Though he was often concerned with documenting the diversity or the more endangered phenomena, his selections did not always please fellow environmentalists. George

Marshall charged, in a 1965 letter to Porter about the artist's Adirondacks project,

> What has troubled me is that few of them seem to represent or symbolize what seem to me to be the major characteristics of the Adirondacks which have made them for many of us a region unsurpassed in beauty. These unique characteristics are to be found, I believe, in its so-called High Peaks, its other mountains in places, its large lakes and ponds, its spagnum marshes . . . and first growth forests. . . . Some of this is represented in your photographs, but frankly, as I recall them, very little.

And to David Brower, Marshall wrote, "Most of the photographs as I recall them are of second growth forests which have been burnt or lumbered. I feel little in this book as it now stands . . . justifies the title 'forever wild.' " That they represented the consequences of logging rather than of forest succession is evident only to the ecologically knowledgeable; human traces are not always so visible as petroglyphs or pavement. The same second-growth forests had been shown in *In Wildness*; perhaps it was because the new photographs were meant as a portrait of a specific place rather than generalized evocation that such details mattered. Marshall seemed to think that the trees should have been left out or should have been photographed as something other than beautiful since they represented something other than an ecosystem in its ideal state (Michael Cohen has commented that perhaps Porter, like Thoreau, felt that second-growth forests represented healing). Marshall raised the enduring conflict of environmental photography: that what is ecologically good is not necessarily beautiful, and vice versa.

Marshall wanted a more "Ansel Adams" treatment, it seems, with more majesty, more unusual features, less celebration of the quotidian. But Porter found the young trees beautiful, so he photographed them. The work of Ansel Adams and Eliot Porter generates instructive comparisons on many grounds: the two were nearly the same age, crossed paths as both artists and activists, and became perhaps the most famous American photographers of the second half of the twentieth century (though Adams's reputation has not faded as Porter's has). The differences are obvious: Adams was a successful, confident artist in an established medium, while Porter was still experimenting in relative isolation; Adams was ensconced in both artistic and environmental communities, as Porter was not; Adams's work, with its taste for grandeur and spectacle, has ties to the great Western landscape photogra-phy of the nineteenth century, whereas Porter was exploring the new medium of dye-transfer color photography as both a technical medium and a compositional challenge and drawing from new developments in painting.

Adams, like Porter, has suffered from becoming famous for a portion of his work now thought of as the whole. Adams also made portraits and took many close-up photographs of flora and other natural details, as well as creating series about entirely different subjects. Still, he did make the definitive majority of his pictures in the classic landscape-photographic tradition, emphasizing deep space, strong contrast, dramatic light, and crisp delineation—almost sculptural qualities that black and white was suited to portray. Porter, in contrast, often flattened out a subject and sought a painterly subtlety of color range.

Adams's pictures often depend on the drama of a revelatory light that appears almost divine; Porter often preferred cloudy days to make his images that speak of the slowness of careful attention. In other words, Adams would usually photo-graph the balancing rock of Balancing Rock Canyon, but Porter would usually ignore it. One result is that Adams's work locates itself through landmarks such as Half Dome or the Grand Tetons, while Porter's does so through representative specimens—the sandstone of the Southwest, the warblers of the Midwest, the maple leaves of New England. Adams prized the most spectacular and unique aspects of a place; Porter focused on the representative and quotidian aspects of even the most exotic places he went. With Adams's monumental scenes, viewers at least felt that they were remote from civilization (though cropping out the peo-ple and infrastructure in Yosemite Valley must have been a challenge at times); with Porter, they could be a few feet from it—his close-ups might speak of an intact natural order, but not necessarily of an unviolated wilderness space.

Porter had his own restrictions about what should be represented and what should be found beautiful. In 1977, he saw *The End of the Game*, an exhibition of African images by the fashion and wildlife photographer Peter Beard, at the

International Center for Photography (ICP). Beard took a radically nonmodernist tack in his book of the same name, writing on photographs, using his own work together with older images, and collaging them scrapbook-style with other material in the style of Victorian travel journals. Porter, who brought the Victorian texts of Thoreau together with his own images, could conceivably have been sympathetic, but he exclaimed in a letter that the project "was supposed to influence people for conservation but played to morbid curiosity and violence. It memorialized killing and death with dead animals, dying animals, a half eaten human body. and 100 elephant carcasses."

Porter had gone to the ICP to discuss an exhibition of his Antarctic photographs, which also included dead animals—seals that had died after becoming stranded inland, then been mummified and partially flayed by the arid winds. But Beard's images were not so gracious: elephants dying in a far warmer zone were a far messier business, and he attempted to suggest the sheer scope of the disaster with his copious images of elephant herds, corpses, and skeletons. He intended to shock and hoped to change minds by doing so. The huge die-off had been caused by a population explosion that denuded the landscape—ultimately it was caused by the unnaturalness of game protection laws born out of Euro-American ideas about wilderness as a place apart from humans (echoing the mistakes made by American game management that had led to the Kaibab Plateau defoliation and deer die-off decades earlier).

It could be said that Porter photographed uneventful cyclical time, Adams an almost Biblical sense of revelatory suspension of time, and Beard the turbulent time of the news. Elsewhere Porter had argued that photography "almost always unintentionally softens rather than exaggerates the unpleasant aspects of the conditions it attempts to dramatize most forcefully. The same is true when photography is used to show the devastations produced by man's works. The utter desolation visible on the scene of operation is almost impossible to reveal in photographs." Although, concerning Beard, he argued that the photographs were not softened at all, but sensationalistic, the same principle—that a photography makes the most reprehensible things pleasant to behold, even fascinating—remains. This assertion justified Porter's own strategy of showing what can be saved and what remains intact, rather than what has been ravaged, of photographing nature as existing in cyclical time rather than history (though looming catastrophe had been the unseen subject of *The Place No One Knew*).

Porter and Adams functioned in a unique way at a unique time: their aesthetic work had a kind of political impact that is hard to imagine in any other arena. Even those who were not great supporters of the publications program of the Sierra Club acknowledged that it was the books—particularly the photographic books, and among those particularly Porter's—that first made the Sierra Club a visible force nationwide. It was a rare moment in history when art could achieve political ends so profound, when the mere sight of such images and reminder of such places became a powerful motivating force, when a pair of artists who were much admired in museum circles could do heroic work in environmental ones. No artist can ask for more than to live in a time when art can change the world.

LEGACY

Today's well-respected landscape photographers are making very different work, and few of them have the role within environmental organizations or the broad popular success that Porter did. The terrain has changed. Almost two decades after *In Wildness Is the Preservation of the World*, the landscape photographer Robert Adams wrote,

> More people currently know the appearance of Yosemite Valley and the Grand Canyon from having looked at photographic books than from having been to the places themselves; conservation publishing has defined for most of us the outstanding features of the American wilderness. Unfortunately, by perhaps an inevitable extension, the same spectacular pictures have also been widely accepted as a definition of nature, and the implication has been circulated that what is not wild is not natural. . . . There are now far fewer unpublicized wilderness areas, and there are relatively few converts, with the exception of children, left to be won to the general idea of wilderness preservation.

Adams argues here that the same images mean different things at different points in history. By the time he wrote, the popular imagination had reached a point where such imagery had achieved what success it could; a new generation of photographers, he argued, ought instead to "teach us to love even vacant lots out of the same sense of wholeness that has inspired the wilderness photographers of the past twenty-five years."

Of course, it can be argued that Porter photographed backyards, if not vacant lots, along with people, ruins, and signs of rural life from Maine to Mexico, but this Adams has a point. Whatever images Porter made, the images of his that proved most memorable and influential were of a pristine nature, a place apart. Though Porter's pictures may have been primarily of the timeless seasonal world of natural phenomena, they existed in historical time; and their influence, even their appearance, has changed over the decades. Later in his career, Porter himself came to believe that his photographs were as likely to send hordes of tourists to an area as to send hordes of letters to Congress in defense of that area, countering Fox's argument that the books could substitute for visits to wilderness. Far more Americans had become familiar with the remote parts of the country, and recreational overuse as well as resource extraction and development threatened to disturb the pristine places. It may be precisely because Porter's work succeeded so spectacularly in contributing to American awareness and appreciation for remote and pristine places that different messages may now be called for. This invisible success is counterbalanced by a very visible one: thousands of professionals and countless amateurs now produce color nature photography more or less in the genre first set out by Porter.

The professional work is not quite like his (nor is the amateur, though for different reasons). For the most part, Porter seemed to value truth more and beauty—at least showy, bright beauty—less. He was concerned more with representing processes, systems, and connections than many of his followers are. He often made photographs of reduced tonal range, and some of his images of bare trees in snow are not immediately recognizable as being in color: "Much is missed if we have eyes only for the bright colors." The contemporary nature photographers whose work is seen in calendars and advertisements tend to pump up the colors and portray a nature far more flawless and untouched than anything Porter found decades earlier (though the best defense for such images is that some of them continue to raise money for environmental causes). Their work tends to crop out anything flawed and to isolate a perfect bloom, a perfect bird, a perfect icicle, in compositions usually simpler than Porter's. Looking at these images, one has the sense that if Porter founded a genre, the genre has become narrower rather than broader since.

Porter photographed dead animals and mating Galapagos turtles, but Barry Lopez, who himself once photographed animals, noted: "In the 1970s came, ironically, a more and more dazzling presentation of those creatures in incomplete and prejudicial ways. Photo editors made them look not like what they were but the way editors wanted them to appear—well-groomed, appropriate to stereotype, and living safely apart from the machinations of human enterprise." A kind of inflationary process has raised the level of purity, of brightness, of showiness each image must have. Some of this may be about the continued evolution of technologies; with improvements in film and cameras and innovations like Photoshop, more technical perfection is possible now than in Porter's time. And images that were relatively original in his work have now become staples, even clichés.

The thing least like an original is an imitation; they look alike, but they are not akin at all in their function in the world. Porter's work is innovative, responding imaginatively to a new medium and the new way of representing the world that the medium made possible. Imitating Porter is not responding to the world but to a now-established definition of it. As the decades go by, these images tend to look more and more like each other and less and less like what we actually see most of the time we go to natural places. The photographers who are most like Porter in their innovations of composition, their definition of nature and the human place in it, as well as the role of photography in the preservation of the world, may be those whose work looks least like his, who make work that responds to their beliefs, the crises of the day, and their outdoor encounters with the same imaginative integrity as Porter did to his. But Porter's primary legacy may not be photographic but something far more pervasive, a transformation of how we see and what we pay attention to.

The Botanical Circus, or
Adventures in American Gardening

⟦2003⟧

Eden is the problem, of course. Eden stands as the idea of nature as it should be rather than as it is, and in attempting to make a garden resemble Eden, the gardener wrestles the garden away from resembling nature—nature, that is, as the uncultivated expanses around it, the patterns that would assert themselves without interference. If gardens were actual nature, we would just have a plot of land outside, left alone, that wind and birds and proximate plants would seed and rain would water. Even in the humid temperate zones, let alone in America's desert Southwest, a good deal of manipulation of soil and water is necessary to make something nonnative grow. Eden serves as the phantasmagorical plan, as the ideal nature, to which every gardener cleaves. But no two gardeners have quite the same vision of it, and some versions of paradise are very fabulous and unrestrained indeed. There are both individual variations and historical evolutions in the ideal of the garden as an improved nature, a paradise; and of course paradise itself originally meant an enclosed garden, the kind of formal Islamic garden whose floor plans can be seen on most Persian carpets.

We love nature as a child loves a parent, but gardeners love their gardens as parents love children, with a preoccupied, hectoring, imposing love, not unlike that of museum curators, editors, animal tamers. Thoreau fretted over it in *Walden*, writing of the crop he grew with gardeners' contemplativeness:

> I came to love my rows, my beans, though so many more than I wanted. They
> attached me to the earth, and so I got strength like Antaeus. But why should I

raise them? Only heaven knows. This was my curious labor all summer,—to make this portion of the earth's surface, which had yielded only cinquefoil, blackberries, johnswort, and the like, before, sweet wild fruits and pleasant flowers, produce instead this pulse. What shall I learn of beans or beans of me? I cherish them, I hoe them, early and late I have an eye to them; and this is my day's work. It is a fine broad leaf to look on. My auxiliaries are the dews and rains which water this dry soil. . . . My enemies are worms, cool days, and most of all woodchucks. . . . A long war, not with cranes, but with weeds, those Trojans who had sun and rain and dews on their side. Daily the beans saw me come to their rescue armed with a hoe, and thin the ranks of their enemies, filling up the trenches with weedy dead.

Thoreau wrote with such wryness because, as an American romantic, he admired the unaltered landscape, and that admiration itself was the fruit of a long European history of garden evolution and the control of nature. Nature was sufficiently abundant, even overwhelming, throughout most of human history that it did not need to be referenced as an ideal, exactly. Some cultures assumed that nature was fine as it was, making gardens unnecessary; others thought that nature was fallen and yearned for an absent paradise whose parameters they sketched with herbs and flowers and walls or, in Asia, with pines and pools and stones. Usually they yearned for a more visibly ordered nature. Our horticultural ancestors the Romans had topiary and espaliered trees and neatly patterned beds; their ideal nature partook of geometry reminiscent of military formations. After them, one could say that nature relaxed into boudoirlike sanctuaries for all the senses until safety, wealth, and a returning preoccupation with geometrical order prompted the explosion of the formal garden in the seventeenth century. Gardens—aristocratic gardens, gardens of extraordinary expense—then reached a sort of Euclidean-Cartesian apogee of conical trees and long allées and managed fountains, and spread into the surroundings as they grew larger and larger: Versailles with its avenues to the horizon is the ultimate example, a garden that competes with the world. A 1712 English guide described part of an ideal garden's layout:

two Squares, each having four Quarters, with Basons. It is terminated by a long Arbour, with three Cabinets facing the Walks and Pavilions. On the Right are Green-Plots cut, to answer the walks, having Water-works, as on the other Side. These are bounded by a double line of Cases and Yews, and behind, by green Niches for Seats and Figures. On the Side is a Parterre of Orange-Trees walled in, having Iron Grills against the Walks; and at the End is a Bason, with Cabinets and green Niches for Seats.

The notion that for every action there is an equal and opposite reaction is as true of gardening as anything else: the English in the eighteenth century began to link the formality of such gardens to despotism and generated a notion of nature as ideal that is still with us. It was a tremendous reversal, full of its own contradictions.

The idea that unaltered nature might be worthy of contemplation as gardens was always slipping into the collective imagination in that century, and nature— or rather, Nature—became a goddess constantly invoked. A year after the above-cited garden manual, Alexander Pope effused, "There is certainly something in the amiable Simplicity of unadorned Nature, that spreads over the Mind a more noble sort of Tranquility, and a loftier Sensation of Pleasure, than can be raised from the nicer Scenes of Art." All the garden geometry of paths and parterres and, particularly, topiary had come to seem obnoxiously or at least ridiculously *unnatural*, that new term of condemnation, and Pope condemned the last with famous verve in an imaginary catalogue of topiaries: "Adam and Eve in Yew; Adam a little shatter'd by the fall of the Tree of Knowledge in the Great Storm; Eve and the serpent very flourishing. St. George in Box; his Arm scarce long enough, but will be in a Condition to stick the Dragon by next April. A green Dragon on the same, with a Tail of Ground-Ivy for the present. N.B. These two not to be Sold separately," and so on. The naturalistic garden known as the English garden evolved by degrees; parterres and topiary were done away with, and the gridded landscape gave way to serpentine paths and meanders, but sculpture and architecture still abounded until mid-century, when the inimitable Capability Brown began to do away with them as well.

Of course, the English garden was imitating a very particular notion of nature, one that at least at first was found more in the paintings of Claude and Poussin and sometimes Salvator Rosa than in the countryside all around. So one of the great contradictions is that the English garden is imitating art in its attempt to imitate nature, and the nature it is willing to imitate is once again a very specific idealized thing, though at least it's a flowing, complex thing. The radical idea was that nature was already orderly (an idea that cleared the way to start questioning the Fall or even to go with Rousseau and see it as a fall from natural innocence into civilized corruption). One thing led to another, as plenty of garden histories recount at length, and the culmination of this naturalizing process was that the surrounding landscape was by the 1770s found worthy of contemplation and suitable for strolling. Scenic-appreciation guidebooks by the likes of William Gilpin replaced garden-books as the manuals of appropriate aesthetic responsiveness.

To some extent, the world ever since has been regarded as once only gardens were. It's a tremendous history, out of the garden and into the landscape, and from thence originate both the outdoor industries and the environmental movement, perhaps even the idea of the national park. It's about a knight's move toward democracy—first toward gardens that, if they required less maintenance, required more space: a thousand-acre garden is only so democratic. But it opened the way to regard the whole world as a garden, at which point one no longer needed privileged access: Hampstead Heath would do, or an excursion train, or a long walk away from the factory districts (the latter two assiduously utilized into the mid-twentieth century in England, though nature never achieved that kind of populist status in America, perhaps because too many populists were still busy fleeing the farm). It recalls a parallel evolution in the visual arts in the second half of the twentieth century, in which, as Robert Irwin put it long before he himself became a garden designer, "the object of art may be to seek the elimination of the necessity of it."

The eighteenth-century dissolution of the garden into the landscape is a spectacular history that left only one unresolved question: what kinds of gardens were people going to have around their homes after that apotheosis of Nature? Christopher Thacker writes, "For several decades the nineteenth century had no distinctive garden style, but remained unsettled, eclectic and searching, as it did in architectural form, in furniture and in clothing." If the great eighteenth-century impulse came out of the growing control that human beings had over the world, a control that meant it was safe to let down the garden walls and satisfying to be occasionally overwhelmed by nature rather than to overwhelm it, then the nineteenth century came from very different impulses. Letting well enough alone was one of the few pastimes the Victorians never entertained. A new fussiness returned, as did the formalism of bright flowerbeds that no longer spoke of great Euclidian expanses of aristocratic order, just of the obsession with pattern and the bourgeois anxiety to sort it all out. And there was so much more to sort out. The Victorian garden comes perhaps from the botanical garden rather than the pleasure garden or landscape garden. And the botanical garden was less about the beauty of Eden per se than its symbolic and literal abundance. This is a shift in part from the garden as primarily a composition to the garden as a collection, and with that shift the garden regained its details—its flowers and unusual plants—that had been lost in the rush toward naturalism. (One of the peculiarities of garden history is how little it is plant history, particularly the landscape gardens, in which everything was meant to become pleasing composition at a suitable distance; flowers were banished in part because such gardens were not about details and close-ups and individual phenomena, and they were certainly not about brightness.)

Early botanical gardens were sometimes divided into quarters, echoing both the paradise garden of the Islamic world (with its central fountain and four streams echoing Eden's own hydrological arrangements) and the idea that the world's four continents were present as the four quarters of the garden. (Though the continents were eventually found to be less symmetrical in number, other, more practical versions of this order survive in, for example, Kew Gardens, with its greenhouses representing climates of varying degrees of intemperate pleasantness, or the Huntington Garden in California, with the continents reiterated as clusters amid the winding paths.) John Prest writes in his history of the botanical garden, "It was as though the creation was a jig-saw puzzle. In the Garden of Eden, Adam and Eve had been introduced to the completed picture. When they sinned, God had put some of the pieces away in a cupboard—an American cupboard—to be released when mankind improved, or he saw fit." This is part of why Thoreau was uncomfortable with "making the earth say beans": because America was already an Edenic garden in the rhetoric of his time, and because he took to an extreme the idea of noninterference implicit in the English landscape garden.

But the botanical garden was all about interference, eventually about the max-imum interference of colonialism and conquest (these movements spread plants in all directions, so that apples and roses grew in the colonies, while chrysanthe-mums and maize and monkey puzzle trees came to Europe). Plants poured in from around the world in increasing profusion in the nineteenth century, helped along by the growing availability of glass for greenhouses, which allowed one to grow delicate and tropical plants in northern Europe and by, in the 1830s, the Wardian case (of which no less an authority than Thacker says, "The Wardian case is, with the ha-ha and the lawn-mower, one of the great inventions in garden history"). The Wardian case, which we nowadays might call a terrarium, was a sealed glass box or bottle that made it possible to keep plants alive for the arduous months on board ship from Australia or Brazil.

There was a sort of golden age of plant hunters (echoed by the rainforest plant hunting now conducted by pharmaceutical companies and resisted as biocolonial-ism by the residents of those forests). Orchids and other tropical flora were arriv-ing in the first world, and their status as trophies of conquest, as prizes of the hunt, was well recognized, especially by Victorian gardeners. Such gardens were didactic and imperial, small local places about colonies and continents and expedi-tions far away. It's hard to recapture the shock some plants, like the first giraffes and elephants, must have produced. The American explorer John Wesley Powell, on his first encounter with the flora of the southwestern deserts, exclaimed in what sounds close to horror, "The few plants are strangers to the dwellers in the temperate zone. On the mountains a few junipers and piñons are found, and cac-tuses, agave, and yuccas, low, fleshy plants with bayonets and thorns. The land-scape of vegetal life is weird—no forests, no meadows, no green hills, no foliage, but clublike stems of plants armed with stilettos. Many of the plants bear gor-geous flowers." The jungle was equally alarming to the temperate-adjusted, with its dense, humid landscape of vigorous life, vivid color, and perilous species.

Only over time did these plants become part of the standard vocabulary, just as words like *jodhpur* and *raccoon* and *canyon* have. Almost no one thinks of Mexico when they look at dahlias (which the Aztecs called *cocoxochitl*). Marigolds and zinnias and rubber plants and bottlebrushes became standard nursery offerings. Only through this history did we arrive at the present ahistorical anything-goes moment of gardens, in which topiary and exotics and wildernesses and abundance and zen gardens and statuary all jostle each other. It is as though all the aesthetics, traditions, and regions have collapsed into an enormous polyglot vocabulary, a vocabulary in which anything may be said.

The United States was already wildly excessive and uninhibited on two fronts when it came time to make gardens. For one thing, the landscape itself was of a spectacularly un-European scale in its individual features, its Niagara Falls and Grand Canyons and ten-mile-long bison herds and mile-wide Mississippi and sequoias more like skyscrapers than other trees, and in its overall vastness and variety of mountains, deserts, prairies, forests, wetlands, and so forth. Second, within this expansive terrain, the Euro-Americans were living off largely introduced crops, though corn, squash, potatoes, and chilies had come over from Native agriculture, and life was already hybrid, jumbled, patchwork. The terrains, the climates, the hybrid populations and plantings all encouraged an unorthodoxy that was harder to come by than in the old countries; the American lack of a past always made the future seem more available, and more wide open. The difference between Britain and America is the difference between Alice, daughter of a don, falling down a rabbit hole (a very expansive, peculiar rabbit hole, admittedly), and Dorothy, an orphan raised by Kansas farmers, taken up by a tornado. Alice wanders a dreamland of decorous delirium, with its playing-card chattels, its nervous small animals, rose gardens, tea parties, chessboards, railroads, and nursery rhyme characters. The landscape of the Wizard of Oz, with the angry apple trees, the endless expanse of poppies (sunflowers in the movie), live scarecrows, talking lions, witches, midgets, Emerald City, tornados—the scale of peculiarity, the available vocabulary of strangeness, the volatility is that much more vast. (American excess is evident, too, in the way L. Frank Baum spun the story of Oz out into more than a dozen books that other writers continued after his death, while Alice's history has its Old Testament in Wonderland and its

New through the looking glass and no more.) English gardens are sometimes Wonderland, but American gardens easily slip into Oz.

Thomas Brayton, for example, acquired a seven-acre parcel of land in New England in 1872 and began a topiary garden, one whose scope would have dizzied even the sarcastic Alexander Pope. Though topiary was a strictly European tradition, Brayton's Green Animals garden is a global menagerie with a topiary giraffe, bear, swan, ostrich, hippopotamus, and peacock (and a stray terrier, out of scale, of course, though not as out of scale as Jeff Koons's). The peculiarity of the place is that it isn't aspiring to the aim of the old topiary gardens, a kind of gracious harmony that made their makers seem an estimable part of the place. Rather, it's a literal zoological garden, an eclectic collection of images from all over the world. This is a far more reckless revolt against good taste than all the garden gnomes in Northumbria could organize, one that isn't merely kitschy but heroically preposterous. In Brayton's time, county fairs were at their apogee, and they exhibited not only exemplary but extreme examples of local agriculture. (Giant pumpkins particularly are a hallowed American tradition going strong today; the iconic American children's author Laura Ingalls Wilder tells a tale of her spouse in his youth exhibiting one at a New York county fair, in what must have been the 1850s or thereabouts, and the comic strip *Peanuts* featured a Great Pumpkin deity for Halloween akin to Santa and the Easter Bunny.) Brayton started out just as Buffalo Bill was becoming the performer whose theatrics would culminate in Buffalo Bill's Wild West Show, a sort of bioregional circus that toured North America and Europe. A couple of years later, P. T. Barnum's efforts culminated in the founding of Barnum and Bailey's circus, still touring today.

Think of P. T. Barnum as a gardener for a moment. Gardeners seek to alter their plants and push them to extremes, and Barnum sought out human beings who were similarly unusual. He began his career exhibiting an African American woman who claimed to be the 161-year-old nurse of George Washington's father, soon acquired a mermaid skeleton, and was truly launched when he enlisted the services of young Charles Stratton, still remembered well as General Tom Thumb, a midget who eventually reached the height of 33 inches (84 cm). Thus began the Golden Age of circuses and the American sideshow or, as it was known at Coney

Island in New York, freak show: a sort of botanical garden of human variety from around the world, often including Siamese twins (seldom Siamese but always so designated after the conjoined Chang and Eng, two of Barnum's performers), giants, dwarfs, midgets, fat ladies, thin men and living skeletons, pinheads, hermaphrodites, strong men, bearded ladies, contortionists, sword-swallowers, fire-eaters and tattooed, limbless, and otherwise unusual people. The botanical equivalent might be bonsai, sequoia, grafts, dwarf and espaliered fruit trees, barrel cacti, banyan trees, hybrid tea roses such as the Racy Lady and Scent Sation, tropical flowers bred to yet more extravagant displays, tulip breaks, and, of course, topiary and outsized pumpkins. (Just as in the sideshow, most of the freaks need do nothing more than be their unusual selves, so sunflowers and azaleas and the largest fig tree in the United States may sit serene in their fabulousness; but topiary is performative flora, akin to sword-swallowers and acrobats in its achievement of an effect that is the result of effort, not essence—topiary is, after all, usually nothing more exotic than box or yew.)

Whole forests have been laid waste to discuss beauty and, in the eighteenth and early nineteenth centuries, the sublime and the picturesque. All of these aesthetics can be configured as being uplifting, enlarging, somehow in good taste. But there are other aesthetics, not least among them what could be called the exuberant, the appetite for the peculiar, the disproportionate, the unusual and exotic, the outsized, the gaudy, the excessive, the appalling. The United States, as Barnum and Brayton and Chesty Morgan (the stripper and B-movie star whose breasts were, more or less, the size of prize pumpkins) and a thousand Las Vegas designers all demonstrate, is the true home of this aesthetic. Familiar as part of the freak show, the hot dog stands shaped like hot dogs, the roadside dinosaur statuary— this is the aesthetic that would describe why we like to look not only at really beautiful people but also at really obese, tall, or tiny ones. It's a curiosity that seems somehow connected to the botanical garden, which attempts to catalog the expanse of creation's flora as the sideshow does its human fauna. It suggests not a nature of harmony and continuity, but of extravagant experimentation, endless variety, a never-a-dull-moment nature, a wide-open nature. And perhaps a democratic one, which brings us back to Americanism.

This nature can be seen as democratic because it achieves its effect not through exclusion but through inclusion, and because exuberance itself is generally considered to be a little déclassé. There is a whole language of class in the garden—when they returned to the garden, flowers were redeemed with the tasteful monochromatic schemes of the likes of Gertrude Jekyll; and, as gardening essayist Michael Pollan points out, there is a whole class war of the roses, in which old roses—more fragrant, more softly shaped, less abundant in their bloom, more limited in their palette—are the exiled aristocracy. Good taste is about renunciation: you must have enough to restrain in order to value restraint, enough abundance to prize austerity. After all, it was only after aniline dyes made bright clothing universally available that the privileged stopped dressing like peacocks; spareness is often the public face of excess. For those for whom too much is still a shining promise, brightness, quantity, and size are not yet dubious qualities. And good taste could also be an aestheticization of the limited-palette moderation of the temperate zone, in contrast to the vividness of the tropics and the starkly sculptural stand-alone forms of desert plants and the desert's periodic wild bloomings. Moderation, the Greek philosopher said, is pleasant to the wise, but it's not necessarily fun. Eleanor Perényi writes in her book *Green Thoughts: A Writer in the Garden*,

> Looking at my dahlias one summer day, a friend whose taste runs to the small and impeccable said sadly, "You do like big, conspicuous flowers, don't you?" She meant vulgar, and I am used to that. It hasn't escaped me that mine is the only WASP garden in town to contain dahlias, and not the discreet little singles either. Some are as blowsy as half-dressed Renoir girls; others are like spiky sea-creatures, water-lilies, or the spirals in a crystal paperweight; and they do shoot up to prodigious heights. But to me they are sumptuous, not vulgar.

Exclusion seeks harmony, familiarity, tranquility, all those things that might be essential to a landscape garden and inimical to a circus—but why can't a garden be like a circus and yield up a circus's gorgeous pleasures? This is the question raised by John Pfahl's garden photographs, and what makes the answer unusual is that it is entirely botanical.

Often, eccentric gardeners seeking self-expression leave plants behind to make gardens of found objects and accretions. The folk art environments that proliferate most in the American South but can be found almost everywhere often speak of religion, particularly the Book of Revelation. They are still gardens, but they have somehow left nature behind, perhaps because it requires a more patient manipulation than bottles and planks and old tires, perhaps because we tend to think of nature in general as restrained and subdued despite examples of nature in particular like Perényi's dahlias and Brayton's giraffe or yuccas whose spray of long leaves looks like fireworks in slow motion. There are other versions of nature that are vibrant, extravagant, even lurid and sensational, and though the most common approximation of paradise emphasizes its serenity, are not its variety and abundance equally essential? And does not the Book of Revelation, with all its architecture of jewels and uncanny beasts suggest that the landscape of revelation is going to be more like the Las Vegas Strip in its neon glory days than, say, the Lake District or the Roman campagna? Was not a long allée of tall trees always secretly offering the pleasures that a row of Vegas showgirls, each six feet tall, now proffers? In which case, plants best approach the ideal nature when the horticulture becomes extreme, an Eden of weirdness and democracy and large appetite for dazzle.

A Murder of Ravens

On Globalized Species

⟦2006⟧

Saudi jihadists weren't the only ones with a penchant for crashing into the upper levels of the World Trade Center. Songbirds did too, migrating by night and mistaking the lights high above the city for stars, with approximately the same disastrous results as moths attempting to navigate by candlelight. At least one ornithologist used to regularly stroll along the base of the towers in the early morning, removing small corpses and rescuing the living. A lot of species have been too fragile, too particular in their requirements, to survive our wholesale transformation of their environment. In my own corner of it, the brown satyr butterfly, endemic to San Francisco, became extinct sometime in the nineteenth century, and the Xerxes blue vanished during World War II when its Golden Gate habitat was overtaken by military expansion. A number of other local species—the bay checkerspot, the San Francisco garter snake, the mission blue butterfly—are near extinction. Farther afield, the California condor with its ten-foot wingspan, or rather the few dozen surviving specimens, continues to hover near the brink of disappearance; after an ingenious captive breeding program, a few have been reintroduced in the wild—where they show an unfortunate penchant for flying into power lines and eating the lead shot in game killed by guns. On the other hand and the other side of the country, one of North America's showiest and most famously extinct birds, the ivory-billed woodpecker, reappeared in 2004; its existence was publicly announced in the spring of 2005, amid a media circus, bouts of scientists' tears, and a lot of astonishment and rapture (and a little Arkansas forest protection). Whether there is a breeding pair rather than just a single individual remains to be seen, as does the bird's ability to make do with what habitat it has left.

Other species have rebounded, notably elephant seals, who were hunted nearly into extinction at the turn of the twentieth century, when at most a few hundred survived in Mexican waters. They first returned to their California coastal breeding grounds in the 1950s and have flourished since, north and south of San Francisco, where their spectacular sex and violence—the bellicose males weigh up to three tons—can be observed every winter. Dozens of species of birds once threatened by DDT have increased in number since the pesticide was banned, as have whales since the 1949 near-ban on hunting, though many, many species continue to lose ground. Yet others, notably a lot of omnivores and carnivores that once feared humans and were hunted by us, have begun not just to rebound but to expand their territory, their diet, and their habits. They are joining us.

Thus the mountain lions of Silicon Valley: a Palo Alto naturalist reports that after sixteen unconfirmed sightings in nine years, there were suddenly thirty sightings in the first nine months of 2004, two of which were so flagrantly out in the middle of suburbia that police decided the predators had to be shot. One primary school sent warnings to parents about letting kids walk to school alone. In a few spectacular cases in the past decade or so, mountain lions have hunted, killed, and partially eaten solitary runners. In several others, they have stalked children who were out with their parents. We are, after all, as food units, sized much like deer and not nearly as speedy. More often the lions, which reach up to 150 pounds, dine on the housepets (as do alligators in Florida, another population on the rebound). California offered a bounty on mountain lions into the 1960s, and they were wary, seldom-seen beasts in those days; but in 1990, we voted to make them a protected species. In 1920, there were about six hundred of them in the state; like the state's human population, they have increased tenfold since. There are now four to six thousand of them, and they have changed their behavior, no longer shunning human beings and habitation.

In this past decade, we have seen the emergence of the new nature that will likely survive while the more fragile primordial nature falls. It includes a weedy, flexible, tough set of species who thrive on the disturbances that send other species into flight or extinction. And they're becoming increasingly urban. For a long time, cities had little but pigeons and rats for urban wildlife; but while foxes move into London, coyotes, raccoons, skunks, ravens, crows, and more have moved into North American cities. For one thing, they like garbage. For another, we have stopped killing them and everything else that moves; we have, from their perspective, become a relatively harmless species (except for our cars, but roadkill is a popular food source for crows, ravens, coyotes, vultures, and more). So they're no longer afraid of us. And then, too, we've cleaned up: the toxic sewers that surrounded Manhattan in the 1960s have gradually become something resembling rivers again, in which fish can swim and herons can hunt. The urban air is cleaner too. And the garbage!

A lot of these species are enchanting to a lot of us urbanites, who are unworried on account of lambs or crops. When a coyote appeared on Bernal Heights in San Francisco, it became a local celebrity, though other coyotes in the city have remained relatively incognito. (Angelenos must have scoffed at our excitement, since choruses of howling coyotes are old hat in the canyons and hills that edge Los Angeles.) Bandit-masked raccoons have soared to bear-cub sizes on their garbage diet and become bolder and bolder; I often see them out strolling, or rather waddling, across streets, under cars, and up fences around the time the bars begin to thin out. Ecologically speaking, these species are mostly harmless: the supply of housepets, runners, and garbage is not endangered.

Ravens and crows are another story. About seventy-five miles up the coast from San Francisco, Alfred Hitchcock made *The Birds*, in which a Coalition of the Winged attacked human beings en masse, a fantasy in its achievement of unity between avian species as much as anything else. Some birds have proliferated amazingly in the past decade or so, notably ravens and crows, but they threaten the survival of more fragile species. One of the still-endangered species of the West Coast is the snowy plover; by 1995, ravens were plundering more than two-thirds of the plover eggs on the seashore north of San Francisco, as well as raiding nests of other at-risk species. Ravens have also been observed preying on other endangered species, including bank swallows in the Bay Area and the marbled murrelet in the Pacific Northwest. A pair of Bay Area ornithologists trying to protect other birds reported, "We go to great lengths: hiding the traps, hiding ourselves, starting before dawn. It's difficult to outsmart them." They are very smart and, unlike most birds, great learners and interpreters.

A young naturalist who grew up birding in San Francisco—we have quail and great blue herons in Golden Gate Park and a considerable seabird population on the coast—told me he considered ravens and crows to be tantamount to a "second Silent Spring" (the first being the decimation of birds by DDT and other pesticides, which Rachel Carson addressed in her landmark *Silent Spring* of 1962). When I came to San Francisco, ravens and crows were rarely sighted in urban spaces—they had become rare altogether in the 1920s, but populations since the 1980s have exploded. In the 1983 San Francisco Christmas count of birds, ornithologists found 14 ravens; in the 1999 count, they found 239. Oakland went from 5 to 101 in the same period. They appear to have increased far more since then. There is a raven explosion afoot here and elsewhere. I see them everywhere these days, in the country, in the city, on campuses, in downtown plazas, and sitting on the power lines outside my windows, their bulk of ruffled feathers making them look middle-aged, disheveled, unlike their sleek corvid cousins the crows, who are also all over these days.

In the deserts east of Los Angeles, ravens are even more devastating. There the highly endangered desert tortoise still roams, and though habitat loss and being run over by cars and off-road vehicles have reduced its numbers, ravens may matter more. The birds have become what wildlife biologist Michael Soule calls a "subsidized species," meaning that they have a stable food source in garbage, as house cats preying on songbirds do in cat food. Urban garbage dumps around the edges of the deep desert have encouraged a population explosion among ravens, one of the many ways population centers destroy habitat at a distance. Adult desert tortoises are as tough as anything in a shell, but the thinner-shelled young are, for the first five or six years of life, extremely vulnerable to ravens. Beneath one raven's nest in the Mojave desert, naturalists found 250 baby tortoise shells.

The success of the raven means the failure of other species, also valuable, so the very sight of these creatures, particularly in new places—like outside my window—is bad news. Tortoises are sacred to some of the Mojave's local tribes, while Raven is, in the mythology of the Northwest Coast, a creator deity. That something sacred or symbolic can become a weed and a pest is disturbing. A raven used to be an oracular sight, an omen, impressive, noble, wild; now they are bad news, weeds, menaces. This decline is troubling not just in what the birds do but in what they mean. They have shifted from being part of an ecosystem into being its destroyer, the birds acting as agents of our own disruption. Ravens, like coyotes, may have been creator deities because they are rather humanlike in their ability to adapt, improvise, and change, to trick and to shift (which is why Coyote is also Trickster in the old myths of this continent). Perhaps in seeing ravens go wrong, we might see ourselves—if we looked hard enough.

In recent years, a number of books have reported on ravens and crows, members along with jays and magpies of the family *corvidae*. Biologist Bernd Heinrich's 1989 *Ravens in Winter* took on the communitarian survival strategies of those birds, while Candace Savage's 1995 *Bird Brains: The Intelligence of Crows, Ravens, Magpies, and Jays* took a wider look at the workings of the complex corvid mind, which learns and adapts: some crows can even figure out how to make and use tools, and others become skillful mimics of other birds and of humans. Savage's book cites at least one scientific study by Tony Angell and several by John M. Marzluff, the co-authors of a new illustrated book, *In the Company of Crows and Ravens*. It is a generalist's book written by experts, whose text meanderingly considers the role of crows in the human cultural imagination and provides some information on their behavior. The accompanying drawings by Angell sometimes sink into cuteness, as in one picture of crows picking dead insects off the grill of a car whose license plate reads "CORVID." Marzluff and Angell know their subject intimately, but not their readers, and they often stoop to overexplaining basic concepts.

At times engrossing—for example, when revealing the ancient tradition of raven keeping in the Tower of London as a recent forgery—their book is more often dilatorily bland, as when they mention for the second time (on p. 134, after illustrating the stuff on p. 10) the Three Crows brand of spices in Maine, to bolster their case for the cultural importance of crows. And even in debunking the myth that ravens have been kept in the London Tower since the time of Charles II, they conclude, "The power of ravens to make people believe the impossible and survive difficult times is obvious" (p. 112). With such enthusiasm, the authors fall into the trap of all those popular science books in recent years, each of which claims that its subject is a world-changing pivotal event, phenomenon, or invention. Crows and ravens matter; they're in the Bible and Norse mythology and the Northwest creation stories, as well as on the wire outside my window. But they're not that central or powerful or cheering; the likelihood that the idea of protective ravens really spurred on the British during the blitz seems a little far-fetched.

Bird Brains does a better job of describing the remarkable intelligence of these birds, and neither book quite describes their threat. In fact, *In the Company of Crows and Ravens* often becomes a defense of the birds, as when Marzluff and Angell write that "demonstrating an ability to find and prey on nests efficiently does not necessarily mean that crows or ravens limit other bird populations" (p. 232). Sixteen pages later, the authors note that the house crows imported to Zanzibar by a British governor in 1891 have "reached half a million in Dar es Salaam alone. They are spreading across Africa, threatening rare birds and annoying people." Tokyo, they report, has seen its crow population quadruple since the 1980s, fueled by accessible garbage.

In and of themselves, ravens and weedy plants like the Himalayan tree of heaven that is all over the rubbly and neglected margins of cities from Berlin to Detroit are admirable and even beautiful. But they function as a biological equivalent of Burger King or Microsoft; they threaten to become transnational monopolies that force out the local versions. In fact, you can see the one almost as a byproduct of the other: the industrialized world that creates garbage, cities, and shipping (which often transmits the weedy species from one continent to another) encourages these species to move out of their former niches and proliferate. It's not coincidental that the crows invading Africa came as part of the imperialist package.

The industrial age's climate change will root out other species of animals and plants—the yellow-bellied marmot, which lives in the high Rockies, is dying out because the thaws now often come too early, before the plants the marmots eat have started to grow. Wolves, too, who have been successfully reintroduced after being hunted into near-extinction in the United States, get through the winter by eating elk who have been weakened by the cold and the snow that covers their foodstuffs; with warmer winters, however, the elk thrive and the wolves starve. Red foxes are moving north to compete with arctic foxes. What will be left in most places will be a brutally simplified ecology, with lots of trees of heaven, dandelions, robins, ravens, and raccoons, what the science writer David Quammen calls "a planet of weeds," though if we ourselves, the chief weed, go extinct or get scaled back, even these weedy species may begin evolving into creatures more delicately adapted to specific niches. But that is the million-year view, not the thousand-year version. In the meantime, what's sauce for the raven is poison for the snowy plover.

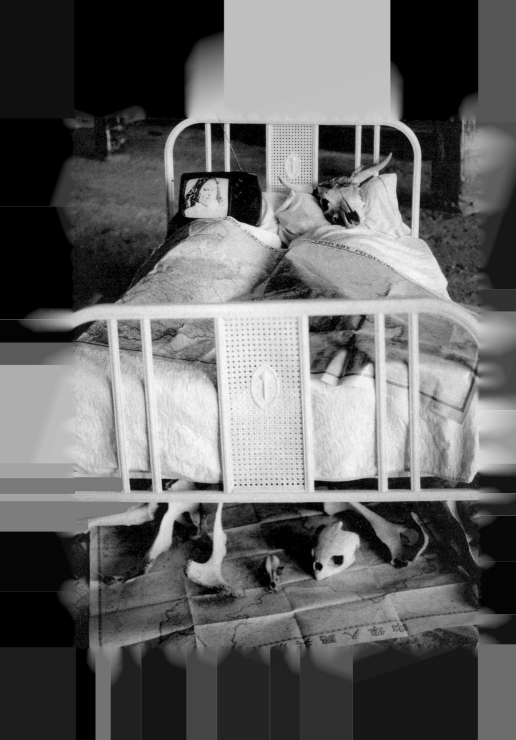

7
WOMEN'S PLACE

Tangled Banks and Clear-Cut Examples

[2003]

In retrospect, I realize I should have made the connection right away. I was investigating Sequoia National Forest for an environmental magazine. Half the naturally occurring sequoia groves in the world are there, but the forest's managers
seemed to be doing everything they could to service the one logging company that
was profiting from the place. Since commercial logging as such had come to an end
in 1990, the administrators had come up with various reasons why the forest
needed to be logged for its own good, and fire prevention was the latest rationale.
The plan that year, 1996, prescribed belts of clear-cutting called Defensible Fuel
Profile Zones across the ridgetops of the million-acre place that Bill Clinton would
later partially protect during his last days in office. One of the tough women
who'd been fighting the Forest Service for fifteen years called the DFPZs a plan to
give the forest a "17 million board feet Punk Rock Haircut!!!! Quarter mile wide
logged strips snaking MILES all along major ridgetops!" It was a fun assignment
in its way, not least because I apparently looked gullible enough that the Forest
Service managers I interviewed damned themselves volubly into my tape recorder.

I stayed in an outback motel for a couple of days during my research, and the
TV there got three channels: the local news, the Weather Channel, and the
Playboy Channel. So I checked out the latter for a while. The perky, corn-fed
houris were pretty much unchanged since the days of my older brother's crumbling pillars of rummage-sale *Playboys* piled up in the garage, though the bodies
were a little different. Everyone was toned, and in a Busby Berkeley number,
when the camera panned all the women lying with feet to the center like so many

daisy petals, you could see that each one had identical scars under her breasts. But what really surprised me was that they'd all shaved their pubic hair into neat rectangles. Probably it was about the exigencies of high-cut bikinis, but sans bikinis their rectangles recalled both Hitler's moustache and topiary shrubbery from the age when yew and box were trimmed into Euclidean forms. Landing strips, I was told they were called, and it would be easy to connect them to the helicopter logging and linear clear-cutting in the Sequoia National Forest, and to the geometricizing, rationalizing aesthetics of Versailles in that era when trees came in cubes, cones, and spheres.

Around that time, I wrote an essay called "Uplift and Separate," which used the aesthetics of the girlie calendar to illuminate the aesthetics of the nature calendar.

The pinup girls and waterfalls in these calendars have some curious things in common, not least among them a highly defined aesthetic that narrows down the categories of Woman and Nature to some very specific subspecies and representational styles. Both are usually portrayed in a kind of photography that calls attention not to its own status as representation, but to what is represented, and like much such "realism" wishes to function as a transparent window onto what is supposed to be represented: the real. Yet what one sees through these windows is a vision of perfection from which death, time, decay, action have been excluded as flaws. Both are souped-up, sleek, flawless, passive; in both the orthodoxy of beauty has produced a curious homogeneity of visual reference to pleasures that are not altogether visual. The chaos of thought and action has been replaced with a stale vision of delight, and the landscapes seem to loll alluringly in much the same way the women do.

I'm now looking at the 2003 Sierra Club wilderness calendar, and nothing there has changed. The aesthetics are pretty much what they were in 1997, or 1987, and if I could remember 1977, I suspect that it would look like this, too. Nature is clean, unpeopled, brightly lit, abundant, and peculiarly tidy. It's an aesthetic that comes straight out of the work of Eliot Porter, the pioneer of color photography who rocked the world in 1962 with his best-selling Sierra Club Exhibit

Format book *In Wildness Is the Preservation of the World*. Porter's book, a break-through in color printing technology, practically gave birth to the coffee-table book and to nature photography; it appeared the same year as Rachel Carson's *Silent Spring* and seems to have worked in concert with it to create a new environmental consciousness in the United States.

Success for some artists is disastrous: so many imitators crowd upon their heels that it soon becomes impossible to look at that work and see that it was ever fresh, startling, or even individual. Such a fate has befallen Porter's oeuvre, but he took far more interest in natural processes, in complexity, in landscapes with human traces, and in signs of death and decay than his army of imitators has done. Animal corpses, human traces, leaf litter, and subdued tonal ranges were part of his territory.

The legions who trample in his footsteps dispense with everything that isn't bright, comfortable, and clean; and they push his interest in what I think of as Busby Berkeley formations to an extreme: in the 2003 calendar, April is a lurid hill-side of California poppies in sharp focus from close-up to rolling distance; in August, weirdly abundant wildflowers recede into the Rocky Mountain distance; and by November, the entire frame is full of monarch butterflies, like stained glass on Ecstasy. The world doesn't tend to look like nature calendars. In fact, the beauty nature photography describes seems to be about technology—the improvements in color photographic processes, darkroom and filter tricks, a flawlessness that seems somehow machined, and probably nowadays refinements wrought by Photoshop. Maybe this is because that moment of epiphany that a single wildflower or a pretty nice sunset even with a freeway overpass in it can arouse can't be aroused by a photograph of same; the photograph needs to be fifty times as spectacular. And perhaps so do the bodies and acts in what seem to be the most popular kinds of porn, since photographic porn leaves out at least four of the senses and a certain sense of involvement. Which might be to say that photo-graphic porn and nature photography are in some ways formalist, about the limits and essences of the medium.

I'm not quite sure why, but along with e-mail alerts notifying me that two-thirds of all women are dissatisfied with the size of my penis (which raises interesting questions about the other third), I get sent the occasional sample of Internet porn, and I've been interested to see that the landing strips of 1997 have been clear-cut. The loins of women in Internet porn, according to these unsolicited samples, are as hairless as those of Barbie. This is the era of the Brazilian wax, whose name is supposed to reference Rio bathing suits but might well recall some trouble with the Amazonian rainforest canopy as well. Body manipulation, when it becomes a ubiquitous orthodoxy, is the opposite of self-expression, and this particular manipulation seems to reveal a squeamish desire for tidiness on the part of the waxers' audience that's interesting to find in pictures once thought of as dirty. Dirt recalls soil, fecundity, generation, life—and, of course, its opposite, death and decay, along with the smudginess of contact. The social developments that have made the acts of mainstream porn ever more dirty while the bodies become ever cleaner and more prepubescent and plasticlike are interesting to contemplate, as is the possibility that the former may compensate for the latter.

In 1749, at the start of the golden age of landscape gardening, which would open the gates to wilder and wilder tastes in landscape and eventually beget romanticism, mountaineering, and the Sierra Club (if not exactly Sierra Club calendars), John Cleland's novel *Fanny Hill* offers us this landscape: "that central furrow which nature had sunk there, between, the soft relieve of two pouting ridges, and which in this was in perfect symmetry of delicacy and miniature with the rest of her frame. No! nothing in nature could be of a beautifuller cut; then, the dark umbrage of the downy spring-moss that over-arched it bestowed, on the luxury of the landscape, a touching warmth, a tender finishing, beyond the expression of words, or even the paint of thought." A hundred and ten years later, Darwin wrote his famous passage about the tangled bank in *The Origin of Species*. His image of this moist, overgrown site that generates biological complexity is akin to Cleland's description of an intricate reverie-provoking terrain.

What's entertaining about Cleland's language is that it's not pornographic, because it pulls you away from the putative subject into the viscerality of its metaphor, asking us to feel not desire which moves closer but admiration which stands back for the fine view. It suggests the extent to which landscape was already a superlative, an ideal to which other things could be brought, so that these genitalia are offered up, as it were, on the altar of landscape beauty and metaphoric adventure, back then when the geometrical lines of formal gardens were breaking up into an aesthetic of wilderness. It's not very far removed from William Gilpin's essay on the superlative gardens at Stowe, published a year earlier: "A Mile's riding, perhaps, would have carried me to the Foot of a steep Precipice, down which thundered the whole Weight of some vast River, which was dashed into Foam at the Bottom, by the craggy points of several rising Rocks: A deep Gloom overhung the Prospect, occasioned by the close Wood that hung round it on every Side."

I wonder if it's that complex language makes it possible to appreciate complexity, or if the aesthetics of gardens extended to bodies back when Pope said "painting, poetry and landskip gardening" were sisters. Or brothers, because in that era, which cultivated the aesthetic experience of the sublime and the beautiful (which Edmund Burke in his treatise on the sublime carefully delineated as, respectively, masculine and feminine), Cleland could make men into landscape with equal felicity. Here's the key portion of a tumescent guy "whose exquisite whiteness was not a little set off by a sprout of black curling hair round the root through which the jetty springs of which the fair skin shewed as in a fine evening you may have remark'd the clear light aether through the branchework of distant trees overtopping the summit of a hill: then the broad and bluish-casted incarnate of the head, and blue serpentines of its veins."

There is a huge body, so to speak, of literature and art that portrays nature and landscape as feminine, from the *Song of Songs*'s "A garden enclosed is my beloved" to Edward Weston's blank nudes in blank dunes. This could simply be about the heterosexual male voice, since the beloved is always nature. Imogen Cunningham's honeymoon pictures, from her soft pictorialist phase before she cofounded the sharp-focus-committed f/64 movement, not only portray the man as the spirit of the land but make the actual man do all that uncomfortable self-exhibition that female models have spent so much time doing. Cunningham's groom stands in lakes a lot. They look cold, and so does he. In fact, it's just as easy to cast the landscape as masculine, at least if that landscape is big, austere, and sublime. Saguaro cacti are also helpful.

I don't believe women are more like nature, but I believe we often share a political fate, not least as the sites on which a dominant culture exercises its fears and desires. Did *Fanny Hill* prefigure the Lake District and the aesthetics of wildness? And if that is so, then what about these bodies that are as much the result of toil by waxers and surgeons as the happy result of genetic dice and exercise? Do they represent the mall, the space capsule, the superhighway, the laboratory, the gated community, the prefab home, drive-through fast food, virtual space, the security state? Is that also what the nature calendars represent, since in them there is, as in porn, life without death, bodies without functions, results without processes, access without roads? If the beloved is always nature, then what are these landscapes and bodies without biology, without threat, without mystery, without darkness?

Where did the complexity go? Landscape photography in what we might have to call the art world has for more than a quarter century been striving to embrace a more complex, compromised vision of the organic world, an organic world whose human traces are not necessarily scars or damage, a landscape of processes as well as spectacles, of beauty without perfection. This undoes the virgin-whore dichotomy calcified out of Porter's and Ansel Adams's vision, which cannot imagine the works of human beings as other than violation and therefore fetishizes nature as a place apart (it's this that made nature photography seem more like girlie calendars—in which the subject is solitary but inviting—rather than like action porn). This is a nature whose existence is more dubious than ever before, as well as a kind of alienation environmental thought is getting over pretty nicely.

We might also ask where the hair went. To imagine the quantities of waxed women toiling on behalf of the Internet's most successful business is to imagine a collective clear-cut that might, were some web nerd to do the calculations, amount to acres. The answer is also to be found in the art world, which at this point is beginning to seem like some sort of wilderness preserve for all kinds of tangled banks. Ann Hamilton, in a mid-1990s show at the Dia Foundation, covered a vast area of floor with swathes of horsehair that visitors had to come into contact with, if only with their feet. A plethora of women artists has affirmed a different female body in art, one that might be beautiful, but not safe or simple, a body that is full of hair, organs, processes, fluids, consciousness, and will. They've represented, as I once said, "everything classical marble removes: the squishy, mobile, mutable stuff of and the traffic of appetites through bodies in process." This work has had fun with hair, again and again, and if anything affirms that hair is political it's this abundance, this tangle, this forest of it in the feminine avant-garde while the stuff is vanishing from the bodies of mainstream porn.

Which is to say, in sum, that if there's anything to complain about in these mainstream photographic territories, it's that they're about sex and wilderness in which wildness is proscribed.

Seven Stepping Stones down
the Primrose Path

A Talk at a Conference on Landscape and Gender

⟦2002⟧

1

When I first started looking into gender and landscape, the questions seemed metaphysical—about which sex had what relationship to nature, or, rather, whether women really had a special relationship to nature. I was young and easily converted to the ecofeminist essentialist position that women are closer to nature or more like nature or one of those warm, fuzzy positions. That was the era of the book *When God Was a Woman* and a general sense that Near Eastern agricultural matriarchies were paradise lost—one thing about this culture, no matter how much it excoriates the Judeo-Christian tradition, it can't resist retelling the tale of Eden and the fall from grace, even if Judeo-Christianity becomes that fall from grace. In this When-God-Was-a-Woman version, women were better than men in all kinds of ways you already know about, and when women ruled, everything was peachy.

Of course, there were critiques of this all along—the feminist art magazine *Heresies* put Mount Saint Helens on the cover of its nature issue as if to say that if we're like nature, she's not delicate, sweet, and passive. And later on, the notion came to prevail that hunter-gatherer life, with all its pantheistic anarchy and low levels of labor, was paradise, and that, in comparison, even matriarchal agriculture seemed like earning your bread by the sweat of your brow, and how fun was that? By that point in the late eighties/early nineties conversation, gender was seen as constructed, so that male and female were only points on a social spectrum, like straight and queer, with a lot of range in between, rather than essential truths of human nature. And of course race entered the picture—which makes me think of environmental justice leader Carl Anthony's great question, "Why is it that white people find it easier to think like a mountain than like a person of color?"

But I was looking through the lens of landscape photography mostly in those days, and what I saw was this, as I wrote in the mid-1990s:

> Through the mid-1980s, it seemed possible to propose a relationship between gender and landscape ideology. While many of the men were taking pictures premised on an irreconcilable schism between nature and culture (or at least emphasizing the occasions where culture violated nature), a lot of women were making images of a bodily and spiritual communion with landscape/nature, one which didn't respect nature and culture as useful categories (a radical departure in the West, whose federal land policies and conservation movements have both been based on belief in a pristine, uninhabited land distinct from civilization). Even compositionally, the genders seemed distinct, with the women's work abandoning the sweeping prospect for more intimate and enclosed scenes.

I think that much of the critique of wilderness as the only nature, as a place apart, came from feminism; but postulating gender as an absolute category just erected another Berlin Wall, while so many were coming down. Since then, things have changed in photography—and, of course, once you broaden your gaze, a lot of other things sneak in.

2

Portraying landscape as masculine is, so to speak, just as natural as portraying it as feminine, as Jane Tompkins points out in her book *West of Everything:*

Men may dominate or simply ignore women in Westerns, they may break horses and drive cattle, kill game and kick dogs and beat one another into a pulp, but they never lord it over nature. Nature is the one transcendent thing, the one thing larger than man (and it is constantly portrayed as immense), the ideal toward which human nature strives. Not imitateo Christi but imitatio naturae. What is imitated is a physical thing, not a spiritual ideal; a solid state of being, not a process of becoming; a material entity, not a person; a condition of object-hood, not a form of consciousness. The landscape's final invitation—merger— promises complete materialization. Meanwhile, the qualities that nature implic-itly possesses—power, endurance, rugged majesty—are the ones that men desire while they live. And so men imitate the land in Westerns.

3

So essentialist constructions of gender and nature are misleading maps. But there are some places in the territory of the imagination where feminism, postmod-ernism, multiculturalism, and environmental critique overlap, and that is still valuable. As I wrote in "Elements of a New Landscape,"

Here the word landscape itself becomes problematic: landscape describes the nat-ural world as an aesthetic phenomenon, a department of visual representation: a landscape is scenery, scenery is stage-decoration, and stage decorations are static backdrops for a drama that is human. The odalisque and the pleasure ground are acted upon rather than actors, sites for the imposition rather than generation of meaning, and both are positioned for consumption by the viewer within works of art that are themselves consumable properties. As a social movement with specific social goals, feminism sought to acquire rights and representation for women as other social justice movements before it had sought them for hitherto marginalized classes, religions, and races of men; as an analysis of entrenched structures of belief, feminism reached far deeper to disrupt the binary relation-ships around which the culture organized itself. The subject/object relations of modern art and science I've been trying to describe align a number of beliefs: the gap between subject and object, observer and observed, creator and creation; the essential immateriality of mind and mindlessness of matter; and the association of men with energy, form, mind, and women with substance, nature and earth.

I don't think it's a coincidence that Rachel Carson's *Silent Spring* and Betty Friedan's *The Feminine Mystique* appeared only a year apart, in 1962 and 1963 — and we could easily switch the titles, to the *Silent Feminine* and *The Chemical Mystique*. Feminist, environmental, and postmodern theories have sometimes converged, at least in some basic ideas about the inadequacies of dualistic and binary descriptions of the world; the interdependences of a world better imagined as networks and webs of interconnected processes than as a collection of discrete objects; the value of diversity, whether cultural or biological; the intricate interpenetrations of mind and body, individual and environment. The worldview that emerges is less about discrete objects and more about interwoven processes.

Another way to put their commonality is in an emphasis on place: literal place for environmentalism, the location from which one can speak for feminism and postmodernism. By grounding voice, such thinking deconstructs authoritative versions, voices, histories; by denying the possibility of a voice that is nowhere, voices begin to arise everywhere, and the hitherto silenced speak. Feminism has both undone the hierarchy in which the elements aligned with the masculine were given greater value than those of the feminine and undermined the metaphors that aligned these broad aspects of experience with gender. So, there goes women and nature. What does it leave us with? One thing is a political mandate to decentralize privilege and power and equalize access, and that can be a literal spatial goal too, the goal of our designed landscapes and even the managed ones — the national parks, forests, refuges, recreation areas, and so on.

4

What's interesting about Tompkins is that she makes it clear that no matter which way the nature/culture construct is genderized, men come out ahead—in the Western, nature is not the chaos that needs to be subdued but the sublimity to which we must submit, and women are just the schoolmarms and parasol-toters who, like Aunt Sally in *Huckleberry Finn*, are out to civilize the hero, giving him grounds to flee farther into the landscape. And really, in practical terms, this ability to flee deep into the landscape as John Muir did has been much more available to men than to women, and it's this practical stuff that interests me most.

Even in that fabulous Inuit movie this summer, *The Fast Runner (Atanarjuat)*, it's clear that hunters often get to roam farther and more often than gatherers, but it's as though they move through two different landscapes, noting different things, and perhaps the gatherers know less terrain with greater depth and intensity. In the book *The Geography of Childhood*, Stephen Trimble writes,

> Once children reach adolescence, American girls typically never catch up to boys in spatial competence (perceptions of the relationships of objects that determine our understanding of place, as tested by working with models and maps). Remember, though, that we build all our cultural biases into experimental design; in Eskimo culture, both girls and boys accompany their fathers on extensive hunting trips, and both sexes perform equally well on spatial tests. Roger Hart studied what he called "the geography of childhood" in a small New England town in the early 1970s. He found that boys were allowed to range freely more than twice as far away from home as girls in all grades. In fourth grade, as children took on their first jobs, the boys delivered papers and mowed lawns, learning the lay of the town; girls hired out as babysitters. Boys broke their parents' rules about boundaries more than girls. . . . Hart and his co-researcher Susan Saegert summarize the depressing and inevitable result of such control of girls: "Not only is environmental exploration and freedom denied to them, but also their confidence and ability to cope with environmental matters are likely to be undermined."

So my question nowadays is not what gender is the landscape but what gender gets to go out into the landscape.

The Pueblo writer Leslie Marmon Silko, who has written a great many more lyrical and spiritual things about landscape, declares, "Women seldom discuss our wariness or the precautions we take after dark. . . . We take for granted that we are targeted as easy prey by muggers, rapists, and serial killers. We try to avoid going anywhere alone after dark. . . . I used to assume that most men were aware of this fact of women's lives, but I was wrong. They may notice our reluctance to drive at night to the convenience store. . . . but it is difficult for me to admit that we women live our entire lives in a combat zone."

In my book *Wanderlust*, I asserted:

> Women have been enthusiastic participants in pilgrimages, walking clubs, parades, processions and revolutions, in part because in an already defined activ- ity their presence is less likely to be read as sexual invitation, in part because companions have been women's best guarantee of public safety. In revolutions the importance of public issues seems to set aside private matters temporarily, and women have found great freedom during them (and some revolutionaries, such as Emma Goldman, have made sexuality one of the fronts on which they sought freedom). But walking alone also has enormous spiritual, cultural, and political resonance. It has been a major part of meditation, prayer, and religious exploration. It has been a mode of contemplation and composition from Aristotle's peripatetics to the roaming poets of New York and Paris. It has sup- plied writers, artists, political theorists and others with the encounters and experiences that inspired their work, as well as the space in which to imagine it, and it is impossible to know what would have become of many of the great male minds had they been unable to move at will through the world. Picture Aristotle confined to the house, Muir in full skirts. Even in times when women could walk by day, the night—the melancholic, poetic, intoxicating carnival of city nights—was likely to be off limits to them, unless they had become "women of the night." If walking is a primary cultural act and a crucial way of being in the world, those who have been unable to walk out as far as their feet would take them have been denied not merely exercise or recreation but a vast portion of their humanity. Virginia Woolf's famous *A Room of One's Own* is often recalled as though it were literally a plea for women to have home offices, but it in fact deals with economics, education, and access to public space as equally necessary to making art. To prove her point, she invents the blighted life of Shakespeare's equally talented sister, and asks of this Judith Shakespeare, "Could she even get her dinner in a tavern or roam the streets at midnight?"

The answer is clear, and its contemporary American corollary is, "Could she go backpacking by herself in the Rockies or roam Central Park without spending most of her time thinking about safety?" I think it's important to remember not only that every designed landscape is a place that expresses its maker's imagination but also that the best measure of its success is how it invites, inspires, and liberates the imagination of its visitors. There's a massive history of writers, poets, musicians, philosophers, physicists working out their ideas while walking, and so making places to walk is making places to dream, imagine, and create, a relation to the shaping of others that is perhaps more direct than any other medium. Virginia Woolf thought up her novel *To the Lighthouse* "in a great, involuntary rush" while walking around Tavistock Square.

One of the functions of landscape is to correspond to, nurture, and provoke exploration of the landscape of the imagination. Space to walk is also space to think, and I think that's one thing landscapes give us: places to think longer, more uninterrupted thoughts or thoughts to a rhythm other than the staccato of navigating the city.

5

I think one of the primary goals of a feminist landscape architecture would be to work toward a public landscape in which we can roam the streets at midnight, in which every square is available for a Virginia Woolf to make up her novels. There is a wonderful anecdote about Seoul, Korea, in Elizabeth Wilson's *The Sphinx in the City*:

> At night these restrictions were reversed. After the city gates were closed, it was men (save for officials and the blind) who were forbidden to appear on the streets, and the city was turned over to women, who were then free to walk abroad. They strolled and chatted in groups with their friends carrying paper lanterns. Even in this dim light, however, they used unfurled fans to protect themselves from being seen, or held their silk jackets over their faces. So often,

this has been women's experience of the city: to live in it, but hidden; to emerge on sufferance, veiled.

Just before I became a student at UC Berkeley in the early 1980s, some feminists pulled off a wonderful prank. There had been rapes on campus, and the campus authorities had responded the usual way, by telling women to curtail their freedom of movement, particularly after dark, so that all women lost some freedom of access, some public space. A guerrilla group responded with faux-official posters warning men that they would not be allowed on campus after dark—a perfectly reasonable approach to the problem, and one that took away no more freedom than the authorities' approach did—but men are not used to losing their freedom because of violence, and many of them became outraged. Women, on the other hand, are used to losing their freedom, as long as it stops a little short of where the Taliban cut it off. We've heard a lot about driving while nonwhite the last few years, but we need to hear as well about walking while female—particularly walking while young and female. I don't get harassed on the street anymore, but I think that's less because the world has changed than because I have; young women still receive lots of that attention that is officially erotic and unofficially threatening, a reminder to know their place and to know that this street or path or plaza is not it.

What would a landscape of equal access look like? I'm not sure, but I think that's a question for landscape architects to consider. And I think it's important to remember that parks and gardens are also social space, and social space is always at least potentially political space as well as imaginative space. Talking in San Francisco earlier this week, Mike Davis mentioned working in a poor Latina neighborhood in L.A. where the locals were ready to form a tenants union—or at least the mothers staying home with their young children were—but there was no place to meet. If they had had a public park, that space would have become not only play space for the children but also organizing community space for the adults, Davis said, noting that the ACLU is preparing a lawsuit for equal access to nature and open space in L.A. It's a right, the right of the people peaceably to assemble, that implies democratic open space, and like most rights nowadays it's not distributed equally without regard to gender, race, class, or location. Being out in public is being part of the community, and it's not so far a stretch from those women Davis met to the Mothers of the Plaza de Mayo in Argentina, demonstrating against the silence and repression of the dictatorship when no one else would—and though the plaza was transformed by the Mothers, the Mothers needed the plaza in which to be in public, to speak as the public, with their feet as well as their signs and voices. Could you have that movement without a highly visible and symbolically loaded public space? I think that the unique task of landscape architects is to design not only space to think but space in which we are in public—the space of democracy.

Again from *Wanderlust:*

> Only citizens familiar with their city as both symbolic and practical territory, able to come together on foot and accustomed to walking about their city, can revolt. Few remember that "the right of the people peaceably to assemble" is listed in the First Amendment of the US Constitution, along with freedom of the press, of speech, and of religion, as critical to a democracy. While the other rights are easily recognized, the elimination of the possibility of such assemblies through urban design, automotive dependence and other factors is hard to trace and seldom framed as a civil-rights issue. But when public spaces are eliminated, so ultimately is the public; the individual has ceased to be a citizen capable of experiencing and acting in common with fellow citizens. Citizenship is predicated on the sense of having something in common with strangers, just as democracy is built upon trust in strangers. And public space is the space we share with strangers, the unsegregated zone. In these communal events, that abstraction the public becomes real and tangible.

So I think that landscape architecture is in part about democracy, but I think that democracy can't be protected and maintained only by design.

6

Another crisis is facing those of us who care about democracy and public space. I once heard the acerbic critique that the death of the author was announced just as authors were ceasing to be almost exclusively white and male. We are at a paradoxical point in the history of public space: women have made great leaps forward in rights, including rights of access, just as the places to which we might have access are withering away from neglect or being eliminated by design or not even being built. In some situations, like the one Mike Davis identified, it's a problem of people without public space, and this is a far-reaching problem. But it has a corollary, public space without people. The linked acceleration, mechanization, privatization, and disembodiment of everyday life have removed a lot of people a lot of the time from the public sphere. In my decades in San Francisco, I have seen a profound shift in how people value and use space—a shift toward what I could as shorthand call suburbanization: dependence on cars, busyness, sequestration in controlled interiors, fear of contact with people who are different.

People without public space is a problem we've identified pretty well. It's pervasive in the suburbs, which are intensely privatized spaces and have become ever more so as the super-sized home is expanded to include your own gym, your own home entertainment center, DSL, cable, and other amenities that make leaving home less and less necessary. But you can see in this last example that there's some slippage—the home is designed to keep you from having to leave it, but choosing not to leave it is not a spatial or design matter so much as it's a social and political one. The principal alarm that has been rung says that we do not have space in which to have certain kinds of time; but instead nowadays it seems equally likely that we will not have time to accept the invitations such spaces issue—or we think we don't, or we don't, as they say, make the time. Equally seriously, we no longer perceive, many of us, our own bodies as adequate to navigate the spaces of everyday life. Quite a lot of people will ski or go to the gym but don't think they can buy milk or the newspaper without mechanical assistance; I think of cars as prosthetics for the conceptually disabled, disabled in their perception of space and self. We also need to make the case that there are benefits to going out on foot, the only way most landscapes and gardens can be fully experienced.

Much of the rhetoric of the Internet, particularly during the boom years, was that efficiency and convenience were the highest goals humans could aspire to—adios, truth and beauty—and these were best served by replacing face-to-face contact and errands run in public space with online access. In fact, a good many ads implied that actually standing in a line or moving along a street with actual strangers was a sinister and unpleasant business as well as a waste of time. The thoughts that fill your mind when you're between tasks is like the space that fills our lives when we're between destinations: this is the open space, the free space, the space in which the subversive and inventive and inspired stuff might happen. Open space is space to think. Cell phones, too, are about a withdrawal from public space—the person talking loudly on a cell phone in a park is saying that he or she is not in this communal space with strangers, but in a privileged space with those who are already known to him or her, and is also saying that this time out in public between things is just emptiness to be filled up. The corollary is that phone booths, the public transportation system of conversation, are disappearing—just as public transit vanished in L.A. when the automobile asserted dominance. And car alarms likewise value individual private property over community tranquility. Privatization is not only an economic but a social mandate, though the irony is that the dot-com boom happened in San Francisco because the new high-tech workers prized the public space of streets and nightclubs that was exactly what their technologies were designed to eliminate. And indeed if efficiency and convenience are your demigods, then the minutiae of life out in public—time to think, contact with others, sense of place, neighborliness, community, the minor epiphanies and revelations being out in the world brings—no longer matter. Or at least you no longer have a language with which to appraise and value them.

Another justification for the Internet a few years ago was that in disguising gender and appearance it was democratizing, though my impression was that a lot of that democratizing allowed middle-aged men to go into smutty chat rooms pretending to be nubile lesbians. And if the body of the beloved is nature, the body of Internet porn is a nature that makes Versailles look like the Bitterroot Wilderness Area. The implication of the freedom argument was that the only way to have freedom from oppression based on bodies, genders, races, was to become bodiless, genderless, raceless—another elimination of the very ground on which we sought to succeed, for I think that embodiment—the recognition that consciousness is situated—is a feminist position. It is not efficient to have a body. It is not, by the same criteria, efficient to be alive. Life is inconvenient, but that's hardly the best measure of what it's for.

When we're talking about landscapes and public spaces, we're talking about space in which people do two things—one is to pass through them, and another is to loiter for pleasure. The rhetoric of efficiency demands that people pass through them as rapidly as possible, and of course it delegitimizes loitering in them: that's for bums. As Reclaim the Streets put it a few years ago, advancing an idea that I believe could be extended to parks, plazas, promenades, piers, paths:

> Vacated, the street seems dangerous, indefensible; sped through, it becomes a haze of fumes and a grating of brakes. But when populated, the street can be a clash of viewpoints, a mess, a morass that can challenge our little orthodoxies and take us out of ourselves. . . . As a communication line between the familiar and the strange, between those we know too well and those we don't know at all, the street can still be the place where the most important connections are made. In it, we begin to see how our home is connected to that home, this house to that house, this street to that street, this city to all those other cities, my experience to yours.

The phenomenon Jane Jacobs identifies is key here: a place is made safe by having many people in it, so we create or abandon public space together—is a plaza truly public space without a public in it? Recall Roger Hart's studies on the "geography of childhood" from the 1970s, which I cited earlier, concerning gender disparity in children's access to their surroundings—by now, I suspect, it's evened out, not because of feminism but because of fear. That is to say, girls have not gained what boys had; rather, boys are losing what girls lost. The fear of child molesters and child abduction has put most American children in a kind of prison: locked down and supervised at all times. I worry a lot about this because I think that free roaming develops imagination, independence, resourcefulness—and a formative taste for free roaming that's going to encourage kids to become environ-

mentalists, gardeners, landscape architects, urban designers, civic activists, ethnobotanists, adventurers of all stripes out under the open sky.

The new technologies are marketed to fear: SUV owners, for example, have a
disproportionate fear of crime, though their cars themselves constitute a legal
form of threat—against other drivers, pedestrians, the environment, and independence from the OPEC nations. (The *San Francisco Chronicle* reported that
SUV drivers have a tendency to run over children—often their own—in the
driveway, because they can't see that space.) And one study demonstrated that
the more you stayed home and watched local news, which hypes crime stories, the
more afraid you were to go out—so TV news became a self-perpetuating isolation, even as actual crime has dropped in the past decade. It's become increasingly
clear that there's another corollary to all this staying home with television and
advertisements and super-sized sodas and Oreos and Doritos and crème brûlée and
the Cooking Channel and microwave popcorn: obesity. The United States is in
the midst of an epidemic of obesity and related health problems, and that creates
another reason why too many people aren't going to go roaming around on foot in
beautiful landscapes.

I hear the phrase "too far to walk" a lot, and it functions as a kind of percep-
tual imposition on the ability of the body to navigate space. It's worth remembering that people can and do walk thousands of miles, that a friend of mine just photographed a manic female athlete running a hundred miles in Yosemite in a
thirty-six-hour period. In cities, on foot is the best way to move large crowds, and,
to kowtow to efficiency, walking is as fast or faster than driving for short and
medium distances, as is walking coupled with decent public transit for long ones.

David Ehrenfeld writes more positively of the suburbs than I do, up to a
point, in *Orion* magazine,

> We have built in our suburbs an elaborate new kind of habitat, pleasing to us
> and to wildlife alike. It is complete with food sources such as bird feeders, succu-
> lent ornamental plantings, and garbage cans; and it has open spaces, clumps of
> trees, and various kinds of shelter under and around houses—the whole area
> interspersed with stream corridors, forested strips, and vegetated rights-of-way.

One might think that we would spend every possible moment outside enjoying the paradise that we have made for ourselves at such great expense. Not so. We have gone indoors to sit in front of our television sets and computer monitors, surrendering the outdoors to the deer, turkeys, crows, coyotes, foxes, bobcats, bears, and others. In the winter of 2001, [a friend] was driving a class along a street with single-family houses bordering on a sixty-acre nature preserve belonging to Rutgers University. It was noon of a glorious sunny day after a fresh snowfall. There were deer tracks everywhere around the houses. But not a single human footprint could be seen.

Paradise on the day before God created man, except that man, and woman, and child are all indoors, microwaving some nachos during the commercial.

7

So, what's to be done? I think we need to think about the conversation. At this point, there is not a lot of language to value the slow over the fast, the scenic detour over the information superhighway, the many small pleasures over the big convenience, the difficult over the easy, the public over the private, the stranger over the friend, the unfamiliar over the familiar, the risky over the safe, the adventure over the routine—or at least not a lot of language to value these things in daily life as opposed to, say, an Everest expedition or a book about checkbook pastoralism in Provence. There's not a lot of language to weigh the infinite pleasures and actualities of embodiment against disembodiment, the meanings that arise from difference over homogenization, to find a balance between freedom and being grounded—in the actual ground that is the foundational landscape.

So we need to stake out actual territory, but this territory can be perceived, enjoyed, realized only if it corresponds to the territory of the imagination, where all artists work, whatever their medium. Feminism did spectacular work in addressing and reappraising an earlier set of dichotomies by which experience was organized; it proved that it's possible to transform the conversation, and I think that it makes a beautiful foundation for continuing to do so. Some of that language we need now is in the antiglobalization movement, the slow food movement, the organic agriculture movement, the democracy movements, the rethinking of urbanism. But some of it, even more profoundly, is in the landscape itself. For landscape invites and inspires a language of complexity and contemplativeness, and it's that we need most right now.

Other Daughters,
Other American Revolutions

〚2006〛

At a dinner table last fall, I mentioned that Women Strike for Peace did some extraordinary things in the early 1960s, not least helping to bring down the House Un-American Activities Committee (HUAC). A well-known political writer sitting across from me sneered that the women in WSP were insignificant and that HUAC didn't exist by then anyway. He was wrong on both counts, but his remark wasn't surprising. The way people talk in decades suggests that the 1950s and '60s never overlapped and thereby blanks out the first half of the latter decade to make the second half into "the sixties," that era popularly imagined as a revolutionary romp by a bunch of antiwar young men. In fact, those young men took up a revolutionary challenge raised in part by middle-aged women, who launched some of the key ideas and fought some of the first battles in their defense. The radical and powerful Women Strike for Peace did it in the streets (and in the hearings chamber—Eric Bentley, in his history of HUAC, credits WSP with striking the crucial blow in the fall of "HUAC's Bastille" in 1962). Jane Jacobs, Rachel Carson, and Betty Friedan did it in books.

Jacobs's *The Death and Life of Great American Cities* appeared in 1961, Carson's *Silent Spring* came out the following year, and Friedan's *The Feminine Mystique* appeared in 1963. These three intellectual bombs collectively assailed almost every institution in American, and indeed in industrial and Western, society. Jacobs ripped into the reinvented postwar city as well as urban planners' obsession with segregating home from work, rich from poor, urban dwellings from the street and from commerce, people from one another, making cities over in the new image of suburbia—and, by implication, challenged the belief in progress and technology and institutional control. Carson radically questioned faith in big science and its disastrous new solutions to age-old problems, and maybe even the old Cartesian worldview of isolated fragments, which she replaced with a precocious vision of ecosystems in which contaminants like DDT and fallout kept traveling from their origins to touch and taint everything. Friedan took on the women's half of the American dream, gender, patriarchy, and the middle-class suburban family, bringing the assault full circle. After all, the suburbanization Jacobs excoriated was designed to produce the all-too-private lives Friedan investigated. Together, these three writers addressed major facets of the great modern project to control the world on every scale, locating it in the widespread attacks on nature, on women, and on the chaotic, the diverse, the crowded, and the poor. Their work transformed our perceptions of the indoor world of the home, the outdoor world of cities, and the larger realm of the biosphere, opening vast new possibilities for social transformation.

It's true, as some critics have argued, that Jacobs, Carson, and Friedan mostly avoided a deeper systemic analysis. Yet such an effort is implicit in Friedan's constant references to the marketers and advertisers who wish to keep women as good consumers, in Jacobs's scorn for top-down solutions and grand-plan developers, in Carson's condemnation of the chemical manufacturers and pest-prone monocropping of agribusiness. *Silent Spring* declares, "There is still very limited awareness of the nature of the threat. This is an era of specialists, each of whom sees his own problem and is unaware of or intolerant of the larger frame into which it fits. It is also an era dominated by industry, in which the right to make a dollar at whatever cost is seldom challenged." Rereading their books, I wonder if they didn't name the beast because their old-left contemporaries who did proffered such an unappealing alternative to corporate capitalism and were being persecuted for doing so. Or perhaps they just weren't interested in that kind of broad prescription—their books, after all, were broad enough.

What's more, the standard-issue socialism of the era was far less radical than the ostensible "reformism" of these three writers, insofar as it accepted the premises of a civilization that was flawed from birth. Lurking as an unexpressed and possibly inexpressible idea in these three books is a searching critique of industrial civilization as a whole, and maybe some other aspects of Western civilization all the way back to when Adam blamed Eve. If these authors failed to join the revolution of their time, they laid the groundwork for the far grander one that was coming: the one rethinking nature, agriculture, food, gender, sex, race, domestic life, home and housing, transportation, energy use, environmental ideas, war, violence, and a few other things—the one that has made it possible to question every authority and tradition.

Death and Life and Silent Spring are still magnificent, still readable, though only the former seems contemporary. Jacobs's book describes with brilliant specificity what works and what doesn't in cities, in language that is fearless and crisp as a trumpet blast: "The pseudoscience of city planning and its companion, the art of city design . . . have not yet embarked on the adventure of probing the real world." She describes the social ecology of cities, enumerating what generates safety, pleasure, liveliness, complexity, civilization as an everyday outdoor experience. Many concessions have been made to her hugely influential arguments—the building of Le Corbusier-style housing projects for the poor has more or less ceased; and my own city, San Francisco, has made a number of decisions one suspects she approves of, such as rebuilding an earthquake-damaged stretch of elevated highway as a broad surface street with pedestrian amenities.

But much of what Jacobs describes as wrong is still wrong, and places like Las Vegas and Phoenix seem to have devoted themselves to defying her every insight and prescription. Often viewed as conservative for its lack of enthusiasm for big government, Death and Life was not about the virtues of free enterprise but of local control. What it celebrated most was life in public, the everyday life of the streets that seven years later would become the extraordinary life of the streets in protest, demonstration, and revolt, in Prague, in Paris, in Mexico City, and in cities and on campuses across the United States. (Jacobs was so opposed to the Vietnam War that she moved her family to Toronto, getting her draft-age sons out of reach of the army.)

Carson's book is extraordinary to revisit. To read its early passages is like listening to God call the world into being during the days of its creation, even if this is only the world of environmental ideas: a passage here evokes issues taken up by

Alfred Crosby in *Ecological Imperialism*, one there recalls Vandana Shiva's critiques of biotechnology, another seems to prefigure Michael Pollan's *The Botany of Desire*, another Sandra Steingraber's *Living Downstream*, and Carson's strong clear voice is still audible in Terry Tempest Williams's environmental writing. Carson wasn't the first to come to grips with many of the environmental crises looming at the end of the 1950s; her brilliant achievement in *Silent Spring* was to synthesize technical information hitherto unavailable to the general public and to make that newly awakened public understand and care.

The book had a colossal impact from the beginning and is often credited with inspiring the DDT ban that went into effect nationwide in 1972. Though some now challenge the relationship between DDT and eggshell-thinning in wild birds, species from brown pelicans to bald eagles and peregrine falcons have rebounded from the brink of extinction since the ban. Conservatives such as Michael Crichton prefer to blame Carson and environmentalists for "millions of deaths" from malaria, but the ban was never applied worldwide, and DDT is still used selectively overseas. (Carson pointed out that since mosquitoes quickly develop resistance to DDT, as insects do to many other pesticides, the stuff is hardly a cure-all.) But picking on Carson over DDT misses the point that she was the first to describe the scope of the sinister consequences of a chemical society, the possibility that, with herbicides, pesticides, and the like, we were poisoning not just pests—or pests and some songbirds and farmworkers—but everyone and everything for a very long time forward. As one chapter opening puts it, "For the first time in the history of the world, every human being is now subjected to contact with dangerous chemicals, from the moment of conception until death." Still true. And if the particulars of the chemicals identified by Carson have changed enough that her book no longer has the currency Jacobs's does, that may be one measure of its success. Another is the far greater environmental literacy of the public, the necessary precursor to any broad environmental movement.

In *The Feminine Mystique*, Friedan, who died earlier this year at age eighty-five, described an array of nebulous social forces—women's magazines, Freudian psychology, politicians' speeches, advertising, and more—that were pressuring and persuading women to be stay-at-home mothers, producing the baby boom, pushing the consumption of household and beauty products, and promoting demeaning, demoralizing ideas about women's capabilities. Her job was hardest of all, because these forces weren't technically coercive; to prove that they were, she had to argue against the powerful façade of contented domesticity, a façade not only men but many women were (and are) bent on preserving. Simply by demonstrating the forces that had pushed women back into the home after the war and into a more retrograde version of female identity, Friedan was digging deep and fighting hard; if her book now seems overly focused on middle-class married white women with kids, it carved out wholly new territory to think about what we might nowadays call the production of identity and the possibility of resistance.

In many respects, *The Feminine Mystique* seems dated now. Friedan's background in psychology seems to have made her susceptible to a lot of the era's clucking over "delinquency," homosexuality, adultery, and promiscuity, as though she were witnessing the first stirrings of what would become feminist and sexual revolutions without seeing the implications. Nor does she question the foundations (if not the delights) of marriage, affluence, or suburbia. Still, there are fleeting moments when she recognizes the links between the "feminine mystique" and consumer capitalism, as in her observation that "in the suburbs where most hours of the day there are virtually no men at all . . . women who have no identity other than sex creatures must ultimately seek their reassurance through the possession of 'things.'"

Friedan's inchoate solution to "the problem that has no name" seemed to be that these educated middle-class women needed careers or some kind of intellectual stimulation, a solution far less profound than her analysis of the problem, and one that overlooked the women who were already invading politics. In *The Feminine Mystique*, she said of the 1950s, "It was easier to look for Freudian sexual roots in man's behavior, his ideas, and his wars than to look critically at his society and act constructively to right its wrongs." Of course, Friedan would go on to think more radically about what women's lives could become and what we could change, and of course in writing for women's magazines and then taking up a five-year residence at the New York Public Library's Allen Room, where she wrote her landmark book, she was having more of a career than she let on—not to mention a history of youthful activism in left and labor politics that she seldom discussed.

Jacobs and Carson were also working—the former as an editor at *Architectural Forum*, the latter as an independent writer. Indeed, they and the WSP activists seem like the women Friedan imagined but did not actually portray in her book. Married with three children, Jacobs continued a professional life of writing, engaging in the world of ideas and, by the time her book appeared, fighting Robert Moses's plan to put an expressway through Greenwich Village's Washington Square. Indeed, she was able to shame the nation's anointed urbanist, Lewis Mumford, into supporting the cause, even though he had just patronized her book in the *New Yorker* as "Mother Jacobs's Home Remedies" and reduced her description of the rich social life an urbanite might experience on the street to "the little flirtations that season a housewife's day."

Sexism in those days went around undisguised; *Time* magazine, in the course of asserting that DDT posed no human health problems, brazenly portrayed "Miss Carson" as "hysterically overemphatic" with a "mystical attachment to the balance of nature," her book as an "emotional and inaccurate outburst." Carson, who never married but raised a couple of nieces and a great-nephew, had been a successful scientist and writer within the federal government before she became an independent, full-time, and best-selling author in 1952. *Silent Spring* was published in September 1962. The Cuban missile crisis began a month later, and for a while people in the United States thought they wouldn't have the luxury of dying slowly from chemicals rather than suddenly from bombs.

A year earlier, the United States and the Soviet Union had decided to resume nuclear testing after an informal three-year moratorium. In response, six women met in Washington, D.C., and began to organize what became, on November 1, 1961, a nationwide strike of tens of thousands of women in sixty cities across the country—mostly married-with-children, middle-class, white women whose radical potential would grow with the decade. The aboveground tests were already known to create radioactive clouds that drifted over the earth, dropping radioactive by-products as they went. Strontium 90 was seeping into mothers' milk and thereby into newborn children; the weapons that were supposed to protect civilians in case of an all-out war were routinely contaminating them. Using their status as middle-class moms as a shield, WSP activists plunged into the fray, taking risks no one else had dared, refusing to screen out potential communists and reaching out to women in the USSR. Within a couple of years, they had helped bring into being the Limited Test Ban Treaty (an achievement acknowledged by United Nations chief U Thant and President John Kennedy) and made a mockery of HUAC's anticommunist inquisitions. In early 1964, they were among the first to oppose the Vietnam War.

Epochal insurrection was breaking out all over during what is often seen as the nation's most repressive era. The civil rights movement was in full swing (though the contributions of key players such as Ella Baker and Rosa Parks would be marginalized and/or downplayed). In the 1950s, the Mattachine Society and Daughters of Bilitis organized, respectively, gays and lesbians; the Daughters held their first national conference in San Francisco in 1960, the year students and labor protested HUAC's anti-educator hearings in that city in one of the first confrontations that looked like "the sixties." Tom Hayden spent the summer of 1960 with students in SLATE, the Berkeley student activists' organization, and brought what he learned back to Michigan and Students for a Democratic Society. The history of SDS is well-enough known at this point; that WSP was working side by side with SDS on antidraft and antiwar organizing has been airbrushed out of history's official portrait. But the later '60s only reaped what the more daring had sown at the beginning of the decade. And among the most visionary sowers were those women whose achievements, those books and bans and changed roles, are still here.

An e-mail arrived as I was finishing this essay, detailing the work of four or five women who are researching and deploying new bioremediation technologies in the cleanup of toxic residues in New Orleans. Based at the Common Ground community center, these women are scientists, environmentalists, and urban activists all at once, and the e-mail goes on to describe them conferring while a young man reads a book to three girls in daycare. It's hard to imagine this guerrilla cleanup team now without Carson, Friedan, and Jacobs then. "Only a book" is a popular epithet, implying that writing always takes place on the sidelines, but these three make it clear that books can change the world.

8

INFERNAL MUSEUMS

California Comedy, or Surfing with Dante

⟦2004⟧

Dante's Inferno, illustrated by Sandow Birk, text adapted by Sandow Birk and Marcus Sanders (San Francisco: Chronicle Books, 2004), 240 pp.

Many years ago, I was supposed to move to Los Angeles, but every time I went there, something about the light and space convinced me that life was basically meaningless and you might as well abandon hope right away. I was still an art critic in those days, and I would drive from northeast of Los Angeles, where I was supposed to settle into my new suburban existence, over to the downtown museums, look at some art, and drive back. But when I came home, I would find that the hours I'd spent negotiating freeway merge lanes and entrances and exits and parking garages were, in some mysterious way, more memorable than the museums. I was supposed to have a head full of paintings or installations. Instead, I had a head full of the anonymously ugly spaces that are not on the official register of what any place is supposed to be, the infrastructure of what for me in those days of my youth was despair.

Every city has them. If you think of Paris, you're more likely to envision gracious rows of mansard-roofed apartment buildings on chestnut-lined boulevards or the Eiffel Tower than the long cement passages of the metro lit by bad fluorescence and smelling of piss or the dank passageways descending from cafés into Turkish toilets. Even national parks situate the sedentary visitor in an asphalted world of public toilets, parking lots, and thou-shalt-not signage, stuff that almost every visitor is good at fast-forwarding past to the sublimity of waterfalls and forest glades and elk doing ungulate things in public. Certainly a waterfall is more striking than the parking lot near its base, but I wonder how it is that visitors can be so sure they saw what they were supposed to and so oblivious to what they are not.

Wordsworth wrote in "Tintern Abbey" of those rural places, saying that, in "the din of towns and cities, I have owed to them, / In hours of weariness, sensa-tions sweet" and speculating that such places contributed "unremembered pleas-ure: such, perhaps, / As have no slight or trivial influence / On that best portion of a good man's life." It isn't hard to speculate on what he would think of multistory parking garages—he fought to keep a railroad out of the Lake District—but one wonders if he ever felt the weight of the din of cities amid the pastoral places and calculated what *their* effect might be. Not that I'm categorically against din or cities, but I wonder about these leftover spaces. Someone remarked to me recently that the reason you lose your recent memory after a blow to the head or similar catastrophe is that you haven't had time to edit it yet. We edit, but life lies also in the outtakes. And they get grimmer and grimmer. Perhaps what's terrifying about these new urban landscapes is that they imply the possibility of a life that would be one long outtake.

The world sometimes seems to be made more and more of stuff we're not sup-posed to look at, the whole banal infrastructure that supports the illusion of auto-motive independence, the largely unseen places whence come our materials—strip mines, industrial agriculture, automated assembly lines, abattoirs—and whence they go: the dumps. A city is a theatrical space, and its parliaments and museums and courthouses are the stage sets, while the sewer systems and trash cans are in the wings. But we are not audience (though tourists try); we are all actors, wandering on and off stage, seeing what we're supposed to and what we're not. Los Angeles just happens to consist mostly of these drably utilitarian spaces, in part because cars demand them, and it is a city built to accommodate cars to the nth degree. These spaces tend to be gray, the gray of unpainted cement, asphalt, accumulated grime, and steel; they tend to be either abandoned or frequented by people who are also discards, a kind of subterranean realm hauled to the surface. Or not.

When the new Getty Museum opened off the stretch of the 405 Freeway that connects Los Angeles proper to the even more suburban San Fernando Valley, much was written about Richard Meier's architecture and Robert Irwin's gardens. Remarkably little was written about the parking garage, though this was the first structure one encountered on arriving at the Getty. (Theoretically, you could take a bus to the place, but this was, after all, a museum in L.A., up on the bluff above the deep canyon the 405 runs through; it wasn't close to anything, except some mansions up in the heights with it, and public transit is largely an underclass phenomenon there.) The old Getty in Malibu had been modeled after a Roman villa, all colonnades and porticoes; and it became clear to me that the new one was, wittingly or otherwise, also full of Europeanate historical reference. It was Dante's *Divine Comedy* as a theme park, and, just as in the *Divine Comedy*, the Inferno was the most compelling part. You, brave cultural adventurer, were Dante. Or a dead soul with a thing for art, anyway.

You took the Getty exit and, if you'd been heading north, swung over the overpass and after a few wriggles dove into the garage. You came out of the smog-filtered Los Angeles light (which always gave me the impression that a thrifty God had replaced our incandescent sun with diffused fluorescent light) into a dark passage. The garage was underlit, with a low-slung ceiling and construction that evinced the massive weight first of the cement slabwork and then of the floors and earth above. The weight pressed down on your soul, and the directions urged you onward. Down you went, and down, and further down, spiraling into the seismically unstable bowels of the Los Angeles earth, in these circles of looming darkness, questing for a parking space of your own, farther and farther down. I believe there were nine circles, or levels, in this vehicular hell. Finally you found a place for your car in this dim realm, staggered to an elevator, and moved upward more quickly than Dante ascended purgatory.

But you weren't in purgatory yet. The elevator opened onto a platform where you could catch a monorail up the hill to the museum. Disneyland too has a monorail, and though on our first visit to the Getty I thought of it as a nice tribute to its sister amusement park, we perplexed everyone around us by walking up the unfrequented road the quarter mile or so to the museum. Altitude, I should add, correlates neatly to economic clout in urban and suburban California; and so, though the presumed point of the Getty was to let people look at art, first they parked, then they looked at the mighty fortress of the Getty hunched up on high, and then up there at various junctures they got the billionaires' view. The museum was purgatory. There you went through the redemptive exercise of experiencing art, lots and lots of it, from ancient times through the early twentieth century, room after room of altarpieces and portraits and still lifes and drawings. I knew the British Museum and the Louvre before I ever went to New York's museums, and those two august institutions are about looting Greece and Egypt, about imperial power; in New York's Metropolitan Museum for the first time, I caught myself wondering when the United States conquered Europe so as to take home all that plunder, a question the Getty Museum also raises.

Having soaked up more art than you could possibly recall once you were back on the 405, you reached the gardens at the far end of the property. From a strictly real estate point of view, what made the place so imperial was what the San Francisco Bay Area artist Richard Misrach calls "the politics of the view," a sub-ject he discovered when he moved from the plebeian flats of Oakland to the profes-sorial heights of the Berkeley hills and discovered that what he'd been missing all those years was vista (this resulted in his book *The Golden Gate Bridge*, a series of photographs of the Turneresque-tourist view of the iconic red suspension bridge from his front porch, or rather of the atmospheric effects swirling around it). Irwin is thought to have chosen, out of contrariness, to make a garden at the Getty in which the splendidly commanding and even more splendidly expensive view disappears.

Paradise is a Persian word that originally meant an enclosed garden, and here you walk downhill, accompanied by a stream in a stony bed, to a garden that, like the garage, is circular, though in this case the circles are truly concentric, a shallow basin whose outer ground level becomes its horizon by the time you've descended a few rings through the bright erratic plantings that Irwin, who is no gardener, had selected. Annoying Richard Meier by obscuring the view and cluttering up the rugged modernist space with a fussy garden was one thing; Irwin chose to annoy the rest of us by putting in the center of his garden what looks like a hedge maze but is, unlike any proper garden maze, inaccessible because of a water moat.

But it's the parking garage that is most memorable of all these three spaces, and it's the parking garage to which you must return before getting back onto the 405 to enter and merge and exit and otherwise wend your way onward. Symbolically, I suppose, it's because you can't quite reach the center of heaven that you end up back in hell.

California has often been imagined as paradise, hell, and everything in between. Paradise is, actually, a small town in northeastern California; I know two filmmakers who grew up there, and it's now filling up with conservative retirees. Hell is nowhere explicit on the map, though Death Valley, Devils Postpile National Monument, and a few other sites have satisfyingly infernal names. And probably the whole place is purgatory, since nearly all of us are so, so to speak, hell-bent on self-improvement. Something about my dear weird Golden State obliges it to assume allegorical and oracular proportions. A quarter century ago, everyone from Jean Baudrillard to Umberto Eco scanned it as a sort of crystal ball in which the future could be seen; the *New York Times* routinely portrays it not as Bosch's *Garden of Earthly Delights*, but as another painting by the same master, *The Ship of Fools*. (Arnold Schwarzenegger's election as governor has deeply gratified the rest of the nation, which can now reflect even more confidently that, though we have better weather and really are inventing their future, we're totally feckless freaks.)

One of the oft-cited reasons for the American film industry to settle in Hollywood is Southern California's ability to simulate almost any part of the world: the place has lush agricultural districts, deserts, mountains, forests, oceans, and open space in which to build Babylon or Atlanta, all drenched in endless light. That is to say, to be in California is to be everywhere and nowhere and usually somewhere else (in the posher parts of L.A., every house seems to be dreaming of elsewhere: this half-timbered job is in the Black Forest, and that one next door is the Alhambra). And, as Los Angeles writer Jenny Price recently remarked, to say, "I ate a doughnut in Los Angeles" is a different thing altogether than to say, "I ate a doughnut." The invocation of L.A. throws that doughnut on a stage where it casts a long shadow of depravity or opportunity (which might be the same thing here). She added that just as Claude Lévi-Strauss once remarked that animals are how we think, so Los Angeles, and by extension California, are also how we think—think about society, about urbanism, about the future, about morality and its opposite. It's as though in the golden light, everything is thrown into dramatic relief, everything is on stage acting out some drama or other.

Sandow Birk, who early in his career restaged the great watery paintings of history—*The Raft of the Medusa, Washington Crossing the Delaware*—as surfing scenes, has long been picking California's allegorical crops. A Southern California surfer himself (and one who insistently foregrounds his surfing as Robert Irwin a few generations before did his car-customizing and hot-rodding), he painted a brilliant series some years before in which the cultural clashes between San Francisco and L.A. were depicted as a duly multiethnic battle, complete with fast food sponsors and gang colors carried by the armed factions, published as *In Smog and Thunder: Historical Works from the Great War of the Californias*. Another of his series, a more serious inspection of the state as heaven and hell, represents all thirty-three state prisons in this incarceration-crazy state (published as *Incarcerated: Visions of California in the 21st Century*). Each is a landscape painting, harking back to all the finest traditions of that genre; they just happen to have, in the foreground, middle ground, or background, a prison (whose architecture, come to think of it, has much in common with airports, parking garages, shopping malls, and the other new spaces of human management, now that ordinary life in the United States is more and more like prison, at least in terms of security and surveillance technologies). New hell surrounded by old heaven, though the prisoners were not put out there for the scenery but for the cheapness and the obscurity that rural places offer.

And now comes Birk's California *Divine Comedy*. His *Dante's Inferno* is in print as a large-format paperback; the *Purgatorio*'s artwork is completed (purgatory is my own hilly hometown, San Francisco), and that book should appear in another year; and *Paradise*, presumably—location undisclosed—will come in 2006. Hell, naturally, is Los Angeles. Literally Los Angeles: Birk's edition of the *Divine Comedy* is faintly reminiscent of Gustave Dore's, and its line drawings depict not a landmark Los Angeles, but the back-alley L.A. of anonymous dead-ends. Every canto has a frontispiece above the argument and a full-page illustration inside. Canto I sets the stage nicely with a tipped-over shopping cart on the cobbled ground of what appears to be a vacant lot. The words *Canto I* appear to be spray-painted on one of those oblong, cement wheel-stops that mark the front end of a parking space—Dante's dark woods become desolation-row parking lot.

Birk's editor told me that he initially considered approaching a rapper to translate the *Divine Comedy*'s terzarima into street slang, but when he was told that this would turn the project into, for example, Ice T's *Comedy* with illustrations by Sandow Birk, he took on the project himself with a friend, surf journalist Marcus Sanders. Their translation is into the vernacular of guy inarticulateness, with a little slang, which is to say its frequent awfulness must be intentional and is certainly appropriate. Throughout most of the English-speaking world, citizens speak English like, well, native speakers, and the ability to speak well is a pleasure and a power. But from George W. Bush on down, the United States, particularly its male portion, is fraught with inarticulateness and often committed to it as well.

Jane Tompkins, in her wonderful *West of Everything: The Inner Life of Westerns*, traces some of this to a frank distrust of language and an association of speaking with opening up, compromising, and otherwise surrendering alpha-male status. John Wayne, she points out, spoke in monosyllables, often to denounce communication and chatter. Yup. Nope. Silence was very golden (it was, after all, gay men who would argue in the heyday of AIDS activism that silence equals death, an equation that goes well with Tompkins's argument that speech equals the unmanly opening up of an orifice). I sometimes think that a certain kind of right-wing belief system is propped up on syntactical delusion: conspiracy theories and accusations rest on beliefs and associations that don't make sense politically but can be swallowed by those who can't make sense grammatically. (Thus when television interviewer Diane Sawyer asked Bush some months ago whether the administration knew that Saddam Hussein had WMDs or thought that he could "move to acquire those weapons," he answered, "So what's the difference?") And this very inarticulateness seems to lead to other means of resolving conflict, so much so that I once caught myself thinking that if these Americans speak English like a second language, perhaps guns were their first language. Of course, a steady diet of television's sentence fragments helps. Complex thoughts require complex syntax. I'm not sure Birk's is always up to the challenge. Thus does Birk's Dante begin: "About halfway through the course of my pathetic life / I woke up and found myself in a stupor in some dark place. . . . I can't really describe what that place was like. It was dark and strange, and just thinking / about it now gives me the chills."

In C. H. Sisson's superb 1980 translation, Virgil says of himself and the other pagans in limbo, "We are lost; there is no other penalty / Than to live here without hope, but with desire." Dante goes on, "It grieved my heart when I heard him say that." In Birk and Marcus Sanders's version, Virgil says, "We're all now eternally lost. That's why / you hear the sighs and despair. We're barred forever from any hope, and everyone is despondent about it." Dante cuts in, "Shit, that doesn't seem right, I thought. How is it fair / that even righteous, decent guys like Virgil should be / trapped in Limbo, forever? I was totally confused, and / I needed to figure out this whole unfair Christianity / thing." More lifeless than deathless, this version is full of editorials (like the unfair Christianity bit), but true to the Dante figure in the drawings, a white homeboy in shades.

Birk is brilliant at architecture and topography, but his bodies are always a little awkwardly realized, like the language. But this works toward a truly California Comedy, one of inarticulate attempts to realize truth, meaning, and complexity. "Text adapted by" is how Birk and Sanders are credited on the cover. Nobody will read their Divine Comedy as an ideal translation, though perhaps it will draw in young readers who might otherwise not read it at all. But there's an odd awkwardness to the street language embedded with the rolling names of medieval Italian sinners and the elaborate scenarios of Dante's tortures. The classics freely adapt—the Odyssey to Dublin in 1904 or to the southern United States during the Civil War (in Cold Mountain)—but Birk's book is too literal to be a real reinvention and too reinvented to be a functional translation. Turning Dante's greyhounds (in Canto XIII) into pit bulls gives local color, but it doesn't really do much for the landscape of souls turned into suffering trees. The text is too weighed down by the power and the particulars of the original, and they are there only to situate the arena where Birk is at ease and inspired: the free visual interpretation of the Inferno.

So Birk's book is better looked at than read. His pictorial contribution is more to the critique of urbanism as embodied by L.A., in the vein of Mike Davis's *City of Quartz*, than to Dante studies or theology. L.A. has little to give Dante, in other words, but Dante via Birk has much to give L.A. His tour through L.A. in thirty-four cantos is a scrutiny of the invisible territories that so fazed me when I was a young freeway-riding critic, punctuated by the phantasmagoria of Dante's torturescapes. They go together beautifully: in Canto XXI, the winged devils of the fifth ditch fly over a freeway toward the clifftop Dante and Virgil. There is a Cyclone fence behind them, a one-way sign in the lower right, another shopping cart, this time full of the possessions of an evidently homeless demon, and the flying demons carry the signs that beggars often do, "Will Work for Food," "Homeless Veteran." The darkness isn't just nocturnal. In another full-page picture, hypocrites form a long line winding toward downtown, with more freeway and mini-mall signage in the middle ground. Among the hypocrites are quite a few Los Angeles cops. For most of us, there are days when a few demons circling around the pilings holding up an overpass would be perfectly apt. Birk has also got at the parts of L.A. that recall Piranesi, not David Hockney, the sinister noir terrain of freeway overpasses and cuttings and drainage ditches that create a stacked-up, tangled, vertical landscape far from the flat, sunshiny L.A. of the usual iconography.

So it goes, genre-scene frontispieces and supernaturally writhing full-page illustrations, and in some ways the latter are relief to the former. In hell, something happens; in the genre scenes, all is quiet, and a sense of inertia, inevitability, pure doom is there, the doom that disaster alleviates. The frontispiece to Canto VII is a gas meter, one of those metal contrivances disgorging pipes and meters like some sort of mechanical heart, and this one is stuck into a wall full of cracks. Sometimes they're more cheerful. One is a drum set. Another is a police motorcycle. In one cheerful one, however, a skateboarder flies through the air, only feet and board with the canto number on it visible in the oval engraving.

California is a tangible place with products and square miles and per capita income, but it is also an oracular landscape, like those in the *Divine Comedy*, a place people look to for signs and portents of what's to come. A crime, a trend, a culinary innovation that shows up here is anxiously scanned for omens and meanings; hardly any place is more overinterpreted (even if the interpretation tends to dwell on the same places over and over again: L.A. for depravity, San Francisco for freaks, the Salton Sea for unnaturalness, and so forth; and even many people in the state don't know that most of the water spread over the fields and the suburban lawns started out as snowpack or any of the other material conditions of the overlooked Californias). Birk's book gets at this oracular California, finding that even an underpass can flood with demons and meanings.

The cover of his book is also its masterpiece. It remodels Frederic Church's gargantuan 1862 luminist painting *Cotopaxi, Ecuador* into a vision of all California as hell. The same belching volcano is there on the horizon, filling the sky with sunreddened smoke, the same vast gorge in the central foreground; but Birk has turned the gorge's sublime waterfalls into a sort of terraced lava-bottomed mining pit around which emblems of all California gather. There are palm trees and oil derricks and power lines in the foreground, along with signs for chain stores and, rather in the mode of Poussin's *Et in Arcadia Ego*, a skull sitting on a plinth inscribed "Inferno." (That Birk's text can only reference humdrum homeboy life says as much about the verbal limitations of this project as its Dore, Church, and Poussin references do about its visual power.) In the middle distance, a shattered Golden Gate Bridge reaches toward the gorge and then breaks off, and birds black in the backlight fly through the ruddy scene and perch on the power lines. Freeways snake all through this vision of hell, the red tail lights of departing traffic balanced with the yellow-white of approaching headlights in what looks like California's most frequent invocation of hell: the rush-hour traffic jam.

Sandow Birk's ongoing project has been to revamp the whole legacy of painting and the language of history painting as something that fits California. This means both bringing a California sensibility (surfer jokes, burger-joint references) to reiterations of history paintings and attempting to come to terms with a place where the very idea of history is problematic. The mythology would have it that California went from pristine wilderness to suburban paradise in a single uneventful bound—and thus are erased the hideous injustices of the genocide of the Native Californians and the marginalization of the Californios who lived here when California was still Mexico, to say nothing of the environmental disaster and drive-by shooting that was the Gold Rush and the epic corruption of the railroad corporation that ran California into the twentieth century. But Birk has attempted to revive history painting without painting the California past. Or is it that Birk has revised history painting to reflect the reinvention of history as being about places and classes and bodies rather than epic moments and heroic men? He has done what the new historians do: look at what has been overlooked—literally in the architecture of odd corners, figuratively in the history of class and consumption—and seek out patterns of meaning.

His surfer series only mocked histories unfolded elsewhere; but his *In Smog and Thunder: Historical Works from the Great War of the Californias* portrayed a comic battle in a fictional future that said much about the present (and included images of "The Bombardment of the Getty Center" as well as the San Francisco Museum of Modern Art in ruins); and his prison paintings were situated in the absolute present tense. History is what gives a place meaning, generally, and Birk has wrestled with the conundrum of California, a place full of amnesiac erasures of history and impositions of histories that never happened, a place whose roots are, in some strange way, in the future. Rome was the eternal city; perhaps California as heaven, hell, and purgatory is the eternal present tense.

The Wal-Mart Biennale

[2006]

It isn't that, when Wal-Mart heiress Alice Walton purchased Asher B. Durand's 1849 painting *Kindred Spirits* last year, she got the state of Arkansas to pass legislation specifically to lower her taxes—in this case, about $3 million on a purchase price of $35 million. It isn't that the world's richest woman and twelfth richest person (according to a *Forbes* magazine 2005 estimate) scooped the painting out from under the National Gallery and the Metropolitan Museum of Art, which had banded together to try to keep it in a public collection when the New York Public Library decided to sell it off. It isn't that Walton will eventually stick this talisman of New England cultural life and a lot of other older American paintings in the Crystal Bridges Museum of American Art, the Walton family museum she's building in Bentonville, Arkansas, the site of Wal-Mart's corporate headquarters—after all, people in the middle of the country should get to see some good art too. It might not even be, as Wal-Mart Watch points out, that the price of the painting equals what the state of Arkansas spends every two years providing for Wal-Mart's 3,971 employees on public assistance; or that the average Wal-Mart cashier makes $7.92 an hour and, since Wal-Mart likes to keep people on less than full-time schedules, works only twenty-nine hours a week, for an annual income of $11,943—so a Wal-Mart cashier would have to work a little under three thousand years to earn the price of the painting without taking any salary out for food, housing, or other expenses (and a few hundred more years to pay the taxes, if the state legislature didn't exempt our semi-immortal worker).

The trouble lies in what the painting means and what Alice Walton and her personal fortune of $18 billion or so mean. Art patronage has always been a kind of money-laundering, a pretty public face for fortunes made in uglier ways. The superb Rockefeller folk art collections in several American museums do not contain any paintings of the 1914 Ludlow Massacre of striking miners and their families in Colorado, carried out by Rockefeller goons, and the J. Paul Getty Museum in Los Angeles doesn't say a thing about oil. But something about Wal-Mart and *Kindred Spirits* is more peculiar than all the robber barons and their chapels, galleries, and collections ever were, perhaps because there's no redemptive Carnegie library-building urges behind Walton's acts, or perhaps because, more than most works of art, Durand's painting is a touchstone for a set of American ideals that Wal-Mart has been directly savaging. In an era when oil companies take out advertisements proclaiming their commitment to saving the environment, halting global warming, promoting petroleum alternatives, and urging conservation, while many of them also fund arguments against the very existence of climate change, nothing is too contrary to embrace. But *Kindred Spirits* is older, more idealistic, and more openly at odds with this state of affairs than most of the hostages to multinational image-making.

Kindred Spirits portrays Durand's friend, the great American landscape painter Thomas Cole, with his friend, the poet and editor William Cullen Bryant. The two stand on a projecting rock above a cataract in the Catskills, bathed, like all the trees and air around them, in golden light. The painting is about friendship freely given, including a sense of friendship, even passion, for the American landscape itself. In the work of Cole, Durand, and Bryant, as in the writing of Henry David Thoreau and Walt Whitman, you can see an emerging belief that love of nature, beauty, truth, and freedom are naturally allied, a romantic vision that still lingers as one of the most idealistic versions of what it might mean to be an American.

Cole was one of the first American painters to see the possibilities in American landscapes, to see that meaning could be greater rather than less in a place not yet full of ruins and historical associations, and so he became an advocate for wilderness nearly half a century before California rhapsodist and eventual Sierra Club co-founder John Muir took up the calling. Bryant had gained a reputation as a poet before he became editor-in-chief of the *New York Evening Post* and thereby a pivotal figure in the culture of the day. He defended a group of striking tailors in 1836, long before there was a union movement, and was ever after a champion of freedom and human rights, turning his newspaper into an antislavery mouthpiece and eventually becoming a founder of the Republican Party, back when that was the more progressive and less beholden of the two parties. He was an early supporter of Abraham Lincoln and of the projects that resulted in New York's Central Park and the Metropolitan Museum—of a democratic urban culture that believed in the uplifting power of nature and free access. Maybe the mutation of the Republican Party from Bryant's to Walton's time is measure enough of American weirdness. Or maybe the details matter, the details of what the painting is and what Wal-Mart and its heiress are.

Kindred Spirits was commissioned by the wealthy dry-goods merchant Jonathan Sturges as a gift for Bryant, in commemoration of his beautiful eulogy for Cole, who died suddenly in 1848. Bryant left it to his daughter Julia, who in 1904 gave it to what became the New York Public Library. It was never a commodity exchanged between strangers until the library, claiming financial need, put it and other works of art up for sale. And so now a portrait of antislavery and wilderness advocates belongs to a woman whose profits came from degrading working conditions in the United States and abroad and from ravaging the North American landscape.

Maybe the problem is that the Crystal Bridges museum seems like a false front for Wal-Mart, a made-in-America, artisanal edifice of idealism for a corporation that is none of the above. The museum will, as such institutions do, attempt to associate the Wal-Mart billionaires with high culture, American history, craftsmanship, beautifully crafted objects—a host of ideals and pleasures a long way from what you find inside the blank, slabby box of a Wal-Mart. One of the privileges of wealth is buying yourself out of the situation you helped to make, so that the wealthy who advocate for deregulation of environmental standards install water purifiers and buy cases of Perrier, while those who advocate for small government simply hire their own security forces and educators.

Walton, it seems safe to assume, lives surrounded by nicer objects, likely made under nicer conditions, than she sells to the rest of us. Perhaps Crystal Bridges will become one of the places we can go to revisit the long history that preceded industrialization and globalization, when creation and execution were not so savagely sundered, when you might know the maker of your everyday goods, and making was a skilled and meaningful act. One of the pleasures of most visual art is that linkage between mind and hand, lost elsewhere as acts of making are divided among many and broken down into multiple repetitive tasks. Perhaps Walton could build us the Museum of When Americans Made Stuff Locally by Hand for People They Knew, or perhaps that's what Crystal Bridges, along with the rest of such institutions, will become. Or she could just plan to open the Museum of When Americans Made Stuff at some more distant date, though about half of what's in Wal-Mart, sources inform me, is still actually made here—for now. The world's richest woman, however, seems more interested in archaic images of America than in the artistry behind them.

She has already scooped up a portrait of George Washington by Charles Wilson Peale and paintings by Winslow Homer and Edward Hopper for her museum. That museum, reports say, will feature many, many nineteenth-century portraits of Native Americans—but it would be hard to see her as a champion of the indigenous history of the Americas. The Wal-Mart that opened last November in Teotihuacán, near Mexico City, is built so close to the great Pyramid of the Sun that many consider the site desecrated. The Wal-Mart parking lot has eradicated the site of a smaller temple. "This is the flag of conquest by global interests, the symbol of the destruction of our culture," said a local schoolteacher. Thanks to free trade measures like NAFTA, Wal-Mart has become Mexico's biggest retailer and private-sector employer.

Imagine if Walton were more like Jonathan Sturges, supporting the art of her time. Imagine her supporting artists who actually had something to say about Wal-Mart and America (and Mexico, and China). Imagine that, in the mode of the Venice Biennale or the São Paolo Biennale, there was a Wal-Mart biennale. After all, Wal-Mart is itself China's seventh-largest trading partner, ahead of Germany and Russia and Italy; if it were a nation, it would be the nineteenth-biggest economy in the world. Since it's on the same scale as those countries, why shouldn't it have its own contemporary art shows? But what would the Wal-Mart nation and its artists look like?

Rather than the open, luminous, intelligent architecture Moshe Safdie will probably bestow on Bentonville, Arkansas, imagine a shuttered Wal-Mart big box—of which there are so many, often shut down simply to stop employees from unionizing—turned into a MOCA, a museum of contemporary art, or, better yet, a MOWA, a Museum of Wal-Mart Art. Or Wal-Art. After all, Los Angeles's MOCA was originally sited in a defunct warehouse. You could set the artists free to make art entirely out of materials available at Wal-Mart or to make art about the global politics of Wal-Mart in our time—poverty, consumerism, sprawl, racism, gender discrimination, exploitation of undocumented workers.

Imagine a contemporary artist, maybe using Photoshop, reworking *Kindred Spirits* again and again. Imagine that Cole and Bryant are, this time, standing not on a rocky outcropping but in, say, one of the puzzle and art supply aisles of a Wal-Mart near Kaaterskill Falls, dazed and depressed. Or imagine instead some sweatshop workers, a little hunched and hungry, on that magnificent perch amid the foliage and the golden light, invited at last into some sense of democratic community. Imagine paintings of Edward Hopper's old downtowns, boarded up because all the sad and lonely people are shopping at Wal-Mart and even having their coffee and hot dogs there. Imagine video-portraits of the people who actually make the stuff you can buy at Wal-Mart, or of the African American truck drivers suing the corporation for racism, or of the women who are lead plaintiffs in the nation's largest class action lawsuit for discrimination. Imagine if Alice Walton decided to follow the route of Kmart with Martha Stewart or Target with architect Michael Graves and commissioned some cutting-edge contemporary art about these issues: videos and DVDs you could buy, prints for your walls, performance art in the aisles, art that maybe even her workers could afford. Imagine if Wal-Mart would acknowledge what Wal-Mart is rather than turning hallowed American art into a fig leaf to paste over naked greed and raw exploitation. But really, it's up to the rest of us to make the real Museum of Wal-Mart, one way or another, in our heads, on our web sites, or in our reading of everyday life everywhere.

The Silence of the Lambswool Cardigans

[[2003]]

There was a time not so long ago when everything was recognizable not just as a cup or a coat, but as a cup made by so-and-so out of clay from this bank on the local river or a coat woven by the guy in that house out of wool from the sheep visible on the hills. Then, objects were not purely material, mere commodities, but signs of processes, human and natural, pieces of a story, and both the story and the stuff sustained life. It's as though every object spoke—some of them must have sung out—in a language everyone could hear, a language that surrounded every object in an aura of its history.

"All commodities are only definite masses of congealed labor-time," said Marx, but who now could dissolve them into their constituent histories of labor and materials, into the stories that made them about the processes of the world, made them part of life even if they were iron or brick, made them come to life? For decades, tales have circulated of city kids who didn't know that milk came from cows, and, more recently, reports of the inability of American teenagers to find Iraq on a map have made the rounds; but who among us can picture precisely where their sweater or their sugar comes from?

I've been thinking about that because a new shopping mall has opened up at the eastern foot of the Bay Bridge, in what was once, according to the newspaper, the biggest shell mound in Northern California. From the 1870s to the 1920s, this place was Shellmound Park, an amusement park, racetrack, dance hall, and shooting range; but Prohibition put the pleasure grounds out of business, and the mound was bulldozed for industry. The remains of seven hundred Ohlone people that an archaeologist snatched from the construction site in 1924 are still at the University of California at Berkeley. The site became industrialized, hosting paint and pesticide factories that eventually made it into a wasteland so toxic that those venturing into it wore moon suits. Now it has been reclaimed for shopping, and the cleanup has disturbed the remaining Ohlone burial sites.

The street that goes out to the shopping center is still called Shellmound, but the outdoor mall itself includes the usual chains that make it impossible to know if you're in Phoenix or Philadelphia: Victoria's Secret, Williams-Sonoma, Express, the three versions of the Gap corporation, including Old Navy and Banana Republic, all laid out on a fake Main Street. Anti-Gap protestors haven't arrived yet, though they are frequent presences in downtown San Francisco, decrying both the Gap's reliance on sweatshop labor and the clear-cutting of old-growth redwood forests in Mendocino by the Gap's and those forests' owners (see www.Gapsucks.org). But the day the mall opened, activists from the International Indian Treaty Council handed out flyers protesting the desecration of a burial ground. The mall is a doubly modern site, a space that could be anywhere, into which commodities come as if out of nowhere.

In *The Condition of the Working Class in England*, Friedrich Engels recounts the crimes behind the production of everyday things—ceramics, ironware, glass, but particularly cotton cloth. He wrote in a time when objects were first becoming silent, and he asked the same thing that the activists from Gapsucks.org do, that we learn the new industrial languages of objects, that we hear the story of children worked into deformity and blindness to make lace, the story of the knife grinders with a life expectancy of thirty-five years, or today the story of the Nike workers who are paid less than living wages to work long hours in excruciating conditions. These industrial stories have always been environmental stories too, about factory effluents, cotton chemicals, paper dioxins, the timber industry, the petrochemical industry, on and on.

Somewhere in the industrial age, objects shut up because their creation had become so remote and intricate a process that it was no longer readily knowable. Or they were silenced, because the pleasures of abundance that all the cheap goods offered were available only if they were mute about the scarcity and loss that lay behind their creation. Modern advertising—notably for Nike—constitutes an aggressive attempt to displace the meaning of the commodity from its makers, as though you enter into relationship with very tall athletes rather than, say, very thin Vietnamese teenagers when you buy these shoes. It is a stretch to think about Mexican prison labor while contemplating Victoria's Secret lavender lace boy-cut panties. The objects are pretty; their stories are hideous; so you get to choose between an alienated and ultimately meaningless world of consumption and one that makes terrible demands on you. And to tell the tales is to be the bearer of bad news—imagine activists as Moses coming down from Sinai but cutting straight to Leviticus, with forty thousand or so prohibitions: against shrimp (see www.montereybayaquarium.org), against strawberries (methyl bromide, stoop labor), against gold (see www.greatbasinminewatch.org), and on and on. It's what makes radicals and environmentalists seem so grumpy to the would-be consumer.

Maybe the real questions are which substances, objects, and products tell stories that don't make people cringe or turn away and how to take these items from the margins to the mainstream. For the past half century, the process of artmaking has been part of its subject, and this making becomes a symbolic act that attempts to substitute for the silence of all the other objects. But nobody lives by art alone. There's food from the wild, from your own garden, from friends, ancient objects salvaged and flea-marketed, heirlooms and hand-me-downs, local crafts, and a few things still made with the union label, but it's not easy for anyone to stay completely free of Payless or Wal-Mart. Too, good stories—such as those told by pricey organic and free-range and shade-grown food that is available only in the hipper stores of the fancier regions—can be a luxury.

Some of the enthusiasm for farmers markets, which are springing up like mushrooms after rain, arises from meeting objects that aren't mute, because you see the people who grew the produce and know that the places they come from are not far away. This alternative economy feeds people who want to be nourished by stories and connections as well as by food, and it's growing. Some farmers markets are like boutiques, with little bunches of peas or raspberries displayed and priced like jewels, but I go to an intensely multiethnic mob scene called Heart of the City

Farmers Market in which the food, even some of the organic stuff, is pretty cheap and everyone is present, including the homeless, who frequent that space all week anyway, and the locals use the market to make up for the way supermarkets boy-cott poor neighborhoods. Seeing the thorn scars on the hands of the rose growers there was as big a step in knowing what constitutes my world as realizing that, in this town where it never snows, our tap water is all Sierra snowmelt.

What bothers me about the new mall is its silence, a silence we mostly live in nowadays; what cheers me are the ways people are learning to read the silent his-tories of objects and choosing the objects that still sing. It's a small start, but it's a start.

Locked Horns

[2003]

One day not long ago, I went to see a show of animal skulls at the local science museum. I like skulls. What's ordinarily hidden under the upholstery of flesh, skin, hair, and other tissue is revealed in bones, the foundations of bodies and, in the size of craniums, perhaps the seat of consciousness, a sort of naked essence of what makes each animal so distinctly itself. The barn-size room was full of them, from the gray throne of an elephant's head to the yellowish hacksaws of crocodile smiles, all the same raw ingredients of teeth and craniums and eye sockets in spectacularly different proportions corresponding to vision and diet and defense and thought. A wall was covered with a grid of hundreds of sea lion skulls to show their subtle variation, and antlered and horned creatures were lined up on other walls, all the splendor of what in that room seemed apt to call the animal kingdom.

Something I'd missed on a previous visit stopped me cold and made me think for days afterward: a glass case containing four stag skulls, or, rather, two pairs of stag skulls. Each pair of opponents had locked antlers and, unable to disentangle themselves, had died face to face, probably of hunger. The antlers were intricately intertwined like branches of trees that had grown together, and it must have taken only an instant of coincidence when the antlers were angled to fit together like two pieces of a puzzle rather than to clash, a moment when the stags sealed their fates. Such a tangle is fairly common among antlered creatures and some horned ones, such as bighorn sheep, and it's given rise to the phrase "lock horns," which I'd never thought about, any more than I had ever thought why a penknife is called a penknife until I came across Wordsworth mentioning that he used one to trim his quill pen.

Language is full of such fossils of the actual and the natural, but what struck me on this visit was the grimness of the stags' fate and the ease with which it turned to metaphor and to warning. I quickly reviewed my own life to see if any conflicts were so intractable and vowed not to let any so consume me. A lot of people have died of being right, and some of them have taken their opponents with them. Everyone's encountered bad divorces, noise-obsessed neighbors, monomaniacs who let a grievance take over their lives to the exclusion of everything else, a sort of psychological starvation. It's not hard to expand this notion to politics, to the locked horns of the cold war between the Soviet Union and the United States. Nor is it hard to extend the idea to the way the United States seems lost without an opponent abroad—an evil empire, an axis of evil—with which to lock horns, so that rather than reap a peace dividend since 1989, we've watched political leaders look for the familiar embrace of an enemy's antlers.

But it's important to remember that it's a metaphor, that stags are no more prone to divorces than to first-strike missile deployment. Theodor Adorno objected to astrology (or, more specifically, to the astrology column in an American newspaper) because people thought that the stars were about them; better to say that we are about the stars. That is, it's not that stags are like us but that we are like stags. One of the uses of the natural world is the generation of striking images and actions that let us define and redefine ourselves and connect ourselves to everything else. That the natural world gives rise to metaphors by which we understand ourselves is, I have long thought, one of the most neglected reasons for protecting it and paying attention to it. It's important to remember too that biological determinism is just bad analogy: all that stuff claiming we are like our primordial selves, therefore we must eat raw food or copulate with those who look this way or act out that way, is just saying that the stars are about us.

The definition is always partial; the door at the far end is always open for something else to happen, for redefinition. "My love is like a red, red rose," wrote the poet Robert Burns; we assume that there is something about roses—sweetness, redness, delicacy, beauty, ephemerality—that he has in mind and do not picture his sweetheart with thorns, roots, and maybe aphids. Partial resemblance, because metaphor takes us only so far; then we must travel by other means.

The same week I saw the skulls of the stags who'd starved of intractable com- bat, I went downtown to meet my friend Claire and see the last day of a big show of Yoko Ono's art. It was a magnificent show, and Ono's work managed to do all the things the conceptualists of that era most prized, but with a kind of tender hopefulness that wasn't theirs but hers. At the entrance to the exhibition were two tables, each with two chairs, and the tabletop was a chessboard set with chess pieces, ready to play. But all the chessmen—and the tables, and the chairs, and the board—were white, whiter than the stags' antlers, than their skulls, than their teeth, pure white. In Ono's game, your opponent was no longer different from yourself and maybe no longer your opponent. Can you fight yourself? How do you know when you're winning?

Claire, who has gone around the world doing antinuclear and peace work and now heads Oakland's Martin Luther King Jr. Freedom Center, has many surpris- ing talents, and it turned out that she is an avid chess player. I am not, and I was tired, but that was all to the good, because she was delighted that it took only three moves for me to mistake her rook for mine and move it against her—at which point the game was over, we had unhooked antlers, and Ono had firmly suggested that difference is negligible and conflict avoidable, in this artwork that was about remaking the games and metaphors for war into a playful merging. Further in the exhibition was documentation of Ono's billboards and placards from the Vietnam War era, which said things like "The War Is Over If You Want It." Ono makes it clear not only that we could disengage from conflict but also that with open imagination we could transform it into something else—perhaps into love, a word that crops up all over her work. Stags are stags, but chess doesn't have to be war. Neither does war.

9
CITY AT THE END OF THE WORLD

The Orbits of Earthly Bodies

⟦2003⟧

"I live in the city but I dream of moving to the country
at least once a week." This thought is expressed in our mix
of sepia-toned photos and plain-spoken text. Black text is silk-
screened on a white background; the frames are black-painted
wood. 14–4420873 Catalog/Internet only $149.
Pottery Barn Holiday 2002 catalog, p. 71

Each of the past several summers, I've spent a month or two at a friend's small house in rural New Mexico. Every year, I'd come back to the city joking that I wasn't sure I was closer to nature, but I was definitely closer to my car. Really, it depends on how you define nature. In the country, there's more wildlife to be seen—though this place surrounded by cattle ranches was not so prolifically populated as many far more suburbanized places I know, where the deer come down and eat the tulips (or, even more thrilling, the mountain lions eat the cocker spaniels).

Around the New Mexico house, coyotes sometimes howled at night; vultures, ravens, and swallows all had their appointed rites from dawn to dusk; and last summer a vivid violet-blue bird I eventually pinned down as a male blue grosbeak arrived like a minor hallucination. Most of all, there was the changing light and sky. Without lifting my head from the pillow, I could watch the summer sun rise in the northeast near where the constellation Cassiopeia made her regular nighttime appearance. I watched the transition from sunset to dusk every evening; the one time I went to a movie instead, I sat there thinking, "I'm missing the show! I'm missing the show!" With views to the horizon and dark, dark nights, the sun, the moon, and the stars lived with me, or I with them, and with the lightning and the wonderful cloud operas that passed by. That was glorious.

But my own life was strictly unnatural. Everything practical I did involved getting into a car, because there wasn't a newspaper, a stamp, or a bottle of milk for sale for many miles. It would have taken me a full day to walk to the nearest grocery store. So I drove there, and drove to the houses of my friends, aunts, and uncles, to hikes in places less restrictive than the ranchlands, to everything. Out there in the little house on the car-alarm-free prairie, I had a great sense of cosmic time and a certain kind of slowing down—until it came time to hit the highway at seventy miles an hour, and that time came often.

Driving a whole hell of a lot is the unspoken foundation of most rural life in America, as well as a lot of wilderness adventuring (a backpack trip of a hundred miles begins with a single parking spot?). We talk about transportation as though the question is whether you drive a Yukon or a hybrid, but the question could be whether you drive, and if so, how often. I know people who really went back to the land, grew their own food, made staying home their business, ranchers whose work is really "out there"; but most people who claim to be rural have just made the countryside into a suburb, from which they commute to their real communities, jobs, research, and resources.

Ed Marston, publisher emeritus of the great environmental newspaper *High Country News*, once remarked that the West won't be destroyed by ranching, mining, or logging, but by ten-acre ranchettes. And those ranchettes seem to preserve the frontier individualism of every-nuclear-unit-for-itself; they're generally antithetical to the ways in which community and density consolidate resources. The urbanist Mike Davis talks of "public luxury"—the shared libraries, pools, parks, transit of urban life—as the way to sustain a decent quality of life that's not predicated on global inequality.

The "new urbanism" can be a solution when it is really about public luxury and pedestrian space, not about dressing up suburbs like Disney's Main Street USA. The old urbanism was a solution before we really had a problem. Today, most of the United States is designed to make driving a necessity, turning those who don't or can't into shut-ins, dependents, and second-class citizens. As my own neighborhood went from working-class African American to middle-class white, it too became much more car-dependent. A lot of people seemed to exit their houses only to get into their cars, depriving themselves of the expansive sense of home that pedestrian urbanism gives you, or the democratic social space that's created by coexisting with strangers from, as they say, all walks of life. Watching this transformation taught me that urbanism and suburbia are defined as much by the way you perceive and engage your time and space as by where you live. And it made me wonder if New York City isn't, in a few key respects, the most natural and democratic space in America, one where stockbrokers and janitors daily coexist in the same space and much of the travel doesn't involve any machines whatsoever.

I've had the rare luxury of living, with rustic intermissions, in the heart of a genuine pedestrian-scale city since I was a teenager, and though the house by the creek might have been natural habitat for a blue grosbeak, the city might be mine. Scratch pedestrian-scale; call it human-scale, since humans are pedestrians when not fitted with vehicular prosthetics.

And in this city with wild edges, I can and do walk to the beach and the hill-tops (from which I can see the peaks of five counties, and where blackberries, miner's lettuce, and a few other wild comestibles grow). Sometimes I think that the intermittent stroll of shopping, people-watching, and errand-running is a pleasantly degenerate form of hunting and gathering, that the city with its dangers and invitations and supplies is more like a primordial wilderness than a predator-free parkland where one leaves only footprints and takes only pictures.

Really, it's about how you define nature. I think we have tended to define nature as things to look at, and we think we're natural when we're looking at nature, however unnatural our own circumstances at the time. If you think of yourself as a species, the question arises of what your natural habitat is: it should be a place where you can forage, where your body is at home, where your scale is adequate, where your rites and sustenance are situated. And then, of course, cities host a kind of human biodiversity that delights me. San Francisco is not only one of the most multiethnic places in the world, but one of the most eclectic. The elderly Asian man in a rose-covered picture hat who strolled down my street one day rivaled the blue grosbeak when it came to provoking amazement.

I love wilderness, wildlife, views straight to the horizon, dark nights, the

Milky Way, and silence, though I love my large libraries and pedestrian practices too. I wish I could have it all all the time. But we choose, and I think that if we changed the way we define nature and imagined our own bodies as part of it, we might more enthusiastically choose the places of public luxury and human scale, not as a sacrifice but as a kind of sanity. Besides which, I saw a golden eagle in Oakland the other day.

San Francisco

The Metamorphosis

[2003]

San Francisco is bounded on three sides by water and on the fourth by the San Bruno Mountains, a small kingdom whose heights lift you up above the concrete to see the hills, the bay, the sea beyond, with a grid of straight avenues that become lines to the horizon, light shafts, and axes: you always know that there's a beyond to this city, America's second most densely urban city, after New York. I've been walking it for three decades, since the days when I'd cut school to catch the bus into the city, and now the place is layered with ghosts—of my own life, of the events of my lifetime, and of the histories that unfolded there before. Everything used to be something else. This mutation itself seems to be a definitive condition of the place. Where the Batman Gallery showed avant-garde art by the likes of Bruce Conner in the 1960s, a Starbucks now serves up Frappuccinos; and where the African Orthodox Church of St. John Coltrane survived into the twenty-first century, a boutique now showcases ironic denim creations and stretchy sweater items. That's gentrification's cultural degradation for you, but the longer stretches of metamorphosis get really interesting.

The particular stretch of South of Market where photographer Eadweard Muybridge lived in the 1870s while he was laying the foundations for motion picture technology was, by Jack Kerouac's time, "the poor grime-bemarked Third Street of lost bums even Negroes so hopeless and long left East and meanings of responsibility and *try* that now all they do is stand there spitting in the broken glass sometimes fifty in one afternoon against one wall at Third and Howard." Third and Howard, not far from downtown's shopping and financial districts, is now the location for the San Francisco Museum of Modern Art, across the street from Yerba Buena Center, a strange mix of nonprofit arts and corporate entertainment that was built where the residential hotels of Kerouac's time stood.

Those hotels were full of the old white guys who'd launched the great dockside strikes and union drives of the era from the 1910s through the 1930s, and when redevelopment came to their neighborhood, they fought the toughest battle in the country against it and won a lot of concessions that, for example, the African American community across town in the Fillmore didn't. When I was a young punk, this central place where the old men had lived out the ends of their lives or had been evicted to die elsewhere was nothing but a vacant lot. Moscone Center, named after the progressive mayor assassinated in 1978, along with gay supervisor Harvey Milk, by ex-cop Dan White, opened in time to host the Democratic convention of 1984; but what would become Yerba Buena Center, to the north, was just a huge expanse of gravel and dirt where we held demonstrations against the Democrats. I still remember watching MDC (whose initials initially stood for Millions of Dead Cops but, as their political education progressed, came to signify Multi-Death Corporations) play there, that summer of my brother David's War-Chest Tours of the downtown corporations that backed the Democrats and built nukes. The vacant lot is now Yerba Buena Center, a strangely dislocated place with an airportlike atmosphere that only once recovered its soul: when the gallery exhibited Ira Nowinski's extraordinary No Vacancy photographs of the old men, their homes, their struggle, and the ruins through the years of the redevelopment fight.

Kerouac continued: "and here's all those Millbrae and San Carlos neat-necktied producers and commuters of America and steel civilization rushing by" to catch the train. The commuter train still runs, but the huge Mission Bay railyard that was long the headquarters for America's first spectacularly corrupt megacorporation, Southern Pacific, is no more. It was actually a bay, once, a fact preserved, after all the landfill dumping, only in its name, Mission Bay; and it was thus named because Mission Creek emptied into it for all those millennia when Ohlone Indians were paddling their reed boats there, looking for shellfish. Mission Creek was long ago driven underground, but the mission that gave the creek and the bay their names still exists—Kim Novak visited its cemetery in Alfred Hitchcock's *Vertigo*—in the core of the hipster zone of the Mission District. As for Mission Bay, after being a rail hub, it became a spacious, morose hobo jungle; and now it's halfway to being a huge biotech campus. Southern Pacific money begat Leland Stanford's fortune, and that fortune begat Stanford University, which begat Silicon Valley and, as a sort of by-blow, a fair bit of biotechnology, come back as another form of colonization where the railroad Frank Norris described as the "Octopus" once sat.

The Bay Area has generated plenty of octopi: Bank of America, Wells Fargo, Chevron, and Bechtel, the last recently hit with protests for being such a war profiteer under the Bush administration and targeted by activists a year before for its attempt to privatize water supplies in Bolivia. In the 1880s, it was *Santa Clara County v. Southern Pacific Railroad* that laid the legal basis for corporations to claim the privileges of human beings. If we generate octopi, however, we also generate their opposite as activism, and not all the trajectories are downward. In 1877, when all across the country the riots of the Great Railroad Strike were breaking out, San Francisco's white working class, underpaid and unemployed, failed to join that Commune of anti-corporate action and instead started anti-Chinese riots. They blamed the Chinese for taking jobs and undercutting wages, though they eventually ended up on Leland Stanford's doorstep atop Nob Hill anyway, facing off against the real reasons they were being squeezed. The riots were organized in the Sandlots next to City Hall, a sort of oratorical equivalent to Hyde Park, and where those sandlots stood, the new San Francisco Public Library stands, across the street from the old library, which was damaged in the earthquake of 1989 and reborn as the Asian Art Museum, one of the finest of its kind outside Asia, a victory over a past almost no one remembers. Everything metamorphoses; some things don't decline; and much is reborn.

San Francisco was destroyed by fire six times in its first few years, destroyed on a far grander scale when it was a far grander city by the 1906 earthquake and fire. Its buildings, populations, and continuities have been ravaged by redevelopment and gentrification since World War II; and around the time of the millennium, it was raided by the dot-com kids, before the recession fixed them. The image on the state flag is the California grizzly, which became extinct several decades ago; but the creature on San Francisco's flag never existed at all: it's the phoenix, the bird that rises from its ashes. San Francisco is forever being destroyed, forever reinvented, and some thread of continuity always runs through. The naked peaks of the highest hills are reminders of the bleak windswept expanse of dunes, the original terrain, that underlies much of the city, and nearly every development project begins by peeling the city back to the sand.

In some ways, the tip of the San Francisco peninsula seems like an island waiting for its fourth side to be sawed loose from the North American continent. The city has, since its Gold Rush birth, been an anomaly and a sanctuary from the American way of pretty much everything except the pursuit of happiness and profit—and even the happiness is likely to take the form of religious and sexual practices and self-expressions that might not be so available in Ames, Iowa. It is its own place. After all, the Pacific gave the whole Bay Area a mediterranean climate and left San Francisco particularly prone to fog, and this has made the region to some extent, and the city far more so, an island ecology. As San Francisco developed, two of its endemic species of butterfly became extinct, and several species of plants are imperiled. Some days, I think our eclectic artists and activists demonstrate that the place's talent for developing unique species didn't stop when it was paved over: we do have, for example, more AIDS educators cross-dressing as nuns, more deployment of giant puppets in antiglobalization demonstrations.

But some of this eclecticism has been evident throughout all Northern California: if you look at a map of Native California, you see that the tribes and language groups were incredibly diverse—more languages were spoken in indigenous California than throughout the rest of the continent, and this diversity reflected the diversity of bioregions, from desert to mountain to several kinds of forest to grassland, with countless variations in between. Among those languages were ones in which men and women spoke different dialects, in which there were no words for right or left because you specified your body's relation to the cardinal directions instead, or in which there were no cardinal directions because, in the twisty terrain, *upriver* and *downriver* were more useful terms. There's more biotic change and biodiversity in a few miles uphill from the coast than in a thousand miles of prairie, and somehow this seems to have lived on even in the Gold Rush city full of Chileans and Chinese and French and Missourians and New Englanders and in contemporary California, with its Hmong and Portuguese and Samoan communities. San Francisco became the nation's first white-minority city decades ago, complicatedly enough as it stopped being a blue-collar port city, and whites will achieve the same status statewide in the next decade. To say that Latinos will be the new majority is to flatten out the complexity of Colombians and Salvadoreans and Mexicans and those old southwesterners who can say, "We didn't cross the border; the border crossed us."

Speaking of that crossing, on a big hillside of grass and oak facing San Pablo Bay, not far north of the town where I grew up, thirty miles north of San Francisco, was Rancho Olompali. It had been a big Miwok village before the Spaniards came, then a Spanish-style rancho run by a Miwok guy named Camilo Ynitia, who had a knack for adaptation. In a precursor of drive-by shootings, a bunch of Yankees rode by one day in 1846 and shot up the place while the ranchers were having breakfast. The Yankees were part of the Bear Flag Revolt, which merged with the war that extracted Mexico's northern half for the United States, but Ynitia survived annexation so nicely that his daughter married a Harvard man. By the turn of the century, the ranch belonged to a wealthy dentist, who surrounded his house with exotic plantings—a pomegranate hedge and some palms live on— and by the late 1960s, it was a hippie commune called The Family, where Grateful Dead lead singer Jerry Garcia, speaking of assimilated Latinos, had an acid trip awful enough to make him swear off it. The rancho buildings and the surrounding hillside became a state park not long ago, where I still hike for its shaded groves, gracefully cascading native grasses, and wildflowers.

Olompali's evolution from indigenous hamlet to battlefield to dental estate to bad trip sometimes seems like an encapsulation of Northern California's evolution to me, where things are always mutating, where erasure and replacement are the only constants. What's erased, though, tends to reappear. Maybe it's easier to imagine this part of the state as a deck of cards constantly being reshuffled into royal flushes and losing hands, where we play poker with memory and identity and meaning and possibility, which are not quite four of a kind. When I was growing up, the Coast Miwoks of Olompali and elsewhere were supposed to have vanished. Now not only are they resurgent, as the Federated Indians of Graton Rancheria, whose attempts to build a casino in the next county north are contested by environmentalists, but the tribe's chair is the brilliant novelist and screenplay writer Greg Sarris. Things are like that here: mixed-up, forever metamorphosing, but returning when you think they're gone. We thought the dot-com invasion had eviscerated radical San Francisco, but during the first days of Gulf War II, activists by the thousands shut down downtown, the Federal Building, and traffic arteries in the most powerful demonstration of outrage in the country.

If the tip of the San Francisco peninsula seems like an island, the whole Bay Area seems like a laboratory where America invents itself—what comes out of here counts because it spreads. Some of it is pretty obvious: environmentalism from the Sierra Club, founded in downtown San Francisco in 1892, and from Global Exchange and Rainforest Action Network more recently; the Black Panthers from Oakland; California cuisine from Berkeley's Chez Panisse and its vegetarian version from San Francisco's Greens, itself an offshoot of San Francisco Zen Center, one of the major sites for the arrival of Buddhism in the West; mountain bikes from Marin County; the nation's major wine supply and wine culture from Sonoma and Napa; silicon stuff, beginning with Hewlett-Packard through Oracle and Netscape and Apple to Google, from what used to be a big orchard land called the Valley of Heart's Delight; the Free Speech Movement from the students of San Francisco State and UC Berkeley; inspiration for Native American activists nationwide from the late sixties occupation of Alcatraz Island; beat poetry from the Fillmore and North Beach. (And, if you go farther north, south, and east, you arrive at the vast factory farms—and more and more little organic ones—from which a huge percentage of the nation's produce comes; fruit and nut jokes are antiquated fixtures here.)

Some of it is not so obvious, not movements but individuals—Jack London and Maxine Hong Kingston and Jello Biafra and Congresswoman Barbara Lee, ideas, scents on the wind, shifts in ideas about sexuality, about citizenship, about spectacle. Sometimes I think of the place as "amateur hour," because so many people are committed to creative expression as a pleasure rather than a discipline, and that involves more costumes and pop-culture ironies than, say, writing history. Consider, for example, the hundreds of thousands of revelers at Halloween in the queer Castro or Nevada's Burning Man festival, born in and organized from the city.

The important thing about the Bay Area being a laboratory is that this is just an extension of its being a port city: we import people from Peru and Indiana and send them back educated or out of the closet, and our definitive figures are often, like Kerouac or Muybridge, people who are just passing through for a few years or decades, but who will be indelibly stamped and will stamp back. Or they are people like Gary Snyder, who came down from the Pacific Northwest to the Bay Area in the 1950s, studied and wrote poetry and hiked around the mountain on which mountain bikes would be invented, went to Japan, came back, and moved into the Sierra foothills. From there, with books like his Pulitzer-winning *Turtle Island*, he forecast the hybrid of Asian philosophy and indigenous place-sense and ecological ideas that would become how we think around these parts.

The factors that make it a good laboratory might include what another poet, Snyder's forebear Kenneth Rexroth, once snarled: "It is the only city in the United States which was not settled overland by the westward-spreading puritanism or by the Walter-Scott fake-cavalier tradition of the South. It had been settled mostly, in spite of all the romances of the overland migration, by gamblers, prostitutes, rascals, and fortune seekers who came across the Isthmus and around the Horn. They had their faults, but they were not influenced by Cotton Mather." Long the "Capital of the West" and the biggest city west of the Mississippi, San Francisco never faced Europe but was instead at the center of an unequal triangle of influences formed by the wild interior of the continent, Mexico, and Asia. These influences and the peculiar balance of the region between the provincial backstage in which experiments are safe and coterie-culture encouraging such flowering has made it peculiarly productive of ideas on all fronts.

The city achieved a European density that allowed it to function as a true city rather than the amorphous, suburban diffusion of almost every other Western city, and thus it has a lively street life, civic and cultural life, public institutions, and nightlife. I've always thought we were the most radical city in the nation not because of our inherent virtue but because of our good fortune: who would demonstrate in a Chicago winter or Houston summer; where would you march to in Los Angeles or Phoenix, and who would notice? Whereas eternally room-temperature San Francisco is full of boulevards connecting parks and plazas, full of places where it's possible to be a member of the public acting in concert with your fellow citizens, an opportunity absent elsewhere. This is the anti-America America draws from in its eternal reinvention.

The Heart of the City

[2004]

Imagine traveling like a seabird in from the gray Pacific on a windy day, sailing across the sand of Ocean Beach, which marks the western boundary of Western civilization, and then following the long line of Fulton Street past Golden Gate Park, past St. Ignatius and its twin spires, past the poetically named New Stranger's Home Baptist Church, angling downhill through the Western Addition. The first obstacle on Fulton is City Hall, but send that bird in the west door of City Hall and out the eastern one, across Civic Center Plaza, that nearly featureless plot of tired grass from which the mayor removed the benches a few years back, down the corridor where the Asian Art Museum and the library face each other, over the rearing bronze horse that a formidable bronze Simón Bolívar rides, into United Nations Plaza.

Land on the golden letters laid into the paving of the plaza, the part that tells you that you're 122–24–45.1 degrees west of Greenwich and 37–46–48.3 degrees north of the equator. These inscriptions tell you that you're not just standing in the city but on the earth. And now that you know exactly where you are in the world, look up into the huge mural the local artist Rigo '03 dedicated a couple of years ago, the black, white, and silver one on the side of the Odd Fellows Hall that says, in the plainest possible letters, big enough to read from City Hall, TRUTH. Fulton Street lies across Market at a slight angle, like an arrow on a bowstring, ready to fire into the sunset; U.N. Plaza is the nock of the arrow. This is San Francisco's plaza, and maybe Northern California's, and perhaps even the West's, the spiritual and geographical heart of a considerable territory. It's not just because it launches that long axis running from Rigo's mural across the street from U.N. Plaza to the Pacific, though any place that can tie together truth and pacifism is already symbolically loaded. It's because the human transactions there bear out the messages of the place.

I have been there on a day when a group of well-dressed South American men suddenly arrived with flowers to place at the statue of Bolívar, the liberator of much of South America. I remember the many years that an AIDS tent encampment stood there outside the Department of Health—part of the Federal Building, on the plaza's north side—as a protest. Since the 1980s, I have been on myriad peace marches that started or ended there. I was there when Rigo dedicated his mural to the Angola Three, a trio of African American men put in solitary confinement in Louisiana for political work in the early 1970s (one of the three, a quietly intense man named Robert King Wilkerson, was freed and attended the dedication). For the past ten years or more, I have gone there on Wednesdays and Sundays, for the Heart of the City Farmers Market, and bought cherries in early summer and pomegranates in late autumn and fine organic produce all year, among the bustle of inner-city dwellers and farmers. And lately I've been joining San Francisco Zen Center there on one of the weekdays when they, or we, offer the homeless takeout cartons full of food we've just cooked.

When the Spanish laid out cities in the Americas, they began with the plaza. Every place had a center, and when a place has a center, you know where you are. What terrifies me about sprawl is the sense that there are no centers and no edges, just a random quilt of strip malls and subdivisions all the way to the horizon. Such places make me feel adrift, without a sense of meaning or direction. I've always thought that San Francisco's livelier public life wasn't about our virtue, just our geography, symbolic and practical. We're full of centers and boulevards, starting points, destinations, and alluring routes between them. The place just seems to encourage marching and gathering and walking. This might be what people mean when they call San Francisco the country's most European city, though it could also be called one of the most Latin American big towns.

"The importance of the main plaza in the history of the cities and towns of Hispanic America cannot be overemphasized," says *Spanish City Planning in*

North America. "Its role as the center of civic life has endured ever since its creation as the pivotal space around which the entire town's plan evolved. Indeed, from the early days of the Spanish conquest, the plaza was a center for secular, religious, political, social, and other ceremonial activities, so that it was not merely the point of convergence of main streets, but was also the point at which civic identity was expressed." Some of these original Latin American central squares still exist. Probably the northernmost such square is in the town of Sonoma, though there it's so vast and tree-shaded that it's more like a New England village green or a town park than a plaza. Santa Fe has a beautiful public square, very much like the one in Antigua, Guatemala—down to the fact that it belongs mostly to tourists, meaning that gathering at the center may be largely a memory for locals. But centers are hardly outdated: Mexico City's vast zócalo and, for that matter, Beijing's even more vast Tiananmen Square are places where national politics are played out by citizens and where locals and visitors mingle every day.

If you imagine the city as a body, plazas are not, like streets, mere arteries of activity; rather, a plaza is the heart, the central place from which the lifeblood of a community issues. This means, of course, that many American cities have had fatal coronaries, or equally fatal coronary bypasses, and that we face a crisis of heartless cities. In 1966, that great historian of the American landscape J. B. Jackson wrote that the federal government "is everywhere destroying public gathering places near or around Federal buildings. Small-town post offices, formerly congenial gathering places, have been landscaped and isolated; and the very term 'public building' has become a contradiction: no one in his right mind goes into a public building except on business. One thing can be said: there must be many more such places, large and small, scattered throughout our communities."

When San Francisco was Yerba Buena, a dusty hamlet on the northeastern edge of the San Francisco peninsula, the place had a center: Portsmouth Square. During the Gold Rush era, it was lined with gambling houses. The Indian trader James Savage came to town in 1850, camped out there, and reputedly started an Indian war when he bet his weight in gold on the turn of a card, since that gold belonged to his entourage of Native Californians. Portsmouth Square was eviscerated by a parking garage and a concrete bridge to the Holiday Inn across Kearny

Street, though it's still a nice park for Chinatown. And San Francisco? Any place so big really has multiple centers. There's the Market and Powell cable car turn-around, where emergency marches have long met, most notably the evening the Gulf War broke out in 1991, and where tourists and street performers meet. There's Dolores Park, the green space for the Mission. There are key spots for each neighborhood—small parks, shopping streets, other plazas. But U.N. Plaza is different. It's not just a symbolic center of the city, but of the world. Not the center—there are infinite such places—but a center, a local center of the globe, a place where you know where you stand in the world in the most practical and metaphysical senses. The longitude and latitude written in the concrete are just a beginning.

The United Nations, of course, was founded in San Francisco in 1945, inside the War Memorial Building over on McAllister and Van Ness. For the U.N.'s fiftieth anniversary, the city redesigned the plaza to reflect this history. As you walk from Bolívar to Market Street, you pass some of the principal statements from the founding document, inscribed in huge metal letters inset into the ground. "We the people of the United Nations determined to save the world from the scourge of war . . . to reaffirm faith in basic human rights, in the dignity and worth of the human person." On either side of this processional space are cement pillars on which are inscribed the years various nations joined up: you can see the fall of the Soviet empire part way down, with nations like Kazakhstan liberated to become members. Most days, homeless people sit around the fountain, on the low cement walls of the flanking grassy beds, and on the base of the Bolívar statue. In some parts of the world, housing is considered a basic human right.

One afternoon not long ago, a shy boy in a knit cap took one of the neat take-out cartons of hot food and a donated carton of Juicy Juice and called me ma'am when he thanked me, in an accent so sweet I had to ask where he was from. Kentucky, he said. Then the bowed-down old woman across the plaza, hearing that I was handing out food from a Buddhist organization, told me that she had been stationed in Tibet during World War II. "Really?" I said, and she unzipped her plastic carryall and showed me the ivory Buddha she said she'd been carrying ever since. A dark-skinned man cheerfully greeted me in a British accent: "Is that dinner, tea, or supper you're offering?" Which would you prefer, I asked, and he said, "Supper, please," and I handed over the goods.

A recent letter to the editor referred to these people "as the multitude of winos, junkies, and crack heads who have infected our city streets and transformed San Francisco into an open sewer." One of the nice things about handing out food is that I've been approaching the crackheads and finding that even they have a graciousness less evident in many more affluent people. Undoubtedly there are criminals among them, as there are among CEOs and Catholic priests these days, and it's clearer that many of them are suffering deeply. Occasionally I see one of them shooting up (not nearly the threat to me that, say, seeing a Range Rover running a light is, remember, please), but even these characters tend to be well-mannered. But seeing them here in the heart of the city reminds me of the medieval Christian and still-pervasive Asian belief that giving alms is a spiritual duty and that beggars provide us with our opportunity to fulfill it, to make a society that is by definition interdependent.

Twice a week, the interdependence of the city and the country is clear. Farm booths and tables form two long lines in front of the columns of United Nations members, and the plaza becomes a kind of United California conference. Some farmers markets are upscale, but this market is down home. It serves the Tenderloin's Asian communities, who, like inner-city dwellers across the nation, have to get by without a nearby supermarket, and it also sells to downtown workers and to people catching the bus back to the Richmond, who leave laden with plastic bags sagging with the bounty. There are Southeast Asian families who set up tables piled high with cilantro, basil, mint, and other herbs less familiar to me; the Grandpa's Sweetness honey people from Turlock with their jars of gold; the Safest Dates on Earth stand with organic and fresh dates from the Mojave; the organic farmers from Davenport, near Santa Cruz, in season; the Latino flower growers who show up some of the time; and the big stand that always anchors the northeast end, staffed by an older woman and her Latino assistants from Half Moon Bay, selling everything from onions to roses. I love it. Where else can you meet the people who grow your food? Where else can you get the feeling that the food might come out of a real place, where people make a living wage, rather than the unsavory mysteries of agribusiness? Where else can you find out that the pomegranate season will be short because of early rain in the San Joaquin Valley or learn why dry-farmed tomatoes are so tasty?

And where else does good food coexist with free speech in such a resonant way? The huge peace march on February 16, 2003, the one with two hundred thousand people, a Korean youth drum group, a Chinese New Year's dragon, stilt-walkers, Palestinian women, a lot of baby carriages and white-haired people— mostly turned off at McAllister Street to fill up Civic Center Plaza, a pleasant dead zone that comes alive only at such times. I broke through the ranks of watchers on the curb to go to the farmers market that Sunday and saw that a few booths were still open, and demonstrators were lining up to buy samosas from the Indian food stand and kettle corn from the popcorn booth. The homeless, the farmers, and the peace marchers were all in it together.

Cities are where people are citizens, where they coexist in public, generating that public life so vital to a democracy, which depends on our sense of connection and trust in strangers, who become less strange when we move among them every day. Too many American cities are just vast suburbs, with people segregated by race, income, and avocation, and by their dependence on private automobiles to get around. Even in true cities, democracy, citizenship, public life can be just words. But in U.N. Plaza, you can stand and look east at TRUTH or west past Bolívar to imagine the curve of the earth over the blue horizon toward Asia; or you can just look your fellow human beings in the eye and know that you're a citizen, of a city, of a state, of the world.

The Ruins of Memory

[[2006]]

Panoramic photographs taken after the 1906 earthquake show that the old San Francisco was gone, replaced by jagged, smoldering spires and piles of ruins. Photographs made a century later demonstrate that the ruins are likewise gone, erased more definitively than the earthquake erased the nineteenth-century city. Ruins represent the physical decay of what preceded them, but their removal erases meaning and memory. Ruins are monuments, but while intentional monuments articulate desire for permanence, even immortality, ruins memorialize the fleeting nature of all things and the limited powers of humankind. "Decay can be halted, but only briefly, and then it resumes. It is the negative image of history," wrote landscape historian J. B. Jackson. It is the negative image of history and a necessary aspect of it. To erase decay or consciousness of decay, decline, entropy, and ruin is to erase the understanding of the unfolding relation between all things, of darkness to light, of age to youth, of fall to rise. Rise and fall go together; they presume each other.

In another sense, everything is the ruin of what came before. A table is the ruin of a tree, as is the paper you hold in your hands; a carved figure is the ruin of the block from which it emerged, a block whose removal scarred the mountainside from which it was hacked; and anything made of metal requires earth upheaval and ore extraction on a scale of extraordinary disproportion to the resultant product. To imagine the metamorphoses that are life on earth at its grandest scale is to imagine both creation and destruction, and to imagine them together is to see their kinship in the common ground of change, abrupt and gradual, beautiful and disastrous, to see the generative richness of ruins and the ruinous nature of all change. "The child is father to the man," declared Wordsworth, but the man is also the ruin of the child, as much as the butterfly is the ruin of the caterpillar. Corpses feed flowers; flowers eat corpses. San Francisco has been ruined again and again, only most spectacularly in 1906, and those ruins too have been erased and forgotten and repeated and erased again.

A city—any city, every city—is the eradication, even the ruin, of the landscape from which it rose. In its fall, that original landscape sometimes triumphs. One day, I looked up from an intersection in San Francisco's densely urban Mission District and saw down the street to the south the undomesticated crest of Bernal Heights, with its coyote and wild blackberries, and up the street to the west the ridgeline of Twin Peaks and with a shudder perceived, still present as a phantom, the steep natural landscape that underlay the city, the skin beneath the clothes, the landscape that reappeared amid the miles of ruins of the 1906 earthquake and that someday will reassert itself again. Another day, I walked down Hayes Street west of City Hall and saw suddenly the surprising view of Bernal Hill across half the distance of the city, a vista opened up by the belated removal of the freeway overpass damaged by the 1989 earthquake. Some months before, I had watched the wrecking ball smash that overpass into chunks of rebar-threaded concrete small enough to truck away. The concrete mined from some place out of sight was being sent back over the horizon. A place like San Francisco could be imagined not as one city stretching out since 1846 but as dozens of cities laid over each other's ruins, the way that archaeologists experience the unearthed ruins layered in strata, the several cities that lay above Homer's Troy. Dolls, whiskey and medicine bottles, buttons, sometimes ships and skeletons reappear along with the sand whenever a new foundation is dug in central San Francisco.

To make this city, much of a windswept, fog-shrouded expanse of sand dunes and chaparral-covered hillsides was smoothed over, dunes removed, hilltops flattened, bays and marshes filled in, streams forced underground, endemic species driven into extinction. Even the view of the resultant simplified topography was obscured by the buildings everywhere, though one of San Francisco's charms is its still-surviving steepness: the crests and heights offer views of the distance—not only of the rest of the city, but the sea, bay, and hills beyond it. Another is the pure geometry of its grid, often criticized for being an overly two-dimensional response to a wildly three-dimensional terrain, but these straight axes also open up the distance visible at the end of the long shafts of streets. San Francisco is the least claustrophobic of cities. Both big earthquakes of the twentieth century shook the place loose of its bonds—the carpet of architecture in 1906, the ugly shackles of the Embarcadero and Central freeways in 1989.

In natural disasters, the natural landscape reasserts itself and reappears, not only as force but as the contours beneath the cityscape. Cities are always main-tained, for natural processes of decay produce ruins as surely as violence and fire, flood and earthquake do; and only maintenance and replacement postpone the inevitable ruin—the entropy of the built and the return of the organic. In his *Arcades Project* notes, Walter Benjamin quotes a Victor Hugo poem:

> I think I see a Gothic roof start laughing
> When, from its ancient frieze,
> Time removes a stone and puts in a nest.

Stone to nest may be the death of a piece of architecture, but it is also a coming to life. Cities are a constant assertion against the anarchic forces of nature, and a dis-aster like an earthquake is the opposite, nature's assertion against the built world. San Francisco is the ruin of a lonely, untrammeled landscape, its buildings the ruin of forests, stony landscapes, gypsum deposits, veins of iron deep in the earth—and after 1906 all these sources were raided again, with urgency and intensity. A few trees were snapped by the earthquake, but forests were laid low for the hasty rebuilding of San Francisco.

The catastrophe of earthquakes is largely the catastrophe of built structures. Trees fall down or snap or split only in the most extreme earthquakes (as a few did here and there from the Santa Cruz Mountains to the Sonoma coast in 1906); under the open sky, creatures may lose their balance, but they are not likely to be crushed. Large earthquakes can also split open the ground and dam and redirect streams, but these are not catastrophic effects. Before the Franciscans brought adobe architecture and the Gold Rush brought more massive development, the Bay Area's Ohlone and Miwok and other indigenous Californians likely regarded earthquakes with wonder and terror but suffered little physical damage. Any lightweight structures that fell down could easily be rebuilt, and little damage to life would result from such a collapse.

Architecture is the principal victim of earthquakes, architecture and infra-structure and anything alive that is in their way when they come down. Crumbling freeway overpasses and other structures built on soggy land are among the major wreckage of recent California quakes—witness the collapse of the Nimitz Freeway over bay landfill in Oakland in 1989, apartments in the infilled Marina District of San Francisco that same year, and Los Angeles's Santa Monica Freeway above La Cienega (which means *the swamp* in Spanish) in the 1994 Northridge quake. These are victims, as a recent book by David Ulin has it, of "the myth of solid ground." Still, the ruins and tragedies in California are dwarfed by quakes of comparable size in other parts of the world—Mexico, Turkey, China, Iran, Algeria—where old and poorly built structures have crushed citi-zens by the thousands.

Man proposes, earthquake disposes, the maxim might be revised to say, though earthquakes are only one small source of the ruins that are in some ways the inevitable corollary of the very act of building. That nothing lasts forever is perhaps our favorite thing to forget. And forgetting is the ruin of memory, its col-lapse, decay, shattering, and eventual fading away into nothingness. We don't quite recognize how resilient cities are, how they arise over and over again from their own ruins, resurrected, reincarnated, though every Rome and London is such a resurrection, or reinvention. So it seems strange to see the ruins of then become the smooth façades of now, to see not the entropy that leads to ruin but the endeavor that effaces it so thoroughly that its ruinous past is hardly believ-able. Yet this happens again and again: Frank Gohlke's 1979–1980 photographs of the Wichita Falls, Texas, tornado show a place torn apart by wind and the same place a year later, restored as though nothing had happened (or so that the same thing can happen again?). Ruins are evidence not only that cities can be destroyed but that they survive their own destruction, are resurrected again and again.

Ruins stand as reminders. Memory is always incomplete, always imperfect, always falling into ruin; but the ruins themselves, like other traces, are treasures: our links to what came before, our guide to situating ourselves in a landscape of time. To erase the ruins is to erase the visible public triggers of memory; a city without ruins and traces of age is like a mind without memories. Such erasure is the foundation of the amnesiac landscape that is the United States. Because the United States is in many ways a country without a past, it seems, at first imagining, to be a country without ruins. But it is rich in ruins, though not always as imagined, for it is without a past only in the sense that it does not own its past, or own up to it. It does not remember officially and in its media and mainstream, though many subsets of Americans remember passionately.

The Pueblo people of New Mexico remember the conquistadors, and Native Americans generally remember the genocides and injustices that transformed their numbers and their place on this continent. Southerners remember the Civil War; African Americans remember slavery and Jim Crow; labor remembers its struggle for the right to organize and a living wage; too few women remember the battle to get the vote and basic human rights. Memory is often the spoils of the defeated, and amnesia may sometimes be the price of victory (though Germany in its postwar era proved that the vanquished can erase even more vehemently—but most vanquished can think of themselves as wronged, and being wronged is all too fine a foundation for identity).

Much of the North American continent is the ruin of intact ecosystems and indigenous nations, absences only history and its scant relics recall, for most of this ruin consists of absence: the absence of bison, the disappearance of passenger pigeons, the reduction of the first nations to reservation dwellers and invisible populations. These nations built lightly and out of organic materials, more often than not, so their own ruins are faint, except perhaps for the great mounds of the Midwest and the stone architecture of the Southwest, Mesa Verde, Chaco Canyon, and the other Anasazi/Pueblo ruins. The Southwest's ruins are considerable, and even its mesas and buttes were often interpreted as resembling the architectural ruins of medieval Europe—or, rather, of romanticism's taste for medieval Europe.

Manhattan is a city founded in the seventeenth century, but it is hard to find traces of the city earlier than the nineteenth century there. Santa Fe is older, and it too contains little that predates the past couple of centuries. But Paris, famously ripped up and redeveloped in the third quarter of the nineteenth century, is still full of buildings from the twelfth to the eighteenth centuries. Peru has Machu Picchu, the ruins of a Quechua city. Guatemala has Antigua, the former capital largely abandoned after the great earthquake of 1773—now a small city or large town, its colonial grid intact, and ruins of splendid baroque convents and churches standing in between the one- and two-story houses—along with Tikal, the Mayan city abandoned long before and visible only because the devouring jungle was pared back some decades ago. Mexico has the ruins of the Aztecs. The United States is curiously devoid of acknowledged and easily recognized ruins. Perhaps some of the amnesia is the result of mobility; people who are constantly moving are constantly arriving in landscapes that do not hold their past and thereby are often read as not holding any past. History is opaque to the deraci-nated, and enough moves can obliterate both history and the knowledge that every place has a history. (I have learned in my own San Francisco neighborhood that people who move every few years believe that they move through a static cityscape; those of us who sit still for longer periods know that it is forever changing.)

Think of ruin in two stages. One is the force—neglect or abandonment, human violence, natural disaster—that transforms buildings into ruins. Ruins can be created slowly or suddenly, and they can survive indefinitely or be cleared away. The second stage of ruin is the abandonment or the appreciation that allows the ruin to remain as a relic—as evidence, as a place apart, outside economies and utilitarian purposes, the physical site that corresponds to room in the culture or imagination for what came before. The forces that create ruins have been plentiful in the United States, but the desire or neglect that allows the ruins to stay has been mostly absent. The great urban ruins have been situated on what is, first of all, real estate, more than it is sacred ground or historical site; and real estate is constantly turned over for profit, whereas a ruin is a site that has fallen out of the financial dealings of a city (unless it has become a tourist site, like the Roman Colosseum).

Poverty, Lucy Lippard once remarked, is a great preserver of history. From New England through the Rust Belt, the poverty of lost jobs and old industries has left behind a ruinous landscape of abandoned factories and city centers, as has white flight and urban disinvestment in cities such as Detroit. We detonate our failed modernist housing projects, along with outdated Las Vegas casinos, as though we were striking sets; demolition telescopes the process of ruination from damage to disappearance. Only in the remote places—the abandoned boomtowns of nineteenth-century mining rushes, old plantation mansions, the withering small towns of the Great Plains—is nature allowed to proceed with its program of ruin. And in the destitute ones: descriptions of a ruinous and half-abandoned inner-city Detroit suggest that it is becoming our Pompeii, or perhaps our Antigua, destroyed not by earthquake or lava but by racially driven economic abandonment and its side effects.

This is the paradox of ruins: they represent a kind of destruction, but they themselves can be destroyed and with them the memory of what was once there and what it confronted. Munich and Cologne in Germany, Birmingham and Coventry in England, and many other European cities keep traces of their war-time ruins on hand as reminders of not only the past but the present insecurity and uncertainty of all things, the architectural equivalent of vanitas paintings, those *ubi sunt* and *sic transit gloria mundi* statements. Hiroshima's Peace Dome is a well-known monument to the atomic bomb dropped on that city, a monument with far more meaning than the building had before the bomb, when it was the Prefectural Industrial Promotion Hall.

In the haste to remove the hundreds of thousands of tons of wreckage of New York's World Trade Center buildings and replace them with a newly made monument, one can see a deep anxiety about what ruins commemorate: ephemerality, vulnerability, and mutability. The singular urbanist and ex–New Yorker Jane Jacobs commented that we don't know what the disaster means yet and that it is too soon to build something; the instant memorial seems part of the therapeutic language of "closure" that was deployed again and again in the immediate after-math of the towers' collapse, a word that seemed to mean that meaning itself could come to an end, a conclusion. Ruins are open to the eye, the sky, the elements, change, and interpretation.

When the World Trade Center fell on September 11, 2001, a kind of American innocence, a widespread belief in American impunity, fell with it. This belief was itself shocking, premised as it was on the notion that we were somehow beyond the reach of the forces, natural and political, that devastate other countries, situated in an ignorance or inability to identify with the victims of death squads, genocides, wars, industrial disasters, with the inhabitants of Bhopal, Chernobyl, Guatemala, Rwanda, Iraq. This belief was rooted not only in American exceptionalism but in amnesia—about the swath of devastation Sherman left across the Civil War South; about the devastation of Galveston, Charleston, Chicago, and other major cities by natural forces; about the essential vulnerability of individuals and communities; about mortality itself; and perhaps about the devastation the United States has wrought elsewhere (Kabul and Baghdad were ravaged on a far grander scale than New York, with far more deaths, many eyes for an eye, in devastations that again seemed unfelt and unimagined for many in whose name they were carried out). There is always an implication in American discourses on death and illness that they are optional, that the cure for cancer or heart disease is in some way a cure for death. As a hospice worker once told me, in this country we regard death as failure.

But death is as inevitable to life as ruins are to buildings, and the death of individuals is not the death of communities. The 2002 movie *Gangs of New York* contains a small commentary on this in its closing frames. Two characters look across the water at southern Manhattan, afire in the draft riots of the 1860s, and a dissolve turns the skyline into the pre-9/11 view dominated by the Trade Towers. This too, these last frames seem to say, shall pass; we shall rise again, as New York has from the far more pervasive devastation of the 1970s and 1980s. Of these destructions, only photographs stand as memorials now.

San Francisco evicted even the dead from its land in the first half of the twentieth century (only a small military cemetery, an even smaller Spanish missionary church cemetery, and the Richmond District Columbarium of cremated remains survive). This was done essentially for economic reasons, but the effect was to eliminate death from the scene along with the dead, those who had inhabited the earlier versions of the city. Of the San Francisco earthquake, no clear evidence exists, only absences: the lack of nineteenth-century buildings throughout most of the city (though in 1906 the southern and western edges were still undeveloped). A number of landmark structures survived the earthquake and fire and were rebuilt, often almost into unrecognizability. But of 1906 ruins as ruins, nothing survives except the "Portals of the Past," the neoclassical portico from a ruined Nob Hill mansion that was transported to Golden Gate Park, where it looks more like a stage set than a relic, for it now frames foliage whereas once it framed a mansion's entryway and then the smoldering wreck of the city beyond where the mansion stood. Before and after the 1906 earthquake, the portals framed no vista, opened onto no long view: it is as though only for that moment of disaster was another vision, a more far-seeing sense of place and time, opened up, and the haste to reconstruct was in part haste to close that vision. Perhaps that vision is the view that all ruins offer us.

Ironically, it was earthquake rubble that became the ground of the Marina District so devastated in 1989; landfill liquefies in an earthquake, which is why the downtown and Mission Bay buildings rest on massive pilings driven below the landfill layers. Mission Bay was once a bay into which Mission Creek drained after its meander from near Mission Dolores. That bay was filled in to build the central railyard of the Southern Pacific Railroad, the great octopus that held all California's politics and economy in its tentacles, and it fell into ruin when the age of the railroads came to an end. The ruins made the place haunted and abandoned—for *abandoned* is our term for places inhabited by outcasts and wildlife— an open space in the most densely populated U.S. city outside New York. *Dream* said the graffiti on an old boxcar, and it was a kind of dreamspace, open to memory, possibility, danger, outside the economy, as ruins almost always are. These ruins were destroyed to build the Mission Bay biotechnology facilities at the end of the twentieth century. The railroads tamed the earth on one colossal scale; the biotech industry seeks to do so on another, more intimate one; and the one thing certain is that the labs atop the landfill will lie in ruins someday, by earthquake or by time itself. Perhaps even the buried bay will reappear, carved out again when Mission Creek reasserts itself and rises from its subterranean passages.

THE FIRST TEN DESTRUCTIONS OF SAN FRANCISCO

San Francisco was in its infancy during the fire on Christmas Eve 1848, which destroyed more than a million dollars' worth of property (at 1848 values) and burned down most of the buildings around Portsmouth Square, then the central plaza of the rough little boomtown risen from the Gold Rush. The authors of the *Annals of San Francisco* described the situation:

> This was the first of the great fires which devastated San Francisco; and it was speedily to be followed by still more extensive and disastrous occurrences of a similar character. Something of the kind had long been anticipated by those who considered the light, combustible materials of which the whole town was constructed. . . . Scarcely were the ashes cold when preparations were made to erect new buildings on the old sites; and in several cases within a few days, and in all, within a few weeks, the place was covered as densely as before with houses of every kind. These, like those that had just been destroyed, and like nearly all around, were chiefly composed of wood and canvas, and presented fresh fuel to the great coming conflagrations.

After this first great fire of San Francisco, five more would follow in the subsequent three and a half years, with the sixth erupting on the summer solstice, June 22, 1851. The third, the *Annals* recorded, destroyed five million dollars' worth of property.

> But in proportion to the unusual depression was the almost immediate reaction, and the ruined citizens began forthwith to lay the foundations of new fortunes instead of those so cruelly destroyed. . . . As the spider, whose web is again and again destroyed, will continue to spark new ones while an atom of material or a

spark of life remains in its body, so did the inhabitants set themselves industriously to work to rear new houses and a new town. . . . From this time forward, we therefore began to notice, that the street architecture gradually assumed a newer and grander appearance.

It also assumed a more fireproof appearance, as brick replaced wood, though brick was a far worse material in earthquakes.

By 1850, the writers could say of a fire damaging about a million dollars' worth of property, "Elsewhere such a fire might well be called a great one; but it was not so reckoned in the 'Annals of San Francisco.'" The fifth fire was the largest of all, coming after eight months of "comparative immunity from conflagration." This arson fire began on the night of May 3, 1851, on the south side of Portsmouth Square. It created a firestorm, burning between fifteen hundred and two thousand structures, most of the central city. Then the rebuilding began. ("Sour, pseudo-religious folk on the shores of the Atlantic, might mutter of Sodom and Gomorrah, and prate the idlest nonsense," said the Annals writers, asserting that the catastrophe was no punishment and that there was no reason why the city should not rise again.)

The sixth great fire came about six weeks after the fifth one. These six fires "successively destroyed nearly all the old buildings and land-marks of Yerba Buena," the original hamlet overtaken by the Yankees. There's a saying to the effect that "this was my grandfather's ax, though it's had four new handles and three heads since his time," the idea being that the continuity of use and of tradition is more powerful than the incessant replacement of materials. Something similar could be said of cities, except when memory is swept away with the masonry rubble. Memory is what makes it my grandfather's ax rather than some worn-out piece of detritus; memory is meaning.

The seventh destruction of San Francisco was the great and oft-forgotten earthquake of October 21, 1868, a rupture on the Hayward Fault estimated at 7.0 on the Richter scale. Five people died, spires and chimneys fell, walls tumbled down, some brick buildings collapsed entirely, cracks opened up in the ground, the Custom House was damaged, and City Hall was devastated. And the city was rebuilt, with little regard for the *San Francisco Morning Call*'s editorial warning against shoddy construction, the use of cornices and other ornaments that could fall in a quake, building on landfill, and other seismically precarious practices: "The lives lost yesterday are not chargeable to the earthquake, but to the vanity, greed and meanness of those who erected the buildings." When San Francisco was largely destroyed by the 1906 earthquake and fire, the sixty-year-old city had already survived a series of destructions and rebuildings. After 1906—the city's seventh fire and eighth destruction—the destructions would be about social forces out of control rather than natural ones.

At one o'clock in the morning on July 27, 1943, the British Air Force, with support from the U.S. Army, began bombing the city of Hamburg. "The aim of Operation Gomorrah, as it was called," writes W. G. Sebald, "was to destroy the city and reduce it as completely as possible to ashes." In this, it was eminently successful, and thousands died. On the eve of Valentine's Day 1945, the same forces began dropping nearly four thousand tons of bombs on the city of Dresden, best known for its manufacture of china dishes, though it also produced gun sights, plane parts, and gas masks. Sixteen hundred acres of the central city, more than twenty-four thousand buildings, and somewhere between thirty and one hundred thousand people were destroyed in the firestorm, the fire so powerful that it incinerated people underground, created its own wind and weather, and moved faster than human beings could run. (Almost twice as many acres, nearly three thousand, were destroyed in San Francisco in 1906.) On August 6, 1945, in the culmination of the Manhattan Project, the first inhabited nuclear ground zero was created when the Enola Gay dropped an atomic bomb on the city of Hiroshima. The bomb killed somewhere in the neighborhood of a hundred thousand people in various terrible ways, some instantly, some slowly, and vaporized, shattered, irradiated, and ignited the central city. Three days later, another atomic bomb was dropped on Nagasaki. In the photographs of Yosuke Yamahata, Nagasaki doesn't look ruined, as San Francisco did after the earthquake; it looks shattered. Buildings have been torn into splinters and shards in which bodies lie, some of them charred; the force of the bomb is furious, vicious in ways the earthquake was not.

Hamburg, Dresden, Hiroshima, and Nagasaki are still cities, though not the cities they were. But World War II also changed even American cities that were far out of reach of the war's violence. The war did much to lift the Great Depression and created a huge demand for factory and shipyard workers, prompting a colossal migration of African Americans from the rural South to the industrial cities. San Francisco's African American population increased ninefold between 1940 and 1950, and still more of these southerners migrated to nearby Oakland, Richmond, and Marin City to fill shipyard jobs. Pushed by discrimination and economics, many ended up in San Francisco's Western Addition, the flatlands west of City Hall and Van Ness Avenue, which had been partly vacated by Japanese Americans forced into prison camps for the duration of the war.

Ironically, this was the most central neighborhood to have survived the 1906 earthquake. It was made up of wooden Victorian row houses with intricate ornamentation, bay windows, and, often, storefronts built into the ground floor. After the quake, businesses and city administration had relocated to Fillmore Street, the central artery of the Western Addition, while the city to the east was rebuilt. Through World War II and afterward, Fillmore was a lively street of theaters, dance halls, and music clubs, frequented in the postwar years by some of the greatest jazz musicians of the time.

By 1947, however, plans were being laid to erase this neighborhood. The word used over and over until it became a mantra and a justification was "blight," a word that was supposed to describe the poor condition of the housing and its alleged infestation by vermin but that was in fact a code word for the human inhabitants, just as "urban renewal" was recognized as code for what was also caustically described as "negro removal." The San Francisco Redevelopment Agency declared, "San Francisco is now developing programs to correct blighted and congested conditions and to deal with an accumulation of housing that is continuously aging and deteriorating faster than it is being rehabilitated or replaced. . . . More than 50 percent of the structures are past middle age with an estimated average age of sixty-seven years. It is this condition which results in neighborhood blight and calls for both major public improvement and private rehabilitation and reconstruction." Hundreds of wooden Victorian buildings were reduced to splinters, though preservationists managed to relocate some. The "past middle age" houses that survived redevelopment are now more than a century old, handsome, and worth more than a million dollars apiece.

Into the 1960s, campaigns to devastate this neighborhood were carried out. The rhetoric of urban renewal was that bad housing would be replaced with good housing—and good was defined in those squeamish modernist terms as efficient, up-to-date, and orderly. The truly urban mixing of classes, activities, and households was seen as disorderly, as almost a form of blight itself. (Interestingly enough, proponents of the "new urbanism" and other contemporary urbanists seek to restore those qualities of mixed use and vibrancy to the anesthetized cityscapes and suburbias of the modern era.) In fact, though a number of barrack-like housing projects were built (most of which have been destroyed in the past several years as inimical to safety and well-being, to be replaced by townhouses more closely resembling the earlier dwellings), many square blocks of the heart of the Fillmore were left vacant for decades, lots full of weeds, surrounded by Cyclone fences.

The agenda all along had not been the creation of better housing for the inhabitants but their replacement by more affluent inhabitants and increased profits for developers and landowners. This debacle and urban renewal's subsequent destruction of the South of Market residential hotels, inhabited largely by poor single retirees, particularly union longshoremen, constitute the ninth destruction of San Francisco. Like the earlier destructions, this devastation was not complete, but it turned once densely inhabited expanses into wastelands and signified the end of an era—in this case, the era of San Francisco as a blue-collar town. (Earlier, some of San Francisco's elite had hoped to use the 1906 earthquake as an opportunity to relocate Chinatown, which had been pretty comprehensively destroyed, from the east flank of Nob Hill to a remote edge of the city; happily, they hoped in vain.)

Poverty as neglect produces ruins in itself—lack of maintenance leads to decay and eventually to ruins. But wealth is a more powerful scourge of cities, removing both buildings and inhabitants to replace them with more profitable versions of same. The Western Addition before urban renewal was shabby, but it was not in ruins. The wrecking balls, the splintered heaps of what had once been

Victorian houses, the vacant lots, the displaced people—all were produced not by the poor but by the wealthy, who controlled urban policy. Or perhaps "wealth" and "poverty" are terms that create a false dichotomy; perhaps "resource alloca-tion" embraces both ends of a spectrum whose pervasive injustices produced urban renewals across the country, produced the ruins that still stand in Detroit and St. Louis and the erasures that made way for the shiny new Manhattans and San Franciscos of the present. Let me again define "ruin." There is the slow pro-cess of entropy that transforms buildings into ruins, and there are the speedy acts of violent nature and violent social forces that immediately shatter buildings—earthquakes, bombs, wrecking balls. But whether the ruins stand, as the ruined abbeys of Henry VIII's Protestant Reformation stand all over rural England, is another question; when the land is valuable, the ruins themselves are often ruined, destroyed, erased.

One of the principal problems in making human beings face our history is that sudden events get our attention while slow ones do not—even though the cumu-lative force of, for example, global warming will prove far more dire for the Arctic than the Exxon-Valdez oil spill. Our minds are better suited to oil spills than to cli-mate change, and so are our media and our stories. The crash of the airplanes into the World Trade Center on September 11, 2001, is unforgettable, but the violent destruction of the South Bronx on a far larger scale throughout the 1970s and 1980s is barely remembered and will likely never elicit a memorial. Yet tens of thousands of intentionally set fires—many of them landlord arsons—devastated this community and turned block after block into ruins. Between 1960 and 1974, the number of fires tripled, from 11,185 to 33,465. There were an average of 33 fires a night in the first half of the 1970s; and in the last year that insurance com-panies paid out claims for fires, the Bronx lost about thirteen hundred buildings to flames. Then, "in the first year without payoffs," Marshall Berman reported, "it lost twelve. In the second year, it lost three." But the fires were never blamed on economic interests. Senator Daniel Patrick Moynihan voiced a typical senti-ment when he wrote, "People don't want housing in the South Bronx, or they wouldn't burn it down."

The fires also raged on the Lower East Side and the Upper West Side, where a concerted program of urban renewal was also creating a huge wave of displace-ment. "For years," Berman recalled, "midnight fires ate up not only buildings but whole blocks, often block after block. Then we found out that, even as big parts of the city were burning down, their firehouses were being closed. . . . Through all these happenings, dozens of ordinary nice neighborhoods, like the one I grew up in, metamorphosed into gigantic, twisted, grotesque ruins. Diverse populations brought up to lead pallid but peaceful lives found themselves engulfed in patholo-gies, ending in unending early death." Later in this essay of searing outrage and stubborn loyalty, Berman added, "In the 1970s and 1980s, New York's greatest spectacles were its ruins. We couldn't believe the enormity of these ruins. They went on and on, for block after block, mile after mile. Some blocks seemed almost intact; but look around the corner, and there was no corner." Cardinal Terence Cooke—the Catholic Church was one of the few powers to fight the Bronx blitz—declared that "whole areas look like the burnt-out ruins of war. The omi-nous wail of sirens has become a terrifying part of people's lives. There is one building in the Bronx in which families live in constant fear because just last week the building next door was set on fire seven times."

Another writer, Luc Sante, came of age in New York in its age of ruins:

Already in the mid-1970s, when I was a student at Columbia, my windows gave out onto the plaza of the School of International Affairs, where on winter nights troops of feral dogs would arrive to bed down on the heating grates. Since then the city had lapsed even further. On Canal Street stood a five-story building empty of human tenants that had been taken over from top to bottom by pigeons. If you walked east on Houston Street from the Bowery on a summer night, the jungle growth of vacant blocks gave a foretaste of the impending wilderness, when lianas would engird the skyscrapers and mushrooms would cover Times Square. At that time much of Manhattan felt depopulated even in daylight. . . . In 1978 I got used to seeing large fires in that direction every night, usually set by arsonists hired by landlords of empty buildings who found it an easy choice to make, between paying property taxes and collecting insurance. By 1980 Avenue C was a lunar landscape of vacant blocks and hollow tenement shells.

What happened in New York was more dramatic and more visible (though it since seems to have been forgotten), but it paralleled the slow, violent death of the modern city and the industrial age across the United States, a death that was itself part of the larger passing of the utopian (and often socialist) belief in a rationalist, technological future that those cities once embodied. The old blue-collar cities of manufacturing and shipping were dying, to be replaced in some cases by sleek new cities dealing in information, of which San Francisco and Manhattan are among the most prominent. New York's ports moved to New Jersey; San Francisco's ports moved to Oakland and Long Beach; railyards closed, as did countless small urban manufacturing sites; jobs went overseas. A sort of forest succession stage took place: the abandoned sweatshops and manufactories became artists' lofts in San Francisco's South of Market and New York's Soho, and then lawyers and others more powerful than artists priced them out. Artists represented a sort of lull between two economies, as did the ruins, and perhaps both represented a moment of openness in the meaning and imagination of the city, a pause in urban busyness to wonder and reflect. Artists in these circumstances often became their communities' historians, servants of memory and thus of ruin.

The ruins: they were part of the San Francisco I came to inhabit in 1980. They no longer exist. They were a significant part of the cityscape of my youth, a cityscape of vacant lots and empty factories, of low-pressure zones in which housing was not so hard to come by and economic choices were not so anxiety-ridden. The ruins signified much to us in the 1980s, as under Ronald Reagan's nuclear brinksmanship we anticipated the end-of-the-world war. The apocalypse seemed close at hand, and the post-apocalyptic landscape was imagined as a landscape of ruins, the landscape of road warriors and terminators. But the ruins lay in the present, not in the future: we were not living before ruin but after it, after the ruin of the old cities that had been written about by people like Joseph Mitchell in his decades of *New Yorker* reportage, the blue-collar cities with room for everyone, the muscular, industrial cities that looked like the future in the first decades of the twentieth century and became the abandoned past by the last two or three.

The ruins were the backdrop—often literally—of punk rock and performance art; San Francisco's Survival Research Labs performed their rites of mechanical failure, their avant-garde demolition derbies between handcrafted machines, in parking lots, in vacant lots, and, at least once, at the site of an abandoned brewery that has been replaced by a Costco. (The movement from local beer production to the consumption of transnational products is one way to trace the trajectory of cities over the past several decades.) And the ruins were our psychic landscape: like Luc Sante, we who were young gloried in the liberatory spaces of abandonment and destruction, found in the ruins a mirror for our own wildness, our own desire to locate an outside to the strictures of society. I think back to that moment when the Portals of the Past framed not a mansion, not a garden, but a whole smoldering terrain, more tragic but also more wide open than before or after, a long pause between two phases, as ruins often are.

And then the ruins were gone—not all at once, but incrementally, throughout the nineties, first in slow stages, then, in San Francisco, in a sudden rush of money as dramatic as any disaster. At the turn of the century, at the height of the dot-com boom, twenty million dollars of venture capital was being pumped into the Bay Area each day, and it swept away not just empty and abandoned spaces but also the poor, the eclectic, the alternative, small businesses, and nonprofits; drowned countless continuities, the small stores and elderly residents and longtime denizens who constituted the place's memory and links to the past. After decades of neglect, vacant lots everywhere filled up, as though the long, sighing exhale of loss had become a quick, choking inhale of cash. You walked down the street and saw a new hair salon or a Starbucks and tried to remember what it had replaced—a fried-chicken shop? an upholstery store? a storefront gospel church?—and then one day you walked down the street and didn't remember how new all this new San Francisco was. Photographers ran around like ethnographic photographers a century before, trying to preserve some sense of the disintegrating communities. Sometimes, as if it had been a neutron bomb, this onslaught of wealth just destroyed the contents of buildings, their fragile residents forced out with their souvenirs and memories; sometimes it tore down less valuable buildings to replace them with ones that would yield more profit and accommodate other populations.

Tens of thousands of newcomers arrived to live not in the San Francisco they found but the San Francisco built out of their paychecks and stock options, a place full of brand-new bars and restaurants and boutiques, a place where condomini-ums—particularly pseudo-industrial lofts—were springing up by the thousands, where nonprofits and small businesses, the economically marginal, and seniors and families were being evicted at a rate several times that of a few years earlier. I am never sure whether these newcomers were the barbarians sacking our Rome or whether they were the Romans—after all, they represented order and homogene-ity and a consolidated future—sacking our Barbary Coast. But they came and they ravaged the city. Then, early in 2001, their technology bubble burst, leases went into default, rental prices that had increased astronomically sagged slightly, restaurants folded, and the boom became a bad memory or a bad case of amnesia. It was as though that futurist technological utopianism that had died out with mod-ernism had lurched back to life, but not for long, not with a credible foundation.

The 1989 earthquake is not what I count as the tenth destruction of San Francisco. For me, that destruction was, like the ninth, economic: the sack of the city by wealth during the heyday of the dot-com boom, circa 1998–2001. Wealth did to us what poverty did to New York—or perhaps both could be identified as the same force, as greed (for it was not the poor but the landlords' profiteering that caused those Bronx and Lower East Side fires). Like all the previous destruc-tions, this one did not destroy the city, but it destroyed *a* city, a slightly rougher, more diverse, more creative city that is gone forever (though the current city too is temporary, and not all of us were uprooted).

The first nine destructions created ruins; the tenth erased them in a frenzy of development, demolition, eviction, and replacement.

Where ought one to situate another invisible age of ruin, the generation of the armies of the homeless, who camp out as though the city was ruined, bombed, as though they are not the species for whom it was built, a crisis that has in two decades become the ordinary state of things, these people who are themselves a ruin of sorts, not of their own lives but of the civility that we used to believe aligned with citizenry and cities? Perhaps they are refugees from the cities that no longer exist, the industrial cities with uncomplicated jobs, unions, job security, blue-collar housing, New Deal and Great Society social programs, and stable net-works. The structure of the Hibernia Bank at McAllister and Market Streets survived the 1906 earthquake. I believe it was still a bank at some point in my tenure in San Francisco, and then it was a police substation. But for many years it has been empty, and homeless people have sat on its steps, as though the city had never been rebuilt after the 1906 earthquake, as though generations had come of age in the ruins. And then, the other day, I passed it and a set of mobile barricades had been erected around the broad, inviting corner steps so that it was truly abandoned, inside and out.

W. G. Sebald wrote of the erasure of Germany's wartime damage: "From the outset, the now legendary and in some respects genuinely admirable reconstruction of the country after the devastation wrought by Germany's wartime enemies, a reconstruction tantamount to a second liquidation in successive phases of the nation's own past history, prohibited any look backward. It did so through the sheer amount of labor required and the creation of a new, faceless reality, pointing the population exclusively towards the future and enjoining on it silence about the past." This is the silence more devastating than ruin.

Gaping Questions

⟦2002⟧

Construction in San Francisco is always a reminder that this place was once little more than dunes: under nearly every building is sand. Around noon on September 10, 2001, I went to see the great oaken rib cage of a 409-ton merchant ship that had been excavated from the sand of a construction site at Battery and Clay, in the heart of the financial district. The dark curved beams were huge, speaking both of forests ancient at the time of their cutting more than a century and a half ago and of the skill and brute exertion that shaped forests into ships. Office workers on their lunch break peered through the Cyclone fence at the site, somehow drawn out of themselves in this place where ordinarily even eye contact is an expenditure few will make; they seemed to feel part of something, and the place was somehow enlarged—not only in its sense of time, as the ship's hull made visible the ruined city of 1851, but also in its sense of community. It was an enchanted moment.

During the Gold Rush, hundreds of ships were abandoned in San Francisco's harbor because so many sailors deserted to head for the mines. Some vessels rotted in the water, but several were hauled ashore and used as warehouses and homes. As the city filled in downtown's shallow cove to create more prime real estate, strangers "were astonished to see the hull of a large ship located in the very heart of the city, surrounded on all sides with large blocks of substantial stone and brick edifices." It was a wild, provisional city, built not only on sand and landfill but on greed, the greed of those hoping to make a killing in the gold mines or in the frenzy of real estate speculation and retailing from which most of the real fortunes came. Only disaster drew people out of themselves, notably the fires that plagued the

371

early city: San Francisco's first fraternal societies were companies of volunteer firemen.

The ship we stood around and looked at on September 10, the *General Harrison*, had burned to the ground in one of those fires. That fire, the fifth great fire of San Francisco, was thought to have been started by an arsonist near midnight on May 3, 1851. Violent winds turned it into a general conflagration, and when it was over, about ten million dollars' worth of goods and property and two thousand buildings—all downtown—had burned. Citizens by the hundreds or thousands rushed to the scene to fight the fire. Hoping to protect themselves and their goods from the frequent blazes, some had built masonry and iron structures, but those who took refuge in them mostly died, and died horribly: masonry collapsed, temperatures in intact structures became unbearable, and the iron doors swelled in the heat and could not be opened. The hulls of the old ships below ground survived, to be buried beneath the new city that arose on top of them, the city that would burn down again in 1906.

Late on the morning of September 11, 2001, unable to concentrate on anything else and frustrated by the uninformative repetition on the radio—I don't have a television—I went to the gym at the college up the street from me. The TVs that usually play rock videos were tuned to CNN, and the dozen or so of us there wavered between working out and gathering around the screen when something new or dramatic occurred. The towers collapsed over and over. The footage taken by a camera held backward by a fleeing cameraman played again and again, and we watched his shadow jolt after him down a New York street full of figures chased by boiling white dust. In the gym, a muscle-bound young man went around and told everyone in a voice tense with emotion where the nearest blood bank was. In the hours and days that followed, everyone agreed that the world was changed, though no one knew exactly how. It was not just the possibility of a war, but the sense of the relation between self and world that changed, at least for Americans.

To live entirely for one's self in private is a huge luxury, a luxury countless aspects of this society encourage; but like a diet of pure foie gras, it clogs and narrows the arteries of the heart. This is what we're encouraged to crave in this country, but most of us crave, more deeply, something with more grit, more substance. Since my home county was faced with a disastrous drought when I was fifteen, I have been fascinated by the way people rise to the occasion of a disaster. In that drought, the wealthy citizens of that county enjoyed self-denial for the public good more than they enjoyed private abundance the rest of the time. The 1989 Loma Prieta quake shook San Francisco into the here and now: I remember how my anger at someone suddenly ceased to matter, and so did my plans. The day after the quake, I walked around town to see people I cared about, and the world was local and immediate. Not just because the Bay Bridge was damaged and there were practical reasons to stay home, but because the long-term perspective from which so much dissatisfaction and desire come was shaken too: life, meaning, value were close to home, in the present. We who had been through the quake were present and connected—connected to death, to fear, to the unknown, but in being so connected one could feel empathy, passion, and heroism as well. We could feel strongly, and that is itself something hard to find in the anesthetizing distractions of this society.

That first impulse everywhere on September 11 was to give blood, a kind of secular communion in which people offered up the life of their bodies for strangers. The media dropped its advertisements, leers, and gossip and told us about tragedy and heroism. Giving blood and volunteering were the first expression of a sense of connection; the flag became an ambiguous symbol of that connection, ambiguous since it meant everything from empathy to belligerence. In Brooklyn that week, a friend reported, "Nobody went to work, and everybody talked to strangers." What makes people heroic, and what makes them feel like members of a community? Years ago, I studied public art that sought to create such a feeling by providing outdoor commemorations of local history and community, as the brief exposure of the hull of the *General Harrison* did. But the larger purpose of public art is to make people participants in their communities, their cities, their politics—to make them citizens. For me, activism itself is a more direct form of that art, the spirit of activism that made the Forty-Niners rush to help put out the flames in San Francisco, that turned Manhattan into an island of volunteers and the United States into a nation of donors and patriots, even though the question of what people felt connected to was itself open to question. I hoped that one thing to come out of the end of American invulnerability would be a stronger sense of what disasters abroad—massacres, occupations, wars, famines, dictatorships—mean and feel like, a sense of citizenship in the world.

There were spectacular heroes in this disaster, the firefighters, police, medical and sanitation workers, those who died trying to save others in those first hours and those who did what could be done at the site afterward. But I mean *heroism* as a comparatively selfless state of being and as a willingness to do. Wartime and disaster elicit this heroism most strongly, though there are always volunteers who don't wait until disaster comes home, the volunteers and activists who engage with issues that don't affect them directly—land mines, discrimination, geno- cide—the people who want to extend their own privilege and security to those who lack such comforts. In its mildest form, that heroism is simply citizenship, a sense of connection and commitment to the community; and for a few months after 9/11, we had a strange surge of citizenship in this country. In a small way, that sense of optimism and camaraderie I felt from the office workers at the *General Harrison*'s hull prefigured it and suggested that it can exist without conflict, without threat; that it can come into being in those pauses in daily life that are filled with art, history, memory, shared time in public space; that public ceremony and public space can bring it about.

Shortly after the bombing, the president swore to "eliminate evil" from the world. With this declaration, he seemed to promise that the goodness that filled us would not be necessary in the future, a future in which we could return to preoc- cupation with our private lives. Though oil politics had much to do with what had happened, we were not asked to give up driving, or vehicles that gulp huge amounts of fuel; rather, we were asked to go shopping, and this summer we were asked to spy on our neighbors. The United States has been a peculiar kind of democracy, one in which we enshrine and pay homage to certain rights and free- doms, though they grow dusty from lack of use. Less than half the eligible voters participated in the 2000 presidential election, which collapsed in chaos before the Supreme Court stepped in; in the wake of September 11, the fact that so many

Americans did not understand their own country's foreign policy or how it is perceived abroad was recognized as a catastrophe of its own, one that contributed to this one. Calling for further restrictions on those rights and freedoms in the wake of the catastrophe seemed another way to consign us to the dreary luxury of private life just when we had emerged into public life with a wholeheartedness unseen since World War II. And that public life is where real democracy could take place.

The hull of the *General Harrison* has been buried again, and a commercial hotel is being built atop it, a hotel that doesn't ask much of us or tell us anything transformative. That beautiful rupture in the fabric of downtown is gone. In Manhattan, the hole is infinitely vaster and more painful, and it can't and won't be buried in the same way. It's an open question, to which there are many answers, none as simple as war, none as quick as bombs, answers that must be given again and again in the choices we make about what we know and how we participate, or don't.

CODA

The Pacific

Seashell to Ear

⟦2001⟧

The seashore is an edge, perhaps the only true edge in the world whose borders are otherwise mostly political fictions, and it defies the usual idea of borders by being unfixed, fluctuant, and infinitely permeable. The seashore is the place that is no place, sometimes solid land or, rather, sand, sometimes the shallow fringe of that huge body of water governed by the remote body of the moon in a mystery something like love or desire. A body of water is always traveling, and so the border between the land and the sea is not a Hadrian's Wall or a zone of armed guards; it's a border of endless embassies, of sandpiper diplomacy and jellyfish exportation, a meeting or even a trysting ground. An open border but a dangerous one between the known and the unknown, which only a few sibyls, amphibians, crustaceans, and marine mammals traverse with impunity. The shore is also the site of the mutual offerings of the dead, our drowned, their beached, another edge effect, this washing up of corpses, metaphors, myths. The mind is such a meeting ground: its ideas are less often laboriously thought out than suddenly washed up from unknown hatcheries and currents far beneath the surface, the dry ideas of logic that drown in the sea; the dreams that, like whales, die crushed by their own weight when they wash up on shore in the morning; and amphibious poetry in between, for the seashore also suggests the border between fact and imagination, waking and sleeping, self and other, suggests perhaps the essential meeting of differences, essential as in primary, essential as in necessary. Wandering the coastline with downcast eyes to find what there is to be found, a material correlation to composing and thinking, is a disreputable profession with its own word, beachcombing. Shopping at one's feet for stories, for the unknown, for the thing lost so long one can no longer name it, for treasure that will transform, for that inhuman material that sets free whatever is most human and immaterial. For adults, there is the question of how to set the eyes—whether to beachcomb or more upliftedly regard the view of sea and land—but for children, who have not yet learned that rocks and shells will generally dwindle into rubbish away from the shore, combing the beach is irresistible. Beachcombing, to comb the beach as though it were the hair those mermaids are forever combing with one eye on the sailors, for there is a litter of images, metaphors, inspirations that are more portable and better-looking removed from the beach than its physical stuff. Generative graveyard, this coastline littered with shells from which the dwellers have been evicted, sailor-strangling seafoam, and, says Rachel Carson at the beginning of her book *The Sea around Us*, Mother Sea. "The sea floats her, ripples her, flows together with her daughter, in all our ways," writes Hélène Cixous. "Then unseparated they sweep along their changing waters, without fear of their bodies, without bony stiffness, without a shell . . . And sea for mother gives herself up to pleasure in her bath of writing." Fluidity, the biological body, Aphrodite of the unsanitary seafoam rather than of marble, generated when Chronos, or Time, threw Uranus's severed genitals upon the open sea. The sea is a body in a thousand ways that don't add up, because adding is too stable a transaction for that flux, but the waves come in in a roar and then ebb, almost silent but for the faint suck of sand and snap of bubbles, over and over, a heartbeat rhythm, the sea always this body turned inside out and opened to the sky, the body always a sea folded in on itself, a nautical chart folded into a paper cup. A person who nearly drowns is more readily revived if her lungs are full of seawater rather than freshwater, for the sea, just as salty as the body, does not dilute the blood and burst the cells. It was the sea in which all life evolved, we were all told long ago; and somewhere further along in biology, blood became one kind of salty ocean circulating nutrients, oxygen, flushing toxins and detritus along the estuaries and channels of the body, and amniotic fluid another sea in which each floated in darkness the first nine months of life until, as they say, the waters broke. But where I come from, the first people say that originally Coyote or Raven or Creator drew solid land up as a fistful of mud from the spreading waters, and the ones who live on the coast say that the dead go west over the sea when they die, the place that every river on this Pacific slope runs to. Another story from this terrain has the earth as Turtle Island, a swimmer forever afloat in the sea, and all these stories assert that the liquid is primary and solidity merely floats on it (and the night before I go to this coast to think out this essay, I dream I am carrying a tortoise or turtle before me in two hands, held out before me like an altarboy's Bible, and the creature keeps leaking water, far more water than ought to be in its body, and only upon waking do I realize that the room around which we proceeded was my childhood bedroom). One thing leads to another: there are the seashells children are told to hold to their ears to hear the sea, and only later are they told that they are listening to the inward sea of their own body's pulses echoing in the seashell that was itself once a favorite metaphor for a delicate ear: these are pearls that were his eyes, but seashells that were her ears. Pearly-eyed Alice cries an ocean and then swims in the sea that flowed from her eyes to the strange world on the other side of her tears, and the American artist Robert Gober's Madonna comes flanked by two suitcases full of tidepool life that seem like allegorical wombs; for though it is obvious enough that rivers are veins and arteries, the ocean is everything. Call it a sea of amniotic fluid, the fluid in which life generated, but uterine hardly describes this most open space under the sky unless to the most wide-open imagination. The seashore, everything always in motion, a place that seems the essence of change, but the pelicans that skim the waves look like pterodactyls, and the trilobites scuttled blindly through the coming and going of the dinosaurs without any more interest than they take in, say, photography, with its womblike darkrooms and amniotic developing washes, or in politics or in poetry. The sea lapping like a cat at a saucer of milk or, rather, since it is the liquid which acts, the sea like a vast saucer of milk lapping at a recumbent cat. The sea laps at the land, or the sea is in the lap of the land, the ancient earth whose unseen depths cradle the seas and whose heights we inhabit mostly at the altitude called sea level, which global warming is due to change and with it outdate all the coastal maps. This is not quite the allegory meant in old movies when sex was implied by a cut to the waves whose steady rhythm had more to do with hips than lips. "Yes, as everyone knows," remarks *Moby Dick*'s Ishmael when he's still on shore waiting to ship out, "water and meditation are wedded for-ever," asking us to accept the play on the liquidities of language in which the substance and the cerebral act can be imagined as married like two members of the same species, a pairing like love's parentage of severed genitals and seafoam. "In all rivers and oceans," says Melville a little later, "is the image of the ungraspable phantom of life; and this is the key to it all." The linear narrative of following the coast, the plot, the history, the sequence of pages versus the steady rhythm of the tides, the waves, the desires. The book and the sea turn into each other at the end, a stranding of black letters on the paperwhite shore, and the pages of a book at the windy seashore blow one over another like waves, a curl, a comb of pages. The box of a book is a misleading shape, call it a pirate chest made to be opened, call it the long thread of a story wound up on the spool of a book's solid shape, every page spread a valley landscape, though the term *gutter* urban-izes the intimate central cleft between the pages. Open a book and look at it end-wise and it looks like a bird seen in flight far away, spine for body and pages for wings, a fat black Bible like a raven, slender art books with thinner curves of pages to either side like albatrosses. This book could be bound as a circle, the pages like spokes on a wheel, a turning investigation of the sea, a continuity that folds back on itself, a walk that went all the way around an island to end at its beginning; or it could be imagined as an aquarium, every page like the Madonna's tidepool suit-cases a sample so fresh that some pages seem to splash, to have depth the hand could plunge into to seize some of their treasure. Walk on the seashore: strands of seaweed lie hieroglyphically upon the strand and are sucked up by the sea and, like words turned back into fluid ink, waver in the water before being cast up on the sand in another equally unreadable version, roll of the dice, toss of the yarrow sticks. Reading the sea, transparent at one's feet, green as arching wave and white as spray, its depths an opaque accumulation of transparencies with blue borrowed from the sky. Building a museum case and filling it with types of mussels is one way of knowing mussels; but on the shore, a mussel leads to a crab or a curious stone, which leads to another thing and eventually leads back to mussels, which is another and perhaps a more far-reaching way to know mussels. The sea that always seems like a metaphor, but one that is always moving, cannot be fixed, like a heart that is like a tongue that is like a mystery that is like a story that is like a border that is like something altogether different and like everything at once. One thing leads to another, and this is the treasure that always runs through your fingers and never runs out.

Acknowledgments

Seen alone, an essay or a book bears an uncomfortable resemblance to a monologue, but it is most often born amid conversations with fellow writers, editors, publishers, friends, and with history and earlier books and works of art. Imagine it instead as a long-winded reply to an invitation, a provocation, a problem, or a revelation, and you begin to imagine the crowd to whom the solitary writer is indebted. I have been fortunate in editors over the years, and some of my best had much to do with various pieces here, including Tom Engelhardt of Tomdispatch, Paul Rauber of *Sierra* magazine, Jennifer Sahn of *Orion*, and Gary Kornblau of the late, much-mourned *Art issues*. Others served less as editors per se than as traveling companions and instigators; thanks also go to Iain Boal, Alec Finlay, Michael Sorkin, and John Rohrbach of the Amon Carter Museum of American Art. Though I long ago ceased to be an art critic, I never gave up my attachment to artists and visual art. Because artists ask the biggest questions about everything from perception to political possibilities, they have remained an important part of my thinking; and more thanks go to Richard Misrach, John Pfahl, and Meridel Rubenstein, in particular, for asking me to work with them. My thanks as well to the other artists whose beautiful images will help readers reimagine the world around them and also to the editors on this project. Niels Hooper and Rachel Lockman at the University of California Press have proceeded with an old-fashioned degree of intellectual involvement and diligence that has much improved the rough sheaf of stuff I put together in 2005 and have made production a pleasure.

As did copyeditor Mary Renaud and production editor Kate Warne, who with thoughtfulness and precision improved the manuscript further. Finally, my agent Bonnie Nadell has much improved my working life for more than a decade now, for which I am more than thankful.

Notes

THE STRUGGLE OF DAWNING INTELLIGENCE

40   "The celebration of the past . . .": Lucy Lippard, *The Lure of the Local: Senses of Place in a Multicentered Society* (New York: New Press, 1997), p. 107.

40   "This site possesses national significance . . .": cited in Robert Dawson and Gray Brechin, *Farewell, Promised Land: Waking from the California Dream* (Berkeley: University of California Press, 1999), p. 17.

42   "The group of figures fronting the City Hall . . .": City of San Francisco, Municipal Report of 1893–1894, archives of the San Francisco Arts Commission.

42   "We request the removal of a monument . . .": letter from Martina O'Dea to the San Francisco Arts Commission, January 30, 1995, archives of the San Francisco Art Commission.

42   "In 1769, the missionaries first came to California . . .": draft document for plaque text, archives of the San Francisco Arts Commission.

43   "many of us, including myself . . .": letter from Consul General of Spain Camilo Alonso-Vega to Mayor Willie Brown, May 24, 1996, archives of the San Francisco Arts Commission.

43   "a Franciscan missionary directs the attention . . .": letter from Archbishop William J. Levada to Mayor Willie Brown, April 17, 1996, archives of the San Francisco Arts Commission.

44   "How can San Francisco . . .": fax from Kevin Starr and John P. Schlegel (president of the Jesuit University of San Francisco) to the San Francisco Arts Commission, April 30, 1996, p. 4, archives of the San Francisco Arts Commission.

44   "that a war of extermination would continue to be waged . . .": Governor Peter Burnett, "Message to the California State Legislature," January 7, 1851, *California State Senate Journal, 1851;* quoted in Alberto Hurtado, *Indian Survival on the California Frontier* (New Haven: Yale University Press, 1988), p. 135.

44   "At least 300,000 Native people . . .": text from the plaque on the monument itself; also included in archives of the San Francisco Arts Commission.

45   "The law also stated that the memorial should provide visitors . . .": official Little Bighorn Battlefield National Monument web site, www.nps.gov/libi (accessed 1999).

45   "enraged critics . . .": *Times* of London, August 26, 1997.

45   "It's like erecting a monument to the Mexicans killed at the Alamo": quoted in Chris Smith and Elizabeth Manning, "The Sacred and Profane Collide in the West," *High Country News,* May 26, 1997.

46   "carefully described key landmarks and locations of fresh water . . .": Leslie Marmon Silko, "Interior and Exterior Landscapes: The Pueblo Migration Stories," in *Yellow Woman and a Beauty of the Spirit: Essays on Native American Life Today* (New York: Simon and Schuster, 1996), pp. 32, 33.

46   Keith Basso, "'Stalking with Stories': Names, Places, and Moral Narratives among the Western Apaches," *Anteus,* no. 57 (Autumn 1986), special issue, "Nature."

47   "the precise date of the incident is often less important than the place": Silko, "Interior and Exterior Landscapes," p. 33.

47   "Americans ought to know . . .": Patricia Nelson Limerick, essay in *Sweet Medicine: Sites of Indian Massacres, Battlefields, and Treaties,* by Drex Brooks (Albuquerque: University of New Mexico Press, 1995), pp. 125, 151.

48   "I grew up going to Devils Tower. . . .": Lakota leader Charlotte Black Elk quoted in *High Country News,* May 26, 1997, sidebar/editorial.

48   "Climbing on Devils Tower is a religious experience for me. . . .": Andy
        Petefish quoted in *High Country News*, April 27, 1998.

50   "I began to realize that for them the religion . . .": Malcolm Margolin,
        remarks as part of a panel titled Where Holiness Resides, April 11, 1992,
        at the Headlands Center for the Arts, in a series organized by Ann
        Chamberlain; quoted in *Headlands Journal*, 1992, p. 13 (annual publication
        of the Headlands Center for the Arts, Sausalito, Calif.). He was speaking of
        the proposed capping of the San Joaquin Valley's Coso Springs for geother-
        mal energy production, noting that "in that spring dwells a particular god,
        one of the gods that created the world. Frog, one of the gods, dwells in that
        spring, and if you cap that spring, what is going to happen to that god?"

50   Work by Edgar Hachivi Heap of Birds is cited in Lippard, *Lure of the Local*,
        p. 86.

50   "All of the state of Oklahoma is Indian Territory. . . .": Edgar Hachivi Heap
        of Birds, presentation at the Headlands Center for the Arts, in a series orga-
        nized by Ann Chamberlain, May 9, 1992; quoted from transcripts courtesy
        of the Headlands Center for the Arts.

THE GARDEN OF MERGING PATHS

51   "You are in a maze . . .": cited in Michael Shallis, *The Silicon Idol: The Micro
        Revolution and Its Social Implications* (New York: Schocken Books, 1984).

51   "Place your right (or left) hand . . .": Julian Barnes, "Letter from London,"
        New Yorker, September 30, 1991.

51   Another United Technologies landscape was underground . . . : Ted Smith,
        executive director of the Silicon Valley Toxics Coalition in San Jose, tele-
        phone interview with the author, September 8, 1994.

52   Langdon Winner, "Silicon Valley Mystery House," in *Variations on a Theme
        Park*, ed. Michael Sorkin (New York: Noonday Press, 1993).

53   "If machinery be the most powerful means . . .": Karl Marx, *Capital, The
        Communist Manifesto, and Other Writings* (New York: Modern Library,
        1932), p. 104.

53   Jerry Mander, *In the Absence of the Sacred: The Failure of Technology and the Survival of the Indian Nations* (San Francisco: Sierra Club Books, 1991).

54   Silicon Valley itself is an excellent check . . . : On Silicon Valley's social problems, see Winner, "Silicon Valley Mystery House"; and Dennis Hayes, *Behind the Silicon Curtain* (Boston: South End Press, 1989).

55   On relations between the Ohlone and the Spanish missionaries, see Malcolm Margolin, *The Ohlone Way: Indian Life in the San Francisco–Monterey Bay Area* (Berkeley: Heyday Books, 1978); and Albert L. Hurtado, *Indian Survival on the California Frontier* (New Haven: Yale University Press, 1988).

55   "For almost twenty miles . . .": Vancouver quoted in Yvonne Olson Jacobson, *Passing Farms, Enduring Values: California's Santa Clara Valley* (Los Altos, Calif.: William Kaufmann and California Historical Center, 1984), pp. 20–21. Jacobson is the granddaughter of the founder of the Olson orchards.

55   One successful raider, Yoscolo . . . : ibid., p. 26.

57   "Santa Clara County is fighting a holding action . . .": Santa Clara planning department report is quoted in ibid., p. 230. Jacobson's volume is also the source of the 1980s acreage statistics.

57   "Perhaps the most significant, enduring accomplishment of Silicon Valley . . .": Winner, "Silicon Valley Mystery House," p. 59.

60   "Ts'ui Pen must have said once . . .": Jorge Luis Borges, "The Garden of Forking Paths," in *Labyrinths* (Harmondsworth: Penguin Books, 1970), p. 50.

61   "VR is reverse Calvinism . . .": Norman M. Klein, "Virtually Lost, Virtually Found: America Enters the Age of Electronic Substance Abuse," *Art issues* (Los Angeles), September-October 1991.

63   "Humans intuitively see analogies . . .": Paul Shepard, *Nature and Madness* (San Francisco: Sierra Club Books, 1982), p. 102.

64   These are the tentacles, the winding corridors, the farthest reaches of Silicon Valley, and the hardest to imagine: Hayes, *Behind the Silicon Curtain;* and "Coming Clean in the Semiconductor Industry," an interview with Ted Smith by Anita Amirrezvani, *Bay Area Computer Currents*, June 1–13, 1994.

64   the rest of the Olson orchard is on its way out: "Last Call for the Last Sunnyvale Orchard," *San Francisco Chronicle*, August 1, 1994, p. A17.

EXCAVATING THE SKY

This essay accompanied a book of Richard Misrach's sky photographs. *The Sky Book* (Santa Fe: Arena Editions, 2000) includes pictures of clouds; of constellations, comets, and planets (slow exposures of their curving trajectories, often interrupted by the straight lines of military flights); and of the cloudless sky, identified by the exact time and place at which they were made ("Paradise Valley [Arizona] 3.22.95 7:05 P.M.," for example, or "Dead Sea 4.3.93 5:01 A.M.," "Warrior Point 6.27.94 5:25 A.M.," "Jerusalem Mountain 10.28.94 7:52 A.M."). The titles of the sky pictures were chosen to call attention to the peculiar naming practices deployed across the American West, and the names of the heavenly bodies were also resonant ("Mars and Air Traffic over Las Vegas," "Cygnus over Ak-Chin").

143   "Don't show the sky . . .": Eliot Porter, quoted by David Brower in a letter reminiscing about Porter, to curator John Rohrbach of the Amon Carter Museum, September 1999.

144   "Somehow the sky seems important . . .": Beaumont Newhall, in a letter to Nancy Newhall (including cloud contact prints in the original), June 20, 1944; quoted in the alternative monthly newspaper *Geronimo* (Taos, New Mexico), August 1999, p. 23.

144   "a traveling deity who was everyplace . . .": Paul Shepard, *Nature and Madness* (San Francisco: Sierra Club Books, 1982), p. 51.

145   "These series are not meteorological records . . .": Sarah Greenough and Juan Hamilton, *Alfred Stieglitz: Photographs and Writings* (Washington, D.C.: National Gallery of Art, 1983), p. 24.

146   "A metaphor is a word with some other meaning . . .": Aristotle, *On Poetry and Style*, trans. G. M. A. Grube (Indianapolis: Bobbs Merrill, 1976), pp. 44–45.

146   "Metaphors are the means by which the oneness of the world . . .": Hannah Arendt, introduction to *Illuminations: Essays and Reflections*, by Walter Benjamin, trans. Harry Zohn (New York: Schocken Books, 1969), pp. 13–14.

146 "The rib bones are the closed ellipses of the planets . . .": Peter Hoeg, *Smilla's Sense of Snow*, trans. Tina Nunnally (New York: Farrar, Straus and Giroux, 1993), p. 253.

146 a comet moving through the pudenda of a constellation . . . : Italo Calvino, "Man, the Sky, and the Elephant: On Pliny's *Natural History*," trans. Patrick Creagh, *Anteus*, no. 57 (Autumn 1986): 73.

146 On alternative readings of the Big Dipper, see Dorcas S. Miller, *Stars of the First People: Native American Star Myths and Constellations* (Boulder, Colo.: Pruett Publishing, 1997), pp. 285–287; and Dan Heim, *Easy Field Guide to the Southwestern Night Sky* (Phoenix, Ariz.: Primer Publishers, 1997), p. 20.

147 "When Orion and Sirius are come to the middle of the sky . . .": Hesiod, quoted in Anthony Aveni, *Stairways to the Stars: Skywatching in Three Great Ancient Cultures* (New York: Wiley, 1997), p. 20.

148 "It is a strange thing how little in general people know about the sky . . .": John Ruskin, *Modern Painters*, vol. 1 (New York: Merrill and Baker, n.d.), pt. 2, pp. 205–206.

149 "that beside the planet there were three starlets . . .": Galileo, *The Starry Messenger*, in *Discoveries and Opinions of Galileo*, trans. Stillman Drake (Garden City, N.Y.: Doubleday, 1957), p. 51.

149 "four planets swiftly revolving about Jupiter . . .": part of the subtitle of *The Starry Messenger*, in ibid.

151 "The streams were timbered with the long-leaved cottonwood . . .": John C. Fremont, "Journal of the First Expedition," in *The Expeditions of John Charles Fremont*, vol. 1, *Travels from 1838 to 1844*, ed. Donald Jackson and Mary Lee Spence (Urbana: University of Illinois Press, 1970–1980), p. 459.

151 On Solomon Nunes Carvalho, see Robert Schlaer's definitive book *Sights Once Seen: Daguerreotyping Fremont's Last Expedition through the Rockies* (Santa Fe: Museum of New Mexico, 2000).

152 "From the Dalles to the point where we turned . . .": Fremont, May 23, 1844, *Expeditions*, vol. 1, pp. 696–697.

153 "Massacre Rocks and Battle Mountain tell their stories . . .": George R.

Stewart, *Names on the Land: A Historical Account of Place-Naming in the United States*, rev. ed. (Boston: Houghton Mifflin, 1967), p. 252.

154   "The Indian name of the lake is Mini-wakan . . .": Fremont, *Expeditions*, vol. 1, p. 62.

154   *Minnesota* means "muddy water . . .": Stewart, *Names on the Land*, pp. 278–279. For the history of Yosemite place-names, see Rebecca Solnit, *Savage Dreams: A Journey into the Landscape Wars of the American West*, 2nd ed. (Berkeley: University of California Press, 1999), pp. 219–220, 309–327.

155   "Most place-names today are what could be termed 'linguistic fossils' . . ." A. D. Mills, *Dictionary of English Place-Names* (Oxford: Oxford University Press, 1991), p. v.

155   "The poets made all the words . . .": Ralph Waldo Emerson, quoted in Susan Morrow, *The Names of Things* (New York: Riverhead Books, 1997), pp. 126–127.

156   "Nullagvik, Pauktugvik, Milliktagvik, Avgumman, Aquisaq, Inmaurat. . . .": Richard K. Nelson, "The Embrace of Names," text of a 1998 talk, courtesy of the Lannan Foundation.

156   "the entire North American continent in a time before living memory . . .": ibid.

157   "Monument Valley's Navajo name is *Tse Bii' Nidzisigai* (White Rocks Inside). . . .": Mike Mitchell, Navajo medicine person, opening text in Skeet McAuley, *Sign Language: Contemporary Southwest Native America* (New York: Aperture, 1989), unpaginated.

160   "And ultimately, the basic configuration of Rothko's abstract paintings . . .": Robert Rosenblum, *Modern Painting and the Northern Romantic Tradition* (New York: Harper and Row, 1975), pp. 214–215.

162   "so lavishly, engagingly visual . . .": Rebecca Solnit, "Scapeland," in *Crimes and Splendors: The Desert Cantos of Richard Misrach*, by Anne Wilkes Tucker (Boston: Bulfinch Press in conjunction with the Museum of Fine Arts, Houston, 1996), p. 53.

162   "I wanted to deconstruct the conventions of landscape . . .": Richard Misrach in Tucker, *Crimes and Splendors*.

225   "As I became interested in photography in the realm of nature . . .": Eliot Porter, *Eliot Porter*, Photographs and text by Eliot Porter, foreword by Martha A. Sandweiss (Fort Worth and Boston: New York Graphic Society and Amon Carter Museum, 1987), p. 83.

225   "cannot be categorized . . .": Guy Davenport, *National Review*, December 18, 1963.

225   "A kind of revolution was underway . . .": Stephen Fox, *John Muir and His Legacy: The American Conservation Movement* (Boston: Little, Brown, 1981), p. 317, quoting the October 1974 issue of *Smithsonian* magazine.

226   Porter's pictures of nature look, so to speak, "natural" now: A parallel history might be that of the eighteenth-century English landscape garden, which imitated nature and then became what people looked for in nature— that is, they looked for landscapes whose features resembled those celebrated in the gardens. By the nineteenth century, the gardens had become unneces- sary as specific locations and intentional constructions; they had evolved into how people looked at unaltered landscapes. In other words, the garden was no longer a constructed place but a constructed frame of reference for looking at places. (Yosemite Valley, for example, was often praised for resembling an "English park.")

227   "The very existence of mankind . . .": cited in Spencer R. Weart, *Nuclear Fear* (Cambridge, Mass.: Harvard University Press, 1988), p. 258.

228   "Their presence casts a shadow . . .": Rachel Carson, *Silent Spring* (New York: Houghton Mifflin, 1962), p. 188.

228   "Conservation has rather suddenly become a major issue . . .": Eliot Porter, letter to Aline Porter, April 11, 1961, in Stephen Porter file, Eliot Porter Archives, Amon Carter Museum, Fort Worth, Texas.

228   "The world of systemic insecticides . . .": Carson, *Silent Spring*, p. 32.

229   "the geography of hope": This phrase appears in a letter from Wallace Steg- ner to Dave Pesonen, originally titled "The Wilderness Idea"; it was read by Secretary of the Interior Stewart Udall as part of his presentation "Conserva- tion in the 1960s: Action or Stalemate?" at the Sierra Club's 1961 wilderness

conference. The proceedings were published as *Wilderness: America's Living Heritage*, ed. David Brower (San Francisco: Sierra Club Books, 1961). "What I want to speak for is not so much the wilderness uses, valuable as those are, but the wilderness idea, which is a resource in itself. Being an intangible and spiritual resource, it will seem mystical to the practical-minded—but then anything that cannot be moved by a bulldozer is likely to seem mystical to them" (Brower, *Wilderness*, p. 97; the phrase "the geography of hope" appears on p. 102). The letter in its original version is printed in Stegner's anthology *The Sound of Mountain Water* (New York: Dutton, 1980). Of course, in the very different times of the early twenty-first century, it can be argued that hope is sometimes misplaced—that images like Porter's were and can be reassuring, when reassurance is far from what's needed. But on January 28, 1969, a James W. Moorman of Washington, D.C., wrote to the Sierra Club, "I learned of the Club about four years ago when "In Wildness" and "These We Inherit" caught my eye in a New York bookstore. These wonderful, transcendent books touched me as few things have. I am not ashamed to say they restored hope. . . . If man created such books, then perhaps man could be persuaded to stop the destruction" (folder 2:25, Publications, Ansel Adams Papers, Sierra Club Archives, Bancroft Library, University of California at Berkeley). The books in this case worked exactly as intended.

229   a way to bring the wilderness to the people: "The club's Exhibit Format books offered an ironic variation on Muir's old scheme of creating conservationists by depositing them in the Sierra. Instead of bringing people to the wilderness, Brower's publishing program brought the wilderness to people— with much the same conversion effect—through books that were hard to put down. Over the first four years, fifty thousand were sold, 80 percent through bookstores and mainly to nonmembers of the Sierra Club. The number of buyers was further increased by a distribution arrangement with Ballantine Books of New York. A cheaper edition of *Wildness* was the best-selling trade paperback of 1967. By 1969 total sales amounted to $10 million" (Fox, *John Muir and His Legacy*, p. 319).

229   "Hundreds of books and articles . . .": *Sports Illustrated*, November 22, 1967.

229   "If those who believe in progress . . .": Joseph Wood Krutch, "Introduction," *In Wildness Is the Preservation of the World* (San Francisco: Sierra Club Books, 1962), p. 13.

231   "When I explored the Colorado Plateau . . .": Stephen Trimble, letter to the author, January 3, 2000.

231   "The message was clear . . .": Stephen Trimble, "Reinventing the West: Private Choices and Consequences in Photography," *Buzzworm*, November-December 1991, pp. 46–54. Michael Cohen pointed out (in a note to the author) that the Glen Canyon book sent people in search of that sense of place throughout the Colorado Plateau, generating, among other things, a "plethora of Antelope Canyon pictures."

232   "I did not consider those years wasted . . .": Porter, *Eliot Porter*, p. 29.

232   "During my career as a photographer . . .": ibid., p. 83.

232   "Over the many years that I worked with him . . .": Eleanor Caponigro, interviewed by John Rohrbach, January 16, 1995, typescript, p. 3, Eliot Porter Archives.

234   "of comparable sensibility . . .": Porter, *Eliot Porter*, p. 45.

234   "The enclosed clipping is a letter I wrote . . .": Eliot Porter, letter to Stephen Porter, November 29, 1958, Stephen Porter file, Eliot Porter Archives.

235   "Photography is a strong tool . . .": Eliot Porter, "Photography and Conservation," manuscript in Notes on Conservation file, box 40, Eliot Porter Archives.

235   "changed Dave's whole way of looking at the conservation movement. . . .": Edgar Wayburn cited by Michael P. Cohen, *The History of the Sierra Club, 1892–1970* (San Francisco: Sierra Club Books, 1988), p. 293.

236   "The conspicuous success of *Wildness* . . .": Fox, *John Muir and His Legacy*, pp. 318–319.

237   On the links between the books and the club's campaigns, see Cohen, *History of the Sierra Club*, pp. 424–426. The Earth National Park ad was one of the last straws in Brower's relationship with the Sierra Club board, who perceived it as both an unauthorized expenditure and a far too vague and

utopian idea to mesh with their commitment to concrete protections and realizable goals.

237 "The idea of playing hardball with big corporations . . .": Philip Berry, oral history interview, Sierra Club Archives. The club was accustomed to cordial relations with the sources of power; *In Wildness Is the Preservation of the World* was underwritten by a philanthropic arm of the giant Bechtel Corporation—which built Hoover Dam, countless oil pipelines around the world, and Glen Canyon Dam and now manages the nuclear weapons program at the Nevada Test Site.

238 "was most eloquently stated, really, by Eliot Porter . . .": ibid., p. 27.

238 "Every acre that is lost . . .": Eliot Porter, *Sierra Club Bulletin*, 1969, from Short Statements on Conservation 1958–1971 file, box 41, Eliot Porter Archives.

239 For Hildebrand's criticism of Porter, see Alex Hildebrand, oral history interview, *Sierra Club Leaders, 1950s–1970s*, p. 21, Sierra Club Archives. Hildebrand was a Standard Oil executive and part of the club's old guard.

239 Adams—who had mixed feelings about color photography: Porter often depicted Ansel Adams as an intimidating and difficult figure, and certainly Adams made many disparaging comments about color photography over the years. But Virginia Adams apparently tried to get an early version of *In Wildness* published, and Adams's letter of congratulations to Porter for *The Place No One Knew* is generous. Perhaps because of his many years of involvement with the club, Adams took a more pragmatic view on everything from publications to Diablo Canyon. In those years, Brower annoyed the two artists with his oft-repeated comment that "Porter is the Sierra Club's most valuable property" (in, for example, a letter of November 16, 1966, in the Publications files of the Sierra Club Archives); Porter did not regard himself as property, and Adams felt disparaged by the focus on Porter. During those years, the Sierra Club letterhead featured an Ansel Adams photograph.

239 "There was a great deal of opposition to the proposal . . .": Porter, *Eliot Porter*, p. 53.

239   "other projects have higher conservation priority . . .": Edgar Wayburn, letter, September 9, 1967, file 2, box 30, David Brower Papers, Sierra Club Archives. Many other Sierra Club board members felt that books should be tied to conservation objectives. Martin Litton tartly recalled, "Along came the exhibit format books. They were done in black and white which, of course, was cheap. In those days not too much color was done anyway. That was the perfect stage for Ansel Adams's material. You had these terrific books, most of which did not pinpoint any subject. They were just all over the place, like *This Is the American Earth*. Pretty pictures of America with a little message by Nancy Newhall or whoever under each one about how lovely it is we still have Mount Whitney there. It didn't do anything political. It showed the Sierra Club could publish books, and books like that weren't all that common then as they are now" (Litton, oral history interview, p. 79, Sierra Club Archives). Board member August Frugé agreed with Adams and Wayburn when he wrote to Brower on February 2, 1969: "We have little need for coffee table books on the Alps and the Scottish Highlands (planned for 1969), but we desperately need books that will help us save Lake Tahoe, San Francisco Bay, the Everglades, Lake Superior, and many other places" (folder 2:26, Ansel Adams Papers, Sierra Club Archives).

239   "The publications committee of the Sierra Club . . .": Porter, *Eliot Porter*, p. 54.

240   "Adams argued that Brower would not accept a position . . .": Cohen, *History of the Sierra Club*, p. 421.

240   "During a board meeting . . .": Porter, *Eliot Porter*, p. 56. In a letter to Brower on March 4, 1968, Porter wrote, "I am getting a little weary of being told one day that I am a valuable property of the Sierra Club and the next day lectured on my responsibilities to the Sierra Club and conservation. Sometimes I think that you would like me to feel guilty for making any money at all from Sierra Club publications. . . . My contribution to conservation may not be enough in your eyes but after all this is a matter that each of us has to decide for himself. My contribution is considerably different from yours and may be judged considerably less, but whatever the judgment is I resent its being down-graded. And this happens when my books are publi-

cized as Sierra Club publications without credit going to me or my name mentioned."

241   "There is no subject and background . . .": Fairfield Porter, *The Nation*, January 1960, p. 39. Art critic Peter Schjeldahl wrote, in a review of Fairfield Porter's paintings, "Porter was born real-estate rich in a suburb of Chicago to a family that had deep roots in New England. His gloomy father was a frustrated architect, his mother a lifelong amateur in social causes and cultural uplift. . . . In 1927, he travelled to Moscow, where he had his first exposure to the paintings of Vuillard and Bonnard, and an audience with Leon Trotsky, who allowed Porter to sketch him. . . . Settling in New York, he became embroiled in radical politics and painted a mural, now lost, entitled 'Turn Imperialist War Into Civil War' " (*New Yorker*, April 17, 2000). Among the differences between the Porter brothers is that Fairfield found his métier early on and eventually the painting became quite separate from the politics, while older brother Eliot struggled to define a new medium that eventually allowed him to bring politics and aesthetics together.

241   first principle of ecology: Carolyn Merchant, "Feminism and Ecology," appendix B, in *Deep Ecology: Living as if Nature Mattered*, by Bill Devall and George Sessions (Layton, Utah: Gibbs Smith, 1985), p. 229. Merchant also quotes Commoner.

242   "Much is missed if we have eyes only for the bright colors. . . .": Porter, *Eliot Porter*, p. 44.

243   "Don't show the sky . . .": Eliot Porter, quoted by David Brower in a letter reminiscing about Porter, to curator John Rohrbach of the Amon Carter Museum, September 1999.

245   "the most distinctive, and perhaps the most impressive, characteristic of American scenery . . .": Thomas Cole, "Essay on American Scenery," in *American Art, 1700–1960*, ed. John McCoubrey, Sources and Documents in the History of Art series (Englewood Cliffs, N.J.: Prentice-Hall, 1965), p. 92.

245   much has been written to revise this idea: My own 1994 book *Savage Dreams: A Journey into the Landscape Wars of the American West* documents

the cost of imagining Yosemite Valley as virgin wilderness—the cost to the Euro-American imagination, Native American rights, and the place's ecology. Ethnobotanists such as Kat Anderson and books ranging from William Cronon's *Changes in the Land: Indians, Colonists, and the Ecology of New England* to Jonathan S. Adams and Thomas O. McShane's *The Myth of Wild Africa: Conservation without Illusion* to Alston Chase's *Playing God in Yellowstone* have done more to complicate our understanding of the eco-systems we sometimes call wilderness and of the human presence in them. Recently, the Native American writer Elizabeth Cook-Lynn published *Why I Can't Read Wallace Stegner, and Other Essays: A Tribal Voice.*

246   "The critique of modernity that is one of environmentalism's most important contributions . . .": William Cronon, "The Trouble with Wilderness," in *Uncommon Ground: Rethinking the Human Place in Nature*, ed. William Cronon (New York: W. W. Norton, 1995), p. 80.

248   "What has troubled me . . .": George Marshall, letter to Eliot Porter, May 11, 1965, Eliot Porter file, carton 11, David Brower Papers, Sierra Club Archives.

248   "Most of the photographs . . .": George Marshall, letter to David Brower, May 6, 1965, Eliot Porter file, carton 11, David Brower Papers, Sierra Club Archives.

250   "was supposed to influence people for conservation . . .": Eliot Porter, letter to Marcie and Stephen Porter, December 17, 1977, Stephen Porter file, Eliot Porter Archives.

250   "almost always unintentionally softens . . .": Eliot Porter, address to Los Alamos Honor Students, p. 4, Eliot Porter Archives. Other color photogra-phers—notably Richard Misrach and John Pfahl—have explored the moral quandary implicit in the way that a color photograph likely to attract atten-tion is likely to endow its subject with beauties of color or composition; these two artists have intentionally deployed this flaw to test ethics against aes-thetics (a subject I have addressed at length in *Crimes and Splendors: The Desert Cantos of Richard Misrach*).

251   "More people currently know the appearance of Yosemite Valley . . .": Robert Adams, "C. A. Hickman," in *Beauty in Photography: Essays in*

Defense of Traditional Values (New York: Aperture, 1981), p. 103. As Michael Cohen has pointed out, Adams's assertion that there are "few converts . . . to be won to the general idea of wilderness preservation" is open to ambiguity now, with the spread of corporate-financed anti-environmentalist groups (such as the Wise Use Movement and People for the West) contributing to widespread suspicion and hostility toward environmentalists among rural, conservative, and working-class people.

253 "In the 1970s came, ironically, a more and more dazzling presentation of those creatures . . .": Barry Lopez, "Learning to See," in *About This Life: Journeys on the Threshold of Memory* (New York: Random House, 1998), p. 233.

THE BOTANICAL CIRCUS, OR ADVENTURES IN AMERICAN GARDENING

254 "I came to love my rows, my beans . . .": Henry David Thoreau, from the "Bean Field" chapter of *Walden*, in *Walden and Other Writings of Henry David Thoreau* (New York: Modern Library, 1937), p. 140.

256 "two Squares, each having four Quarters . . .": A. J. Dezallier D'Argenville, "Theory and Practice of Gardening" (1712), trans. John James, in *The Genius of the Place: The English Landscape Garden, 1620–1820*, ed. John Dixon Hunt and Peter Willis (Cambridge, Mass.: MIT Press, 1988), p. 125.

256 "There is certainly something in the amiable Simplicity . . .": Alexander Pope, 1713 essay from *The Guardian*, in Hunt and Willis, *The Genius of the Place*, p. 205.

256 "Adam and Eve in Yew . . .": ibid., p. 208.

257 "the object of art may be to seek the elimination of the necessity of it . . .": Robert Irwin in conversation with Ed Wortz and James Turrell in Lawrence Weschler, *Seeing Is Forgetting the Name of the Thing One Sees: A Life of Contemporary Artist Robert Irwin* (Berkeley: University of California Press, 1982), p. 128. Irwin designed the very peculiar garden at the J. Paul Getty Museum in Los Angeles, a garden that is a sort of sunken basin in whose center is an inaccessible hedge maze surrounded by water. The plantings are abundant, and the decision to eliminate the commanding view of the site with a descent into the wildly varied floral plantings could be construed

as a pointed rejection of the monumentally ambitious architecture and looming location on a high hill.

257   "For several decades the nineteenth century had no distinctive garden
style . . .": Christopher Thacker, *The History of Gardens* (Berkeley: University of California Press, 1979), p. 239.

258   "It was as though the creation was a jig-saw puzzle . . .": John Prest, *The
Garden of Eden: The Botanic Garden and the Re-Creation of Paradise* (New
Haven: Yale University Press, 1981), p. 39.

259   "The Wardian case is, with the ha-ha . . .": Thacker, *History of Gardens*,
p. 236. A ha-ha is a sunken boundary or fence, which visually eliminates the
boundary though in fact it remains.

259   "biocolonialism": See, for example, Tamar Kahn in the *Johannesburg Business
Day*, March 22, 2002: "For thousands of years the San have used the Hoodia
cactus as an appetite suppressant and thirst quencher. It helped them endure
long hunts, and resist the temptation to eat their kill before they returned to
their camps. The cactus is potentially worth a fortune, because it could very
well be the first plant to give rise to a commercially viable appetite suppressant drug. In the US alone, with an estimated 35-million to 65-million clini-
cally obese people, the market for such a product is huge and growing all
the time. The central issue in the tale of the cactus, the San, and the international drug companies, is what benefits will the San derive from all of this?
That question made international headlines last year, when a British journalist revealed that the Council for Scientific and Industrial Research (CSIR)
had patented Hoodia's appetite-suppressing ingredient, dubbed P57, and
granted the development rights to Phytopharm, a small pharmaceutical firm
in the UK."

259   "The few plants are strangers . . .": John Wesley Powell, *The Exploration of
the Colorado River and Its Canyons* (New York: Dover Books, 1961), p. 22.
On the other hand, consider historian Patricia Nelson Limerick on her first
trip out of the arid West in which she was born: "As I drove across Oklahoma, crossing what I later learned was the ninety-eighth meridian, discovery joined up with its usual partner, disorientation. The air became humid,
clammy, and unpleasant, and the landscape turned distressingly green. The

Eastern United States, I learned with every mile, was badly infested by plants. Even where they had been driven back, the bushes, shrubs, and trees gave every sign of anticipating a reconquest. But the even more remarkable fact was this: millions of people lived in this muggy, congested world . . . and considered it normal" ("Disorientation and Reorientation," *Something in the Soil: Legacies and Reckonings in the New West* [New York: W. W. Norton, 2000], p. 196).

261   Laura Ingalls Wilder tells a tale: Wilder's *Farmer Boy* (1933; New York: HarperCollins, 2004) is a digressive portion of her many-volume fictionalized memoirs of growing up on the American frontier. This book deals with her husband's childhood on a big farm in New York State, during which he raises a prize pumpkin and worries about having cheated by growing it milk-fed (and the book, as I recall thirty years later, gives details of how he fed this early Miracle-Gro formula to the vine). It must be said, however, that at the Findhorn spiritual community in Scotland in the 1970s, overgrown vegetables became an even more explicit sign of the approval of the gods than did all those county fair pumpkins and postcards of freight cars bearing a single peach of America the Promised Land.

263   class war of the roses: "The war of the roses is at bottom a class war. The tracts of old-rosarians bristle with the fine distinctions, winks, and code words by which aristocrats have always recognized one another" (Michael Pollan, *Second Nature: A Plant's Eye View of the World* [New York: Random House, 2001], p. 84).

263   "Looking at my dahlias one summer day . . .": Eleanor Perényi, *Green Thoughts: A Writer in the Garden* (New York: Random House, 1981), pp. 46–47.

THE RUINS OF MEMORY

351   "Decay can be halted . . .": in J. B. Jackson, "Looking at New Mexico," in *Landscape in Sight: Looking at America*, ed. Helen Lefkowitz Horowitz (New Haven: Yale University Press, 1997), p. 62.

353   Victor Hugo poem quoted: Walter Benjamin, *The Arcades Project*, trans.

Howard Eiland and Kevin McLaughlin (Cambridge, Mass.: Belknap Press, 1999), p. 95.

360   "This was the first of the great fires which devastated San Francisco . . .":
      Frank Soule, John H. Gihon, and James Nisbet, *The Annals of San Francisco*
      (New York: D. Appleton, 1855), p. 241.

360   "But in proportion to the unusual depression . . .": ibid., pp. 277–278.

361   "Elsewhere such a fire might well be called a great one . . .": ibid., p. 299.

361   "Sour, pseudo-religious folk on the shores of the Atlantic . . .": ibid., p. 333.

361   "successively destroyed nearly all the old buildings and land-marks of Yerba
      Buena . . .": ibid., p. 345.

362   "The lives lost yesterday are not chargeable to the earthquake . . .": *San
      Francisco Morning Call*, October 22, 1868.

362   "The aim of Operation Gomorrah, as it was called . . .": W. G. Sebald, *On
      the Natural History of Destruction*, trans. Anthea Bell (New York: Random
      House, 2003), p. 26.

363   "San Francisco is now developing programs . . .": Leonard S. Mosias for the
      San Francisco Redevelopment Agency, "Residential Rehabilitation Survey
      Western Addition Area 2," July 1962, unpaginated.

365   Between 1960 and 1974, the number of fires tripled: Jill Jonnes, *We're Still
      Here: The Rise, Fall, and Resurrection of the South Bronx* (Boston: Atlantic
      Monthly Press, 1986), p. 261.

365   an average of 33 fires a night in the first half of the 1970s: Brian Wallis, ed., *If
      You Lived Here: The City in Art, Theory, and Social Activism — A Project by
      Martha Rosler* (Seattle: Bay Press, 1991), p. 288.

365   "in the first year without payoffs . . .": Marshall Berman, "New York (New
      York City)," in *These United States*, ed. John Leonard (New York: Nation
      Books, 2003), p. 299.

365   "People don't want housing in the South Bronx . . .": Senator Daniel Patrick
      Moynihan quoted in Jonnes, *We're Still Here*, p. 92.

366   "For years, midnight fires ate up not only buildings . . .": Berman, "New
      York (New York City)," p. 288.

366   "In the 1970s and 1980s, New York's greatest spectacles . . .": ibid., p. 294.

366   "whole areas look like the burnt-out ruins of war . . .": Cardinal Terence Cooke quoted in Jonnes, *We're Still Here*, p. 264.

366   "Already in the mid-1970s . . .": Luc Sante, "My Lost City," *New York Review of Books*, November 6, 2003, p. 34.

370   "From the outset . . .": Sebald, *Natural History of Destruction*, p. 7.

Permissions

Most of the essays in this book have appeared in print in earlier versions, though often in overseas or local publications, lush books few seem to have found, and other obscure places. They have been edited for this volume; some have been shortened, while in others text that had been cut from the earlier version was restored. Some essays have been retitled or have had their original titles restored.

"The Red Lands," "California Comedy, or Surfing with Dante," and "A Murder of Ravens: On Globalized Species" originally appeared in the *London Review of Books* in 2003, 2004, and 2006, respectively.

"The Postmodern Old West, or the Precession of Cowboys and Indians" was originally published in the September and December 1996 issues of *Art issues*.

"The Struggle of Dawning Intelligence: Creating, Revising, and Recognizing Native American Monuments" is included here courtesy of *Harvard Design Magazine*, where it first appeared in the fall 1999 issue.

"The Garden of Merging Paths" first appeared in *Resisting the Virtual Life: The Culture and Politics of Information*, edited by James Brook and Iain A. Boal and published by City Lights Books in 1995.

"A Route in the Shape of a Question" was published in a truncated version in the *Los Angeles Times* in 2004.

"Thirty-Nine Steps Across the Border and Back" appeared in *Against the Wall*, edited by Michael Sorkin and published by the New Press in 2005.

"Nonconforming Uses: Teddy Cruz on Both Sides of the Border" was originally published as part of *Democratic Vistas Profiles: Essays in the Arts and Democracy* (http://

artspolicy.colum.edu/DVProfiles.html), Center for Arts Policy at Columbia College, Chicago, in 2006.

"The Price of Gold, the Value of Water" appeared in *Sierra* magazine in 2000.

"Meanwhile Back at the Ranch," "Jailbirds I Have Loved," "Fragments of the Future: The FTAA in Miami," "Liberation Conspiracies," "Sontag and Tsunami," and "The Wal-Mart Biennale" all originally appeared at Tomdispatch.com.

"Poison Pictures" and "Other Daughters, Other American Revolutions" were published in *The Nation* in 2003 and 2006, respectively.

"Excavating the Sky" was the essay included in Richard Misrach's *The Sky Book*, published by Arena Editions in 2000.

"Drawing the Constellations" accompanied the photograph "Home" in Meridel Rubenstein's retrospective volume *Belonging: Los Alamos to Vietnam*, published by St. Anne's Press in 2004.

"Hugging the Shadows," "Justice by Moonlight," "Mirror in the Street," "The Silence of the Lambswool Cardigans," "Locked Horns," and "The Orbits of Earthly Bodies" all appeared in *Orion* magazine from 2003 through 2005.

"Making It Home: Travels outside the Fear Economy" was part of the text of a talk delivered by the author at the 2005 Chicago Humanities Festival.

A slightly longer version of "Every Corner Is Alive: Eliot Porter as an Environmentalist and an Artist" appeared in *Eliot Porter: The Color of Wildness*, a book edited by John Rohrbach to accompany an Eliot Porter retrospective, copublished in 2001 by the Amon Carter Museum and the Aperture Foundation; it is included here courtesy of the Museum.

"The Botanical Circus, or Adventures in American Gardening" was the introduction to John Pfahl's *Extreme Horticulture*, published by Francis Lincoln Books in 2003, and appears here by permission of the press.

"Seven Stepping Stones down the Primrose Path past Gender" was the keynote address delivered by the author at a 2002 conference on landscape and gender, sponsored by the Department of Landscape Architecture, University of California at Berkeley.

"San Francisco: The Metamorphosis" was included in *These United States: Original Essays by Leading American Writers on Their State within the Union*, edited by John Leonard and published by Nation Books in 2003.

"The Heart of the City" and "Gaping Questions" were published in the *San Francisco Chronicle* in 2004 and 2002, respectively, though the latter was written in October of 2001.

A longer version of "The Ruins of Memory" was included in Mark Klett's book with
Michael Lundgren, with essays by Philip Fradkin and Rebecca Solnit, *After the
Ruins, 1906 and 2006: Rephotographing the San Francisco Earthquake and Fire*, pub-
lished by the University of California Press in 2006.

"Seashell to Ear" was the text for Helen Douglas's photographic book *Unravelling the
Ripple*, published by Pocketbooks in Edinburgh in 2001.

Index

DESIGNER: SANDY DROOKER
TEXT: 9.75/13 KENNERLY
DISPLAY: AKZIDENZ GROTESK BE
COMPOSITOR: BOOKMATTERS, BERKELEY
PRINTER AND BINDER: SHERIDAN BOOKS, INC.